Philosophy of Mind

When first published, John Heil's introduction quickly became a widely used guide for students with little or no background in philosophy to central issues of philosophy of mind. Heil provided an introduction free of formalisms, technical trappings, and specialized terminology. He offered clear arguments and explanations, focusing on the ontological basis of mentality and its place in the material world. The book concluded with a systematic discussion of questions the book raises – and a sketch of a unified metaphysics of mind – thus inviting scholarly attention while providing a book very well suited for an introductory course.

This Third Edition builds on these strengths, and incorporates new material on theories of consciousness, computationalism, the Language of Thought, and animal minds as well as other emerging areas of research. With an updated reading list at the end of each chapter and a revised bibliography, this new edition will again make it the indispensable primer for anyone seeking better understanding of the central metaphysical issues in philosophy of mind.

John Heil is Professor of Philosophy at Washington University in St. Louis. His previous publications include *The Universe as We Find It* (2012) and *From an Ontological Point of View* (2003).

Routledge Contemporary Introductions to Philosophy
Series editor: Paul K Moser, Loyola University of Chicago

This innovative, well-structured series is for students who have already done an introductory course in philosophy. Each book introduces a core general subject in contemporary philosophy and offers students an accessible but substantial transition from introductory to higher-level college work in that subject. The series is accessible to non-specialists and each book clearly motivates and expounds the problems and positions introduced. An orientating chapter briefly introduces its topic and reminds readers of any crucial material they need to have retained from a typical introductory course. Considerable attention is given to explaining the central philosophical problems of a subject and the main competing solutions and arguments for those solutions. The primary aim is to educate students in the main problems, positions and arguments of contemporary philosophy rather than to convince students of a single position.

Ancient Philosophy
Christopher Shields

Classical Philosophy
Christopher Shields

Classical Modern Philosophy
Jeffrey Tlumak

Continental Philosophy
Andrew Cutrofello

Epistemology
Third Edition
Robert Audi

Ethics
Second Edition
Harry J. Gensler

Metaphysics
Third Edition
Michael J. Loux

Philosophy of Art
Noël Carroll

Philosophy of Biology
Alex Rosenberg and Daniel W. McShea

Philosophy of Language
Second Edition
Willam G. Lycan

Philosophy of Mathematics
Second Edition
James Robert Brown

Philosophy of Mind

A Contemporary Introduction

Third Edition

John Heil

Routledge
Taylor & Francis Group

NEW YORK AND LONDON

First published 2013
by Routledge
711 Third Avenue, New York, NY 10017

Simultaneously published in the UK
by Routledge
2 Park Square, Milton Park, Abingdon, Oxon OX14 4RN

*Routledge is an imprint of the Taylor & Francis Group, an informa
business*

Library of Congress Cataloging in Publication Data
Philosophy of mind : a contemporary introduction / by [edited]
John Heil. — [3rd ed.].
   p. cm.
   Includes bibliographical references and index.
   ISBN 978-0-415-89174-5 (hardback)
   1. Philosophy of mind. I. Heil, John.
   BD418.3.H47 2012   128'.2—dc23
   2012019915

ISBN: 978–0–415–89174–5 [HBK]
ISBN: 978–0–415–89175–2 [PBK]
ISBN: 978–0–203–08110–5 [EBK]

Typeset in Adobe Garamond Pro and Gill Sans
by Bookcraft Ltd, Stroud, Gloucestershire

Printed and bound by CPI Group (UK) Ltd, Croydon, CR0 4YY

For Mark, Gus, and Lilian

Contents

Preface to the Third Edition

Philosophy of Mind: A Contemporary Introduction appeared in 1998 followed, six years later, by a second edition. That second edition included numerous changes, corrections and additions, some in response to philosophical developments in the intervening years, some based on my own experiences in using the book as a text in my own classes. This third edition reflects those two factors, but it reflects as well valuable suggestions from others who have used the book with their own students. I have taken those suggestions to heart. This was not always easy to do because in some cases I received conflicting advice.

The book always aimed at illuminating issues in the philosophy of mind for readers not steeped in the literature. Because philosophy nowadays is conducted in an excessively technical idiom intelligible only to other card-carrying philosophers, this is not an easy task. Over the years, I have come more and more to believe that if you can't explain something clearly without recourse to an esoteric vocabulary, you don't really understand it. Philosophers who lace their writing with jargon and flaunt technicalities intimidating to all but a select group of readers seem, too often, incapable of plain speech. Is this because plain speech would not do justice to the subtle theses being advanced, or is it because all the hard philosophical work is being done by the jargon? A technical term can serve as a useful shorthand for a complex idea. At the same time technical terms encode substantive philosophical theses. The use of jargon masks the extent to which the important moves are occurring behind the scenes, obscured by a specialized vocabulary, familiarity with which is taken for granted.

In my own teaching, I have found myself pulled in two, often incompatible, directions. First, I would like my students to cultivate a clear view of the territory and thereby improve their capacity to evaluate competing ways of thinking about the mind. Second, I would like to familiarize students with the going conceptions and arguments that support them. I have, with dispiriting frequency, felt pangs of guilt in trying to spell out and motivate views that I am convinced are, at best, shallow, and, at worst, incoherent. These views survive and continue to find supporters because smart philosophers are adept at defending almost any idea. I want my students to be familiar with the space of positions in the philosophy of mind, but there are places I cannot bring myself to take them.

I have, in this third edition, made additions, corrections, and changes on every page of every chapter, but four changes deserve special mention.

Chapter 4 of the second edition, 'Non-Cartesian Dualism', was a chapter many readers elected to skip, in part because the position discussed was a difficult and unfamiliar one. Its very unfamiliarity was what led me to include the chapter in the first place. Too much of the philosophy of mind is a rehash of familiar, well-worn, hence comfortable, views. Sometimes it is useful to find inspiration elsewhere. In composing this third edition, I reworked the discussion with an eye toward clarifying the argument and making it more accessible. In the end, however, I decided to eliminate the chapter, mostly in the interest of keeping the book to a manageable length. I have heard from many readers who appreciated the chapter's inclusion. If you are one of those readers, I encourage you not to discard or recycle the second edition.

Much the same could be said about the second edition's Chapter 9, 'Radical Interpretation', which provided an account of Davidson's theory of propositional attitude ascription, a topic that some readers found fascinating, others daunting, and still others hopeless. The chapter does not appear in the third edition.

The second edition's Chapter 13, 'Property Dualism', has been reconceived and appears in the third edition as Chapter 11, 'Non-Reductive Physicalism'.

Chapter 10, 'Consciousness' is almost completely new. The chapter replaces Chapter 9 in the second edition which was more narrowly focused on *qualia*. I discuss various accounts of consciousness and the qualities of conscious experience that previously were either mentioned only in passing or not discussed at all.

Chapters 14 and 15 of the second edition survive, much revised, in the third edition as Chapters 12 and 13. I do not expect instructors who use this book as an introductory textbook in philosophy of mind to assign these chapters. But it seems to me that anyone who takes the trouble to read through some or all of my discussion of various positions is owed an account of how the author himself thinks about the topics under discussion. If nothing else, my putting my cards on the table allows curious readers to factor out inevitable authorial biases. These chapters are meant to be self-contained. They can be read without extensive knowledge of material taken up earlier in the book. One result is that some themes and arguments that appear earlier appear again in modified form.

Once again, I am grateful to all those who took the trouble to pass along corrections and suggestions for improving the first and second editions. This third edition has benefited from the collective wisdom of many philosophers and many of their students. It has benefited, as well, from support from the National Endowment for the Humanities and from Washington University in St Louis.

John Heil
St. Louis
May, 2012

Preface to the Second Edition

The first edition of *Philosophy of Mind: A Contemporary Introduction* appeared in 1998. Since that time, I have had occasion to rethink topics addressed in that volume, to discuss my approach to those topics with many people, and to hear from numerous readers. The result is this second edition.

One aim of the first edition was to make difficult issues intelligible to novices without unduly watering them down. My impression is that the effort was, on the whole, successful. This edition incorporates changes of two sorts. First I have added or supplemented discussions of topics ignored or treated lightly in the first edition. My discussion of eliminativism, of *qualia*, and the Representational Theory of Mind have been expanded, and I have added a chapter on property dualism. Second, I have divided the book into shorter, more self-contained chapters. In so doing, my hope was that this would allow more flexibility for instructors using the book in courses in the philosophy of mind. Chapters, too, have been divided into bite-sized sections. I believe the new divisions make the book more attractive and easier on the reader.

As before, each chapter concludes with a listing of suggested readings. These listings have been expanded and updated (to include, for instance, Internet resources). I have also instituted an author/date citation scheme keyed to a comprehensive bibliography at the end of the volume. Readers' annoyance at having to turn to a separate bibliography to track down references might be offset by the absence of footnotes and endnotes. The first edition contained a handful of footnotes. I came to believe, however, that a book of this kind could, and should, be written without such textual intrusions.

I am grateful to readers who took the trouble to pass along corrections and suggestions for improving the first edition. I hope that the resulting changes have resulted in a better all round book.

Many of the themes taken up in Chapters 14 and 15 (Chapter 6 in the first edition) were subsequently developed in detail in *From an Ontological Point of View* (Oxford: Clarendon Press, 2003), written during a year as a guest of Monash University. Revisions and additions distinguishing this second edition from its predecessor were also undertaken at Monash during two subsequent visits. I am grateful to the University, to the School of Philosophy and Bioethics, and to my magnificent colleagues at Monash for support and encouragement. I am grateful as well to Davidson College for its generous support, material and otherwise.

John Heil
Melbourne
July, 2003

Preface to the First Edition

One aim of this book is to introduce readers with little or no background in philosophy to central issues in the philosophy of mind, and to do so in a way that highlights those issues' metaphysical dimensions. In this regard, my approach differs from approaches that emphasize connections between the philosophy of mind and various empirical domains: psychology, neuroscience, and artificial intelligence, for instance. It is not that I regard empirical work as irrelevant to the philosophy of mind. After years of skepticism, however, I have become convinced that the fundamental philosophical questions concerning the mind remain metaphysical questions – where metaphysics is understood as something more than the a priori pursuit of eternal verities: metaphysics, as I see it, takes the sciences at their word. More particularly, the fundamental questions are questions of ontology – our best accounting of what, in the most general terms, there is.

As in the case of any other systematic pursuit, ontology is constrained formally: ontological theses must be internally coherent. Ontological theses ought, in addition, to be reconcilable with established scientific lore. When we consider every imaginable ontology that is consistent, both internally and with pronouncements of the sciences, however, we can see that the field remains wide open. Something more is required if our evaluation of competing approaches is to be anything more than a bare expression of preference. That something more lies in the relative power of alternative schemes. An ontology that not only strikes us as plausible (in the sense that it is both internally coherent and consistent with science and common experience) but at the same time offers solutions to a wide range of problems in a way that makes those solutions appear inevitable, is to be preferred to an ontology that provides only piecemeal solutions to a narrow range of problems.

At the present time, the field is dominated by David Lewis's ontology of possible worlds. Lewis postulates, in addition to the actual world, an infinity of real, but non-actual, *alternative* worlds. (Lewis calls these alternative worlds 'possible worlds', but the worlds he has in mind are not mere possibilities; they are fully fledged worlds on a par with ours. The 'actual world' differs from the others only in containing us.) Each world differs in some respect from the actual world and from every other possible world. By appealing to features of these worlds, Lewis lays claim to offering explanations of important truths holding in the actual world.

The Lewis ontology of alternative worlds strikes many philosophers (and all non-philosophers) as mad. Nevertheless, many of these same philosophers persist in resorting to alternative worlds to explicate important concepts: the concept of causation, for instance, the concept of a causal power or disposition, the concept of necessity. If you reject the ontology of alternative worlds, however, it is unclear what is supposed to ground such appeals. For Lewis, the truthmakers for claims about alternative worlds are the alternative worlds. If you disdain alternative worlds, however, yet appeal to them in explicating, say, causation, what makes your assertions true or false? If alternative worlds do not exist, then presumably your claims are grounded in features – intrinsic features – of the actual world. But then why not appeal directly to these features? What use is it to invoke imaginary entities?

I believe we have a right to be suspicious of anyone who embraces the formal apparatus of alternative worlds while rejecting the ontology. Indeed, I think we might be more suspicious of formal techniques generally, when these are deployed to answer substantive questions in metaphysics and the philosophy of mind. So long as we remain at a formal level of discourse, it is easy to lose interest in what might ground our claims. And this, I think, has led to the kind of technical sterility characteristic of so much contemporary, analytical philosophy.

I do not deny that formal techniques have their place. I want only to suggest that it is a mistake to imagine that these techniques can be relied upon to reveal hidden ontological details of our world. A good example of the detrimental effects of ungrounded formalism can be found in the tendency to conflate (if not officially, then in practice) *predicates* – linguistic entities – and *properties*. This can lead to specious puzzles. Are there disjunctive properties? Well of course, some reply: if P is a property and Q is a property, then $P \vee Q$ (P or Q) is a property.

True enough, if P and Q are predicates denoting properties, then you can construct a disjunctive predicate, '$P \vee Q$'. What is less clear is whether this gives us any right whatever to suppose that '$P \vee Q$' designates a *property*. The notion of a disjunctive property makes sense, I suspect, only so long as you imagine that a property is whatever answers to a predicate. But this is the linguistic tail wagging the ontological dog.

I mention all this by way of calling attention to the absence of formal devices, appeals to purely modal notions like supervenience, and invocations of alternative worlds in the chapters that follow. If it accomplishes nothing else, my decision to omit such technical trappings will certainly make the book more accessible to non-specialist readers. In any case, the philosophy of mind, indeed metaphysics generally, is not – or ought not to be – a technical exercise. Philosophical theses should be expressible without reliance on specialized terminology. I have tried my best to say what I have to say without resorting to such terminology. This strikes me as an important exercise for every philosopher. Too much can be smuggled in, too much left unexplained when we allow ourselves to fall back on philosophical jargon.

Although this book is written with the non-specialist in view, it is intended to be more than a mere survey of going theories. I take up a number of issues that could be of interest to hardened philosophers of mind and to non-philosophers with a professional interest in minds and their nature. If nothing else, I am hopeful that my approach will encourage others to delve more deeply into the ontological basis of mentality.

Some readers will be surprised at my including certain views, and disappointed at my downplaying or ignoring others. In a book of this sort, however, you must be selective: it is impossible to do justice to every position. I have, then, chosen what seem to me to be central issues and points of view in the philosophy of mind, and concentrated on these. Ultimately I hope to lead open-minded readers to what amounts to a new perspective on the territory.

On a more practical note: I expect instructors who use this book as part of a course in the philosophy of mind to supplement it with readings of original materials. With that in mind, I have included, at the end of each chapter, a list of suggested readings. If nothing else, these readings can be used to fill perceived gaps and to compensate for infelicities in my exposition.

The inspiration for this book came to me as I was completing an earlier volume, *The Nature of True Minds* (Cambridge: Cambridge University Press, 1992). The centerpiece of that volume is an elaborate discussion of the problem of mental causation: if mental properties depend on, but are not identical with, material properties, how could mental properties affect behavior? As I struggled with details of my account of mental causation (an account that owed much to the work of my colleague, Alfred Mele), it gradually dawned on me that any solution to the problem would require a prolonged excursion into ontology. More generally, I began to see that attempts to answer questions in the philosophy of mind that ignored ontology, or depended (as mine did) on ad hoc ontological assumptions, were bound to prove unsatisfying. The upshot was something akin to a religious conversion.

My route to 'ontological seriousness' was occasioned by conversations (pitched battles, really) with C. B. Martin. The first result was a book-length manuscript on metaphysics and the philosophy of mind completed during a sabbatical leave in Berkeley in 1993/94. The book before you is a distant relative of that manuscript. I am grateful to Davidson College and to the National Endowment for the Humanities for their generous support, and to the Department of Psychology, the University of California, Berkeley, for hosting me. I owe a particular debt to Lynne Davisson and Carolyn Scott for their administrative support and to the Berkeley Presbyterian Missionary Homes for providing accommodation for my family.

Countless people have contributed to my thinking on the topics covered here. Martin is foremost among these. My most fervent hope is that readers whose interest is stirred by the ideas discussed in Chapter 6 will take the trouble to track down those ideas' sources in Martin's writings.

I have benefited immeasurably from discussions with John Carroll, Randolph Clarke, Güven Güzeldere, Michael Lockwood, E. J. Lowe, David Robb, Dan Ryder, Amie Thomasson, Peter Unger, and Peter Vallentyne, all of whom provided astute comments on portions of the manuscript. I am especially indebted to participants in my 1996 NEH Summer Seminar on Metaphysics of Mind at Cornell, including (in addition to Clarke and Thomasson) Leonard Clapp, Anthony Dardis, James Garson, Heather Gert, Muhammad Ali Khalidi, David Pitt, Eric Saidel, Stephen Schwartz, Nigel J. T. Thomas, and Michael Watkins. Many of the ideas found in the pages that follow emerged in seminar discussions. I cannot imagine a more congenial, philosophically discerning, and, yes, ontologically serious group anywhere.

A number of people have, in discussion or correspondence, influenced my thinking on particular issues addressed here. David Armstrong, Richard Boyd, Jaegwon Kim, Brian McLaughlin, Alfred Mele, Brendan O'Sullivan, David Robb, and Sydney Shoemaker deserve special mention. Fred Dretsky and Kim Sterelny provided useful comments on a penultmate draft of the manuscript. I am especially indebted to E. J. Lowe for detailed and searching criticisms of every chapter. Lowe is, to my mind, one of a handful of contemporary philosophers whose views on minds and their place in nature reflect a deep appreciation of ontology. Finally, and most importantly, the book would not have been possible without the unwavering support – intellectual, moral, and otherwise – of Harrison Hagan Heil.

The manuscript was completed during a fellowship year at the National Humanities Center (1996/97) and was supported by the Center, by a Davidson College Faculty Grant, and by the National Endowment for the Humanities. I owe these institutions more than I can say.

John Heil
National Humanities Center
Research Triangle Park, N. C.
Spring, 1997

1 Introduction

1.1 Experience and Reality

Does a tree falling in the forest make a sound when no one is around to hear it? The question is familiar to every undergraduate. One natural response is that *of course* the tree makes a sound – why shouldn't it? The tree makes a sound whether anyone is on hand to hear it or not. And, in any case, even if there are no people about, there are squirrels, birds, or at the very least bugs that would hear it crashing down.

Consider a more measured response, versions of which have percolated down through successive generations of student philosophers. The tree's falling creates sound waves that radiate outwards as do ripples on the surface of a pond, but in a spherical pattern. If these sound waves are intercepted by a human ear (or maybe – although this might be slightly more controversial – the ear of some nonhuman sentient creature) they are heard as a crashing noise. If the sound waves go undetected, they eventually peter out. Whether an unobserved falling tree makes a sound, then, depends on what you *mean* by sound. If you mean 'heard noise', then (squirrels and birds aside) the tree falls silently. If, in contrast, you mean something like 'distinctive spherical pattern of impact waves in the air', then, yes, the tree's falling does make a sound.

Most people who answer the question this way consider the issue settled. The puzzle is solved simply by getting clear on what you *mean* when you talk about sounds. Indeed, you could appreciate the original question as posing a puzzle only if you were already prepared to distinguish two senses of 'sound'. But what precisely are these two senses? On the one hand, there is the *physical* sound, a spherical pattern of impact waves open to public inspection and measurement – at any rate, open to public inspection given the right instruments. On the other hand, there is the *experienced* sound. The experienced sound depends on the presence of an *observer*. It is not, or not obviously, a public occurrence: although a sound can be experienced by many people, each observer's experience is 'private'. You can observe and measure agents' responses to experienced sounds, but you cannot measure the experiences themselves. This way of thinking about sounds applies quite generally. It applies, for instance, to the looks of objects, to their tastes, their smells, and to ways they feel to the touch. Physicist Erwin Schrödinger (1887–1961) puts it this way in discussing sensations of color:

> The sensation of colour cannot be accounted for by the physicist's objective picture of light-waves. Could the physiologist account for it, if he had fuller knowledge than he has of the processes in the retina and the nervous processes set up by them in the optical nerve bundles and in the brain? I do not think so.
>
> (Schrödinger 1958, 90)

The picture of the universe and our place in it that lies behind such reflections has the effect of bifurcating reality. You have, on the one hand, the 'outer' material world, the world of trees, forests, sound waves, and light radiation. On the other hand, you have the 'inner' mental world, the mind and its contents. The mental world includes conscious experiences: the looks of seen objects, ways objects feel, heard sounds, tasted tastes, smelled smells. The 'external' material world comprises the objects themselves, and their properties. These properties include such things as objects' masses and spatial characteristics (their shapes, sizes, surface textures, and, if you consider objects over time, motions and changes in their spatial characteristics).

Following a long tradition, you might call those observed qualities properly belonging to material objects 'primary qualities'. The rest, the 'secondary qualities', are characteristics of objects (presumably nothing more than arrangements of objects' primary qualities) that elicit certain familiar kinds of experience in conscious observers. Experience reliably mirrors the primary qualities of objects. Secondary qualities, in contrast, call for a distinction between the way objects are *experienced*, and the way they *are*. This distinction shows itself in student reflections on trees falling in deserted forests. More fundamentally, the distinction encourages us to view conscious experiences as occurring 'outside' the material universe.

You might doubt this, confident that conscious experiences occur in brains, and regarding brains as respectable material objects. But now apply the distinction between primary and secondary qualities to brains. Brains – yours included – have assorted primary qualities. Your brain has a definite size, shape, mass, and spatial location; it is made up of particles, each with a definite size, shape, mass, and spatial location, and each of which contributes in a small way to the brain's overall material character. In virtue of this overall character, your brain would look (and presumably sound, smell, feel, and taste!) a particular way. This is just to say that your brain could be variously experienced. The qualities of these experiences, although undoubtedly related in some systematic way to the material reality that elicits them, differ from qualities possessed by any material object, including your brain. But if that is so, where do we situate the qualities of experience?

Your first instinct was to locate them in the brain. But inspection of brains reveals only familiar material qualities. An examination of a brain – even with the kinds of sophisticated instrumentation found in the laboratory of the neurophysiologist and the neural anatomist – reveals no looks, feels, heard sounds. Imagine that you are attending a performance of *Die Walküre* at Bayreuth. Your senses are assaulted by sounds, colors, smells, even tastes. A neuroscientist observing your brain while all this is occurring would observe a panoply of neurological activities. But you can rest assured that the neuroscientist will not observe anything resembling the qualities of your conscious experience.

The idea that these qualities reside in your brain, so natural at first, appears, on further reflection, unpromising. But now, if qualities of your experiences are not found in your brain, *where are they?* The traditional answer, and the answer that we seem driven to accept, is that they are located in your *mind*. And this implies, quite straightforwardly, that your mind is somehow distinct from your brain. Indeed, it implies that the mind is not a material object at all, not an entity on all fours with tables, trees, stones – and brains! Minds appear to be *non*material entities: entities with properties not possessed by brains, or perhaps by *any* material object. Minds bear intimate relations to material objects, perhaps, and especially intimate relations to brains. Your conscious experiences of ordinary material objects (including your own body) appear to reach you 'through' your brain; and the effects of your conscious deliberations have on the universe (as when you decide to turn a page in this book and subsequently turn the page) require the brain as an intermediary. Nevertheless, the conclusion seems inescapable: the mind could not itself be a material object.

1.2   The Unavoidability of the Philosophy of Mind

You might find this conclusion unacceptable. If you do, I invite you to go back over the reasoning that led up to it and figure out where that reasoning went off the rails. In so doing you would be engaging in philosophical reflection on the mind: *philosophy of mind*. Your attention would be turned, not to the latest results in psychology or neuroscience, but to commonsense assumptions with which this chapter began and to a very natural line of argument leading from these assumptions to a particular conclusion. As you begin your reflections, you might suspect a trick. If you are right, your excursion into philosophy of mind will be brief. You need only locate the point at which the trick occurs.

I think it unlikely that you will discover any such trick. Instead you will be forced to do what philosophers since at least the time of Descartes (1596– 1650) have been obliged to do. You will be forced to choose from among a variety of possibilities, each with its own distinctive advantages and liabilities. You might, for instance, simply accept the conclusion as Descartes did: minds and material objects are distinct kinds of entity, distinct 'substances'.

You might instead challenge one or more of the assumptions that led to that conclusion. If you elect this course, however, you should be aware that giving up or modifying an assumption can have unexpected and possibly unwelcome repercussions elsewhere. In any case, you will have your work cut out for you. The best minds in philosophy – and many of the best outside philosophy as well – have turned their attention to these issues, and there remains a notable lack of anything resembling a definitive, uncontested view of the mind's place in the universe.

Do not conclude from this that it would be a waste of time for you to delve into the philosophy of mind. On the contrary, you can enjoy the advantage of hindsight. You can learn from the successes and failures of others. Even if you cannot resolve every puzzle, you might at least come to learn something important about your picture of the universe and your place in it. If you are honest, you will be obliged to admit that this picture is gappy and unsatisfying in many respects. This, I submit, represents an important stage for each of us in coming to terms with ourselves and our standing in the order of things.

1.3 Science and Metaphysics

Some readers will be impatient with all this. Everyone knows that philosophers only *pose* problems and never solve them. Solutions to the important puzzles reside with the sciences. So it is to science that we should turn if we are ever to understand the mind and its place in a universe of quarks, leptons, and fields. Residual problems, problems not susceptible to scientific resolution, are at bottom phony *pseudo-problems*. Answers you give to them make no difference; any 'solution' you care to offer is as good as any other.

Although understandable, this kind of reaction is ill-considered. The success of science has depended on the enforcement of well-defined divisions of labor, coupled with a strategy of divide and conquer. Consider: there is no such thing as science; there are only individual sciences – physics, chemistry, meteorology, geology, biology, psychology, sociology. Each of these sciences (and of course there are others) carves off a strictly circumscribed domain. Staking out a domain requires delimiting permissible questions. No science sets out to answer *every* question, not even every 'empirical' question. In this way, every science passes the buck. The practice of buck-passing is benign because, in most cases, the buck is passed eventually to a science where it stops. Sometimes, however, the buck is passed out of the sciences altogether. Indeed, this is inevitable. The sciences do not speak with a single voice. Even if every science were fully successful within its domain of application, we should still be left with the question of how these domains are related, how pronouncements of the several sciences are to be calibrated against one another. And this question is, quite clearly, not a question answerable from within any particular science.

Enter metaphysics. One traditional function of metaphysics – or, more particularly, that branch of metaphysics called *ontology* – is to provide a completely general, overall conception of how things are. This includes not the pursuit of particular scientific ends, but an accommodation of the pronouncements of the several sciences. It includes, as well, an attempt to reconcile the sciences with ordinary experience. In one respect, every science takes ordinary experience for granted. A science is 'empirical' insofar as it appeals to observation in confirming experimental outcomes. But the intrinsic character of observation itself (and, by extension, the character of observers) is apparently left untouched by the sciences. The nature of observation – outwardly directed conscious experience – stands at the limits of science. It is just at this point that the puzzle with which this chapter began rears its head.

Scientific practice presupposes observers and observations. In the end, however, the sciences are silent about the intrinsic nature of both. The buck is passed. Our best hope for a unified picture – a picture that includes the universe as described by the sciences and includes, as well, observers and their observations – lies in pursuing serious ontology. The buck stops here. You can, of course, turn your back on the metaphysical issues. This, however, is easier said than done. Many of those who proclaim their independence from philosophical influences, in fact, embrace unacknowledged metaphysical assumptions. In considering the nature of the mind, the question is not whether you are going to engage in metaphysical thinking, but whether you are going to do so self-consciously.

1.4 Metaphysics and Cognitive Science

This book concerns the metaphysics – the ontology – of mind. It revolves around reflections on questions about mind that fall partly or wholly outside the purview of the sciences. I should warn you that this is not a particularly fashionable endeavor. Many philosophers regard metaphysics as sterile and dated. Many more have arrived at the belief that our best bet for understanding the mind and its place in the universe is to turn our backs on philosophy altogether. These philosophers promote the idea that the philosophy of mind is, or ought to be, one component of what has come to be called *cognitive science*. Cognitive science includes elements of psychology, neuroscience, computer science, linguistics, and anthropology. What has a philosopher to offer the scientists who work in these areas? That is a good question.

Perhaps philosophers can provide some kind of unifying influence, a general picture that accommodates finer-grained assessments issuing from the scientific contributors to cognitive science. This, it would seem, is simply to engage in a kind of attenuated metaphysics. The metaphysics is attenuated to the extent that it excludes traditional ontological concerns, and excludes as well consideration of the relation sciences such as physics or chemistry bear on our uncovering the nature of the mind.

If I sound skeptical about attempts to assimilate the philosophy of mind to cognitive science, I am. This book is premised on the conviction that the philosophy of mind is continuous with metaphysics as traditionally conceived. The difficult questions that arise in the philosophy of mind – and some would say the difficult questions *tout court* – are at bottom metaphysical questions. Such questions are, to all appearances, both legitimate and unavoidable. More to the point, philosophers can make (and in fact *have* made) progress in addressing them. This does not mean that philosophers have at hand a catalogue of fully satisfactory answers that could be succinctly reviewed and assessed in an introduction to the philosophy of mind. It does mean that you can reasonably hope to find, in subsequent chapters, some help in sorting through and eliminating options.

Am I just conceding the point: philosophers agree only on questions, not on answers? Not at all. Progress in philosophy, like progress in any domain, can be measured in two ways. You can focus on some definite goal, and ask yourself whether you are approaching that goal. But you can also ask yourself how far you have come from your starting point. And, on this count, philosophy can be said to move forward. In any case, we have little choice. Philosophical questions about the mind will not go away. They occur, even in laboratory contexts, to working scientists. And as recent widely publicized controversies over the nature of consciousness attest, ignoring such questions is not an option.

A final word about the relation philosophy of mind as I have characterized it bears to scientific endeavors. Philosophy of mind, I contend, is applied metaphysics, but metaphysics, like philosophy generally, is itself continuous with science. In engaging in metaphysics, you do not compete with, but complement, the sciences. You could think of metaphysics as concerned with the fundamental categories of being. Sorting out these categories is not a matter of engaging in empirical research, but the categories themselves are shaped in part by such research, and the nature of entities falling under the categories is only discoverable empirically, only in the kind of systematic intercourse with the universe characteristic of the sciences.

Suppose you are attracted, as Descartes and many other philosophers have been, to a substance–property ontology: the universe comprises objects, the substances, that possess assorted properties and stand in assorted relations to one another. Part of the appeal of such an ontology is its meshing with the picture of the universe we obtain from the sciences. What the substances and properties ultimately are is a matter to be determined by empirical investigation. Regarding philosophy of mind as applied metaphysics, then, is not to embrace the notion that philosophy of mind is a purely speculative, wholly a priori endeavor, an endeavor founded on reason alone, a matter of armchair reflection. Our understanding of the fundamental categories unfolds through everyday and scientific engagement with the universe. If science is the systematic investigation of the universe, then metaphysics is an ineliminable accompaniment of science.

1.5   A Look Ahead

The chapters to follow introduce a range of themes preeminent in the philosophy of mind. They do so in a way that presupposes no special background in the subject. The focus is on theories that have formed the basis of what might be regarded as the modern (or is it postmodern?) conception of mind. I have done my best to present each of these theories in a way that makes its attractions salient. Philosophers of mind have, in my judgment, been too quick to dismiss views they regard as quaint or outmoded. One result is that we are apt to forgo opportunities to learn from predecessors who, as it happens, had a good deal to teach. A second result of slighting unfashionable theories is that we risk repeating mistakes that we ought by now to have learned to avoid. I have tried to rectify this situation by providing sympathetic readings of positions that are sometimes caricatured, dismissed out of hand, or simply ignored. In so doing, I have put less weight on criticism of positions covered than do other authors. My job, as I see it, is to illuminate the territory. I leave it to you, the reader, to decide for yourself what to accept and what to reject.

This is not to say that I am neutral on topics discussed. Where I offer my opinion, however, I have tried to make clear that it *is* my opinion, a consideration to be weighed alongside other considerations. In a pair of concluding chapters I say what I think. There, I offer an account of minds and their place in the universe grounded in what I consider to be an independently plausible ontology. Chapter 12 is devoted to sketching that ontology; Chapter 13 spells out its implications for central issues in the philosophy of mind. The aim of these concluding chapters is less to convince you of the details of the view I prefer than to convince you of the importance of serious ontology for the philosophy of mind.

But this is to get ahead of the story. Chapters 12 and 13 follow on the heels of chapters devoted to the examination of a rich variety of conceptions of mind. Before venturing further, it might be worthwhile to provide a brief accounting of what you can expect in each of these intervening chapters.

Cartesian Dualism and Variations

Chapter 2 introduces Descartes's 'dualist' conception of mind. Descartes divides the world into mental and nonmental – immaterial and material – substances. Having done so, he is obliged to confront the notorious mind–body problem: how could mental and nonmental substances interact causally? Dissatisfaction with Descartes's apparent failure to answer this question bred amended versions of the Cartesian framework taken up in Chapter 3: parallelism, occasionalism, epiphenomenalism, idealism.

Parallelism, conceding the seeming impossibility of comprehending causal interaction between nonmaterial mental and material entities, supposes that mental and material substances do not interact, but undergo alterations in parallel. *Occasionalists* introduce God as a connecting link between the mental and the material. God wills changes in both the material world and in minds in such a way that occurrences in each realm are aligned just as they would be were they directly causally related. *Epiphenomenalists* defend one way, material-to-mental causation. Mental occurrences are causally inert 'by-products' of material events (most likely events in the brain). Epiphenomenalism has enjoyed renewed popularity in recent years, especially among philosophers and neuroscientists who take consciousness seriously but see no prospect of 'reducing' conscious experiences to goings-on in the brain. *Idealists* reject the materialist component of the dualist picture. All that exists, they contend, are minds and their contents. Idealists do not simply deny that external, material objects exist; they contend that an external material world is literally *unthinkable*. The thesis that material objects exist outside the mind is judged, not false, but *unintelligible*.

Behaviorism

Idealists reject the materialist side of the dualist conception of mind: nonmental material substance is inconceivable. Materialists hold, in contrast, that every substance is a material substance (and nothing more). Chapter 4 focuses on one historically influential materialist response to Cartesianism, behaviorism.

Behaviorists hoped to show that the Cartesian conception of minds as distinct from bodies was based on a fundamental misunderstanding of what you are up to when you ascribe states of mind to yourself and to others. According to behaviorists, claims about your mind can be 'analyzed' into claims about what you do or are disposed to do, how you behave or are disposed to behave. To say that you are in pain – suffering a headache, for instance – is just to say (if the behaviorist is right) that you are holding your head, moaning, saying 'I have a headache', and the like, or at least that you are disposed to do these things. Your being in pain, then, is not a matter of your being a nonmaterial mind that is undergoing pain; it is simply a matter of your behaving in a characteristic way or being so disposed.

The Mind–Brain Identity Theory

Proponents of the identity theory, the topic of Chapter 5, side with behaviorists against the Cartesian notion that minds are immaterial substances, but stand with Cartesians against the behaviorists' contention that having a mind is nothing more than behaving, or being disposed to behave, in particular ways. Identity theorists argue that states of mind (such as having a headache, or thinking of Alice Springs) are genuine internal states of agents possessing them. These states, as neuroscience will someday reveal, are states of our *brains*. Mental states are *identical with* these brain states: mental states *are* states of brains. The identity theory appeals to anyone attracted to the idea that minds are after all just brains. But, at the same time, the identity theory inherits problems associated with that doctrine, most especially the problem of finding a place of consciousness and qualities of conscious experiences in the brain.

Functionalism

Chapter 6 turns to functionalism, the historical successor to behaviorism and the identity theory, and certainly the present day's most widely accepted conception of mind. Functionalists identify states of mind, not with states of brains, but with *functional roles*. Your having a headache is for you to be in some state (doubtless a state of your brain) that exhibits input–output conditions characteristic of pain. (In this, functionalism resembles a dressed-up version of behaviorism.) Headaches are caused by blows to the head, excessive alcohol intake, lack of sleep, eyestrain, and the like, and they produce characteristic responses that include, but are not exhausted by, overt behavior of the sort focused on by behaviorists: head-holding, moaning, utterances of 'I have a headache'. In addition to behavior, a headache gives rise to other states of mind. (And here functionalists depart from the behaviorist contention that claims about states of mind are fully analyzable in terms of behavior and behavioral dispositions.) Your headache likely leads you to believe that you have a headache, for instance, to wish matters were otherwise, and to want aspirin.

Central to all forms of functionalism is the idea that states of mind are 'multiply realizable'. To be in a particular mental state is to be in a state that has a certain characteristic role. But many different kinds of material state could occupy or 'realize' the very same role. You, an octopus, and an Alpha Centaurian could all be in pain despite your very different physiologies (pretend that Alpha Centaurians have a silicon-based 'biology'). If being in pain were, as identity theorists suggest, solely being in a particular kind of neurological state, then octopodes and Alpha Centaurians, lacking physiologies comparable to ours, could not be in pain – an apparent absurdity. Functionalism affords a powerful model that allows for the 'abstraction' of states of mind from the hardware that 'realizes' them. One result is that dramatically different kinds of material system could all share a common *psychology*.

The Representational Theory of Mind

The Representational Theory of Mind, an important strain of mainstream functionalism, is the subject of Chapter 7. Proponents of the Representational Theory of Mind, regard minds as 'information-processing' devices. Information, in the form of 'mental representations' encoded in a Language of Thought, mediates incoming stimuli and behavioral outputs. On a view of this kind, minds could be thought of as 'software' running, not on factory-assembled computing machines, but on neurological 'hardware' in brains. The appeal of such a picture is obvious: it promises to demystify minds and their operations, neatly integrating them into the material universe.

The Representational Theory of Mind inherits a difficulty widely associated with functionalist theories in general: the difficulty of accommodating qualities of conscious experiences. When you are in pain you are in a state of a kind that has various characteristic causes and effects. But what is salient to anyone undergoing a painful experience, being in this state is *painful*. Painfulness is qualitatively distinctive. Indeed you might think that what makes a state a *pain* state is its having this character. The difficulty is to see how the qualitative aspect of conscious experiences might be reconciled with the functionalist picture.

The Intentional Stance

Daniel Dennett, the hero (or villain!) of Chapter 8, focuses on the 'propositional attitudes': beliefs, desires, intentions, and the like. Dennett holds that the question whether a creature (or indeed anything at all) possesses a belief, or desire, or intention, turns solely on the utility of the practice of ascribing beliefs (or desires, or intentions) to it. We find it useful to describe cats, desktop computers, and even thermostats as believing this or that. Your cat *believes there is a mouse under the refrigerator.* Your desktop computer *believes the printer is out of paper* (and so alerts you to that fact); the thermostat *believes that the room is too cool* (and, in consequence, turns the furnace on).

To the extent that such attributions of belief *work*, cats, desktop computers and thermostats (and, of course, people and many other creatures) are 'true believers'. There is no further question of whether thermostats, for instance, *really* have beliefs, or whether it is just that we can get away with treating them *as though* they do. *All there is* to having a belief is to be so treatable.

The practice of ascribing beliefs, desires, and intentions is, according to Dennett, a matter of taking up a particular *stance*: the 'intentional stance'. In pursuing science, however, you would find surprising differences in creatures' responses to one another and to their environments. An understanding of these requires that you adopt the 'design stance'. In so doing, you discover that mechanisms responsible for behavior differ importantly across species. Actions indistinguishable from the intentional perspective look very different once you consider the 'design' of creatures performing them. Eventually, the design stance gives way to the 'physical stance'. This is the move from considering a creature's software to looking at its hardware.

Having a mind, then, is simply a matter of being describable from the intentional stance. The mystery of how minds are related to bodies vanishes, according to Dennett, once you recognize that truths expressible from within the intentional stance can be explained by reverting to the design stance. For their part, design stance truths are grounded in facts uncovered from within the physical stance.

Reduction and Elimination

The thought that all there is to having a mind is being so describable, could easily lead to the more radical thought that minds are, at bottom, fictions. In Chapter 9 this possibility is explored in some detail. Perhaps our talk of minds and their contents and our practice of explaining behavior by reference to mental goings-on, are simply remnants of primitive animistic forms of explanation. We once explained the weather by the fickleness of the gods who controlled it. Later, we developed a science, meteorology, that enabled us to understand meteorological phenomena purely 'naturalistically' without appeal to conscious agents. Maybe explanations of intelligent behavior should likewise move beyond appeals to states of mind and mental processes.

One possibility is that talk of minds could be replaced by talk of states and processes unearthed by neuroscience. A second possibility takes seriously an important feature of the Representational Theory of Mind. Suppose the mind *were* animated by 'mental representations'. These would be sentences in a built-in, hard-wired 'Language of Thought'. But just as a computing machine cares nothing for the significance of symbols it processes, so minds – or their physical 'realizers', brains – care nothing for the meanings of symbols in the Language of Thought: mental processes are purely 'syntactic'. Representational 'content', central in traditional accounts of the mind, drops out of the picture, taking with it the familiar categories of belief, desire, and intention.

Consciousness

Consciousness is the 800-pound gorilla that inevitably asserts itself in the philosophy of mind. Psychology and neuroscience have made impressive advances in recent years. None of these advances, however, has brought us a step closer to understanding the 'mystery of consciousness'. Or so it seems.

What exactly *is* the 'mystery of consciousness'? It is not easy to say. You can get a feel for it, however, by reflecting on a vivid conscious experience, the sort of experience you might have in strolling on a tropical beach at sunset, for instance. You have visual experiences of the ocean, the sky, the setting sun, the sand; you feel a cool breeze and the warm sand under your feet; you hear the waves lapping the shoreline and the calls of birds; you smell the scent of flowers and salt air. These experiences are the result of your perceptual encounter with your surroundings. Your 'sensory surfaces' are stimulated, and signals are passed on to your brain where, it would seem, they issue in your experiences. If this sequence were blocked at any point or inhibited, your experiences would be diminished.

As a result of your experiences, you respond in various ways. You are led to entertain new thoughts and to continue strolling; you turn your head to find a bird that has produced a particularly striking call. A scientist studying all this could, at least in theory, follow the whole input–output sequence, or at any rate have a detailed picture of what is going on inside your body. The problem is that there is apparently a 'gap' between what a scientist could observe, and what your experiences are like. How are experiences and their 'Technicolor' qualities to fit into the scientific picture? This is the mystery of consciousness.

Faced with this mystery, scientists and philosophers have responded in various ways. Some have chosen simply to ignore the phenomenon, dismiss it as unfit for scientific study. Although a scientist is free to 'bracket' or ignore one topic for the sake of studying others, philosophers do not have this luxury. Philosophers are bound to attempt a unified picture of the universe, a picture that accommodates both the findings of psychology and neuroscience, *and* conscious experiences.

Another option is to accept conscious experiences as they are, but to assimilate them to functional states of agents. To be conscious is just to be in a particular sort of functional state, a state realized in your brain. The question is whether qualities of conscious experience can plausibly be dealt with in this fashion. Many have doubted it.

Other options include *epiphenomenalism* (conscious qualities are causally inert by-products of material processes in the brain), *panpsychism* (what you might regard as qualities of conscious experience are really part of the 'intrinsic nature' of matter), and *representationalism* (what you regard as qualities of experiences are in fact qualities you represent objects you experience as having; qualities of your beach experience are, at bottom, just qualities of objects that you are experiencing).

Clearly, then, if you take *qualia* (the term used by philosophers to designate qualities of conscious experiences) seriously, you will need to say something about what David Chalmers calls 'the hard problem': what relation does consciousness bear to material goings-on? You might, in the end, be driven to embrace a position that seemed antecedently unattractive, epiphenomenalism, for instance, or panpsychism. Before accepting a position concerning which you might have important reservations, however, you should be certain that you have exhausted the space of possibilities. A central goal of this book is to make you aware of the extent of that space and thereby to equip you to choose wisely.

Non-Reductive Physicalism

Cartesian dualism takes consciousness seriously, while at the same time making it clear why conscious experiences are not going to be encountered in scientific investigations of the material universe. That is the good news. The bad news is that Cartesian dualism makes the interface between minds and bodies – mind–body interaction – wholly mysterious. How could substances sharing no attributes causally interact?

Suppose Descartes is wrong, however. Suppose mental properties and material properties *could* be possessed by material substances. Neuroscience research suggests that mental properties are 'grounded in' physical properties. You experience a pain, for instance, *because* your nervous system is in a particular state. Still, pains evidently differ qualitatively from anything in your nervous system. This suggests that, although the presence of mental properties depends on the presence of physical properties, mental properties are nevertheless distinct from physical properties; the mental is not 'reducible' to the physical. The result: substance monism combined with a dualism of properties.

This neat 'non-reductive physicalist' solution to the mind–body problem has recently come under fire. Mental and material properties might be properties of a single substance, but if mental and material properties are genuinely distinct, and if mental properties depend for their very existence on material properties, it is hard to see how mental properties could have a role in the production of bodily behavior. This is the Cartesian problem all over again.

Suppose that your forming the belief that a snake is in the path results in a particular bodily response (your altering course). Suppose that some material event in your brain 'realizes' this belief, and that this material realizer causes you to alter your course. The material realizer might 'underlie' or 'give rise to' various mental properties. Suppose that it does. Those properties need have no part in producing your subsequent behavior; however, they might be 'causally irrelevant'.

A fast-bowled red cricket ball cracks a batsman's rib. The ball is red, but its redness apparently has no role in the cracking. Many have thought that there are excellent reasons to think mental properties are like this; the properties are on the scene, perfectly genuine, but 'causally irrelevant'. In that case you would be left with a virulent new form of epiphenomenalism. Once again, you will need to sort through the options and find the one you regard as the most promising, perhaps only because it is the least objectionable.

Ontology and Mind

The book concludes with two chapters in which, as noted above, I lay out an account of the mind grounded in a particular ontology. The ontology, details of which occupy Chapter 12, regards substances as the basic entities. Substances possess properties, which I take to be *ways* substances are. You could think of a cricket ball as a substance. A cricket ball is red and spherical. The ball's redness and sphericity are ways it – that ball, and nothing else – is. Every property contributes distinctively to its possessor's qualities and causal powers or dispositions. Indeed, every property is *both* qualitative and dispositional: properties are powerful qualities. From this basis, I construct, in Chapter 13, an account of the mind. The construction is tentative and sketchy, but the fundamental ideas will be clear. I regard it as an important feature of the conception I sketch that it accommodates the attractions of its competitors without inheriting (all) their liabilities. There is, as I hope to convince you, something right as well as something wrong in each of the diverse accounts of the mind taken up in earlier chapters.

A final comment. This book will have achieved its purpose if it convinces you that any philosophical account of the nature of the mind includes an important metaphysical component. I am less concerned with your agreeing with me on the details of this component. To my way of thinking, you will have made considerable progress if only you recognize that the study of mind requires a stiff measure of ontological seriousness.

Suggested Reading

A book like this should inspire readers to look more closely at primary sources, the work of philosophers bent on defending (or attacking) positions being discussed. To this end, anthologies in the philosophy of mind can be especially useful. Three new collections and an old standard merit special mention. O'Connor and Robb's *Philosophy of Mind: Contemporary Readings* (2003) assembles essays expressly selected to complement this volume. Rosenthal's *The Nature of Mind* (1991), and its updated replacement, Chalmers's *Philosophy of Mind: Classical and Contemporary Readings* (2002), cover much of the same territory. My own collection, *Philosophy of Mind: A Guide and Anthology* (2003b) includes, in addition to primary source readings, extensive introductory material.

Block, Flanagan, and Güzeldere's *The Nature of Consciousness: Philosophical Debates* (1997) focuses on consciousness and includes a valuable comprehensive introduction by Güven Güzeldere. William Lycan's *Mind and Cognition: An Anthology* (1999), Christensen and Turner's *Folk Psychology and the Philosophy of Mind* (1993), and Geirsson and Losonsky's *Readings in Mind and Language* (1996) contain, in addition to readings in philosophy of mind, selections on topics in cognitive science that will be of interest to readers hankering for empirical enlightenment. Beakley and Ludlow's *The Philosophy of Mind: Classical Problems, Contemporary Issues* (1992) combines selections from towering historical figures with present day sources in both philosophy and psychology, arranged by topic. Godfrey Vesey's *Body and Mind: Readings in Philosophy* (1964), Daniel Kolak's *From Plato to Wittgenstein: The Historical Foundations of Mind* (1997), Peter Morton's *Historical Introduction to the Philosophy of Mind: Readings with Commentary* (1997), and Daniel Robinson's *The Mind* (1999) all incorporate interesting and important historical selections.

Samuel Guttenplan's (1994) *Companion* and Stich and Warfield's (2003) *Guide* to the philosophy of mind are organized topically and provide in depth coverage of particular subjects. Gregory's *Companion to the Mind* (1987) has broader ambitions, and could prove useful on topics in psychology and the neurosciences.

Volumes intended, as this one is, to introduce readers to the philosophy of mind include: Tim Crane's *Elements of Mind: An Introduction to the Philosophy of Mind* (2001), George Graham's *Philosophy of Mind: An Introduction* (1993), Dale Jacquette's *Philosophy of Mind* (1994), Jaegwon Kim's *Philosophy of Mind* (2010), E. J. Lowe's *An Introduction to the Philosophy of Mind* (2000a), and William Lyons's *Matters of the Mind* (2001). D. M. Armstrong in *The Mind–Body Problem: An Opinionated Introduction* (1999), Anthony Kenny in *The Metaphysics of Mind* (1989), Colin McGinn in *The Character of Mind* (1982), and Georges Rey in *Philosophy of Mind: A Contentiously Classical Approach* (1997) advance distinctive views of the mind in the course of introducing the subject. Being opinionated goes with being a philosopher. A clear view of the territory results not from occupying a single, neutral vantage point, but from acquiring familiarity with a variety of perspectives.

Braddon-Mitchell and Jackson's *The Philosophy of Mind and Cognition* (1996) and Paul Churchland's *Matter and Consciousness: A Contemporary Introduction to the Philosophy of Mind*, Revised Edition (1988) incorporate useful discussions of topics in the philosophy of mind and in cognitive science. Readers whose interests tend toward the empirical will benefit from a look at Bechtel *et al.*, *A Companion to Cognitive Science* (1998); Joao Brânquinho, *The Foundations of Cognitive Science* (2001); Cummins and Cummins, *Minds, Brains, and Computers: The Foundations of Cognitive Science: An Anthology* (2000); Jay Garfield, *Foundations of Cognitive Science: The Essential Readings* (1990); Gleitman *et al.*, *An Invitation to Cognitive Science* (1995); and Michael Posner, *Foundations of Cognitive Science* (1989). (As these titles suggest, cognitive science has a certain obsession with its foundations.) These anthologies march alongside introductory texts that include Andy Clark, *Being There: Putting Brain, Body, and World Together Again* (1997) and *Mindware: An Introduction to Cognitive Science* (2001); James Fetzer, *Philosophy and Cognitive Science* (1991); Owen Flanagan, *The Science of the Mind* (1984); Robert Harnish, *Minds, Brains, Computers: An Historical Introduction to the Foundations of Cognitive Science* (2001); Rom Harré, *Cognitive Science: A Philosophical Introduction* (2002); and Paul Thagard, *Mind: Introduction to Cognitive Science* (1996). The online *MIT Encyclopedia of Cognitive Sciences* (Wilson and Keil, 1999) is a useful and reliable Internet resource.

In general, you should be skeptical of materials you turn up on the Internet. Disinformation swamps information; self-proclaimed philosophers often aren't. For this reason, entries in Wikipedia should be approached with extreme caution. In contrast, the online *Stanford Encyclopedia of Philosophy* (Zalta 2002) is a trustworthy source for topics in the philosophy of mind. Marco Nani's (2001) *Field Guide for the Philosophy of Mind* and Chris Eliasmith's (2003) *Dictionary of Philosophy of Mind* contain useful entries. David Chalmers's *Contemporary Philosophy of Mind: An Annotated*

Bibliography (Chalmers 2001) is an excellent bibliographic resource. Web sites of authors included in the bibliography can also contain useful and reliable material. Hint: to locate an author's web page, try typing 'Author Name philosophy' (the author's name, followed by a space, then 'philosophy') into your favorite search engine.

2   Cartesian Dualism

2.1   Science and Philosophy

We all take ourselves and our fellow human beings to have minds. But what exactly is it to 'have a mind'? The question is one with which philosophers and non-philosophers have struggled throughout recorded history. According to some, minds are spiritual entities, souls that temporarily reside in bodies, entering at birth (or maybe at conception) and departing on death. Indeed, death *is* just a soul's taking leave of a body. Others imagine the relation between minds and bodies to be more intimate. Minds, they hold, are not entities. Minds resemble fists or laps: a mind is present when a body is organized in a particular way, and absent otherwise. A mind ceases to exist on the death of the body because the body's internal structure breaks down. Still others hold that minds are indeed entities, physical entities: minds are *brains*.

The aim of this chapter is to make a start at sorting out some of these competing views and thus to make clear what precisely is at stake when you ask what minds are. You will discover that the issues are rarely clear cut. This is scarcely surprising. Puzzles posed by the investigation of minds are some of the deepest in philosophy. In the end, you might find no proffered solution entirely satisfactory. Even if that is so, you will at least have a better understanding of the attractions and liabilities inherent in different ways of regarding minds.

Having said this, I want to head off one natural line of response. A common attitude toward philosophy is that philosophers never answer questions, but merely pose them. Scientists, in contrast, are in the business of delivering answers. Questions, the answers to which elude science, questions that seem scientifically unanswerable, are often dismissed as 'merely philosophical'. It is but a short step from this deflationary depiction of philosophy to the notion that, where philosophy is concerned, there are no settled truths: every opinion is as good as any other.

This conception of philosophy and its relation to science is inadequate, naïve, and, in the end, self-defeating. What eludes science need not be unsettled. The state of the universe immediately preceding the Big Bang, for instance, might be forever unknowable. We are, it seems, evidentially cut off from that state. It would be absurd to conclude, however, that there was no such state, or that every claim concerning its character is as good as every other. Similarly, from the fact that philosophers often disagree as to the status of minds, it does not follow that minds have no definite status or that 'anything goes' when discussing the mind.

As you will see in the chapters ahead, questions that arise in the philosophy of mind are rarely susceptible to straightforward *empirical* answers. (An empirical question is one decidable, at least in principle, by observation or experiment.) Although experimental results tell against some conceptions of the mind's nature, most competing traditional accounts of the mind are consistent with whatever empirical evidence anyone now possesses or might conceivably possess in the future. The philosophical question concerns what you are to *make* of this evidence. And here your guide cannot be purely scientific. Science provides an assortment of frameworks for representing empirical findings, but no strictly scientific principles tell you how to interpret or make sense of those findings. For that, you must rely on 'common sense' and on philosophy.

This does not mean that empirical evidence supports specific philosophical theories. Rather, the activity of sorting through scientific findings and reconciling these with ordinary experience, and with a constellation of beliefs you have adopted on the basis of other findings, *is* a kind of philosophizing: *philosophers are not the only philosophers.* Card-carrying philosophers are just those who do their philosophizing self-consciously.

2.2 Descartes's Dualism

A natural starting point is an influential conception of mind advanced by René Descartes. Descartes held that minds and bodies are 'substances' of distinct kinds that, in the case of living human beings, happen to be intimately related. Human beings are compound entities, entities made up of coupled mental and material substances.

This dualism of substances (subsequently labeled *Cartesian dualism*) nowadays strikes most philosophers and scientists interested in the mind as hopelessly misguided. Until quite recently, it was widely supposed that the source of the notorious mind–body problem – the problem of how minds and bodies could causally interact – stemmed from the acceptance of the Cartesian picture: a solution to the problem could be had by rejecting dualism. As you will see, this diagnosis has not panned out. Nevertheless, you can begin to develop an appreciation of the mind–body problem by examining Descartes's approach to the mind.

As a preliminary, think about some *prima facie* differences between mental and material objects and states. First, material objects are spatial; they occupy a region of space, excluding other bodies from that region; they have a particular shape, and they exhibit spatial dimensions. Mental objects

– thoughts and sensations, for instance – are apparently nonspatial. What is the size and shape of your desire for a Whopper? Might your thinking of Texas be a centimeter long? Such questions evidently make no sense.

You might suppose that bodily sensations – some of them at least – have definite spatial locations. A pain in your left big toe is, after all, in your left big toe. (Does this mean it is big-toe-shaped?) But is this quite right? Consider the phenomenon of 'phantom pain', a phenomenon well known to Descartes and his contemporaries. Amputees often seem to undergo experiences of pains in their amputated limbs. Your big toe could be amputated, and you still might continue to experience the very same kind of throbbing pain you experienced prior to its amputation, and this pain might seem to you to be in a region at the end of your foot once occupied by your big toe.

This suggests that, although you experience pains and other sensations *as* occurring in various bodily locations, it need not follow that sensory experiences occur *at* those locations. Following Descartes, you might say that an experience of pain-in-your-left-big-toe is a *kind* of experience. Such an experience differs *qualitatively* from an experience of pain-in-your-*right*-big-toe. There is no reason to think – and indeed good reason *not* to think – that such experiences must be located where they are felt to be located – or even that they have any definite location at all. Mental states, then, unlike material states, appear to be distinctively nonspatial. This, at any rate, is Descartes's conclusion.

A second important difference between the mental and the material is qualitative. Think of the qualities of your experience of a pain in your big toe. You might find these qualities difficult to describe, but that need not temper your awareness of them. Now ask yourself whether you would ever expect to encounter *these* qualities in a material object. A neuroscientist observing your nervous system while you are experiencing pain will observe nothing qualitatively resembling your pain. Indeed, the possibility seems to make no sense.

The point can be summed up as follows. Qualities of conscious experiences appear to be nothing at all like qualities of material objects. More significantly, they are apparently altogether unlike the qualities of any *conceivable* material object. The natural conclusion to draw is that mental qualities differ in kind from material qualities. Thus, mental qualities are not qualities of material objects.

A third distinction between the mental and the material is partly *epistemological* – that is, it concerns the character of our knowledge of such things. The knowledge you have of your own states of mind is direct, immediate, and unchallengeable in a way that your knowledge of material objects is not. Philosophers sometimes put this by saying that you have 'privileged access' to your own states of mind. Descartes himself believed that this knowledge was *incorrigible*: your thoughts about your current states of mind could not fail to be true. He believed, as well, that the contents of our own minds were 'transparent' to us. In consequence, Descartes can be taken to embrace both

1   *Transparency*: if you are in a particular state of mind, you *know* you are in that state; and
2   *Incorrigibility*: if you think you are in a particular state of mind, you *are* in that state; being in a mental state *is* thinking that you are in that state.

The Cartesian notion that the mind is 'transparent' might strike you as implausible. Freud long ago provided convincing reasons to suppose that particular states of mind could be consciously inaccessible. Today cognitive scientists routinely assume that all sorts of mental states and operations are inaccessible to consciousness. Social psychologists take delight in showing us that we are often poor judges as to what we *really* believe or want.

You could accept all this, however, without jettisoning Descartes's central insight. The access you have to your own states of mind *is* distinctive, if not infallible. You entertain thoughts and experience pains *self-consciously*. An observer, even an observer armed with a brain-scanning device, could only *infer* the occurrence in you of such goings-on. Your access to your own states of mind is direct and unmediated, anyone else's access to your states of mind is invariably indirect, mediated by observations of what you say or do.

Philosophers put this by saying that states of mind are 'private'. They are 'directly available' only by the person (or creature) to which they belong; outsiders can only infer others' mental states from their material effects. You can tell me what you are thinking, or I can guess it from the expression on your face. Neuroscientists might eventually be able to work out what you are thinking by observing patterns of neurological activities in your brain. Another's awareness of your mental life, however, is never direct in the way yours appears to be. A neuroscientist's inferences about your states of mind would be indirect, on a par with inferences about falling air pressure based on barometer readings.

The situation is very different for material objects and material properties and states. If mental items are necessarily private, material things are necessarily *public*. When it comes to a material object, or the state of a material object, if you are in a position to observe it, then anyone else could observe it as well by taking up your observational standpoint. The type of 'asymmetry of access' characteristic of minds is entirely absent.

Again, this suggests that minds and material bodies are very different kinds of entity. Descartes offers an explanation for this difference: minds and material bodies are *distinct kinds of substance*. A mental substance possesses properties that could not be possessed by any material substance, and a material substance possesses properties no mental substance could possess. Indeed, according to Descartes, there is *no* overlap in the properties possessed by mental and material substances.

Before taking up Descartes's view in more detail, it might be useful to chart the three differences between the mental and the material just mentioned (Figure 2.1). In later chapters, I shall reopen discussion of these distinctions. For the present, however, let us accept them as they stand and notice what follows.

Material Bodies	Minds
Spatial	Nonspatial
Material qualities	Distinctively mental qualities
Public	Private

Figure 2.1

2.3   Substances, Attributes, Modes

Descartes assumes, as many philosophers have been inclined to assume, that the world is made up of *substances*. A substance is not, as the term might suggest, a kind of *stuff* like water, or butter, or paint. Descartes, following tradition, regards substances as individual, self-standing *objects*. The desk at which I am now sitting is, in this traditional sense, a substance, as is the pen I hold in my hand, the tree outside my window, and the bird nesting in its branches. These substances are complex: each is made up of other substances, their parts. My desk is made up of pieces of wood, organized in a particular way. Each of these pieces of wood (and each of the screws holding them together) is a substance in its own right. Similarly, the pen, the tree, and the bird are all made up of parts that are themselves substances. And, of course, these substances are themselves made up of distinct substances. (A natural question to ask is whether *every* substance is made up of parts, each of which is a distinct substance.) Substances, note, are individuals – 'particulars' in the jargon of philosophers – as distinct from classes, types, or kinds of thing. This bird and this tree are substances, but the class of birds is a class, not a substance; beech and oak are *species* of substance, not substances.

Substances are to be contrasted, on the one hand, with nonsubstantial individuals, and, on the other hand with properties. Nonsubstantial individuals include 'concrete' items such as events and 'abstract' entities such as sets and numbers. An event (a particular chicken's crossing a particular road on a particular occasion, for instance) could be regarded as a dated, nonrepeatable particular. In this respect, events resemble substances. Just as two exactly similar peas in a pod are nevertheless distinct peas, so your reading this sentence now is one event, and your reading the very same sentence tomorrow is a distinct event. You might think of events as changes substances undergo. Finally, substances and events are *concrete* particulars as distinct from 'abstract entities' such as sets and numbers: the set of cows, the number two.

Properties are *had* or *possessed* (or 'instantiated') by substances. Think of an ordinary substance, a particular red billiard ball. You can distinguish the ball's *redness* from its *sphericity* and its *mass*. In so doing, you consider three of the ball's properties. Similarly, you can distinguish the ball, as *bearer* of these properties, from its properties. On the view I am associating with Descartes, the ball is a substance that possesses a number of properties including redness, sphericity, and a definite mass. Properties and substances are correlative, the one requiring the other. You could not peel off an object's properties and leave a bare unpropertied substance. Nor could properties float free of substances and persist on their own. Some philosophers have argued that substances are nothing more than collections or *bundles* of properties. This is not Descartes's view, however, nor is it a view that will play a role in what follows.

I have mentioned substances and properties. Descartes, in fact, speaks not of properties, but of 'attributes' and 'modes'. An attribute is what makes a substance the basic kind of substance it is. A material (or physical; I shall use the terms interchangeably) substance is a substance characterized by the attribute of *extension*: an extended substance. Extension is, roughly, *spatiality*. Thus, a material substance is a substance that occupies a definite spatial region at any given time and possesses a definite shape and size. The particular shape and size possessed by material substances are *modes* of extension, *ways* of being extended. What you would ordinarily think of as properties of everyday material objects are, for Descartes, *modes of extension*.

On this conception, a billiard ball's sphericity is a mode of extension; its sphericity is the way it is shaped. What of the ball's color? Here Descartes contends that the distinctive visual experience you have when you look at a red billiard ball does not resemble the feature of the ball that produces this experience in us. That feature might be the texture of the ball's surface, a texture that reflects light in a particular way so as to look red. Texture – the arrangement of micro-particles making up an object's surface – is another mode of extension, another way the ball is extended, another material property.

2.4   The Metaphysics of Cartesian Dualism

Descartes puts the attribute–mode distinction to work by supposing that each basic kind of substance is characterized by one, and only one, distinctive attribute. A material substance is a substance characterized by the attribute of extension, a substance extended in various ways. A mental substance, in contrast, is a substance characterized by a very different attribute, the attribute of *thought*. Descartes gives the term 'thought' a broader sense than we would today. Anything you might count in everyday life as a state of mind – a sensation, an image, an emotion, a belief, a desire – Descartes regards as a mode of thought, a *way of thinking*, a mental property. (In another respect, Descartes's conception of thought is narrower than ours. Descartes appears not to countenance the possibility of nonconscious thought.)

Putting all this together, you are now in a position to understand Cartesian dualism. Bodies are material substances, substances characterized by the attribute of extension. Every material body is extended in various ways; every material body possesses various material properties. Minds, too, are substances, but not material substances. Minds are characterized by the attribute of thought; minds possess distinctively mental properties.

One more step is required to yield dualism. Every substance possesses just one definitive attribute. If a substance is characterized by the attribute of extension (and so is extended in various ways), it could not be a thinking substance, one characterized by the attribute of thought. Similarly, if a substance is characterized by the attribute of thought (and thus possesses various mental properties, various modes of thought: feelings, images, beliefs), it could not be extended, it could not be characterized by the attribute of extension. Thought and extension mutually exclude one another. It follows that no extended substance thinks, and no thinking substance is extended. Minds are thinking substances and bodies are extended substances, so minds are distinct from bodies.

Descartes embraces this conclusion, but he does not deny that minds and bodies are, as they clearly seem to be, intimately related. Think for a moment, as Descartes does, of the mind as the *I*: the ego, the self. You are related in an especially intimate way to a particular body, *your* body. When that body's finger comes too near the flame of a candle *you* feel pain. When my body's finger goes near the flame, in contrast, *you* feel no pain, although *I* do. When you decide to get up and walk across the room, it is *your* body that moves, not mine. To be sure you can control my body. You can ask me to get up and walk across the room, or order me to do so at gunpoint, or tie a rope around me and *drag* me across the room. In so doing, however, your decision affects my body only indirectly, only by way of some movement of *your* body. Movements of your own body (your tongue and vocal cords, or your limbs) seem, in contrast, largely under your immediate voluntary control.

Descartes's picture – the Cartesian picture – is one according to which the world consists of two kinds of substance: material substances and mental substances. Material substances are extended and unthinking; mental substances think, but are unextended. Each mental substance bears an especially intimate relation to some particular material substance. (Or at any rate this is the arrangement with which we are most familiar. According to Descartes, it might be possible for a mental substance to persist after the demise of the material substance it once animated: you might survive the death of your body.) Mental and material substances, although utterly distinct, interact causally. Your body is guided by your plans and decisions. Your mind receives signals from your body in the form of sensory experiences that provide you with information about the state of your body and, indirectly, information concerning the state of the world outside your body. The world causally impinges on your mind by way of your senses: your eyes, ears, nose, and your sense of touch.

The Cartesian picture is straightforward. Imagine that you sit on a tack planted in your chair by a malicious practical joker. Your sitting on the tack (a material event involving a pair of material substances, the tack and your body) gives rise to a distinctive sensation of pain (a mental event). This sensation or feeling in turn generates another mental event, a desire to leap upwards, and this desire brings about a leaping (Figure 2.2).

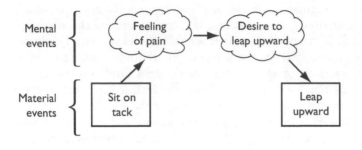

Figure 2.2

On the face of it, Cartesian dualism accords nicely with common sense. You see yourself as *having* a body, but as *distinct* from your body in at least the following sense. You can apparently conceive of your body's changing dramatically, or ceasing to exist altogether, while *you* continue to exist: Kafka's Gregor Samsa awoke one morning to discover he had metamorphosed into a large cockroach. Tabloids are fond of cases in which people report 'out of body' experiences, and cases in which minds move from one body to another are a staple of science fiction.

True, you speak of yourself as 'having a mind' – and, for that matter, you speak of changing your mind. But, while you can perhaps imagine your body's being destroyed while you remain, it is less clear that you could coherently imagine your surviving the demise of your mind or self. You can imagine that you or your mind ceases to exist while your body continues to exist (in a vegetative state perhaps), but that is another matter. You might be able to imagine cases in which you swap bodies, but it seems to make no sense to suppose that you could swap minds or selves. 'Changing your mind' is not akin to changing a lightbulb, not a matter of exchanging one mind for another, but a matter of revising your beliefs. When a chastened Scrooge becomes 'a new person', he does not swap selves, but alters his attitudes.

In addition to meshing with a commonsense conception of the self, Cartesian dualism also promises a reconciliation of our scientific picture of the universe with ordinary experience. Science tells us – or at any rate physics apparently tells us – that the universe consists of microscopic, colorless particles jumbled together to form familiar middle-sized objects. Our experience of the universe is quite different. Your visual experience of the red billiard ball is not an experience of a colorless spherical jumble. Sounds are vibrations in a medium (air or water, for instance). Yet your experience of a performance of an Offenbach overture differs qualitatively from anything science seems likely to turn up in its investigation of the physical universe. Dualism makes sense of this apparent bifurcation. Material bodies are nothing more than collections of minute, silent, colorless objects interacting in space over time.

Such interactions, however, produce in the mind 'Technicolor' experiences sporting lively qualities quite unlike the qualities of any material object.

Qualities of our experiences (at bottom, distinctive modes of thought) appear to differ dramatically from the qualities of material bodies (modes of extension). Despite these apparent differences, however, Descartes holds that experiential qualities and material qualities co-vary. One result of this co-variation is that qualities of experiences can serve as reliable signs or indicators of qualities of material objects and events. Red objects look red, not because they are made up of red particles, but because (let us suppose) they have a particular kind of surface texture. Red objects share this texture, or at any rate share properties that structure light so as to produce, in observers, characteristic experiences of redness.

2.5 Mind–Body Interaction

We seem, then, following Descartes, to be in a position to account for apparently dramatic qualitative differences between our experiences and objects experienced, and for our capacity to infer qualities of the world from qualities of our experiences. Further, we can accommodate our own everyday view of ourselves as housed in, but in some way distinct from, our bodies. All this is to the good. Unfortunately, Cartesian dualism comes at a price, a price few philosophers, even in Descartes's day, have been prepared to pay.

One difficulty, which was immediately obvious to Descartes's contemporaries, is a difficulty that Descartes himself understood keenly. Central to Descartes's view is the idea that minds and bodies causally interact. But if minds and bodies are utterly different kinds of substance, it is hard to see how such causal interaction could possibly occur. Minds or selves, you will recall, are immaterial thinking, but *unextended*, substances. Material bodies, in contrast, are *extended* but unthinking. How could entities of such wholly different kinds affect one another causally? How could an event in an immaterial mind bring about a material effect? How could a physical event beget a change in an immaterial mind? The metaphysical distance Descartes places between minds and material bodies would seem to preclude causal interaction.

Here is how Princess Elizabeth of Bohemia put it in a letter to Descartes: 'It would be easier for me to attribute matter and extension to the soul than to attribute to an immaterial body the capacity to move and be moved by a [material] body' (see Kenny 1970, 140). The difficulty is acute for Descartes for a number of reasons. First, Descartes agrees with many of his contemporaries that motion is transmitted via direct physical contact. If the mind is an immaterial substance, how *could* it make contact with a physical body? How *could* a physical body come into contact with a mind?

Second, Descartes's thinks of causation on the model of *transference*. 'Nothing', he says, 'can be in an effect that is not in the cause.' If a moving body imparts motion to another body causing it to move, the first body cannot impart *more* motion than it already possesses. If minds and bodies share *no* properties, however, how could a mind impart *any* property to a body, or a body impart *any* property to a mind?

A Cartesian might concede the difficulty but contend that causal relations between a mental and a material substance are *sui generis*: mental–material causation is not a species of causation of the sort we encounter in the course of investigating material universe. How *could* it be? Science looks only at interactions among material substances, and these, Descartes thinks, involve spatial contact. Minds are nonspatial, however. So mental–physical causal interaction would have to be something quite different.

Such a response leads us from the frying pan into the fire. Modern science is premised on the assumption that the material universe is a *causally closed* system: every event in the material universe is caused by some other material event (if it is caused by any event) and has, as effects, only material events. (The parenthetical rider allows us to leave room for the possibility of uncaused, spontaneous events such as the decay of a radium atom.)

You could reformulate this idea in terms of explanation: an explanation citing all of the material causes of a material event is a complete causal explanation of an event. If a scientist finds a kind of event, something going on at the sub-atomic level, say, that appears to have no material cause, the scientist does not then posit an immaterial cause. Rather, the scientist looks more closely for some previously unsuspected material cause, or assumes that the event was spontaneous, that is *uncaused*.

A commitment to the causally closed nature of the universe is reflected in physics by conservation principles. Mass and energy are convertible, but the total amount of mass–energy is constant. Mind–body interaction threatens to violate conservation. Intervention from the 'outside' by a mind would increase total energy without a compensating loss of mass, and mass–energy would be lost were material bodies to affect minds.

The notion that the material universe is causally closed is related to our conception of natural law. Natural laws govern causal relations among material events. Such laws differ from laws passed by legislative bodies. A natural law is exceptionless: it could not be violated in the way a traffic law could be violated. An object that behaves in an odd or unexpected way nevertheless perfectly conforms to natural law. Evidence that an object's behavior 'violates' a given natural law is evidence that, either 'hidden variables', unidentified material causes, are at work, or that what we had thought was a law is not.

Return now to Descartes's supposition that minds are nonmaterial substances capable of initiating events in the material universe. This supposition would oblige scientists to give up the idea that the material universe is causally self-contained. To see why this is so, imagine how causal interaction between mental and material substances might work. Suppose your mind acts on your body by instigating changes in a certain region of your brain. Descartes himself speculated that minds might be linked to bodies by way of the *pineal gland*, a small structure near the center of the brain.

Minute alterations in the motions of particles in the pineal gland radiated throughout the body via the nervous system producing muscular contractions and ultimately overt bodily motions.

Pretend for a moment that Descartes was right: your mind influences your body via your pineal gland. Your pineal gland is made up of micro-particles that operate in accord with physical law. If your mind is to initiate a causal sequence in your pineal gland, then, it will have to affect in some way the behavior of these micro-constituents. Its influencing the behavior of micro-constituents, however, would appear to require intervention in their behavior, hence violation of the laws governing the micro-constituents – an impossibility if you take the material universe to be causally self-contained and laws of nature to be inviolable.

(Descartes endorses the conservation of *motion*, not energy or mass–energy: motion, he thinks, can be transformed, as when particles change direction, so long as the total amount of motion is conserved. On such a view, the pineal gland might influence material particles, not by *introducing* motion, but by altering the trajectories of particles. Unfortunately for Descartes, this suggestion is undermined by subsequent conceptions of conservation.)

You might think that physics provides an out here, a way the mind could influence the body without violating laws governing its material constituents. Suppose, as the quantum theory suggests, laws governing those constituents are ultimately probabilistic or statistical in character. Imagine that a micro-system's being in a certain state, S_1, causes the system subsequently to go into state S_2, but only with a certain probability: there is a 65% probability that a particular micro-system in state S_1 will evolve into state S_2 (during a certain period of time).

Now, imagine that you – a mental substance – decide to wave to a friend. You initiate a particular change in your body by making it the case that a particular S_1 micro-system in your pineal gland goes into state S_2. (Imagine that when the constituents of such states 'line up' in this way, the result is a signal sent to your right arm that causes a series of muscle contractions and ultimately a waving motion of your arm. Here you have decided to wave, and subsequently wave.) In this way, you, a mental substance, seem capable of making yourself felt in the material universe without in any sense *violating* laws governing material bodies. After all, sometimes when your pineal gland is in state S_1 it goes into S_2, sometimes not. Your mind's causing your pineal gland to go into S_2 is consistent with this fact.

Consider a sequence of tosses of a fair coin, one that lands heads about half the time. When you toss the coin on a particular occasion, you snap your thumb in a characteristic way sending the coin tumbling through the air in a trajectory that leads it eventually to land on the ground, heads side up. Suppose that there is a completely deterministic basis for the coin's landing as it does on this occasion: given features of the coin, the character of the movement of your thumb, the location and composition of the surface on which the coin lands, and so on, the coin is bound to land heads. Of course you are ignorant of most of these factors. You can only guess how the coin will land on each toss. You might express this ignorance by saying that, on any given occasion, the probability that the coin will land heads is 50%.

Imagine now an outsider who occasionally intervenes in the system by focusing a strong electromagnetic beam on the coin ensuring that it lands heads or that it lands tails. The outsider might do this infrequently and in a statistically undetectable manner: when you evaluate the relative frequency with which the coin landed heads over a long series of tosses, that frequency approaches 50%. The outsider, then, intervenes, but in a way that does not detectably alter the statistical likelihood that the coin will land heads whenever it is tossed, and does not reveal itself when you examine the coin's behavior over time. The outsider 'changes' some heads tosses to tails, some tails tosses to heads. Perhaps this is how the mind affects the body.

This example misses the mark. It misconstrues the nature of statistical or probabilistic causation as it might be thought to apply to the basic constituents of the material universe. If probabilities are written into fundamental laws of nature, these probabilities are not the result of our ignorance in the face of the complexity of physical systems, nor do they simply express statistical frequencies. The probabilities are, as it were, *built into* the fundamental entities. In the imaginary case we are considering, it is an intrinsic – built-in – feature of an S_1 micro-system that it is 65% likely to go into state S_2 (during a particular interval). This does not imply that 65% of S_1 systems go into S_2. It is consistent with this imaginary law that the relative frequency of S_1 to S_2 transitions is much less or much greater than 65%. In fact it is possible, although of course highly unlikely, that no S_1 system *ever* goes into state S_2.

If you imagine a force from outside nature intervening in a physical transaction governed by a statistical law, then you must imagine the force as somehow altering the probabilities that hold for the physical system in question: if the probabilities are not affected, then it is hard to understand what the alleged intervention amounts to. But if these probabilities are built into the system, then their being altered would amount to a 'violation' of physical law.

To grasp this point, it is important to see that the kinds of statistical law thought to govern the elementary constituents of the universe exclude so-called hidden variables. That is, the probabilistic character of these laws is not due to the intervention of some factor the nature of which you might be ignorant of. It is, rather, irreducible, ineliminable, grounded in the nature of the elementary entities themselves. If the mind intervenes in the operation of the material universe in a way that is statistically undetectable, it does not follow that no 'violation' of physical law has occurred. Genuine intervention would require minds to affect in some way the propensity of particular S_1 systems to go into state S_2. And that would necessitate alterations in the character of S_1 systems, alterations the occurrence of which would constitute 'violations' of natural law.

Here is another possibility. Although mental events do not alter S_1, they might, on occasion, *prevent* S_1 from manifesting itself by going into S_2 – in the way you might prevent a fragile vase from shattering when it is dropped by catching it before it hits the floor. Selective 'blockings' of this sort, if suitably fine-grained and strategically placed, might account for the effects of thoughts on bodily goings-on.

Again, it is hard to see how anything like this could work without violating science's conception of the material universe as causally self-contained. (I shall return to propensities – or, as I prefer, dispositions – and their manifestations in more detail in subsequent chapters.)

One further difficulty for Descartes's conception of mind–body interaction is worth mentioning. Cartesian minds are wholly nonspatial. This means that they have no shape or size. Shape and size are spatial properties, and could be possessed only by an extended substance. But if minds are truly nonspatial, they are not *locatable* in space: minds have *no* spatial location. In that case, however, what connects a particular mind with a particular body? This is what Jaegwon Kim calls the 'pairing problem' (Kim 2001). You might think of your mind as being *in* your body, or even *inside* your head, but this could not be so for a Cartesian mind. Your mind is no more in *your* body than it is in *my* body. What, then, is the source of its apparently intimate connection to *your* body? It is not easy to see how Descartes could respond.

2.6 A Causally Closed Universe

Of course it is possible that immaterial Cartesian minds *do* intervene in the material universe. It is possible that the material universe is not in fact causally closed and that natural law *is* subject to contravention. The argument against Cartesian dualism is not that minds do not intervene, therefore dualism must be false. Such an argument would beg the question against Descartes. The argument, rather, is founded on considerations of plausibility. If you accept Cartesian dualism, you must suppose that immaterial minds sometimes intervene in the operation of the material universe. It is hard to see how this could be possible, even on Descartes's own terms.

It might be possible to massage Descartes's principles so as to make the theory internally consistent, but the problem remains. Cartesian-style interactionism conflicts with a fundamental presumption of modern science, a presumption we have excellent independent reasons to accept. To the extent that you regard the intervention of nonmaterial minds in the material universe as implausible, you should regard Cartesian interactive dualism as implausible.

Even if you are prepared to abandon the idea that the material universe is a causally closed system, even if you are prepared to allow events originating outside the material universe to have material effects, problems remain. Assume that Descartes is right about the nature of minds and bodies, and assume that minds and bodies causally interact. How, on Descartes's own terms, is this supposed to *work*? If causation requires that whatever is present in an effect be present in its cause, then how *could* mental substances interact with material substances if these have no properties in common? The idea that mind–body causation is *sui generis*, that it differs from causation in the material universe is just to label a problem, not to solve it.

Or so it would seem. Arguments of this sort are scarcely conclusive. Metaphysical arguments rarely are. You might fairly ask, however, who bears the burden of proof here. The Cartesian dualist offers you an account of mind that fits nicely with much of what you antecedently believe about the universe and with everyday experience. The account has the disadvantage of being both internally dodgy (it makes mind–body interaction hard to credit on its own terms) and implying something (that the physical universe is not causally closed) we have few reasons to believe, and many reasons to doubt. It is up to the Cartesian, then, to show that competing accounts of mind suffer equally serious defects. You will be in a better position to evaluate the Cartesian's prospects when you have examined the alternatives.

Suggested Reading

Substance dualism is given scant attention in contemporary philosophy of mind. The focus has been, instead, on 'property dualism', a view according to which the mental and the physical are not distinguishable kinds of substance, but distinct families of properties (Chapter 11). Dualisms of this sort have troubles of their own, and have been much discussed in recent years. I have elected to dwell on substance dualism here partly in hopes of encouraging a fresh look at a range of well-worn issues. Descartes is probably wrong, but he is not stupidly wrong.

Descartes's views on the mind are developed in his *Meditations on First Philosophy* (1641). This edition of the *Meditations* includes selections from the 'Objections and Replies' that illuminate certain of Descartes's positions. Relevant portions of the *Meditations* and the 'Objections and Replies' appear in my *Philosophy of Mind: A Guide and Anthology* (2003b) and in O'Connor and Robb's *Philosophy of Mind: Contemporary Readings* (2003). A philosophically sophisticated discussion of Descartes's dualism can be found in Daniel Garber's *Descartes Embodied: Reading Cartesian Philosophy through Cartesian Science* (2001). See also John Cottingham's *Cambridge Companion to Descartes* (1992) and Margaret Wilson's *Descartes* (1978) and *Ideas and Mechanism: Essays on Early Modern Philosophy* (1999). On mind–body interaction and physical law, see Daniel Dennett's 'Current Issues in the Philosophy of Mind' (1978). Averill and Keating, in 'Does Interactionism Violate a Law of Classical Physics?' (1981), argue against the prevailing view, contending that interaction *is* compatible with classical physics.

E. J. Lowe defends a version of substance dualism in *Subjects of Experience* (1996). Lowe argues that minds are simple substances distinct from bodies that house them and with which they interact, but with an important caveat: minds are not *immaterial* substances. The position is discussed in some detail in Heil (2004, chapter 4).

3 Descartes's Legacy

3.1 Dualism without Interaction: Parallelism

Cartesian dualism stumbles in attempting to accommodate mind–body interaction. Minds and bodies evidently interact causally. Your decisions lead you to act and so to move your body in particular ways. The material world impinging on your body gives rise to conscious sensory experiences. As you have discovered, however, it is hard to see how such interaction *could* occur if minds are unextended, nonmaterial substances and bodies are extended, material substances.

Some of Descartes's successors sought to massage dualism so as to resolve the problem of mind–body interaction while preserving what you might regard as Descartes's core insights. What would happen, for instance, if you simply dropped the requirement of causal interaction? In so doing, you would move to a doctrine called 'psycho-physical parallelism' or, for short, 'parallelism'. Gottfried Wilhelm von Leibniz (1646–1716) is perhaps the best known proponent of parallelism, although my focus here will not be on Leibniz's considered view but on a simpler alternative.

A proponent of parallelism accepts Descartes's bifurcation of the world into extended material substances and unextended mental substances. Parallelists deny, however, that mental and material substances interact causally. This appears to fly in the face of ordinary experience. It seems obvious that goings-on in your mind affect your body, and through it, the material universe beyond your body. It seems no less clear that events and objects in the universe have an impact on your mind by way of their effects on your body.

Consider again your sitting on a tack planted by a practical joker. You sit on the tack, experience a sharp, painful sensation, and leap from your chair. This sequence of events includes both mental and material events that are, to all appearances, causally related. A defender of parallelism, in contrast, insists that these appearances are deceptive. The parallelist's picture is captured by Figure 3.1 (compare Figure 2.2).

Minds, parallelists grant, *appear* to interact with the material universe, but this appearance is a *mere* appearance. Sequences of events involving minds,

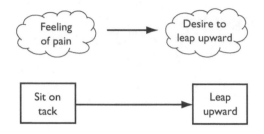

Figure 3.1

mental events, and sequences of material events run in parallel: co-variation without causal interaction. Your sitting on a tack (a material event) precedes your sensation of pain (a mental event). You undoubtedly have the clear impression that the former brought about the latter. In this you are mistaken, however. Similarly, when you form a desire to leap upward and subsequently leap, you have the impression that your feeling of pain and its attendant desire to leap caused your leaping, but it did not. Events in the mind systematically co-vary with events in the material universe, but there are no mental–material causal connections.

Now, you know that *A*'s can co-vary with *B*'s without its being true that *A*'s cause *B*'s. If the co-variation is extensive and systematic, however, it would be natural to seek a causal explanation: perhaps *A*'s and *B*'s are themselves caused by *C*'s. A squeaking from under the hood of an acquaintance's vintage DeSoto is inevitably followed by the motor's quitting. The motor's quitting co-varies with the squeaking, but is not caused by it. Rather some mechanical condition produces both the squeaking and the motor's quitting.

What explanation has a parallelist to offer for the fact that sequences of mental events co-vary systematically and universally with sequences of material events? One possibility is that this is just a 'brute fact' about our universe, a fact not admitting of further explanation. Such a response is scarcely satisfying, however. In the context, it appears embarrassingly *ad hoc*. True, all explanation comes to an end somewhere. Fundamental facts uncovered in physics might themselves be incapable of explanation. Such facts would function as unexplained explainers. But the notion that the delicate pattern of co-variation of the mental and the material is an inexplicable brute fact appears to be motivated solely by a wish to preserve dualism. This is painfully evident given that a straightforward explanation appears to be available: mental events co-vary with material events because mental substances and material substances interact causally! To be sure, this explanation would require that parallelism be abandoned, but that is the parallelist's problem, not anyone else's.

Another defense of parallelism invokes God. God intervenes to ensure that mental and material sequences run in parallel. You might think that an appeal to God to account for the co-variation of mental and material events is obviously unpromising. God is not a material substance. Indeed, according to Descartes, God is not a mental substance either: God is a substance of a third sort (a substance whose defining attribute is perfection). But if that is so, how is it any easier to understand how God could affect the course of material events than it is to understand how finite material substances could do so? All the difficulties associated with Cartesian interactionism appear to arise all over again.

Perhaps this is unfair to the parallelist. A parallelist need not envisage God as continually adjusting or 'tuning' the course of mental and material events. Rather God might create, once and for all, a world containing both material substances subject to unalterable natural law and mental substances, subject, perhaps, to psychological laws. The world is designed in such a way that events in the mental realm co-vary with events in the material realm. The model is a clockmaker who constructs a pair of perfectly synchronized chronometers the movements of which mirror one another, not because they are causally linked, but because the internal adjustments in one clock perfectly match the internal adjustments in the other. (See Sobel 1995 for an account of just such a clockmaker.)

Even so, the parallelist's appeal to God is not much of an improvement over the brute fact account. Indeed, the appeal to God appears to be just a gussied up way of saying that mental–material co-variation is a brute, inexplicable fact. Were there independent grounds for believing that God exists and acts in the way required by parallelism, matters would be different. In the absence of such independent grounds, the appeal to God is an appeal to a *deus ex machina*, a contrived solution to an otherwise intractable problem.

3.2 Occasionalism

A variant of parallelism, 'occasionalism', accords God a more active role in the world. Occasionalism is most often associated with the writings of Nicolas Malebranche (1638–1715), although Descartes himself might have had occasionalist leanings. My discussion will focus on occasionalism as a philosophical doctrine, and omit historical subtleties.

Parallelism envisages systems operating independently, but side by side, in the way an automobile on a highway might shadow a train. Occasionalism makes God actively responsible for the existence and character of *every* sequence of events. When you sit on a tack, God 'occasions' or wills the occurrence of a sensation of pain in your mind (see Figure 3.2). God's acting in this instance resembles, but is taken to be different from causing.

You might have difficulty seeing occasionalism as an advance over parallelism, and difficulty seeing either doctrine as an improvement on Descartes's original version of dualism. The sticking point for Descartes is the difficulty of understanding how unextended mental substances could interact causally with extended material substances. Parallelism and occasionalism concede

Figure 3.2

the difficulty and attempt to cope with it by granting that mental and material substances could not causally interact, and offering an explanation for the *appearance* of interaction. The strategy looks unpromising, seeming merely to push the original problem around without solving it.

3.3   Causation and Occasionalism

How might an occasionalist respond? Occasionalism is motivated in part by a general thesis about causation. Suppose, as most philosophers do suppose, that causation is a relation holding among events: one event, the cause, *brings about* another event, the effect. Your striking a billiard ball with a billiard cue, one event, brings about the billiard ball's rolling in a particular direction, a second event. The difficulty is to understand what exactly such 'bringing about' amounts to. We ordinarily distinguish cases in which one event merely follows or accompanies another, from those in which one event is causally *responsible* for another. But what is the basis of this distinction? This is the problem of the *causal nexus*: when events are linked causally, what is the character of the linkage?

Descartes thought of the causal nexus in terms of *transference*: when you strike the billiard ball with a billiard cue, a quantity of motion is transferred from the cue to the ball. More recent versions of this conception of causation take causal connections to involve energy transference. Appealing as this might seem, it is just this feature of Descartes's conception of causation that leads to difficulties in understanding how mind–body interaction could be possible. If minds and bodies share no properties, how could either cause a change in the other if causation requires the transfer of some quantity?

One possibility is that, with respect to causation, Descartes was mistaken: there *are* no genuine links between events, no transference, only bare event sequences. Scientists, then, might regard two events as standing in a causal relation, not because they observe the first bringing about or inducing the second, but because the event sequence resembles sequences they have previously observed. A view of this kind is associated with David Hume (1711–76).

Note that, although tempting, it would be misleading to describe such a view as one that denies that events are causally related. The idea rather is that this is just what particular causal relations amount to: a causal sequence is *nothing more than* an instance of some universal regularity. Your striking the billiard ball now (a particular, dated event) causes it to roll across the table (another particular event), just in case it is true that, whenever an event of a kind similar to the first occurs, an event of a kind similar to the second occurs as well.

Hume was hardly an occasionalist, but his influential observations on causality bear on the occasionalist hypothesis. (Indeed, Malebranche, the best known occasionalist, advanced 'Humean' arguments long before they occurred to Hume.) If causal relations boil down to nothing more than regularities, the co-variation of events of particular sorts, then it is a mistake to regard the absence of a mechanism, a nexus, or a causal link between mental events and material events as a special problem. On the contrary, there are no such links, not even among events in the material universe. To be sure, we are often under the impression that we have observed connections among events, real bringings about. But according to Hume this is merely a 'projection' of our conviction that, when an event of a given sort occurs (the striking of a billiard ball by a billiard cue), an event of another sort (the ball's moving in a particular way) will follow. And this conviction arises in us after we have been conditioned by prior observations of similar event sequences.

If causal relations boil down to regularities among types of event, then there is nothing especially problematic or mysterious about mental events causing material events. The appearance of a problem stems from the tacit assumption that causal relations require an intervening mechanism or link. If no mental–material links are discoverable, that is scarcely surprising. They are absent as well from ordinary sequences of material events. Cartesian and parallelist pictures of mental causation are, on such a view, indistinguishable.

Where does this leave occasionalism? Occasionalists might argue that, in the absence of a causal nexus, a connecting mechanism or linkage between causes and effects, we require *some* explanation for the pattern of regularities among kinds of event we find in the world. These regularities encompass purely material event sequences as well as sequences involving both mental and material components. When an event of one kind is invariably followed by an event of another kind, this is not because events of the first kind somehow instigate or bring about events of the second kind. Events are discrete, entirely self-contained occurrences; no event has the power to produce another event. How then are we to explain the obvious fact that event sequences are tightly structured, regular, and orderly? Their orderliness is captured by scientific theories, which postulate natural laws, and it is enshrined in everyday causal generalizations.

At this point the occasionalist invokes God. If events are discrete, wholly self-contained episodes, the occurrence of one event cannot by itself account for the occurrence of any subsequent event. The occurrence of *every* event is, in an important sense, miraculous. God, as it were, creates every event *ex nihilo* – from nothing. One way to think about a view of this sort is to imagine that the universe is divided into momentary temporal stages or segments (Figure 3.3).

Alternatively, you could think of the universe over time as comprising a sequence of numerically distinct universes, each universe differing slightly from its predecessor in something like the way each image on a movie film differs from the image preceding it. In the billiard ball example, the cue's striking the ball belongs to one temporal segment (one universe), and the ball's subsequent rolling belongs to subsequent temporal segments (each a distinct universe). Every segment in the sequence that makes up what we commonly regard as our universe must be created anew: continual creation. God provides the connecting thread.

Let me pause briefly to say something about my use of 'universe' here and elsewhere in the book. By 'universe', I mean the all-encompassing totality of material reality of the kind investigated by fundamental physics. Some physicists have speculated that 'our universe' is just one among many universes, each with its own space–time and its own distinctive laws of nature. As I am using the term, however, this 'multiverse' would *be* the universe. Talk of 'our universe' would amount to talk of one constituent of the universe, one self-contained space–time, the one you and I happen to inhabit.

It is widely held that no event *in* the universe could account for the existence of the universe (a universe that includes that event as a part). And if what we call *the* universe is more accurately thought of as a *sequence* of metaphysically independent universes or universe stages, it follows that no event in any stage in the sequence can account for any event in a subsequent stage. You have a choice it seems. You could accept the existence and character of each stage in the sequence as a brute, inexplicable fact; or you could explain the existence of the sequence by postulating a powerful, benevolent God. God wills anew each universe in the sequence of universe stages in accord with a divine plan. You can rest content that the sequence will preserve the kind of complex order you would find were you to engage in scientific inquiry because you can be confident that it belongs to God's nature to do so (Figure 3.4).

Figure 3.3

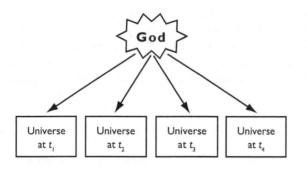

Figure 3.4

The movie analogy can help make this clear. [Although sequences of images on a movie screen *appear* continuous, and events in those images *appear* causally connected, in fact no image-event is causally responsible for any other image-event.] The sequence of events depends on goings-on outside the sequence: the operation of a system consisting of a projector and reels of film. (The projection system fills the role occupied by God in Figure 3.4.) This does not prevent us from making predictions about sequences of images: an image of a falling vase will be followed by an image of the vase's shattering on the floor. But the causal story here is not 'horizontal', not one that holds across sequences of images, but 'vertical': [each image is produced by something outside the sequence.]

This is the picture, but what can be said for it? An occasionalist can point out that it is one thing for a scientist to allow that the existence of a single universe is simply a brute fact, a fact for which there is no explanation. It is quite another matter, however, to hold that each member of a patterned sequence of metaphysically independent universe stages is a brute fact. If no event in any stage accounts for the occurrence of that stage or the occurrence of any event in any other stage, then, it would seem *every* fact is merely a brute fact!

Suppose you find this conclusion unappealing but you accept the occasionalist's conception of the universe as a sequence of momentary, self-contained universe stages. You then seem faced with a choice. Either every fact is a brute, unexplained and unexplainable fact (Figure 3.3), or God exists and provides an explanation for things being as they are (Figure 3.4). In this case, unlike the case of parallelism, God is offered as a plausible explanation of an otherwise baffling state of affairs. Of course, you might question the occasionalist's take on causation, and question as well the notion that the universe is a sequence of metaphysically independent momentary stages. But then it is up to you to provide a plausible alternative.

If nothing else, these reflections make it clear that you cannot hope to evaluate claims about minds and the material universe without first coming to grips with a host of fundamental metaphysical issues. Whatever plausibility occasionalism possesses rests in large measure on a particular metaphysical conception of causation. If the occasionalists are right about causation (and right, as well, about mental and material substances), then they are in a relatively strong position. Before you can evaluate the occasionalist's brand of dualism, however, you will need to build up your grasp of the metaphysical options.

3.4   Idealism

Parallelism and occasionalism imply that our impression that minds and bodies affect one another is an illusion. You make up your mind to wave and subsequently wave. It might seem to you that your decision *brings about* your waving. But that is not so – or, if it is so, it is only because God ensures that, in the universe-segment subsequent to the universe-segment in which you decide to wave, you wave.

Suppose you go further, however, suppose you allow that, not only is the impression of mind–body causal interaction an illusion but that the material universe is itself an illusion! You have experiences that you would describe as experiences of material objects and events existing outside your mind, 'out there', but these are at bottom nothing more than elaborate and prolonged dreams or hallucinations. Of course, everyday activities lack the peculiar dreamlike character of dreams, but that is just because everyday experiences are more orderly, regular, and unforgiving.

On a view of this sort, 'idealism', the world consists exclusively of minds and their contents. (On a variant of idealism, 'solipsism', the world is just a single mind – *your* mind – and its contents.) There are no nonmental material objects or events, hence no worrisome causal interactions between minds and mind-independent material objects, no mysterious parallelism between independent mental and material realms. We explain the regularity and order we find in our experiences, not by reference to a regular and orderly material universe, but by reference to the intrinsic nature of minds (Figure 3.5) or by postulating that the order is secured by a benevolent God who ensures that our ideas occur in orderly, hence predictable, patterns (Figure 3.6). (The Irish philosopher and Anglican bishop, George Berkeley [1685–1753] is the most famous proponent of the latter view.)

Idealism has the advantage of saving the appearances. If idealism is true, then your experiences of the universe would be no different in any way

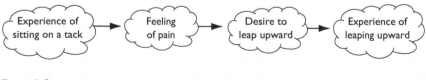

Figure 3.5

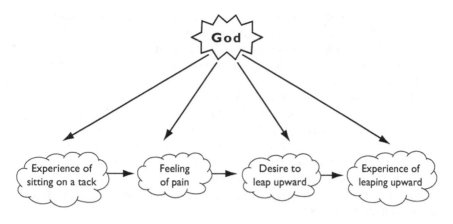

Figure 3.6

from what they would be were the universe populated by material objects. Idealism does not imply that what appear to you to be solid, extended material objects would take on a ghostly air. On the contrary, you would have experiences 'as of' solid extended objects and spatial expanses, just as you sometimes do in dreams.

Suppose you set out to disprove idealism by conducting experiments designed to establish the existence of mind-independent material bodies. These experiments might be crude – as in the famous episode of Dr. Johnson's kicking a large stone and announcing 'thus I refute Berkeley' – or sophisticated – including, for instance, the deployment of expensive detectors to identify the material particles that science tells us are the building blocks of a mind-independent reality.

An idealist will point out that experimentation is a matter of arranging matters so as to yield certain observations. Your kicking a stone provides observational evidence of an especially vivid sort that the stone exists. A scientist's observation of a particular kind of streak in a cloud chamber provides rather more indirect evidence that an alpha particle has passed through the chamber. Observations are conscious experiences, however, and so do not carry us outside the mind. Further, our experimental equipment – stones, Atwood machines, cloud chambers – are, if the idealist is right, no less mental. What is a stone or a cloud chamber other than something that looks a particular way, feels a particular way, sounds a particular way, and so on? Looks, feels, and sounds, are just conscious sensory states! Experiment, the idealist concludes, cannot hope to provide grounds for inferring the existence of anything nonmental.

Idealism certainly covers the bases. It banishes problems associated with causal interaction between minds and the material universe, and it does so in a way that by-passes worries associated with parallelism and occasionalism. Rightly understood, idealism is consistent with all the evidence you could possibly muster. Moreover, idealism has a kind of elegant simplicity of the sort valued in the sciences. Idealism postulates nothing more than minds and their contents and explains all the phenomena by appeals to these without needing to resort to messy theories concerning extra-mental material objects and events.

Even so, you are likely to find idealism hard to swallow. This could be in part because idealism appears to take the easy way out. Idealism explains the appearances by identifying the appearances with reality. Most of us, however, hold out hope that there might be some way to keep the distinction and to reconcile our minds and their contents with a nonmental, mind-independent, material universe. In the end, we might be forced to accept idealism. But until we are forced to accept it, we can continue to seek less dramatic alternatives.

3.5   Mind and Meaning

Having expressed reservations about idealism, I should note that, traditionally, idealists have not offered idealism simply as a happy alternative to Cartesian dualism. At the heart of most species of idealism is a view about meaning and the contents of our thoughts. Idealists argue that opposing views, views that sharply distinguish a mind-independent universe from minds and their contents, are not simply false, but are literally *unintelligible*. True, belief in an 'external world', a world outside the mind, might not immediately strike you as unintelligible. According to the idealist, however, once you understand what is involved in the having of particular thoughts, you can see that such beliefs are in fact nonsense: thoughts of a universe of mind-independent material objects are *literally unthinkable*. The upshot is that there really are no options, no coherent alternatives to idealism!

This is a stunning thesis. If true, idealism would appear to be unassailable. This is not the place to examine idealists' arguments in detail. Let us look, rather, at a streamlined version of the kind of argument to which idealists might appeal.

The line of argument I have in mind was perfected by Bishop Berkeley. Berkeley was not interested in showing that there is, as a matter of fact, no material universe but only minds and their contents, or that idealism enjoys subtle metaphysical or explanatory advantages over its dualistic competitors. His aim was to show that, in the final analysis, there *are* no serious competitors. Berkeley holds that when philosophers attempt to talk about the material universe, they are endeavoring to talk about something literally inconceivable. More starkly: philosophical talk about a mind-independent material universe is not talk about anything at all. Dualistic hypotheses, then, are not merely false or implausible; they altogether lack meaning.

Consider, says Berkeley, what you are talking (or thinking) about when you talk (or think) about familiar objects: tables, stones, cats. You are talking (or thinking) about things that look, sound, taste, smell, and feel a certain way. But the sounds you hear, the looks of things, their tastes, and feels are not external to you, not entities present outside your mind. They are simply *experiences* of certain characteristic sorts. You commonly distinguish your experiences of things from the things, of course, but Berkeley is out to convince you that this is an empty distinction.

Imagine that you are now perceiving a ripe tomato in bright sunlight. You have a particular visual experience of a reddish spherical sort. If you grasp the tomato and bite it, you will have additional tactile, olfactory, gustatory, and auditory experiences: the tomato feels, smells, and, when you bite it, tastes and sounds a particular way. Berkeley argues that your thoughts about the tomato are exhausted by these sensory features. When you think about the tomato, your thought concerns something that looks, feels, smells, tastes and sounds a particular way. But, again, looks, feels, and the rest are, properly understood, nothing more than qualities of conscious experiences; and conscious experiences are mental phenomena.

So your thoughts about the tomato are, in the end, thoughts about certain characteristic mental episodes. It makes no sense to suppose that mental episodes – Berkeley calls them 'ideas' – could exist outside the mind, however. Your thoughts about tomatoes, then, are *really* thoughts about mental goings-on: conscious experiences of particular kinds you have had, or would have under the right conditions. Materialist philosophers tell us that these experiences correspond to and are caused by a mind-independent tomato 'out there'. But, when you examine your conception of tomatoes, you will find only experiences. You will find nothing answering to the expression 'mind-independent tomato'. The expression 'mind-independent tomato', then, is empty of significance. In that regard, it resembles 'colorless green ideas'. You can utter these words, but they signify nothing. You could, as well, entertain a thought that you might describe as a thought of colorless green ideas. But in so doing you entertain an empty thought, a thought with no content.

You might think that there is an obvious response to this line of reasoning. Of course, you say, anyone can think of a mind-independent tomato. Nothing could be easier. Mind-independent tomatoes *resemble* our tomato experiences: they are red, spherical, and acidic. You could think of a mind-independent tomato by entertaining thoughts of the kinds of conscious experience you might normally have in the presence of tomatoes, and appending to these thoughts the thought that they are of something outside the mind, something 'beyond' those experiences.

Berkeley quickly dismisses moves of this kind. Experiences, he contends, could only resemble experiences. In setting out to imagine a mind-independent tomato, you, in effect, call to mind certain familiar kinds of experience, then subtract from these the idea that they are experiences! This, Berkeley argues, is nonsense. It resembles calling to mind the idea of a triangle and then subtracting from this idea that it is three-sided. You are left with nothing but an empty thought. Of course, you still have *words*:

'unexperienced, mind-independent tomato', 'triangle without three sides'. But the words lack significance, lack potential application to anything in the world. In the former case philosophers have not noticed this difficulty. We have persisted in prattling on about a mind-independent universe in the way a child might prattle on about a triangle that is not three-sided.

The conclusion – a universe of material objects residing outside the mind is literally unthinkable – *seems* outrageous. But why? Suppose idealism were true: all that exists are minds and their contents. How would your everyday experiences, or for that matter, experiences of scientists in their laboratories, be different than they would be were idealism false? The answer, according to Berkeley and other idealists, is that nothing would be detectably different. If that is so, however, it is hard to accuse idealists of confuting ordinary expectations. What idealists deny is simply a certain unmotivated philosophical *interpretation* of these expectations. In rejecting material objects, idealists insist that they are not rejecting tables, trees, galaxies, and the like. Rather, they are rejecting the notion that 'table', 'tree', and 'galaxy' designate fanciful mind-independent material objects. The terms in fact designate collections of actual and possible experiences, ideas in Berkeley's special sense.

Idealism, despite its initial implausibility, is notoriously difficult to confront head-on. Rather than rehearsing detailed arguments against idealism here, I propose to move forward and discuss alternative views. It might turn out that there are grounds for preferring one or more of these to idealism, even though there are no obvious chinks in the idealist's armor. My own suspicion is that idealism represents a kind of failure of nerve: unable to reconcile minds and the material universe, the idealist gives up the game and stuffs the material universe inside the mind.

3.6   Epiphenomenalism

Descartes depicts minds as causally interacting with the material universe: events in the material universe produce experiences in minds, and mental events yield bodily motions. You have seen that this kind of two-way causal interaction is difficult to reconcile with the conviction that the material universe is causally self-contained: the causes of every material event are exclusively material. Suppose, however, you granted that the material universe is 'causally closed', but allowed that material events can have mental *by-products*. Mental events exist. Mental events are effects of certain material causes. But no mental event has a material effect; no mental event affects goings-on in the material universe. Mental events are 'epiphenomena', incidental 'side-effects' of material phenomena, that themselves yield no effects of any kind (see Figure 3.7).

Epiphenomenalists regard mental phenomena (conscious experiences, for instance) as by-products of occurrences in complex physical systems. Mental phenomena resemble heat produced by a computing machine, or the shadow cast by a billiard ball rolling across a billiard table, or the squeaking noise

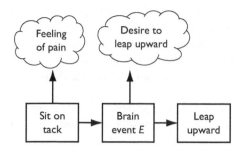

Figure 3.7

produced by a pair of new shoes. The heat, the shadow, and the squeaking noise play no causal role in the operation of the systems that produce them. Of course, the heat, the shadow, and the squeaking noise are themselves material phenomena, and so have straightforward physical effects: the heat triggers a fan, the shadow alters the distribution of light radiation in the region on which it falls, and the squeaking produces minute vibrations in the eardrums of the person wearing the shoes and nearby observers. Mental phenomena, in contrast, are *wholly* epiphenomenal: mental phenomena have no effects whatever – material or mental. (And their production apparently involves no expenditure of energy.)

Epiphenomenalism, at first glance, appears to fly in the face of common experience. Surely your experience of pain as you move your hand too close to the fire is what brings about your snatching it away. And surely your deliberation and subsequent decision to obtain a Whopper are what lead you to pull into the Burger King drive-thru. According to the epiphenomenalist, however, all the causal work in these cases is done by events in your nervous system. Those events have, as a by-product, the production of certain conscious experiences, perhaps. The conscious experiences, however, are causally inert. They *appear* to have causal efficacy because they are caused by, hence invariably accompany, material events that *themselves* reliably produce various kinds of effect. Suppose a loose fan belt causes both the overheating of your friend's DeSoto and a distinctive whistling noise. The whistling accompanies, but does not cause, the overheating. According to the epiphenomenalist, this is how it is with mental phenomena generally.

The fact, then, if it is a fact, that it *feels* to you as though your states of mind make a causal difference in what you do is entirely consistent with the truth of epiphenomenalism. In deciding to reach for a Whopper and subsequently reaching, you have the distinct impression that your decision is responsible for your reaching (or, at any rate, that it contributed to the occurrence of that material event). Certainly, you can count on your body's moving in ways that reflect your decisions. And it could be true that, had you not decided to reach for the Whopper, you would not have done so. It does not follow, however, that decisions – kinds of mental event – themselves move anything. If epiphenomenalism is right, then the cause of your body's moving is some neurological event. This neurological event has, as an inevitable auxiliary effect, a conscious decision – just as, in Figure 3.7, a neurological event, E, yields both a desire to leap – a mental event – and a subsequent leaping.

Neuroscientists have sometimes found epiphenomenalism attractive. In studying brain function, if you accept epiphenomenalism, you can safely ignore 'phenomenal' characteristics of mental phenomena altogether, and focus exclusively on physical mechanisms and processes in the brain. If mental phenomena are epiphenomenal then they are undetectable (except, presumably, by those undergoing them), and they could make no difference to anything that transpires in the material realm. This would leave neuroscientists free to explore mysteries of the brain without having to concern themselves with the messy details of conscious experience.

Epiphenomenalism faces a number of difficulties, however. First, a familiar difficulty, the nature of body-to-mind, material-to-mental causal relations, is none too clear. Many philosophers accept the idea that causal relations hold among events. The epiphenomenalist contends that some material events cause mental events, but mental events cause nothing. You might think that there would be no harm in allowing that mental events could cause other mental events. After all, mental events (according to the epiphenomenalist) have no material effects, so causal relations among mental events would pose no threat to the causal integrity of the material universe. But this possibility is out of step with the epiphenomenalist's broader picture. If mental events could themselves cause other mental events, then a mental event could have a life of its own. It is of the essence of epiphenomenalism, however, that mental events are exclusively by-products of material goings-on.

Epiphenomenalists suppose then that mental events, although themselves causally inert, are induced by material events. 'Dangling' causal relations – the expression comes from Herbert Feigl by way of J. J. C. Smart – of this sort differ from ordinary causal relations, however. In the case of ordinary material causation, events are both effects (of prior events) and causes (of subsequent events). So, causal transactions that include mental events appear to be dramatically different from those encountered elsewhere in the universe. You might wonder, for starters, whether a material event's causing a purely mental event might not after all require energy departing the material universe in violation of conservation principles fundamental to physics.

Perhaps such considerations by themselves pose no serious threat to epiphenomenalism. At most, they are *consequences* of the epiphenomenalist's conception of mental events, so pointing them out amounts to little more than restating the epiphenomenalist thesis. Nevertheless, it seems clear that, if an alternative view were available, one that accounted for all that epiphenomenalism accounted for, but that did so without recourse to a special kind of causal relation, that view would be preferable.

This way of thinking invokes the Principle of Parsimony or Ockham's Razor (named in honor of William of Ockham, 1285–1347). Ockham's Razor bids us not to 'multiply entities beyond necessity'. The idea is that simpler, more parsimonious, accounts of phenomena, accounts that refrain from introducing new kinds of entity or process, are preferred to less simple competitors. The notion of simplicity in play here is notoriously difficult to spell out. And, of course, there is no guarantee that nature is governed by the simplest possible laws. Such matters, however, needn't detain us. We are bound to judge competing theories on their merits. You could think of Ockham's Razor, not as a principle that tells us how the universe is organized, but as one that encourages us to place the burden of proof on proponents of 'less simple' theories. If an alternative to epiphenomenalism avoids 'dangling' causal relations, then the burden is on the proponent of epiphenomenalism to convince us that epiphenomenalism nevertheless affords a better account of the phenomena.

Suggested Reading

Malebranche's defense of occasionalism can be found in *Dialogues on Metaphysics and Religion*, (1688). Leibniz advances a version of parallelism in his *Monodology* (1787). Berkeley's idealism is discussed at length and defended in his *Treatise Concerning the Principles of Human Knowledge* (1713); and in *Three Dialogues between Hylas and Philonous* (1710). John Foster brings idealism up to date in *The Case for Idealism* (1982) and *The Immaterial Self* (1991). Howard Robinson's *Objections to Physicalism* (1993) includes contemporary essays defending various immaterialist doctrines including idealism. For more recent discussion of the territory see Gillett and Lower's *Physicalism and Its Discontents* (2001).

Victor Caston, 'Epiphenomenalisms Ancient and Modern' (1997), provides a historical look at epiphenomenalism. Epiphenomenalism is described and defended by T. H. Huxley in his *Methods and Results: Essays* (1901). See also C. D. Broad's *The Mind and Its Place in Nature* (1925), chapter 3. Nowadays, epiphenomenalism is most often taken to concern, not mental *events*, but mental *properties*: an object's possession of mental properties makes no nonmental difference. Brian McLaughlin's 'Type Epiphenomenalism, Type Dualism, and the Causal Priority of the Physical' (1989) affords an excellent account of what McLaughlin calls 'type epiphenomenalism'. Frank Jackson's defense of property-epiphenomenalism in 'Epiphenomenal Qualia' (1982) has been widely influential. Taking Jackson to heart, David Chalmers, in *The Conscious Mind* (1996), develops an account of consciousness with strong epiphenomenalist tendencies.

Recent work in neuroscience has suggested to some that conscious decisions are in fact epiphenomenal on the grounds that decisions seem to occur *after* the onset of neural processes that lead to actions. The work of Benjamin Libet is most often cited in this regard. See Libet's 'Unconscious Cerebral

Initiative and the Role of Conscious Will in Voluntary Action' (1985) and commentaries accompanying this paper. See also Daniel Wegner's 'Précis of *The Illusion of Conscious Will*' (2004). Alfred Mele's 'Free Will and Science' (2011) discusses this and related empirical work purporting to show that some conscious states are epiphenomenal.

4 Behaviorism

4.1 Moving Away from Dualism

Chapter 2 began with an examination of Descartes's contention that minds and material bodies are distinct kinds of substance, distinct *things*. Chapter 3 took up an assortment of related views, each of which could be spun out from a Cartesian starting point by rejecting or modifying one or another of its trademark components. This chapter and the chapter to follow, explore two *materialist* accounts of the mind.

Materialists deny that the universe includes both mental and material substances. Every substance is a material substance, every property a material property. Minds are fashioned from the same kind of elementary component that makes up rocks, trees, and stars. If you took fundamental particles and arranged them one way, the result would be a granite boulder; differently arranged, the outcome would be a theoretical physicist. The mind is not a separate, nonmaterial entity, but only matter, suitably organized.

Materialism has a long history. Democritus (*c.* 460–370 BC) described the universe as a fleeting arrangement of atoms swirling in the void. Hobbes (1588–1679) and La Mettrie (1707–51) argued that mental phenomena were nothing more than mechanical interactions among material components of animate creatures. On such a view, plants and animals, including human beings, would be complex machines. Nowadays, materialism of one stripe or another is more often than not simply taken for granted; in David Lewis's words, materialism is *non-negotiable*. In any case, the belief that minds are just brains is evidently widespread. Francis Crick's recent characterization of this as 'the astonishing hypothesis' flies in the face of my own experience with undergraduate philosophy students who often seem happy to use 'mind' and 'brain' interchangeably.

Although many philosophers would, if pressed, describe themselves as materialists, materialism is not a single unified doctrine, but a family of divergent doctrines. Indeed, disagreements among materialists tend to overshadow their common rejection of dualism. More significantly for our purposes, dissatisfaction with various materialist precepts has led to a revival of interest in forms of dualism. Surprisingly, much of this renewed interest has been spawned by work in the neurosciences, where difficulties in reconciling characteristics of complex material systems with characteristics of conscious experiences are especially acute (for discussion, see Chapter 10).

In this chapter, the focus will be on one important and influential precursor to the contemporary debate: *behaviorism*. The label 'behaviorism' has been used to designate both a philosophical doctrine and a once prominent research program in psychology. Although both philosophical and psychological behaviorism have common roots, they bear at best a superficial resemblance to one another. (*Verificationism*, the view that the meaning of empirical claims is exhausted by their 'verification conditions', served as an important source of inspiration for both sorts of behaviorism.)

Philosophical behaviorism is associated with a thesis about the nature of mind and the meanings of mental terms. *Psychological* behaviorism emerged from an influential conception of scientific method as applied to psychology. Psychological behaviorism dominated experimental work in psychology in the mid-twentieth century until it was eclipsed by the 'information-processing' model, a model inspired both by the sense that the behaviorist model was hopelessly inadequate and by the advent of the computing machine.

Distinguishing between philosophical and psychological behaviorism brings to the foreground the relation philosophy bears to the empirical sciences, including psychology. Science professes to have little use for philosophy. For their part, philosophers commonly defer to scientists when their interests intersect. This suggests a well-defined division of labor. Matters are not so straightforward, however. For better or worse, philosophers have had an important part in shaping conceptions of mentality that guide empirical investigators. At the same time, philosophers have periodically reevaluated their theories in light of what are taken to be advances in psychology and neuroscience. One result is that philosophical influences on empirical theorizing can find their way back into philosophy. When this happens, a philosophical thesis can gain an undeserved air of empirical respectability in the minds of philosophers eager to embrace the pronouncements of scientists.

Thus, philosophers impressed by behaviorism in psychology largely failed to appreciate the extent to which the behaviorist conception of mind was the product of a contentious philosophical conception of scientific method. Ironically, the roots of that conception lay in a positivist tradition that many of these same philosophers would have found unappealing. One lesson is that it is a mistake for philosophers of mind – or their students! – to accept uncritically, or at face value, claims issuing from psychology or the neurosciences purporting to bear on traditional issues in the philosophy of mind.

4.2 Historical and Philosophical Background

Until the twentieth century, scientific study of the mind was assumed to revolve around the study of conscious states and processes. Subjects in psychological experiments (most often the experimenters themselves or their students) were trained to 'introspect', and report in detail on features of their conscious experiences under various conditions. In this milieu, mental imagery and subtle qualities of sensory episodes had a central place.

At the same time, psychologists were concerned to integrate the study of the mind with the study of the brain. No one could doubt that occurrences in the brain and nervous system were intimately connected to mental goings-on. The difficulty was to understand precisely the nature of this connection. It is tempting to think that minds (or selves: I shall continue to use the terms interchangeably, without intending to suggest that they are synonymous) are nothing more than brains. Properties of brains, however, seem to differ importantly from properties of minds. When you undergo a conscious experience, you are vividly aware of characteristics of that experience. When you examine a living brain, the characteristics you observe appear to be utterly different. These differences are reflected in differences in the vocabularies used to describe conscious experiences and brains or states of brains.

Think what it is like to have a headache. Now imagine that you are able to peer into the brain of someone suffering a headache. What you observe, even aided by instruments that reveal the brain's fine structure, is quite unlike what the headache victim *feels*. Imagine a neuroscientist, intimately familiar with the physiology of headache, but who has never experienced a headache. There is, it would seem, something the scientist lacks knowledge of, some characteristic the scientist has not encountered and *could not* encounter simply by inspecting the brains of headache sufferers. This characteristic – what it is like to have a headache – would appear not to be a neurological characteristic. When you look at the matter this way, it is hard to avoid concluding that mental characteristics are not brain characteristics: minds are not brains.

How *could* minds be brains? You evidently enjoy a kind of privileged introspective 'access' to your conscious experiences that others could never have. Your experiences are 'private'. Your awareness of them is direct and authoritative; a neuroscientist's awareness of those same experiences is, in contrast, indirect, inferential and subject to correction. When you have a headache, form an image of your grandmother, or decide to comb your hair, you are in a position to recognize immediately, without the benefit of evidence or observation, that you have a headache, that you are imagining your grandmother, or that you have decided to comb your hair. An observer could only infer your state of mind by monitoring your behavior (including your linguistic behavior: the observer could interrogate you).

All this is exactly what you would expect were dualism true. But dualism, or at any rate Cartesian dualism, apparently leads to a bifurcation of the study of intelligent, sentient agents. You can study the biology and physiology of such agents, but in so doing you would be ignoring their minds; or you could study their minds, at least indirectly, ignoring their material makeup.

Now, however, you confront an all-too-familiar difficulty. Science is limited to the pursuit of knowledge concerning objective, 'public' states of affairs. A state of affairs is objective if it can be apprehended from more than one standpoint, by more than one observer. The contents of your mind, however, are observable (if that is the right word) *only* by you. The objective, scientific route to those contents is through observations of what you say and do. This appears to place minds themselves outside the realm of respectable scientific inquiry. Scientists can study brains. This might lead scientists to conclude that particular kinds of neurological goings-on are *correlated* with, or in some way responsible for, particular kinds of mental goings-on. Knowledge of such correlations would enable scientists reliably to infer states of mind by observing brain activity. But scientists would not be observing or measuring those states of mind themselves, except in their own case, except when they 'introspected'.

4.3   Other Minds

Once you start down this road, you might come to doubt that states of mind – as distinct from their physiological correlates – are a fit subject for scientific examination. Eventually, the very idea that science is in a position even to establish *correlations* between mental occurrences and goings-on in the nervous system can come to be doubted. Imagine that, every time you have a particular kind of experience – every time you see a certain shade of red, for instance, the red of a ripe tomato – your brain goes into a particular state, S. Further, whenever your brain goes into state S, you experience that very shade of red. (You might go into state S because you are looking at a tomato, or because you are dreaming that you are looking at a tomato, or because your brain is being artificially stimulated by an implanted electrode with the result that you hallucinate a tomato.) It looks as though there must be a correlation between experiences of this kind and neural states of kind S.

Suppose, now, you observe *my* brain in state S. I announce that I am experiencing a certain shade of red, a shade I describe as the red of a ripe tomato. It might seem that this provides further evidence of the correlation already observed in your own case. But does it? In your own case, you have access *both* to the mental state and to its neural correlate. When you observe me, however, you have access *only* to my neurological condition and to my report as to what I am experiencing. What gives you the right to assume that *my* mental state resembles *yours*?

True, I describe my experience just as you describe yours. We agree that we are experiencing the color of ripe tomatoes. But, of course, this is how we have each been taught to characterize our respective experiences. I have a particular kind of visual experience when I view a ripe tomato in bright sunlight. I describe this experience as the kind of experience *I* have when I view a ripe tomato in bright sunlight. You have a particular kind of experience when you view a ripe tomato under similar observational conditions.

And you have learned to describe this experience as the kind of experience *you* have when you view a ripe tomato in bright sunlight. But what entitles either of us to say that the experiences so described are *similar*? Perhaps the experience *you* have is like the experience *I* would have were I to view a lime in bright sunlight – your red is my green! Our *descriptions* perfectly coincide, but our respective states of mind differ qualitatively.

Attempts to correlate kinds of neurological goings-on and kinds of mental occurrences boil down to correlations of neurological goings-on and first-person *descriptions* or *reports* of mental occurrences. You learn to describe the qualities of your states of mind by reference to publicly observable objects that typically evoke them. And this leaves open the possibility that, while your *descriptions* match others', the *states* to which they apply are wildly different qualitatively.

This might seem an idle worry, a 'purely philosophical' possibility. But ask yourself: what earthly reason do you have for thinking that your states of mind qualitatively resemble the states of mind of others? It is not as though you have observed others' states of mind and discovered they match yours. You lack even a single example of such a match. Might you infer *induc-tively* from characteristics of your own case to the characteristics of others? (Inductive inference is probabilistic: reasoning from the characteristics of a sample of a population to characteristics of the population as a whole.) But canons of inductive reasoning proscribe inferences from a single individual case to a whole population unless it is already clear that the individual is representative of the population. If you assume that characteristics of your states of mind are representative, however, you are assuming precisely what you set out to establish!

The problem we have stumbled upon is the old 'problem of other minds'. Granted you can know *your own* mind, how could you know the minds of *others*? Indeed, once you put it this way, you can see that the problem is really much worse than you might have expected. How could you know that others have minds *at all*? What grounds have you to suppose that *they* have conscious experiences? Yes, others behave in ways similar to the ways you behave; they insist they have pains, images, feelings, and thoughts. But what reason might you have for supposing that they *do*? You cannot observe others' states of mind. Nor do you have remotely adequate induc-tive grounds for inferring that they enjoy a mental life from what you can observe about them.

A recent twist on this venerable puzzle introduces the possibility of philosophical 'zombies'. Philosophical zombies, as distinct from cinematic zombies, are not the 'undead', not creatures who stagger about menacing the living. Philosophical zombies are creatures identical to us in every mate-rial respect, but altogether lacking conscious experiences. The apparent conceivability of zombies has convinced some philosophers that there is an unbridgeable 'explanatory gap' between material qualities and the qualities of conscious experience. (This is a topic to which I shall return in § 10.4.)

You are likely to be growing impatient with this line of reasoning. *Of course* we know that others have mental lives similar to ours in many ways – and different as well: it is also possible to know that! Well and good. But it is hard to see how this confidence could be justified so long as you accept the notion that minds and their contents are private affairs, impervious to public scrutiny.

4.4 The Beetle in the Box

Perhaps, as is so often the case in philosophy, our starting point is what is responsible for our predicament. Perhaps we have been led down the garden path by a faulty conception of mind inherited from Descartes. If we begin to question that conception, we might see our way clear to a solution to the problem, a solution that better fits our unshakeable confidence that others have minds and that their states of mind resemble ours.

Wittgenstein (1889–1951), in his *Philosophical Investigations* (1953), § 293, offers a compelling analogy:

> Suppose everyone had a box with something in it: we call it a 'beetle'. No one can look into anyone else's box, and everyone says he knows what a beetle is only by looking at his beetle. – Here it would be quite possible for everyone to have something different in his box. One might even imagine such a thing constantly changing.

The example is meant to evoke the familiar depiction of the relation you bear to your own and others' states of mind, a depiction taken for granted in the previous discussion: your states of mind are 'private' objects to which only you have access.

Wittgenstein argues against this picture, not by presenting considerations that imply its falsity, but by showing that accepting it leads to a paradoxical result: if this is the relation you bear to your own and others' states of mind, then you would have no way of so much as *referring* to them.

> Suppose the word 'beetle' had a use in these people's language? – If so it would not be used as the name of a thing. The thing in the box has no place in the language-game at all; not even as a something: for the box might even be empty. – No, one can 'divide through' by the thing in the box; it cancels out, whatever it is. That is to say: if we construe the grammar of the expression of sensation on the model of 'object and designation' the object drops out of consideration as irrelevant.

What is Wittgenstein's point? You report that your box contains a beetle. Your report is perfectly apt. You have been taught to use the word 'beetle' in just this way. Imagine, now, that the object in *my* box is, in fact, very different from the object in your box: were you and I to compare the objects, this would be obvious – although of course we could never be in a position to compare them. I report that my box contains a beetle. In so doing, I am using the word 'beetle' exactly as I have been taught to use it. My utterance, like yours, is perfectly correct. You and I both report that our respective boxes contain beetles. Is either of us mistaken?

No, says Wittgenstein. In the imagined situation, the word 'beetle' is used in such a way that it makes no difference *what* is inside anyone's box. 'Beetle', in the imagined dialect, means, roughly, 'whatever is in the box'. To wonder whether your beetle resembles my beetle is to misunderstand this use of 'beetle'. It is to treat 'beetle' as though it named or designated a particular kind of object or entity. But 'beetle' is used in such a way that 'the object drops out of consideration as irrelevant'.

Wittgenstein's point is not merely a linguistic one. Any *thoughts* you might harbor that you would express using the word 'beetle', are similarly constrained. Those thoughts turn out not to concern some particular kind of entity. Differently put: if the word 'beetle' does not refer to entities of a particular sort, then neither do thoughts naturally expressible using 'beetle'. In this regard, your beetle is no different from mine.

How is the beetle analogy meant to be extended to states of mind? As a child, you react in various ways to your surroundings. On some occasions, you whimper and rub your head. Adults tell you that you have what is called a headache. Others are similarly taught to use 'headache'. Does 'headache' designate a kind of entity or state?

Maybe not. Maybe when you tell me that you have a headache, you are not picking out any definite thing or private condition at all (think of the beetle), but merely *evincing* your headache. You have been trained or conditioned in a particular way. When you are moved to whimper and rub your head, you are, as a result of this training, moved as well to utter the words 'I have a headache'. When you ascribe a headache to me, you are saying no more than that I am in a kind of state that leads me to whimper, rub my head, and perhaps to utter 'I have a headache'. The private qualitative character of that state, if there is one, could differ in each of its instances. It might continually change, or even, in some cases (zombies?), be altogether absent. The function of the word 'headache' is not to designate a private, qualitatively distinctive entity or episode, however. This 'drops out of consideration as irrelevant'. Your headache, like your beetle, is no different from mine.

Suppose this story of our use of 'headache' is applied to our mental vocabulary generally. Suppose that mental terms are not in fact used to name or designate kinds of entity or qualitatively similar private episodes as Descartes would have it. Their role is altogether different. In that case, the question whether the state you designate by the 'experience I have when I view a ripe tomato in bright sunlight' qualitatively *matches* the state I designate when I use the same expression, could not so much as arise. To raise the question is to mischaracterize the use of mental terminology, and thus to speak nonsense!

4.5 Philosophical Behaviorism

This line of reasoning supports what I have been calling philosophical behaviorism. (A caveat: philosophers usually characterized as behaviorists have rarely applied the label to themselves.) Philosophical behaviorists hold that so long as we treat minds and bodies as distinct entities we err in a fundamental way. Minds are not *entities* at all, not Cartesian substances, not brains. And mental episodes are not goings-on 'inside' such entities. Philosophers have been attracted to the Cartesian picture only because they have been misled by what Wittgenstein calls the 'grammar' of our language.

According to Wittgenstein, words owe their significance to 'language games' we have learned to play with them. An appropriate understanding of any word (hence the concept the word expresses) requires a grasp of its role in these language games. So long as we deploy our language in everyday life we steer clear of philosophical puzzles. When we engage in philosophy, however, we are apt to be misled by the fact that 'mind', like 'brain' or 'tomato', is a substantive noun. We reason that 'mind' must designate a kind of entity, and that what we call thoughts, sensations, and feelings refer to qualitative states or modes of this entity. We can avoid confusion, only by looking carefully at the way our words are actually deployed in ordinary circumstances.

This prescription is intended by Wittgenstein to apply to philosophy generally. Philosophical problems arise 'when language goes on holiday', when we lose touch with the way words are actually used. In our everyday interactions with one another, we are not in the least puzzled by our capacity to know how others feel or what they are thinking. The philosophical problem of other minds arises when we wrench 'mind', 'thought', 'feeling', 'sensation', and their cognates from the contexts in which they are naturally deployed, put a special interpretation on them, and then boggle at the puzzles that result.

Gilbert Ryle (1900–76) extends Wittgenstein's point. According to Ryle, the supposition that minds are kinds of entity amounts to a 'category mistake': 'it represents the facts of mental life as if they belonged to one logical type or category ... when actually they belong to another' (1949, 16). Suppose you take a visitor, Jack, on a tour of your university. You stroll through the grounds; you show Jack various academic and administrative buildings; you take Jack to the library; you introduce him to students and to members of the faculty. When you are done, you ask whether there is anything else he would like to see. Jack replies: 'Yes. You've shown me the grounds, academic and administrative buildings, the library, students, and faculty; but you haven't shown me the *university*. I'd like to see that.' Jack's confusion reflects a category mistake. He has taken the term 'university' to designate something similar to, but distinct from, those things he has seen already.

If Jack persisted in the belief that 'university' designates such an entity despite failing ever to encounter it, he might come to imagine that the entity in question is a spectral, immaterial edifice. An analogous mistake, says Ryle, encourages Cartesian dualism. You begin with the idea that minds are entities. But when you examine all the obvious candidate entities – bodies and brains, for instance – you fail to find mentality. If minds are entities, then, they must be entities of a special sort, *nonmaterial* entities. You come to see the mind, in Ryle's colorful phrase, as a *ghost in the machine*.

But, Ryle holds, the mistake was made at the outset. Minds are not entities at all, ghostly or otherwise, a fact we should immediately appreciate if only we kept firmly before us the way 'mind' functions in ordinary English.

> The theoretically interesting category mistakes are those made by people who are perfectly competent to apply concepts, at least in the situations with which they are familiar, but are still liable in their abstract thinking to allocate those concepts to logical types to which they do not belong.

> (Ryle 1949, 17)

At the risk of confusing matters by piling analogies on top of analogies, an example of Wittgenstein's might help here. Suppose you look into the cab of a locomotive (or the cockpit of a jetliner). You see levers, knobs, buttons, and switches. Each of these operates in a particular way (some are turned, some slide back and forth, some are pushed or pulled), and each has a particular function in the locomotive's (or jetliner's) operation. You would be misled if you assumed that levers or knobs with similar shapes all had similar functions. In the same way, the fact that 'mind' is a substantive noun, or that we speak of 'states of mind' should not lead us to assume that 'mind' functions to designate particular kinds of entity, and that states of mind are states of such entities.

If 'mind', like 'university, does not function as the name a particular kind of material or immaterial ('ghostly') entity, how *does* it function? If the concept of mind is not the concept of an entity, of what *is* it the concept?

According to Wittgenstein and Ryle, minds are ascribed to creatures with a capacity to comport themselves *intelligently*. A creature possesses a mind, not in virtue of being equipped with a peculiar kind of internal organ, material or immaterial, but in virtue of being the sort of creature capable of engaging in behavior that exhibits a measure of spontaneity and a relatively complex organization.

The point here is not to downgrade the brain. No one could doubt that brains are required for intelligent behavior. The point rather is to move beyond the idea that minds are organs, distinctive kinds of entity, and states of mind are states of such organs: minds are not brains, nor are they entities distinct from, but somehow intimately related to, brains. States of mind – headaches, intentions, beliefs – are possessed by intelligent creatures in virtue of what they do or would do. Your believing there is a bear in your path, for instance, is not a matter of your being in a particular sort of inner state. Your believing there is a bear in your path is your taking (or being disposed to take) appropriate evasive measures, your assenting (or being disposed to assent) to 'There is a bear in the path', and the like. Your intending to attend the World Series is a matter of your being moved to purchase tickets, arranging for transportation, announcing 'I'm going to the World Series', and so on. (In Chapter 8, you will encounter Daniel Dennett's updated version of this view.)

4.6 Dispositions

Philosophical behaviorists hold that agents are correctly describable as having states of mind, not only in virtue of what those agents *do*, but also, and crucially, in virtue of what the agents *would do*, what they are *disposed* to do. If you have a headache, you might be disposed to whimper, rub your head, seek out aspirin, and announce when prompted, 'I have a headache'. You might do none of these things, however. Imagine, for instance, that you thought it ill-mannered to speak of one's afflictions. In that case, although you are *disposed* to behave in particular ways, you do not actually behave in those ways.

But now we are confronted with a new question. What is it to be 'disposed' to behave in a particular way? What are *dispositions*? A fragile vase possesses a disposition to shatter. In shattering – when struck forcefully with a tire iron, for instance – this disposition is manifested. A salt crystal possesses a disposition to dissolve in water. In dissolving upon being placed in water, it manifests its solubility. An object could possess a disposition, however, without ever manifesting that disposition. A fragile glass need never shatter; a salt crystal need never dissolve.

I shall have more to say about dispositions in later chapters (see especially §§ 12.6–12.8). For the moment, it is important only to appreciate that any plausible version of philosophical behaviorism requires their introduction. Among other things, dispositions take up the slack between what you do and what you *would* do. You do, presumably, what you are disposed to do; but you could be disposed to do many things you never do because the opportunity to do them does not arise or because you are more strongly disposed to do something else. You might be disposed to act bravely when faced with danger, but pass your life in tranquil surroundings. That need not detract from your bravery. Of course if you never *manifest* your bravery, acquaintances would have no reason to think you brave – nor, for that matter, need *you* have any inkling that you possess this virtue. Similarly, you would have no reason to think that a particular unfamiliar substance was water soluble if its solubility were never manifested, if it never actually dissolved, even if the occasion should arise: a salt crystal disposed to dissolve in water might fail to dissolve if the water is already saturated. Finally, you might act in ways consistent with your possession of a particular disposition, but not because you were so disposed. You might, for instance, be brave but stand your ground, not owing to your bravery, but because you are unaware of impending danger.

4.7   Behavioral Analysis

In what sense, exactly, does philosophical behaviorism 'tie states of mind to behavior'? Many behaviorists hold that assertions concerning states of mind can be *translated* or *analyzed* into statements about behavior or dispositions to behave. You have had a taste of this already. A behaviorist might say that if you believe there is a bear in your path, you are disposed to take evasive action, to assent to 'There is a bear in the path', to warn your companions, and the like. This, according to the behaviorist, is, at bottom, what it *is* to believe there is a bear in your path.

The guiding idea is that, if talk about states of mind could be *analyzed* or *paraphrased* into talk of behavior (and dispositions to behave), then talk of states of mind will have been 'reduced to' – shown to be nothing more than – a shorthand way of talking about behavior (or, more accurately, behavior plus dispositions to behave). Analysis of this sort is meant to replace something potentially contentious with something uncontroversial. To see the point, think of a parallel case. Economists sometimes speak of the average family. The income of the average family in rural areas has declined from what it was a decade ago. Is there an average family? Is there an entity (or, for that matter, a collection of entities) designated by the phrase 'the average family'? Thinking so looks like a category mistake.

In this case, you can see how talk about the average family's income might be reductively analyzed into talk about the income of individual families summed and divided by the number of families. The upshot: there is nothing more to the average family than this. If you could 'paraphrase away' claims about minds and mental goings-on, replacing such claims with descriptions of behavior and dispositions to behave, then (so the thought goes) you would have succeeded in showing that there is nothing more to an agent's possessing a mind than the agent's behaving or being disposed to behave in appropriately mindful ways.

(Berkeley, whom you encountered in Chapter 3 promoting idealism, defends a reductive analysis of talk about material objects to talk about 'ideas', Berkeley's catch-all term for states of mind. If successful, such an analysis would show that you do not need to suppose that material objects are anything 'over and above' ideas in the mind. Behaviorists' analyses run in the opposite direction.)

What are the prospects for behaviorist-style reductive analyses of states of mind? One nagging worry is that behavioral analyses threaten to be open-ended. There is no limit on the list of things you might do or be disposed to do if you harbor the belief that there is a bear on the trail, for instance. What you do, will depend on the circumstances, and the circumstances can vary in indefinitely many ways that resist specification in advance. Moreover, it seems clear that among the things you will be disposed to do is to form new beliefs and acquire new desires. Each of these beliefs and desires will require its own separate behavioral analysis.

This complicates the picture, certainly, but it need not pose an insuperable problem for the philosophical behaviorist. The envisaged analyses could turn out to be non-finite. You might accept a non-finite reductive analysis, provided you can see how it *could* be extended, even when you are in no position to do so yourself.

Another difficulty is less easily dismissed. You see a bear on the path and form the belief that there is a bear on the path. But what you do and what you are disposed to do evidently depends on your *overall* state of mind: what else you believe and want, for instance. And this is so for any state of mind. Suppose you believe that there is a bear in the path, but want to have a closer look (you are curious by nature), or believe that bears are not dangerous, or suppose you have a yen to live dangerously, or to impress a companion.

It would seem that your belief is compatible with your behaving or being disposed to behave in *any way at all* depending on what else you believe and what you want. In that case, it looks as though *no* reductive analysis of states of mind is on the cards. The problem is not just that each of these additional states of mind requires a further behavioral analysis, thus complicating and extending the analytical task. The problem, rather, is that there is apparently no way to avoid mention of further states of mind in any statement of what behavior a given state of mind is likely to produce. It is as though you set out to analyze away talk about the average family only to discover that your analysis reintroduced mention of average families at every turning.

To appreciate the magnitude of the problem, return to your belief that there is a bear in the path. This belief, in concert with the belief that bears are dangerous, and a desire to avoid dangerous animals, might lead you to hurry away. But now imagine that you believe that there is a bear in your path, believe that bears are dangerous, and desire to avoid dangerous animals (your beliefs and desires are as before) but that you believe, *in addition*, that hurrying away would only attract the bear's attention. In this case, you would be disposed to behave, and behave, very differently.

The example illustrates a general point. Any attempt to say what behavior constitutes, or partly constitutes, a given state of mind can be shown false by producing an example in which the state of mind is present but, owing to the addition of further beliefs or desires, the behavior in question does not follow. Nor will it help to try to rule out such cases by means of a general excluder: if you believe that there is a bear in the path, believe that bears are dangerous, and you desire to avoid dangerous animals, then, *providing you have no additional conflicting beliefs or desires*, you will be disposed to turn tail. The problem here is that we have reintroduced mention of states of mind in the italicized exclusion clause. And these are precisely what we were trying to 'analyze away'. The analytical project looks hopeless. (In § 6.11, you will encounter a technique – associated with Frank Ramsey and David

Lewis – for dealing with cases of this sort that a behaviorist could adopt. The question then arises whether this is sufficient to render behaviorism an attractive option.)

4.8 Sensation

A committed behaviorist might regard all these worries as pedantic philosophical details. Perhaps it is unreasonable to expect perfect translations of assertions about states of mind into statements about behavior. Perhaps all we need show is that talk of inner goings-on could be *replaced* with behavioral talk. Perhaps so doing would mesh nicely with scientific accounts of the activities of intelligent creatures.

This 'verificationist' line of response is likely to be attractive to psychological behaviorists (see below, § 4.12). How reasonable is it? In discussing behaviorism's analytic project, I have focused on kinds of mental state that might seem especially apt for reduction: belief, desire, intention, and the like (these are the so-called propositional attitudes). What happens when you extend the analytical enterprise to *qualitatively loaded* states of mind?

To see why there might be a problem with such cases, consider a concrete example. Imagine that you have contracted a mild case of food poisoning as a result of a visit to a local fast-food emporium. You suffer a variety of symptoms including nausea. Your feeling nauseous doubtless leads you to behave in various ways and to be disposed to behave in various others. (You will have no trouble filling in the details.) Could this be *all there is* to your being nauseous? The behaviorist analysis apparently leaves out the most salient feature of nausea: its immediate qualitative character! Most of us would find it hard not to believe that this qualitative character is what *leads* us to behave as we do. The beetle is reasserting itself!

Behaviorism opposes the idea that states of mind are inner states that yield behavioral symptoms. But this seems crazy when you think of nausea, headache, or the 'electric' feeling you have when you bump your funny bone or your foot falls asleep at the cinema. In fact, behaviorism seems to have things backwards when you reflect on any qualitatively vivid state of mind. These can be unpleasant, as in headache or nausea; pleasant, as in feelings of warmth; or both pleasant and unpleasant, as a child's feeling when being tickled by an older sibling. Analyzing talk of such things into statements about behavior or dispositions to behave, apparently omits just what is most distinctive about them.

Is this just more philosophical pedantry? I urge caution here. As you will discover, behaviorists are not alone in wanting to factor out talk of the qualitative character of states of mind. Plenty of materialist philosophers who reject behaviorism reject, as well, the idea that states of mind are what they are owing to their qualitative character. If you are so inclined, if you are skeptical that sensory experiences are qualitatively imbued, you will be in no position to criticize behaviorists on this score.

4.9   The Legacy of Philosophical Behaviorism

If the attempt to analyze talk of states of mind into talk of behavior is unworkable, what is left of philosophical behaviorism? It is true, certainly, that our grounds for ascribing states of mind to one another are largely behavioral. This is an epistemological point, however; a point about what constitutes *evidence* for our beliefs about one another's mental lives, and a point a Cartesian could happily accept.

What of Ryle's contention that it is a mistake – a 'category mistake' – to regard your possessing a mind as a matter of your body's standing in a particular relation to a special entity, your mind? And what of Wittgenstein's suggestion that terms used to ascribe states of mind are not meant to designate definite sorts of object or episode? Both of these ideas are independent of the behaviorist's analytical project, and both survive in accounts of the mind that are self-consciously anti-behaviorist. You might, for instance, think that to have a mind is simply to possess a particular sort of organization, one that issues in intelligent behavior. And you might imagine that to be in a given state of mind is just to be in *some state or other* – the nature of the state could vary across individuals or species – that contributes in a characteristic way to the operation of this organized system.

These themes are central to functionalism, a conception of mind to be examined in Chapter 6. For the moment, I ask you simply to register behaviorism's lack of concern for the *qualitative* dimension of states of mind. If your having a headache is solely a matter of your behaving, or being disposed to behave, in a particular way, then the intrinsic qualitative nature of whatever is responsible for your so behaving, or being disposed so to behave, is irrelevant. This is explicit in Wittgenstein's beetle in the box analogy. And, as you will see, this feature of behaviorism is apparently inherited by functionalism.

4.10   Intrinsic Characteristics

Speaking of 'intrinsic qualitative nature', you are bound to wonder what exactly this phrase is supposed to signify. The notion of an intrinsic quality is best understood in contrast to the complementary notion of an extrinsic characteristic. (I prefer to contrast *intrinsic* with *extrinsic* rather than *relational*. That two liver cells bear a certain relation to one another is a relational feature of the cells, but an intrinsic feature of the organ to which they belong.) An intrinsic quality is a quality an object has in its own right. Being spherical is an *in*trinsic quality of a billiard ball. Being near the center of the billiard table is, in contrast, a non-intrinsic, *ex*trinsic feature of the ball.

Think of intrinsic qualities as being *built into* objects; extrinsic characteristics as being ascribable to objects only in virtue of relations those objects bear to other objects. In the beetle in the box case, imagine that one person's box contains a marble, and another's contains a sugar cube. Then the intrinsic nature of what is in each box differs. And it is precisely this that 'drops out of consideration as irrelevant'.

You can distinguish an object's intrinsic qualitative nature from its dispositionalities or 'causal powers'. The billiard ball has the power to roll across the table, the power to shatter a pane of glass, and the power to reflect light in a particular way. But the ball has, as well, a particular qualitative nature: a particular shape, a particular color, a particular size, a particular mass, a particular temperature. How an object's powers or dispositionalities are related to its qualitative characteristics is a difficult business, as you will see. For the present, you need only appreciate that it seems natural to distinguish an object's qualitative aspects from its causal propensities or powers. And, again, behaviorism regards the intrinsic qualitative nature of a state of mind as irrelevant. What matters is what it does or would do, not what it is.

One way to put this would be to say that, according to the behaviorist, states of mind, '*qua* states of mind', lack an intrinsic qualitative nature. Think again of the beetle in the box analogy. Whatever is in the box *has* some intrinsic qualitative nature or other – how could it not? But this nature is irrelevant to its being true that the box contains a beetle: *qua* beetle – considered solely as a 'beetle' – what the box contains lacks intrinsic qualities.

You might regard a view of this kind as wildly implausible. Surely your headache has an intrinsic qualitative nature, and this is an important part of what makes your headache a *headache*: 'there is something it is like' to have a headache. What it is like to have a headache differs *qualitatively* from what it is like to have other kinds of conscious experience. Part of what makes a given conscious experience a headache is just this intrinsic 'what-its-likeness'.

The denial of all this could strike you as incredible. Yet behaviorists *do* deny it. And, as you will see, many other philosophers, including philosophers dismissive of behaviorism, seem ready to deny it as well. These philosophers argue that states of mind owe their identity, not to their intrinsic qualitative nature (if indeed they have any such nature at all), but exclusively to their causal powers, their dispositionalities. One of the aims of the chapters that follow is to equip you to evaluate such claims.

4.11 'Experimental Methods and Conceptual Confusion'

Philosophical behaviorism is a thesis about the meanings of mental terms and, ultimately, about the significance of mental concepts. Its proponents consider philosophical questions about the nature of mind to be equivalent to questions about the character of mental concepts. They reason that, if you want to know what minds are, you must make explicit what 'mind' and its cognates *mean*. This, they contend, is largely a matter of spelling out how 'mind' and its cognates are used by competent speakers. Minds are whatever answers to ' … is a mind' in common parlance.

A conception of this sort neatly distinguishes the philosopher's interest in minds from the psychologist's. Philosophers are taken to be in the business of making clear the subtleties of the conception of mind enshrined in our linguistic practices. Psychologists and other empirical scientists investigate the character of extra-linguistic reality. Language 'carves up' the universe in a particular way. You are in a position to interpret empirical claims about minds only after comparing concepts deployed in those claims with the concepts encoded in ordinary language. When psychologists speak of belief, or emotion, or mental imagery, do they *mean* belief, emotion, mental imagery, do they mean what is ordinarily meant by 'belief', 'emotion', 'mental imagery'? To find out, you must see how these expressions function in psychological theories and compare this with their use in everyday language.

When you do this, according to philosophers sympathetic to Wittgenstein and Ryle, you discover that psychology has more often than not made use of familiar terminology in surprising ways. This can lead to a systematic misunderstanding of psychological theses. Wittgenstein put it this way: 'in psychology there are experimental methods and *conceptual confusion*' (1953, 232). The charge of 'conceptual confusion' is intended to apply as much to the psychologists' interpretation of their own work as it does to a layperson's grasp of psychological results.

Here is the picture. A theorist introduces a technical notion using a familiar term. The technical notion might differ importantly from the term's everyday significance. The theorist then establishes truths that pertain to whatever the technical notion denotes. Confusion results when the theorist, along with the rest of us, interprets these as applying to whatever the original everyday term applies to. It is as though you decided to give 'pigeon' a strict sense: a four-legged artifact with a flat surface used for supporting objects. You then go on, using rigorous empirical methods, to establish that the common belief that pigeons can fly, mate, build nests, and lay eggs is a myth.

This, according to Ryle and Wittgenstein, is just the *kind* of mistake made by psychologists when, under the guise of making mental terms more precise, they redefine them and deploy the terms thus redefined in experimental settings. If the critics are right, psychology is riddled with such mistakes.

4.12 Psychological Behaviorism

So much for philosophical behaviorism. Behaviorism in psychology was spawned, not by worries about the significance of mental terms, but by a concern that psychology have an appropriately *scientific* status. On a traditional view of the mind, a view accepted without question by psychologists in the nineteenth century, states of mind were taken to be private conscious states not amenable to public scrutiny. You know the story. While 'access' to your own states of mind is direct, others can only observe their effects on your behavior. If you suppose, as pioneering behaviorists J. B. Watson (1878–1958) and B. F. Skinner (1904–90) supposed, that only what is publicly observable is a fit subject for science, you will want to exclude states of mind, as traditionally conceived, from scientific consideration. If you suppose, as well, that talk about items not susceptible to public verification is unsavory, or even meaningless, you will have, in effect, ruled the traditional conception of mind out of bounds for serious empirical consideration. (In fairness, I should note that early behaviorists were reacting to what was widely perceived as the uniform failure of introspective psychology to deliver the goods.)

You could put this by saying that, on the behaviorist conception, talk of minds, conscious experiences, and the like is pointless. Appeals of such things in explanations of behavior reflect only a superstitious past in which observable characteristics of objects were explained by reference to ghosts and spirits taken to animate them. To deny ghosts and spirits – and mental states – is not to deny that objects and intelligent creatures have complex observable traits, nor is it to deny that these are susceptible to rigorous scientific explanation. Just as we have put behind us explanations of pathological behavior that appeal to possession by evil spirits, so we must put behind us explanations that appeal to private inner occurrences. This is what behaviorists set out to do.

The data for psychological behaviorism are instances of behavior, 'behaviors': what organisms do in response to environmental contingencies. A behaviorist explains an instance of behavior, not by postulating unobservable interior states of mind, but by reference to environmental stimuli that elicit the behavior. The governing model is the simple reflex. On a visit to the doctor, you sit in a relaxed position on the edge of an examining table. A doctor taps your knee, and your leg bobs in a characteristic way. Here, a bit of behavior, a response – your leg's bobbing – is explained by the occurrence of a stimulus – the doctor's tapping your knee. What connects stimulus and response is an unadorned 'reflex mechanism'. Behaviorists describe that mechanism exclusively by reference to its role in clear-cut stimulus response (S–R) relations.

Behaviorists hold that *all* behavior, even complex behavior, can be fully explained in S–R terms. The job of the psychologist is to provide a systematic accounting of these S–R relations. As far as the behaviorist is concerned, the organism is a 'black box', something the psychological nature of which is exhaustively describable by reference to its response to stimuli (Figure 4.1). Black boxes and organisms have an internal structure, something capable of being investigated in its own right. But this is the province of the biologist or the physiologist, not the psychologist. The psychologist is, or ought to be, interested only in plotting behavioral contingencies.

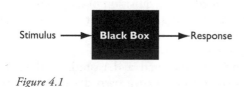

Figure 4.1

Behaviorists proscribe mention of inner mechanisms except in cases in which these are capable of exhaustive decomposition into relations between stimuli (observable inputs) and output responses (observable behavior). Complex responses are to be broken down into patterns of simpler S–R relations. In this way, simple mechanisms operating in concert, could yield recognizably intelligent behavior.

All but the simplest organisms are capable of *learning*, capable, that is, of modifying their S–R contingencies. Again, the mechanism is straightforward. A particular kind of response can be 'reinforced' if its occurrence is 'rewarded'. A rat may not be inclined at the onset of a particular sound – a ringing bell, say – to respond by pressing a bar in its cage. But if, perhaps by accident, the rat, hearing the bell, presses the bar and receives a food pellet, then a bar-pressing response to the aural stimulus will be reinforced. Eventually, the rat comes to 'associate' the bell, the act of bar-pressing, and the reward. As a result, the rat is *conditioned* to press the bar when the bell sounds.

It would be natural to describe the rat as 'discovering a connection' between the bell's ringing, pressing the bar, and the receipt of a food pellet. If behaviorists are right, however, such a description must be purely metaphorical. Taken literally, it suggests an inner mental process of the sort behaviorists disdain. Sticking to the observable facts, you find that the rat presses the bar at the onset of a particular sound and receives a food pellet. Subsequently, the rat's bar-pressing comes to co-vary reliably with the bell's ringing. More precisely: the probability that the rat will press the bar at the onset of the sound increases dramatically. Eventually, the rat presses the bar during, and only during, a period immediately following the onset of the sound. This is, at bottom, what the rat's 'discovering the connection' amounts to.

4.13   The Demise of Behaviorism

Behaviorists were committed to the idea that *all* learning could be explained in terms of simple associative S–R mechanisms. This assumes that complex tasks – your learning to play Parcheesi, for instance, or your acquiring the ability to paint in the manner of Kandinsky, or your coming to master English or Urdu – can be broken down into simpler tasks, each of which can be explained in something like the way the rat's bar-pressing is explained.

In 1959, Noam Chomsky published a review of Skinner's *Verbal Behavior* in which he argued forcefully that Skinner's attempts to extend the behaviorist model of learning to the linguistic abilities of human beings were hopelessly inadequate. Chomsky claimed that acquisition of language could not, even in principle, be explained without assuming that human beings possessed a sizable repertoire of complex cognitive structures that governed their acquisition and deployment of language.

This attack on central behaviorist themes had a devastating effect on the behaviorist program. Many psychologists had grown dissatisfied with rigid behaviorist doctrines, and were already moving in new directions. Chomsky's review, combined with a growing interest in 'rule-governed' activities generally, sealed behaviorism's fate. Behaviorism was never again to possess the kind of scientific cachet it once enjoyed. It became increasingly clear that behaviorism was founded on a view about scientific legitimacy rooted in unappealing philosophical doctrines going back at least to Berkeley. (If that surprises you, recall Berkeley's emphasis on observability as the mark of reality.) By requiring that every scientifically respectable expression be characterizable in terms of observations that would confirm its application, behaviorists foreclosed modes of explanation that had proved fruitful in other sciences. These modes of explanation distinguished, as behaviorists often did not, between entities postulated to explain observable features of the universe and observations that constituted evidence for these entities.

4.14   Behavior

One further difficulty inherent in the behaviorist program is worth mention. Consider the central notion of *behavior*. What constitutes an instance of behavior? When do two 'behaviors' count as instances of the same kind of behavior, and when are they different? Answers to these questions are central to the behaviorist agenda. Behaviorists envisage a rigorous pairing of stimuli with response 'behaviors'. The model we began with was the patella reflex: your knee is tapped, and your leg bobs. This same response – your leg's bobbing – happens whenever your knee is tapped. If your leg's bobbing is an example of behavior, then it would seem that behavior is to be understood as bodily motion. Two instances of behavior are counted the same just in cases they are instances of the same kind of bodily motion.

Once you move beyond simple reflexes, however, matters are not so simple. A rat's bar-pressing is a case in point. Suppose that on one occasion the rat presses the bar with its right paw, then later with its nose, then with both paws. The behaviorist counts these as instances of the *same* behavior – 'bar-pressing behavior' – even though the rat's bodily motions differ markedly. This is to move away from the basic reflex model.

It is relatively easy to envisage a simple mechanism that accounts for your leg's bobbing when your knee is tapped. But the mechanism responsible for a rat's pressing a bar with a bell's ringing is not like this. That mechanism connects the onset of a particular sound with a variety of *different* kinds of bodily motion. What these bodily motions have in common is just that they each result in the bar's being pressed. And now it looks as though any mechanism behind the rat's bar-pressing behavior must be specified by reference to what we non-behaviorists might blushingly describe as the rat's purposes or desires: what the rat *wants* is not to move its right front paw, or both paws, or its nose, but to press the bar. Unfortunately, purposes and desires are 'unobservable' states of mind, and so officially out of bounds for the behaviorist.

When it comes to complex human behavior, the situation is much, much worse. Think of your answering the door when the doorbell rings. Call this door-answering behavior. There need be *no* bodily motions common to all instances of behavior of this kind. Sometimes you walk calmly to the door and open it. On other occasions you might trot to the door, or go on tiptoe, or roller skate, or press a button unlocking the door remotely, or, if the door is unlocked and you are otherwise occupied, merely shout 'Come in!' Again, it is difficult to imagine that the mechanism connecting the doorbell's ring with your door-answering behavior is a simple reflex mechanism, or even an organized collection of such mechanisms. It looks, for all the world, as though your behavior is mediated by a goal-directed state of mind!

Parallel considerations hold of the behaviorist notion of stimulus. When you look at what behaviorists count as instances of 'the same' stimuli, you discover that these lack the sorts of common feature the approach would seem to require. Your 'door-opening behavior' might be elicited by a loud banging on the door, or a soft knock; by the ringing of a doorbell; or by a glimpse through the window of an acquaintance striding up the footpath. These stimuli have little in common beyond being in some respect responsible for your electing to open the door.

Suppose a behaviorist cannot come up with a noncircular, independent characterization of 'door-opening stimulus', one that does not invoke the very thing for which it is the postulated stimulus – 'door-opening behavior'. Then it looks as though appeals to such stimuli in explanations of behavior will be trivial. A response is elicited by a stimulus. Which one? The response-eliciting stimulus! This does not mean that the behaviorist contention that all behavior is explicable by reference to stimulus–response relations is false, or that learning is not explicable purely by reference to contingencies of reinforcement of such relations. But it does strongly suggest that the central notions of stimulus and response gain credence only by taking in one another's washing. And if this is so, the theory is largely uninformative.

Perhaps these worries about the emptiness of behaviorist explanation could be overcome. Even so, there is some reason to suspect that the behaviorist model is fundamentally misguided. Think for a moment of your response to a given stimulus, the appearance of a bear in your path, for instance. Strictly speaking, it would seem not to be the *bear* that elicits your response (whatever it might be), but your *perceiving* or in some way *taking note* of the bear. If a bear appeared in your path, but you remained oblivious to it, you would be unmoved by the bear's presence. Just so, you might be moved to a bear-avoiding response, even if a bear were absent. You might be so moved if, for whatever reason, you *thought* there were a bear in your path.

Such examples suggest that behavioral responses are determined, not by behaviorist-style stimuli, but by your perceptions (or apparent perceptions) of those stimuli. The bear's presence explains your behavior only if it leads you to a perception of a bear. This perception mediates your subsequent behavior. Perceiving (or apparently perceiving: imagining or hallucinating) a bear, however, is a matter of your going into a particular sort of mental state. And it was just such mental intermediaries that behaviorism was supposed to eliminate.

None of these reflections yields a knock down argument against behaviorism. In fact behaviorists have attempted to respond to these and other worries. I shall not pursue those responses here, but push ahead to what appear to be more promising approaches to minds and their contents.

Suggested Reading

Although Democritus's own writings have not survived, his defense of atomism – the view that everything that exists is nothing more than a fleeting arrangement of 'atoms in the void' – is discussed by Aristotle, Plutarch, Galen, and other Greek philosophers. See Jonathan Barnes, *Early Greek Philosophy* (1987), 247–53; and Richard McKirahan, *Philosophy Before Socrates: An Introduction with Texts and Commentary* (1994), especially 322–4 on 'Compounds'. A standard collection of texts can be found in Kirk *et al.*, *The Presocratic Philosophers* (1983), 406–27. The reintroduction of atomism into European culture by way of the rediscovery of Lucretius's *On the Nature of Things* is entertainingly discussed in Stephen Greenblatt's *The Swerve: How the World Became Modern* (2011).

Francis Crick's brand of materialism is developed in *The Astonishing Hypothesis: The Scientific Search for the Soul* (1994). Whether Crick's hypothesis is 'astonishing' is a matter of dispute. Thomas Hobbes defends materialism in part one of *Leviathan* (1651). Julien Offraye de La Mettrie offers another early materialist model in *Man a Machine*, (1747/1994). For the biologically inclined, this edition includes, as well, La Mettrie's *Man a Plant*.

The possibility of a neuroscientist who has mastered the neurophysiology of headaches but has never suffered from a headache touches on an argument that has come to be associated with Frank Jackson: the 'knowledge argument'. The argument moves from the claim that, unless you have undergone an experience, you could not know what it is like to undergo that experience, to the conclusion that qualities of conscious experiences (so-called 'qualia') could not fit the materialist worldview. You can know all the material facts (facts about brain goings-on, for instance) and yet fail to know facts about conscious experiences (what they are like), so facts about conscious experiences are not material facts. See Jackson's 'Epiphenomenal Qualia' (1982) and the discussion in § 10.6.

David Chalmers's account of zombies appears in *The Conscious Mind: In Search of a Fundamental Theory* (1996), chapter 3; see also § 10.4 below. The presence of an 'explanatory gap' between material properties and qualities of conscious experiences – what philosophers call 'qualia' – is discussed by Joseph Levine, 'Materialism and Qualia: The Explanatory Gap' (1983).

Wittgenstein's best known discussion of states of mind occurs in *Philosophical Investigations* (1953). The question whether Wittgenstein's views are behaviorist is much debated. The philosopher most often associated with behaviorism as a philosophical doctrine is Gilbert Ryle. Ryle's position is developed in *The Concept of Mind* (1949). Readers of *The Concept of Mind*, however, might doubt that Ryle's position is accurately described as behaviorist. Some of the same ambivalence extends to the work of Wittgenstein's students and followers (see, for instance, Norman Malcolm's *Dreaming*, 1959).

Reductionist programs in the philosophy of science of the kind advanced by Rudolph Carnap, 'Logical Foundations of the Unity of Science' (1938), and Carl Hempel, 'The Logical Analysis of Psychology' (1949), were more explicitly and enthusiastically behaviorist. Hilary Putnam's 'Brains and Behaviour' (1965) comprises a withering attack on these and other strains of behaviorism. Behaviorism's association with verificationism probably accounts for its lingering well past its heyday. (Verificationists, who trace their ancestry to the British empiricists, hold that the meaning of claims purporting to be about the world must be analyzable into sentences concerning actual or possible observations.) W. V. O. Quine's *Word and Object* (1960) expresses strong behaviorist sympathies, and Daniel Dennett (*The Intentional Stance*, 1987), a student of Ryle's, could be read as advancing a nuanced brand of behaviorism.

On the psychological front, you find less ambiguity. J. B. Watson's 'Psychology as the Behaviorist Views It' (1913) sets out the position clearly. More up to date discussion and defense of psychological behaviorism can be found in B. F. Skinner's *Science and Human Behavior* (1953). See also Skinner's 'Behaviorism at Fifty' (1963). Skinner's *Verbal Behavior* (1957) was aggressively attacked in a famous review by Noam Chomsky (1959). See also Chomsky's *Cartesian Linguistics: A Chapter in the History of Rationalist Thought* (1966). John Staddon's *Behaviourism: Mind, Mechanism, and Society* (1993) contains a more recent assessment of behaviorism in psychology.

5   The Identity Theory

5.1   From Correlation to Identification

Let us, at least for the time being, banish thoughts of behaviorism – philosophical and psychological – and revert to our Cartesian starting point. Let us suppose that states of mind are states of something – some *thing*, a substance – the mind. Descartes argues that minds are distinct from bodies. And if states of mind are not states of the body, they are not states of some part of the body, states of the brain, for instance.

What makes Cartesianism so unappealing to the modern temperament is not Descartes's contention that minds are entities, but that minds are *nonmaterial* entities. The more we learn about the nervous system, the more we discover intimate connections, or at least *correlations*, between mental occurrences and neurological goings-on in the brain. (I follow custom and speak of goings-on in the *brain*. This should, however, be understood as shorthand for goings-on in the central nervous system. Alternatively, you could think of the brain as distributed throughout the body.) Suppose these correlations were perfect: every kind of mental state or process could be matched to a definite kind of neural state or process. Your undergoing conscious experiences of a particular kind – your seeing a particular shade of red, for instance – might invariably be accompanied by brain processes of a particular kind, perhaps the firing of a particular collection of neurons. Finally, suppose the brains of others undergoing similar experiences exhibit similar processes.

What are we to make of this? Cartesians explain the correlations as resulting from causal interactions between minds and brains. Such correlations would resemble correlations between falling barometers and the advent of rain. Another possibility is epiphenomenalism: the correlations are the result of mental goings-on being systematically produced as by-products of neurological activity. Occasionalism offers a third possibility: every mental and material event is willed by God in such a way that occurs in orderly patterns.

Each of these ways of accounting for one–one mental–material correlations is founded on the assumption that mental states or events are, and must be, distinct from physical states or events. Suppose you doubted this assumption, however; suppose you *identified* conscious states with states of brains; suppose you thought mental occurrences were at bottom *nothing more* than goings-on in the brain? This is the *mind–brain identity theory.* Identity theorists hold that mental goings-on are not merely *correlated* with material goings-on in the brain. Indeed talk of correlation here is misleading. Mental goings-on *are* brain processes, and you cannot correlate something with *itself.* Brain events are correlated with subjects' *reports* of mental events (recall the discussion in § 4.3). The 'correlations' are analogous to correlations in the whereabouts of the butler and the murderer, when the butler *is* the murderer.

5.2   Parsimony

Its proponents argue that, other things equal, the identity theory is preferable to its dualist rivals for two reasons. First, and most obviously, the identity theory provides a straightforward solution to the mind–body problem. If mental events *are* neurological events, then there is no special difficulty in understanding how mental events might cause or be caused by material events: a mental event's causing a material event (or vice versa) is simply a matter of one material event's causing another.

A second consideration favoring the identity theory is *parsimony*. Both the identity theory and dualism grant the existence of brains and neurological goings-on. But dualism must suppose that, in addition to – 'over and above' – brains and neurological goings-on, there are minds and mental goings-on. Why posit these additional items unless you are forced to? If you can account for mental phenomena solely by reference to brains and their properties, why follow the dualist in envisaging an independent realm of minds and mental properties?

You have already encountered appeals to parsimony – Ockham's Razor – within the dualist camp (§ 3.6). Epiphenomenalists hold that epiphenomenalism provides a simpler, hence preferable account of the mind and its relation to material bodies than do competing dualist theories. In assessing this line, I noted that appeals to simplicity ought not to be understood as based on the assumption that the *universe* must be simple – whatever that might mean. Parsimony figures in the comparative evaluation of theories or explanations.

Imagine two theories, T_1 and T_2, both of which provide explanations for some particular phenomenon. Suppose, further, that T_1 and T_2 both appeal to familiar kinds of entity and process, but that T_2 appeals, in addition, to a kind of entity not invoked by T_1. In that case, assuming the theories are otherwise on a par, parsimony advises that you choose the simpler ('more parsimonious') theory, T_1. The extra entities appealed to by T_2 are not, it seems, *needed* to explain the phenomenon. Simpler theories are preferred by default.

An example should make this clear. One morning you discover that the milk in the refrigerator has curdled. You recall that you left the milk out the previous night, but it seemed fine when you returned it to the refrigerator. An acquaintance explains that milk's curdling is a matter of its undergoing a particular kind of chemical process. This process is inhibited, but not completely blocked, by refrigeration. The milk began to curdle when it was left unrefrigerated, a process subsequent refrigeration was inadequate to subdue.

Meanwhile, a second acquaintance tells you that the milk curdled because it was left out during a full moon. In this case, a chemical explanation is a more parsimonious explanation than one invoking the moon. Appeals to well-understood chemical mechanisms of the sort involved in milk's curdling are widespread. Appeal to moon effects in this case involves what appears to be a gratuitous – unparsimonious, unmotivated – complication of the chemical picture.

In the same vein, identity theorists contend that, provided the identity theory and dualism *both* account for the phenomena, the identity theory wins by default. Why appeal to nonmaterial entities, states, or processes, to explain the activities of sentient creatures when material entities, states, or processes will do the job? The next question is, *does* the identity theory do the job, *does* the identity theory account for the phenomena?

5.3   Self-Conscious Thought

You might begin by asking, as Descartes does, whether states of mind *could* be states of the body, more specifically, states of the brain or central nervous system. The chief reason for thinking that states of mind not merely *are* not, but *could not* be brain states is that mental and material states appear to be radically different in kind. If A's are different in kind from B's, then there is no chance that A's could turn out to *be* B's. In the case of states of mind and material states of the nervous system, these differences are both epistemological and ontological. (Here it might be helpful to review Figure 2.1.)

On the epistemological front, you need only recall that the 'access' you and others enjoy to your states of mind is notably asymmetrical. Your mental life is 'private' in a way that no material object or state ever is. You are aware of your own states of mind and various qualities of your own conscious experiences directly and without evidence or observation. I, in contrast, have access to your mental life, at best, only indirectly. I infer your thoughts and feelings by observing your circumstances, demeanor, and behavior, verbal or otherwise. Suppose I observe goings-on in your brain, and suppose these goings-on are known to be reliable indicators of your mental condition. In that case I would be in an epistemologically strong position to know what you are thinking and feeling. Even so, my access to your thoughts and feelings differs from yours. I must infer what you experience directly.

A Cartesian would explain this epistemological asymmetry by noting that others' knowledge of your states of mind depends on observations, not of the states themselves, but only of their effects on material bodies. My knowledge of your states of mind is epistemologically on a par with a doctor's knowledge that you have chicken pox based on the doctor's observation of a rash on your stomach. Your knowledge of your own mental life is unmediated, however. Indeed it is at the very least misleading to imagine that you *observe* your own thoughts and feelings.

This last point deserves elaboration. Reflect on your thoughts. Each thought carries with it the potential for self-awareness – an idea implicit in Descartes and explicitly emphasized by Immanuel Kant (1724–1804). Thinking is not something that occurs to you like the beating of your heart, something concerning which you are a mere spectator. Thinking is something you *do*. And, like anything you consciously do, you need not observe yourself in the act to recognize that you are doing it. (I leave aside for the moment consideration of nonconscious states of mind.)

When you entertain the thought that it is raining and consciously recognize that this is what you are thinking, your conscious recognition is not based on some further act of inward observation of the original thought. That thought, rather, is thought *self-consciously*. If every thought is at least potentially self-conscious, then this self-conscious thought could *itself* be entertained self-consciously: you could become aware that you are thinking that you are thinking that it is raining. Try it! And note that this thought is itself perfectly self-contained; it is a single thought, not a sequence of distinct thoughts.

Any account of the mind must, it would seem, accommodate the possibility of self-consciousness. The Cartesian view does so by building it into the nature of the mental: that states of mind are 'self-revealing' is just one way minds differ from material bodies. States of mind, as it were, reflect themselves. Brain states, in contrast, are like any other publicly observable material states. Our access to them is grounded in ordinary observation. How could something epistemologically private possibly be identified with something publicly observable? Anyone who hopes to assimilate minds to bodies – or, more particularly, to brains – must be prepared to answer the Cartesian on this score.

5.4   Locating Mental Qualities

A second hurdle facing anyone aiming to substitute brains for Cartesian minds is *ontological*. Mental events, states, and properties appear to be utterly different *in kind* from material events, states, and properties. The difference is striking when you consider qualities of your own conscious states of mind and compare these with the qualities of material bodies, including the qualities of brains. Your visual experience of a ripe tomato in bright sunlight seems wholly different qualitatively from goings-on in your nervous system.

Neurological occurrences can be observed and described in great detail. But observe the brain as you will, you seem never to observe anything remotely resembling a conscious experience. Indeed, the very idea that you might observe someone else's thoughts or experiences appears unintelligible.

You might hope to sidestep this problem by appealing to the fact that science regularly tells us that things are not as they seem. Take the ripe tomato. You experience the tomato as possessing a particular color. But physicists like to tell us that the experienced color is in a certain sense an illusion. The tomato's surface exhibits a particular microscopic texture. Surfaces with this texture reflect light in a particular way. And reflected light of this sort, when analyzed by the human visual system, gives rise to an experience of red. It would be a mistake to locate a feature of our experience in the tomato. Considered in its own right, the material universe is colorless.

Similar arguments can be concocted to show that sounds, tastes, smells, and the way things feel are, in the sense described, absent from the material universe. A long tradition, going back at least to Galileo, Descartes, and Locke, classifies colors, sounds, and the like, 'secondary qualities'. Secondary qualities could be thought of as *powers* possessed by material bodies to produce experiences of familiar kinds in conscious observers.

Whatever its merits, this train of thought does little to advance the case of the anti-Cartesian. If characteristics of conscious experiences of colors are not characteristics of material bodies, then what are they characteristics *of*? A physicist can banish them to the mind. But this move implies that minds do not themselves belong to the material universe! If you distinguish appearance from material reality by relegating appearances to the mind, you thereby place minds outside the material realm. Assuming that science is devoted to the investigation of the material universe, this line of reasoning would land you back with a Cartesian conception: minds are distinct from material bodies.

Notwithstanding these difficulties, many philosophers (and many more scientists) have been attracted to the view that, at bottom, minds are in fact material bodies. When a material body is organized in a particular way, organized in the way a human brain is organized, for instance, you have a mind. In the end, mental characteristics are, *despite appearances*, material characteristics.

As you have seen, the impetus for such a theory is twofold. First, the more scientists investigate the brain, the more they uncover intimate, fine-grained connections between neurological and mental goings-on.

Second, by far the simplest, most straightforward explanation of these connections is that minds *are* brains, mental states and processes *are* neurological states and processes. The idea that complex actions and reactions among the ultimate constituents of the universe are uniformly physically explicable – *except* for those occurring in the brains of sentient creatures – seems incredible. Thus, a view according to which there is at most one kind of substance, material substance, appears preferable to a dualistic view, on grounds of simplicity – assuming, of course, that it is possible somehow to account for central features of our mental lives without having to introduce nonmaterial substances. But *is* it possible?

5.5   Substances, Properties, States, and Events

What has come to be called the identity theory of mind emerged simultaneously in the United States and Australia in the 1950s in papers published by Herbert Feigl, U. T. Place, and J. J. C. Smart. According to the identity theory, minds are material entities – brains – and mental properties are, as a matter of discoverable empirical fact, material properties of brains and nervous systems. In claiming that mental properties are material properties, Feigl, Place, and Smart were not claiming merely that mental properties were properties of material bodies. You might think this, and yet imagine that mental properties were quite different from nonmental material properties. The result would be a substance monism coupled with a dualism of properties (as discussed in Chapter 11). Identity theorists, however, hold that every mental property, every property you might regard as mental, is in reality a material property, that is, a property of the kind appealed to in the physical sciences.

Earlier, I spoke of mental (and material) characteristics, states, and the like. Identity theorists talk of identifying mental processes with brain processes. Now I am formulating the identity theory as a theory about properties. These terminological vacillations deserve comment.

In Chapter 2, I followed Descartes in distinguishing *attributes* and *modes* from *substances*. Descartes's modes are what are more familiarly called properties; Cartesian attributes are *kinds* of property. To put it somewhat unhelpfully, a substance is an individual possessor of properties; and properties are what substances possess: ways those substances are. Substances themselves differ from one another both numerically, and with respect to their properties. Here is one billiard ball, and here is another, distinct, billiard ball. The balls differ numerically. But they also differ in color: one is red, the other white.

You will recall that Descartes distinguishes material and mental substances by reference to their fundamental attributes: a material substance is extended; a mental substance thinks. Properties possessed by material bodies are, one and all, modes of extension – ways of being extended; and particular thoughts, feelings, or sensory experiences possessed by nonmaterial substances are modes of thought – ways of thinking. No substance that possesses properties of the one sort *could* possess properties of the other sort; the possession of one kind of property *precludes* possession of the other.

You might balk at a substance dualism of this sort, yet join the dualist in insisting on a distinction between mental and material *properties*. You might think, for instance, that there is a single substance, the body, or maybe the brain, and this substance possesses *both* mental and material properties. This is not what identity theorists have in mind, however. Their contention is that [every mental property just *is* – *is identical with* – some material property.] (I shall return to the notion of identity in play here presently.)

So much for properties. What of states, events, processes, and the like? Think of a state as a substance's possessing a property. There is the billiard ball, a substance, and the ball's redness, a property of the ball. The ball's being red is a *state* of the ball. Suppose that being angry is a mental property. Then your possessing this property, your being angry, is for you to be in a state of anger. If the state of anger turns out to be some neurological state, then this is so because the property of being angry is identical with – *is* – a certain neurological property.

You could think of *events* and *processes* as *state transitions*. An object's coming to be in a particular state, the object's coming to possess a certain property, would be an event. Finally, a *process* would be a sequence of events. Now it is possible to formulate an identity principle.

(I) a state, event, or process, α, is identical with state, event, or process β, only if the properties involved in α and β are identical.

Trying to keep all this straight could induce a certain amount of giddiness. Imagine that it does, and that your feeling giddy is a matter of your being in a particular state of mind. Your being in this state is your possessing a certain, possibly elusive, mental property. Now suppose the question arises whether your feeling giddy – your being in this mental state – *is* your being in a particular brain state (and nothing more). If you agree with the identity theorist that this is what your feeling giddy is – your brain's being in a particular state – then you will accept the identification of the mental property, *being giddy*, *giddiness*, with some definite neurological property.

The moral: So long as you bear in mind that state, event, and process identity requires property identity, you can speak indifferently of the identity theory as identifying mental and material states, processes, events, or properties.

5.6 Predicates and Properties

Getting clear on what it means to *identify* properties α and β, requires distinguishing *properties* and *predicates*. Sidestepping assorted complications, you could think of predicates as linguistic devices, *terms* used to ascribe properties to objects. The English expression 'is round' is a predicate used to characterize objects: coins, rings, manhole covers, dinner plates, automobile tires. This predicate holds of a given coin, in virtue of that coin's being a certain way: being round. The predicate 'is shiny' holds of the same coin in virtue of the coin's being another way: being shiny. These distinct 'ways' answer to distinct predicates.

One reason to make the predicate–property distinction explicit is that, as you will see below, it would be impossible to understand what claims about 'properties being identical' amount to otherwise. Another reason is that philosophers all too often assume without argument that every predicate capable of meaningful application to an object designates a property of that object. Such a view is ill-advised.[What the properties are is largely a question for science.]

Predicates can be constructed ad lib to suit all manner of parochial needs and interests, including those of philosophers writing textbooks. Consider the predicate 'is a left ear or made of copper'. This predicate holds of many objects. It holds of anything that is a left ear (so it holds of your left ear) and anything that is made of copper (so it holds of the penny on your dresser). The predicate holds of objects in virtue of properties they possess, ways those objects are. It does not follow, however, that the predicate *designates* a property in the sense that objects that it applies to possess the *very same* property.

These are deep waters. I shall return to them in later chapters. In the meantime, you need only bear in mind that properties and predicates, even those predicates that uncontroversially designate properties, belong to different *orders*: predicates are linguistic, representational; properties are nonlinguistic features of objects.

5.7   Strict Identity

Identity theorists contend that mental properties are *identical with* material, physical properties. It is time to say what exactly this means. Consider, first, how identity applies to objects or *substances* as distinct from *properties*.

Our concept of identity, or self-sameness, is indispensable. This is due in part to the fact that it is common to speak or think of a single object in different ways. You need some way of registering that distinct ways of speaking about something are ways of speaking about one and the same something. John le Carré is an author. Saying that le Carré *is* an author, amounts to saying something *about* le Carré, attributing a characteristic to him. As it happens, John le Carré is David Cornwell. Saying that le Carré is Cornwell is to say that the man called 'le Carré' and the man named 'Cornwell' are the selfsame individual.

1   Le Carré is an author ('is' of predication)
2   Le Carré is Cornwell ('is' of identity: le Carré, is *identical with* Cornwell)

Any object could be given multiple names; any object could be described in different ways. You could know an object under one name or description, but not under another. Imagine that you are traveling in Australia, intending to visit Uluru. En route, you hear talk of an impressive rock edifice, Ayers Rock, and regret not having enough time to visit it as well. Much later you discover that Uluru *is* Ayers Rock. In hiking around Uluru, you hiked around Ayers Rock without knowing it.

If α and β are strictly identical, *α is β*. But debutantes who wear identical gowns to the ball do not occupy the selfsame gown. Wayne and Dwayne are identical twins, but Wayne isn't Dwayne. In these cases 'identical' means, not 'one and the same', but 'exactly similar'. The distinction between strict identity and identity-as-exact-similarity is signaled in English by the use of different prepositions: le Carré is identical *with* Cornwall; Wayne is identical *to* Dwayne. (A word of warning: this grammatical subtlety is often flouted by careless writers, including philosophers writing on identity.)

The identity theory extends the notion of identity – *strict* identity – to properties. Like objects, properties can be the subject of identity claims.

3   Red is the color of ripe tomatoes.

In this case, a single property, a color, is designated by distinct predicates: 'is red' and 'is the color of ripe tomatoes'. And just as you might be familiar with Ayers Rock and with Uluru without realizing that Ayers Rock and Uluru are identical, without realizing that Ayers Rock *is* Uluru, so you might fail to realize that two predicates in fact designate the selfsame property. You might know that a particular color is red without knowing that it is the color of ripe tomatoes – if, for instance, you were ignorant of tomatoes.

Identity theorists focus on what Smart calls *theoretical identities*. Such identities are uncovered by scientists exploring the way the universe is put together. Lightning, scientists discovered, *is* an electrical discharge; water *is* H_2O; temperature *is* mean molecular kinetic energy; liquidity *is* a particular kind of molecular arrangement. An identity theorist holds that it is a good bet that research on the brain will lead to the discovery that certain properties we now designate using mental terms are in fact properties of brains. Pain, for instance, might turn out to be the firing of *C*-fibers in the brain. (This, a standard example, has been empirically discredited, but it will do to illustrate the point.) Were that so, the property of being in pain would be *identified* with the neurological property of being a *C*-fiber firing. Believing this is to believe that pain *is* *C*-fiber firing.

Identity theorists do not set out to advance particular identity claims. The establishment of these would be the job of brain researchers who uncover correlations between goings-on in the brain and subjects' reports of experiences. Rather, the identity theory offers an interpretation of these results: in reporting conscious experiences, you are reporting goings-on in your brain. Details will be revealed as the neurosciences move forward.

5.8   Leibniz's Law

Strict identity is self-sameness. If object α and object β are strictly identical (if $α = β$), then any property of α must be a property of β, and vice versa. This principle – called 'Leibniz's Law' in honor of the philosopher who first articulated it explicitly – provides a test for strict identity. You can decisively establish that some α is *not* identical with some β, if you could show that α possesses some property that β lacks, or that β possesses some property lacked by α. The butler could not be the murderer if the murderer has a limp and the butler does not.

Applying Leibniz's Law to the case at hand, minds could not be identified with brains if minds had properties lacked by brains or brains possessed properties not possessed by minds. Similarly, brain states, events, or processes would fail to be identical with mental states, events, or processes, if brain states, events, or processes involved properties absent from mental states, events, or processes; or if mental states, events, and processes involved properties absent from brain states, events, or processes.

What of properties themselves? Suppose property ψ is strictly identical with property ϕ. Does this mean that every property of ψ must be a property of ϕ and vice versa? That might be so if ψ and ϕ were complex properties, properties that had properties as parts. In that case $\psi = \phi$ only if every constituent property of ψ is a constituent of ϕ and vice versa. If ψ and ϕ are simple, you reach the limit: ψ is identical with ϕ *tout court*.

Suppose ψ and ϕ are properties, you are familiar with both ψ and ϕ, and ψ and ϕ are, as it happens, identical. Could you fail to know that ψ and ϕ are identical? You could fail to know this, presumably, just as a detective could fail to know that the butler is the murderer despite knowing a good deal about both. This is how it is with mental and material properties according to proponents of the identity theory. Mental properties *are* material properties, although this is not something you could discover without expending considerable effort – just as considerable effort was required to discover that lightning is an electrical discharge and that water is H_2O.

5.9   The $64 Question

The question to be faced now, the $64 question, is whether it is even remotely plausible to suppose that mental properties, the kinds of property the having of which might constitute your undergoing a particular conscious experience, for instance, *could* turn out to be properties of your brain? There appear to be powerful reasons to doubt this possibility. As noted earlier, the qualities you encounter when you undergo a conscious experience seem nothing at all like the qualities scientists find when they inspect brains. (For a convenient listing, see Figure 2.1.)

Imagine that it is a sunny day and you are standing in Trafalgar Square watching a red double-decker bus rumble past. You have a visual experience of the red bus, you hear it, very probably smell it and, through the soles of your feet, feel its passing. The qualities of your conscious experience are vivid and memorable. But now, could anyone seriously think that, were neuroscientists to open your skull and observe the operation of your brain while you were undergoing this experience, the neuroscientists would encounter *those* qualities? And if this is implausible, how could anyone seriously hope to identify experiences with brain processes?

Pretend for a moment that the identity theory is correct, pretend that states of mind *are* brain states. Your undergoing an experience – seeing, hearing, feeling, smelling the passing bus – would presumably be a matter of your brain's undergoing a complex sequence of processes (Figure 5.1).

Next imagine that a neuroscientist is observing your brain's undergoing this sequence of processes. The neuroscientist's conscious experiences of your brain would themselves be a sequence of processes in the neuroscientist's own brain (Figure 5.2). (Remember, we are assuming for the sake of argument that the identity theory is correct.)

Now ask yourself, is it really so obvious that the qualities of your experience differ from qualities the scientist observes when the scientist probes your brain?

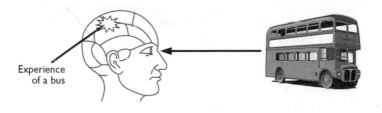

Experience
of a bus

Figure 5.1

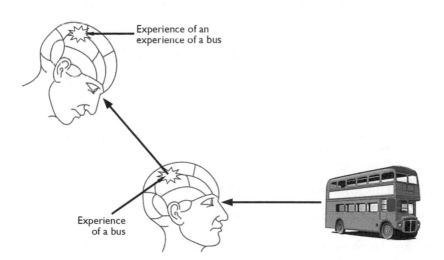

Experience of an
experience of a bus

Experience
of a bus

Figure 5.2

In considering this question, it is vital not to confuse qualities of the *scientist's* experience of your brain with qualities of *your* experience of the passing bus or, what comes to the same thing if the identity theory is true, qualities of your brain. The qualities to consider in this case are qualities of processes in the scientist's brain that (we are assuming) coincide with the scientist's observation of your brain. What needs to be compared is, to put it crudely, how a conscious experience *looks* to an observer and what the experience is like for someone *undergoing* it. This means that you must compare qualities of the observing scientist's conscious experiences of your brain (which, by hypothesis, are themselves neurological goings-on) with qualities of your conscious experiences (also, presumably, neurological events). And, although these will be different – observing a brain differs qualitatively from observing a passing bus – there is no reason to think that they must be dramatically different in kind.

The moral is that, if the aim is to compare the qualities of conscious experiences with the qualities of brains, you must be careful to compare the right things. If the identity theory were correct, your undergoing a conscious experience would be a matter of your brain's undergoing a complex process. If you want to compare qualities of your conscious experience with observations of your brain, then the appropriate target of comparison would be the brain of the observer. Goings-on in the observer's brain are what would constitute, for the observer, the 'look and feel' of *your* brain.

All this is just to insist on a simple point:[undergoing an experience is one thing, observing the undergoing of an experience (a distinct experience) is something else again.]The qualities of these will certainly be different. Looking at a brain, after all, is nothing at all like watching a passing bus] But the qualities need not be radically different in kind – radically different in the way harped on by dualists.

You might think that these remarks completely miss the point of the original worry: when you consider 'what it is like' to observe the passing bus, when you reflect on the qualities of *this* experience, those qualities seem not to be remotely plausible candidates for possible qualities of brains. You know what your conscious experiences are like and you know enough about what brains are like to make it seem obvious that conscious experiences are *nothing at all* like neurological goings-on. If that is so, the identity theory, whatever its scientific appeal, cannot get off the ground.

5.10   The Phenomenological Fallacy

You might be tempted to reason as follows. When you observe the passing bus, you observe something red, loud, and smelling of diesel fumes. But redness, loudness, and that distinctive diesel odor are not found in your brain. If a scientist scrutinizes your brain when you are undergoing this experience, the scientist will not find anything that possesses these qualities. The philosopher Leibniz, who made an appearance earlier as author of

Leibniz's Law, provides an analogy.

> Suppose there were a machine so constructed as to produce thought, feeling, and perception, we could imagine it as increased in size and while retaining the same proportions, so that one could enter it as one might a mill. On going inside we should only see the parts imping-ing on one another; we should not see anything which would explain a perception.
>
> (1787, 181)

(Leibniz goes on to argue that 'the explanation of perception must be sought in a simple substance, and not in a compound or in a machine'.)

Despite its seeming plausibility, this line of reasoning is seriously flawed. When you undergo a conscious experience – when you observe the passing bus, for instance – your experience is qualitatively saturated. But what exactly are *its* qualities, what are the qualities of your *experience*? Whatever they are, they are not to be confused with the qualities of *objects and events observed*, in this case qualities of a passing bus. Your *experiencing* a bus is one thing, the *bus* is another. It is natural, maybe unavoidable, when describing experiences to describe objects experienced and their qualities. [What it is like to experience the bus, however, the qualities of your *experience* of the bus, are not qualities of the bus.]

The identity theory identifies your *experience* of the bus with some occur-rence in your brain. As noted, we typically describe our experiences by refer-ence to objects that typically cause them, what they are experiences *of*. You can convey to me an experience you had at Trafalgar Square by telling me that it was an experience of a passing red double-decker bus. I have a decent idea what it is like to observe passing red double-decker buses, and so I acquire a sense of what you experienced. But, again, the qualities of your experience are not to be confused with the qualities of their objects, qualities of *what* you experience. An experience of something red, massive, and smelly is not itself red, massive, and smelly (Figure 5.1).

This point was one insisted on by both Place and Smart in their respec-tive defenses of the identity theory, but it has not always been fully appreciated. The rhetorical punch of the dualist's contention that it is just *obvious* that qualities of experiences differ from brain qualities relies heavily on your tacitly identifying, as Leibniz apparently does, quali-ties of experiences with qualities of objects experienced. In his original 1956 paper defending mind–brain identity, Place dubbed the mistake of confusing properties of objects experienced with properties of experi-ences, the *phenomenological fallacy*.

Once you distinguish qualities of experiences from qualities of what is experienced (and these must be distinguished on *any* view), it is much less obvious that experiences could not turn out to be brain processes. Anyone who persists in claiming that experiential qualities differ in kind from neurological qualities owes us an argument. What exactly *are* the qualities of experience? And what reasons might there be for thinking that qualities of experiences could not be qualities of brains?

Materialist philosophers sometimes accuse their opponents of mistakenly thinking of conscious experiences as playing out on a kind of internal television screen. Think about what exactly might be wrong with such a conception. Start by considering images on a television screen. These are meant to reproduce important qualities of perceived objects. A televised billiard match results in spherical red and white images on a trapezoidal green background that, on a television screen, correspond to the colors and shapes of billiard balls arranged on a billiard table as you might visually perceive them from a nearby vantage point. The properties on the screen, the colors and shapes, are stand-ins for properties of objects perceived. But it would be crazy to think of *these* properties as themselves properties of conscious experiences. Whatever conscious experiences are like, whatever their properties, they are not like this. (This point will reassert itself in Chapter 10.)

The suggestion on the table is that the distinction between qualities of experiences and qualities of objects experienced is theory-neutral. The distinction must be made by dualists as well as proponents of the identity theory. It is worth pointing out that, provided you keep the distinction firmly in mind, you can begin to make sense of a range of mental phenomena that might appear baffling otherwise. This is so, whatever you ultimately conclude about the status of mental properties.

Consider dreams, mental images, and hallucinations. Some theorists have wanted to downplay such phenomena, or depict them as purely cognitive processes. The worry is that there is no room in the brain for images, hallucinations, or dreams, the qualities of which appear to differ dramatically from qualities discoverable in brains. Suppose you hallucinate a pink penguin (or dream, or form an image in your mind's eye of a pink penguin). Nothing in your brain is pink or penguin-shaped. Indeed, it is entirely possible that nothing anywhere in your vicinity (or, for that matter, anywhere at all!) is pink and penguin-shaped.

But if this is supposed to cast doubt on hallucination, dreaming, or imagery, it succeeds only by conflating qualities of objects hallucinated (or dreamed, or imagined) with qualities of the hallucinatory (or dream, or imagistic) experience. Visually hallucinating a pink penguin ought to resemble having a visual experience of a pink penguin, not a pink penguin. Just as the experience is not pink and penguin-shaped, neither is the hallucinating pink or penguin-shaped. Nor need we suppose that hallucinating, or imagining, or dreaming of a pink penguin is a matter of inwardly viewing a picture-like image of a pink penguin.

My hope is that, your appreciating these points might enable you to relax a bit and think more clearly about the character of hallucination, mental imagery, and dreaming. (I shall have more to say about the importance imagery and the qualities of conscious experiences in Chapters 10 and 13.)

5.11 Epistemological Loose Ends

What can an identity theorist say about the asymmetry of 'access' to states of mind? You have 'privileged first-person access' to your thoughts and sensory experiences. The rest of us have, at best, indirect, 'third-person access' to your mental life. Your mental life is private, but your brain is public. A scientist could observe and measure goings-on in your brain, but only *you* are in a position to be 'directly aware' of your thoughts and feelings. If those thoughts and feelings were brain processes, however, they would be open to public scrutiny, an apparent impossibility!

These are difficult issues. Materialists must somehow accommodate asymmetry of access without backsliding into dualism, without, for instance, resorting to the notion that mental occurrences take place in a private interior chamber, visible only to the agent to whom they belong. (Recall Wittgenstein's beetle in the box example in § 4.4.) But how *else* could the privileged access each of us enjoys to our own states of mind be explained? How else might we account for the asymmetry?

Consider, first, an observation made earlier concerning conscious thought. Thinking is something you *do*. Like anything you do, in doing it, you are in a position to appreciate *what* you are doing. To be sure, you rarely bother to reflect on the fact that you are doing what you are doing. But, when you do reflect, you are not acting as an observer – even an especially well-placed observer – of what you are doing. Your recognition of what you are up to stems from the fact that it is you who are up to it.

Imagine that you draw a diagram on the blackboard to illustrate a point about the economy of pre-Roman Britain. I am in the audience. Compare your understanding of the diagram with mine. I observe what you have drawn and endeavor to interpret it in light of your lecture. You, in contrast, grasp its significance immediately. You are able to do this, not because you have a better, more intimate view of the diagram, not because you are much closer to it, but because it is *your* diagram: you drew it with this significance.

You bear an analogous relation to your own thoughts. You immediately grasp the significance of those thoughts, not because your view of them is especially acute or unimpeded, but because you *think* them. Because you do not always do what you set out to do, your capacity to recognize what you are doing is not infallible. You take yourself to be walking west, when you are, in reality, walking east. In the same way, you might take yourself to be thinking of your grandmother, when in reality you are not: the person you have always assumed was your grandmother is an impostor!

What of your 'access' to your own conscious sensory episodes? Your recognition that you are suffering a headache is apparently direct and unmediated in a way anyone else's access to your headache never is – or could be. Does this imply that headaches are states or processes 'visible' only to those undergoing them?

Two points bear mention. First, in undergoing a conscious sensory experience, you do not (1) have the experience, and (2) observe – perhaps in an especially intimate way by means of an inward-looking perceptual organ – the experience. Your awareness of the experience is *constituted*, at least in part, by your *undergoing* it. This is why talk of 'access' to one's sensory experiences is potentially misleading. Your recognition that you have a headache is constituted, in part, by your *having* or *undergoing* the headache. Differently put: your conscious experience of the headache is a matter of your *having* it. It is not that the headache occurs and, in inwardly observing it, you 'access' it.

Second, and to echo a point made earlier, it is important to distinguish a system's undergoing some process or being in some state, from observations of that system's undergoing a process or being in a state. Your refrigerator probably defrosts automatically. The refrigerator's defrosting on an occasion is, in an obvious way, very different from your *observing* its defrosting. Similarly, your undergoing a pain is very different from someone else's *observing* your undergoing it, even if that someone else has an unrestricted view of the operation of your brain. Now, if 'directly observing a sensation' just amounts to *having* that sensation, then there is no puzzle at all in the idea that only you can 'directly observe' your sensations. This is just to say that only you can have *your* sensations. And this is no more mysterious than the thought that only your refrigerator can undergo *its* defrosting.

Considerations of this sort tell against the Cartesian picture, not by providing a refutation of that picture, but by offering an alternative depiction of what self-awareness might encompass. On the Cartesian model, self-awareness resembles the awareness of 'external' objects and events turned inward. As the foregoing discussion makes clear, however, you need not embrace this way of depicting the situation. And, the Cartesian conception aside, it would seem that you probably ought not to embrace it.

This does not mean that dualists must forthwith abandon dualism and accept the identity theory or some other form of materialism. It does mean that one consideration apparently favoring dualism needs to be reevaluated. It might be possible to accommodate the epistemological asymmetry associated with states of mind without recourse to dualism. (The topic will be revisited in § 13.10.)

5.12   Taking Stock

Materialism, in the guise of the identity theory, offers itself as a replacement for dualism, one that purports to explain mentality, but more parsimoniously, that is, without recourse to nonmaterial substances or properties. I have touched on one respect in which the identity theory is vindicated. Dualists sometimes argue as though it is indisputably *obvious* that the properties of states of mind could not be properties of brains – or indeed properties of *any* material entity.

As it happens, the force of this argument depends in large measure on a tacit conflation of the qualities of experiences and the qualities of *what* is experienced, the objects of experience. This is Place's 'phenomenological fallacy'. The qualities of objects experienced are indeed very different from the qualities we experience in the course of observing brains. This, however, is not something that need trouble an identity theorist. Colorful experiences are experiences of colorful objects, not experiences that are themselves colored. If dualists continue to insist that qualities of conscious experiences could not be possessed by brains, then the ball is back in the dualists' court.

I do not mean to leave the impression that this is the end of the matter. I have suggested that it is not obvious that conscious experiences *could not* be identified material states and processes. But neither is it obvious that they *could* be. I counsel suspicion of anyone who claims that either answer to this question is obvious.

Another worry that I have left untouched concerns the unity of experience. On the one hand, the brain is a complex system encompassing endless subsystems. On the other hand, our mental lives are apparently unified. Although we all possess various distinguishable mental faculties, at any given time each of us confronts the universe as a single ego with a single point of view or perspective. (This is so, I suspect, even for persons said to possess multiple personalities.) How is this unity of experience to be reconciled with the widely dispersed and fragmented character of neural processing?

In recent years, hopes for finding a neurological 'central processing unit', a neurological analogue of a computing machine's CPU, have receded. Even if we were to locate a neurological CPU, however, it is by no means clear that its operation could account for the unity of experience. A point of view is just that: a point, a position in space–time, from which the universe is apprehended. The relation of this point of view to the experienced universe resembles the relation of the eye to the visual field. The eye is not *within* the visual field, but stands at its limit (Wittgenstein 1922, § 5.6331; and see § 13.10 below).

Scientists and philosophers traditionally sought to reconcile appearance with reality by banishing appearances to the mind. Many apparent features of the universe – colors, for instance, or sounds, or odors – were taken to belong not to the universe, but to us, to our point of view on the universe. If your hope is to see minds and universe as parts of a single reality, however, you are faced with the task of finding a place for appearance within that reality. And this requires locating points of view on the universe wholly *within* the universe. The trick, as you have seen in considering the qualities of experience, is to be clear on the nature of appearance, the character of points of view.

Although these strike me as central themes, they have not played an appreciable role in philosophical attacks on the identity theory. Those attacks have centered on the claim that states of mind are functional states of creatures possessing them, not material states. Functionalism takes center stage in Chapter 6.

Suggested Reading

Herbert Feigl provides one line of argument for the identity theory in 'The "Mental" and the "Physical"' (1958). Feigl was a philosopher of science at the University of Minnesota. Working independently at the University of Adelaide, U. T. Place ('Is Consciousness a Brain Process?', 1956) and J. J. C. Smart ('Sensations and Brain Processes', 1959) came at the problem from a different, but complementary, background.

The decade of the 1960s gave rise to a torrent of articles attacking and defending the identification of minds with brains, especially as it had been developed by Smart. Many of these papers are collected in C. V. Borst, *The Mind–Brain Identity Theory* (1970); John O'Connor, *Modern Materialism: Readings on Mind–Body Identity* (1969); and C. F. Presley, *The Identity Theory of Mind* (1967). D. M. Armstrong, in *A Materialist Theory of the Mind* (1968), develops a version of the identity theory – hinted at in his *Perception and the Physical World* (1961) – that, like the account advanced by David Lewis ('An Argument for the Identity Theory', 1966), has functionalist elements.

Christopher Hill, *Sensations: A Defense of Type Materialism* (1991), defends an updated version of the identity theory; Cynthia Macdonald, in *Mind–Body Identity Theories* (1989), provides an exhaustive discussion of 'type identity'. Smart's online piece on mind–brain identity, 'The Identity Theory of Mind' (2000), is clear and on-target; see also U. T. Place's online contribution, 'Identity Theories' (2001). Readers interested in how all this plays out in the neurosciences might look at Gerald Edelman's *Bright Air, Brilliant Fire: On the Matter of the Mind* (1993), and Francis Crick's *The Astonishing Hypothesis: The Scientific Search for the Soul* (1994).

Leibniz's defense of substance dualism, and his insistence that mental substances (selves) must be metaphysically simple, can be found in his *Monodology* (1787).

In 'The Unity of Consciousness: Subjects and Objectivity' (forthcoming) Elizabeth Schechter discusses 'split brain' cases that result in what is sometimes called 'divided consciousness'. Such cases apparently threaten traditional attempts to identify the self with the unity of consciousness. For an interesting and provocative contemporary discussion of the self, see Galen Strawson's *Selves: An Essay in Revisionary Metaphysics* (2009).

6 Functionalism

6.1 The Rise of Functionalism

The identity theory enjoyed a surprisingly brief period of favor among philosophers. Its decline in popularity was not the result of dualist counterattacks, however, but a consequence of the rise of a very different conception of mind: *functionalism*. Functionalists were not put off by identity theorists' commitment to materialism. Although, as you will see, functionalism is not a materialist theory per se, functionalism can be understood as compatible with the aims of materialism; most functionalists would regard themselves as materialists of one sort or another.

Functionalists would allow that, although immaterial substances – Cartesian souls, for instance – are conceivable, in all probability every substance is a material substance. Were that so, every property possessed by a substance would be possessed by a material substance. Does this imply that every property is a material property? Are mental properties a species of material property? The issues here are tricky. They occupy the sections – and chapters – that follow.

These days functionalism dominates the landscape in the philosophy of mind, in cognitive science, and in psychology. Functionalism offers a perspective on the mind that suits the needs of many empirical scientists, a perspective that promises solutions to a host of long-standing philosophical puzzles about minds and their relation to material bodies. Clearly functionalism – the doctrine, if not the label – has etched its way into the popular imagination by way of the press and television. When basic tenets of functionalism are put to non-philosophers, the response is, often enough, 'Well, that's obvious, isn't it?'

This is not to say that functionalism lacks critics. On the contrary, plenty of philosophers and empirical scientists have found functionalism wanting. There is scant agreement among its opponents, however, concerning where exactly functionalism falls down. Indeed, opponents are typically willing to concede that functionalism is right about some things – although, again, what these things are is something concerning which there is little consensus. In the absence of clear competitors, many theorists have opted to stick with functionalism despite what they admit are gaps and deficiencies, at least until something better comes along. In this respect, functionalism wins by default.

6.2 The Functionalist Picture

Functionalism's emergence coincided with the meteoric rise of interest in computation and computing machines in the 1950s and 1960s. When you consider computational operations in a computing machine, you 'abstract' from the machine's hardware. Two very differently constructed mechanisms can be said to perform *the same* computations, run *the same* programs. Charles Babbage (1792–1871) is usually credited with the design of the first programmable computing machine. Although the history is murky, Augusta Ada King (1815–52), daughter of Lord Byron and Countess of Lovelace, appears to have recognized the computational potential of Babbage's machine and formulated an algorithm for calculating a sequence of Bernoulli numbers, making her the first 'computer programmer'.

Babbage's design called for a device made of brass gears, cylinders, rods, levers, and assorted mechanical gizmos. Fully assembled, this mechanical marvel – Babbage christened it the Analytical Engine – would have been the size of a railway locomotive. Although the machine was never completed, had it been, there is no reason to doubt that it could have performed (rather more slowly) the very sorts of computation that twenty-first century computers perform. Where Babbage used gears and cylinders, the first electronic computing machines, constructed in the 1950s and early 1960s, made use of vacuum tubes. Today's computing machines have replaced vacuum tubes with arrays of millions of minuscule transistors embedded in slivers of silicon.

Economies of scale result when you move from brass gears and cylinders to vacuum tubes, and again when you move from vacuum tubes to densely packed transistors. These economies make an enormous practical difference in the range of computations you could expect a given device to perform. When you consider only the computations themselves, however, all such devices are on a par. One might be faster, or more reliable, or less expensive to manufacture than another, but all carry out the same *kinds* of computation. For this reason, when you consider computations – the manipulation of symbols in accord with formal rules – you 'abstract' from the material nature of the device performing them. And in so doing, you characterize the behavior of computing devices at a 'higher level'.

Are computational processes material processes? Philosophers of a functionalist bent prefer to say that computational processes are implemented by or 'realized' in material systems. The material process that realizes a given computational operation in Babbage's Analytical Engine differs from material processes that realize it in a modern transistor-based computing machine or in an antique device equipped with vacuum tubes. If there are immaterial substances, the very same process could well have an immaterial realization. Functionalists sum up these points by describing computational processes as 'multiply realizable'.

Think of a computing machine as a device that operates in a way that could be described by reference to, and whose behavior could be explained in terms of, formal operations over symbols: symbol manipulation, for short. Such a device could be made of any number of materials – or even, perhaps, of immaterial ghost-stuff – and organized in any number of ways. In considering a device *as* a computing machine, you consider it without concern for its actual makeup. Just as you 'abstract' from the size, color, and spatial location of a geometrical figure when it is the subject of a geometrical proof, so you 'abstract' from a computing machine's material composition when you consider it as a computational device.

6.3   Abstraction as Partial Consideration

The notion of 'abstraction' in play here is worth making explicit. Imagine that you are watching Lilian run through a proof of the Pythagorean theorem. Lilian draws a right triangle on a sheet of paper with a red crayon. You attend to the shape of the drawing, not its color, size, or spatial orientation. You attend to the lines and not their wiggliness. In so doing you 'abstract' from the drawing's color, size, and spatial orientation. You engage in what Locke felicitously described as 'partial consideration'. Human beings (and doubtless other intelligent creatures) have a capacity for this kind of selective attention. You can attend to or consider the color of a paint chip without attending to or considering its size or shape. You might do this when, for instance, you are deciding on what color to paint your bedroom.

In thinking of a device as performing computations, you are abstracting in this sense. You are considering the device as a finite symbol processor, not as something made of metal and plastic that operates in accord with laws of physics and chemistry. In describing computational or functional systems as 'abstract', you are not describing nonmaterial abstract *entities*. You are simply describing systems without reference to their material characteristics. In the same way, in describing Lilian's right triangle as a triangle, you are 'abstracting' from the triangle's having wiggly lines or being red, you are not describing a nonmaterial triangle existing alongside or in addition to the red, right triangle.

I am emphasizing this topic because philosophers sometimes leave students with the impression that abstraction is a matter of identifying mysterious *abstract entities* taken to subsist in a realm of *abstracta*, distinct from the realm of 'concrete' material entities. Think of 'abstracting' as a matter of omitting, leaving out of consideration. An abstract description leaves out features of the object described: to abstract is to engage in partial consideration. You can accept talk of 'abstraction' in this sense without imagining that such talk invokes a realm of spectral entities.

6.4 Minds as Programs

Suppose you thought of minds in roughly the way you might think of computing machines. A mind is a device capable of performing particular sorts of operation. States of mind resemble computational states, at least to the extent that they could occur, in principle, in many different kinds of material (and perhaps immaterial, a qualification I shall henceforth omit) system. To talk of minds and mental operations, is to abstract from whatever 'realizes' them: to talk at a 'higher level'.

This preliminary characterization is intended only to impart the flavor of functionalism. You should not be put off by the idea that creatures like us, creatures possessing minds, are 'nothing more than machines'. The point of the computing machine analogy is not to suggest that you are a mechanical automaton, a robot rigidly programmed to behave as you do. The point, rather, is that you might think of minds as bearing a relation to their material embodiments analogous to the relation computer programs bear to devices on which they run. A program is 'embodied' in some material device or other. But the very same program could be compiled to run on very different sorts of material device. In the same vein, you might suppose that every mind has some material embodiment, although minds could be embodied in very different kinds of material. In the case of human beings, our brains constitute the hardware on which our mental software runs. Alpha Centaurians, in contrast, might share our psychology, our mental *software*, yet have very different, perhaps non-carbon-based, hardware.

If something like this were right, then there would seem to be no deep mystery as to how minds and bodies are related. Minds are not identifiable with brains, as an identity theorist would have it; but neither are minds distinct immaterial substances mysteriously linked to bodies. Talk of minds is at bottom talk of material systems at a 'higher level', a level that abstracts from the 'hardware'. Feeling a pain or thinking of Vienna are not brain processes, any more than a computational operation, summing two integers for instance, is a vacuum tube process or a transistor process. Brains and brain processes are analogous to the hardware and electrical processes that, in a particular kind of computing machine, *realize* computations. Thoughts and feelings are, as computations are, *multiply realizable*. They are capable of being embodied in a potentially endless array of organisms or devices. Your mind is a program running in your brain.

6.5 Functional Explanation

Sticking with the computing machine analogy for the moment, you can identify two strands in the functionalist approach to the mind. One strand is explanatory; another is metaphysical. Consider, first, functional explanation.

Imagine you are a scientist confronted with a computing machine deposited on Earth by an alien visitor. You might want to know how the device was programmed. Doing so would involve a measure of 'reverse engineering'. You would 'work backwards' by observing inputs and outputs, hypothesizing computational operations linking inputs to outputs, testing these hypotheses against new inputs and outputs, and gradually refining your understanding of the alien device's program. Functionalists think of the scientific investigation of the mind as an analogous enterprise. Psychologists are faced with 'black boxes', the mechanisms controlling intelligent human behavior. Their task is to provide an account of programs governing the operation of these mechanisms. (Recall Figure 4.1.)

Compare the task of understanding a device's program with that of understanding its mechanical nature. An alien computing machine would attract considerable interest among electrical engineers. They would want to know how it is put together, how it operates. Their interest would be in its physical makeup, not in its software. A programmer's explanation of the operation of a computing machine and an engineer's explanation of its operation are importantly distinct kinds of explanation: one explains at the 'hardware level', the other at a higher level, the 'program level'. These explanations need not be seen to be in competition: the explanations share a target – the operation of a particular device – described at different levels of abstraction.

In the same way, you could imagine neuroscientists examining the nervous systems of intelligent creatures, and offering hardware-level explanations of their operations and behavior. These explanations need not be seen as in competition with the program-level explanations advanced by psychologists.

Although it is convenient to think of hardware and program 'levels' as distinct, in practice you would expect a good deal of cross-level communication among scientists. If you are engaged in an attempt to decipher the program of a particular computing machine, you might be helped by understanding certain things about the machine's mechanical organization. And an engineer trying to comprehend the device's hardware might benefit considerably from understanding of what it is programmed to *do*. Suppose a third party is introduced into the picture, a trouble-shooter, whose job is to repair the device when it malfunctions. A trouble-shooter would need to understand both the device's program and its hardware. A computing machine can 'crash' because of a software 'bug', or because of a hardware defect or failure. (Indeed, the expression 'bug' stems from the days when computing machines took up whole rooms filled with wires and vacuum tubes and could be brought to their knees by real live bugs. Legend has it that the term 'bug' originated when Lieutenant Grace Hopper discovered a moth trapped inside ENIAC, the first modern-day digital computer.)

Similarly, you would expect psychologists and neuroscientists to benefit from looking over one another's shoulders in pursuing their respective enterprises. And trouble-shooters – physicians, clinical psychologists, psychiatrists – must be equipped to diagnose assorted malfunctions as psychological (software bugs) or physiological (glitches in neural hardware).

6.6   Functionalist Metaphysics

Functionalists in the philosophy of mind invoke levels of explanation analogous to hardware and software levels you encounter in explanations of the operation of computing machines. I have explained this in terms of *description*: you can describe a complex system at various levels of abstraction. But functionalism is widely taken to be committed as well to *metaphysical* or *ontological* levels. It is not merely that talk of minds and their operation is a higher-level, more 'abstract' way of talking about what is, at bottom, a purely material system. Rather, higher-level mental terms are taken to designate properties *distinct* from properties designated by lower-level terms deployed by scientists concerned with the material composition of the universe. Although mental states and properties are 'realized' by material states and properties, mental states and properties are not *identifiable* with realizing material states and properties. Pains, for instance, are, according to functionalists, *realized* in the nervous system. But the property of being in pain is not a material property.

Why on earth *not*?

Take a deep breath and reflect, again, on the computing machine analogy. A given computational operation could be realized in a variety of distinct material devices: in Babbage's Analytical Engine, in a room full of vacuum tubes and wires, in a device consisting of silicon and transistors, even in a hydraulic device consisting of water-filled tubes and valves. Brains, and indeed many biological systems, seem capable of performing computations; and if there are immaterial spirits, there is every reason to think that these too could realize computational operations. In fact there is no end to the kinds of device that might be capable of engaging in a given computation. But if this is so, the argument goes, performing a computation could not be some one kind of material process.

Think of the process that realized a particular computational operation – the summing of 7 and 5 to yield 12 – in an early computing machine. This process consisted of electrical goings-on in an array of wires and vacuum tubes. But the summing of 7 and 5 to yield 12 is not a vacuum-tube-and-wire process. If it were, it could not be performed on an abacus (a calculating device consisting of beads strung on rods in a rigid frame) or occur in the brain of a six-year-old learning to do sums. Abacuses and brains contain neither wires nor vacuum tubes.

Now, the functionalist continues, the same point applies to states of mind. Consider being in pain. Although it is perfectly possible that your C-fibers firing are responsible for your being in pain – your being in pain is *realized* by your C-fibers firing – being in pain is *not*, as identity theorists would have it, C-fibers firing. If it were, then creatures lacking C-fibers could not experience pain. Yet there is every reason to think that creatures with vastly different biological constitutions, creatures altogether lacking C-fibers, (and, yes, immaterial spirits, if there are any) could experience pain.

In claiming that mental properties (or, for that matter, computational properties) are not material properties, functionalists are not suggesting that mental properties are *im*material properties, properties of *im*material substances. Fantasies aside, the possession of a mental property (or engaging in a computation) could well require a material 'base': the possession of some material property or other that *realizes* the mental (or computational) property. The functionalists' point is just that higher-level properties such as being in pain or computing the sum of 7 and 5 are not to be identified with, 'reduced to', or mistaken for their realizers.

Figure 6.1 is meant to represent schematically a case of a multiply realizable property. Imagine that M_1 is a mental property – being in pain, for instance – and that P_1, P_2, P_3, P_4 are physical realizers of M_1. (Functionalists allow that the list of realizers of a mental property could be 'open ended', but, to keep the example simple, I shall pretend there are just four.) The idea is that M_1 is a 'higher-level' property, distinct from, but dependent on, its several realizing properties. I shall eventually need to say more about the notion of realization appealed to here. First, however, more needs to be said to fill out this sketchy preliminary account of functionalism.

6.7 Functionalism and Materialism

Earlier I described functionalism as compatible with the *spirit* of materialism, the view that every object, state, and process is a material object, state, or process. In light of what has been said about the ontology of functionalism, you can now see why functionalists resist what they regard as unduly *reductive* tendencies inherent in competing materialist conceptions of mind. Think again of the computing machine analogy. As you have just seen, a computational process could be multiply realized: although a process of a particular sort in a material system might *realize* a given computational process, computational processes are not to be *identified* with material processes of this sort. Suppose, for instance, that Babbage's Analytical Engine sums 7 and 5 by lining up a row of brass gears. You would be off base were you to imagine that the summing operation is a matter of the aligning of rows of brass gears. The iPhone calculator you use to calculate a tip can perform the very same computation, but the iPhone contains no gears at all.

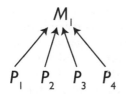

Figure 6.1

Functionalists argue that in such cases [you must distinguish between (1) the computation, and (2) processes that realize or embody the computation.] According to functionalists, the identity theory of Chapter 5 errs in running these together. Doing so, they contend, is to confuse 'higher-level' features of systems with their 'lower-level' realizing features. True enough, in undergoing certain changes of state, your iPhone calculator or Babbage's Analytical Engine perform particular computations. But compare: in moving your arm in a particular way you might signal a left turn. You would not conclude, however, that signaling a left turn *is* a kind of arm motion. (Think how you might signal without moving your arm in that way.) And performing a particular computation is not a kind of silicon state change or a kind of rotational motion of gears.

The issues here are delicate, and it only gets worse. You will need a much clearer view of the metaphysical territory before you will be in any position to evaluate the functionalist picture. I shall return to these matters in due course. Meanwhile, let us conclude tentatively that functionalism, as I have spelled it out thus far, could be true, even if it turned out that there are no immaterial objects, properties, or events; even that immaterial objects, properties, and events are for some reason impossible. To embrace functionalism, then, is not thereby to give up on materialism completely.

6.8   Functional Properties

Functionalism, like most -isms in philosophy, is not a single, univocal view. Functionalists begin with a shared collection of insights and convictions, then spin these out in different ways. Earlier, I noted that functionalism blossomed with the advent of interest in computing machines. It seems uncontroversial to distinguish programs and computations from the hardware said to realize these. You can, functionalists contend, deploy an analogous distinction in explicating the mind. Think of minds as devices running programs on complex chunks of hardware – in the case of human beings, human brains. Just as computational operations are realized by processes in the hardware of a computing machine without being reducible to or identifiable with those processes, so states of mind are realized by states of the brain without being reducible to or identifiable with those states.

The computer analogy is just a special case of a more general idea. Consider Wayne. Wayne is a male human being, 182 cm tall, and a vice-president of Gargantuan Industries, Inc. Wayne, it would seem, possesses a number of properties: the property of being a human being; the property of being male; the property of being 182 cm tall; and the property of being a vice-president.

Let us look more closely at the last of these: the property of being a vice-president. Wayne's being a vice-president is a matter of his satisfying a particular *job description*. Wayne is a vice-president in virtue of his role in the operations of Gargantuan Industries, Inc. Anyone at all who filled the same role, regardless of gender, height, and even biological makeup (we might imagine Wayne's being replaced by a brainy chimpanzee or a more cost-effective robot) would thereby possess the property of being a vice-president, would thereby *be* a vice-president.

You could represent the property of being a vice-president by means of an organizational chart. As the chart illustrates, being a vice-president is not a matter of possessing any particular material makeup. Being a vice-president is a matter of occupying the appropriate niche in the organizational structure. Wayne is vice-president by virtue of occupying the vice-presidential niche (Figure 6.2).

The property of being a vice-president is one kind of functional property. The possession of a functional property by a system is a matter of some component of that system's satisfying a particular job description. To see the point, think of another functional property, the property of being a clock. An object possesses this property (in unadorned English, an object *is* a clock), not because it has a definite kind of composition or internal organization, but because of what it does – its job description. Clocks could be – and have been – made of candles; gears, springs, and pendulums; vibrating crystals; and arrangements of water-filled tubes and valves. An object is a clock, not because it is put together in a particular way or made of materials of a particular sort, but because of what it *does*: it keeps time. So the property of being a clock is, if it is a property, a functional property. (Someone might insist that a clock must be an artifact: a natural object that kept time would not count as a clock. I leave aside this complication; it makes no difference to the point at issue. I leave aside as well, for the time being, whether being a clock or being a vice-president really are *properties*; see Chapter 12).

The example of the property of being a clock, and my describing functional properties as those possessed by entities in virtue of their job descriptions, might engender the impression that functional properties are in some

Gargantuan Corporation

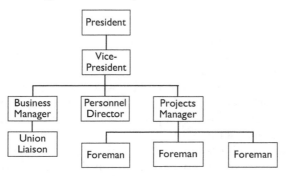

Figure 6.2

way conventional or 'made up'. But consider the biological property of being an eye. To a first approximation, an eye is an organ that extracts information about objects encountered in the environment from light radiation structured by those objects. Eyes can be, and are, made of many different kinds of material, and take many different forms. The compound eye of a honeybee differs from the eye of a horse, and the eye of a horse is unlike the foveal eye of a human being. You could imagine eyes more different still in aquatic creatures, in robots, or in creatures elsewhere in the universe. Something is an eye, something possesses the property of being an eye, just in case it fills a particular role in the system to which it belongs: it extracts information from light radiation and makes that information available to the system it subserves.

An object possesses a functional property when it incorporates a component, or state, or process that fills a particular role. But what is it to 'fill a role'? Functionalists prefer to think of roles causally. Something occupies a particular role if it responds, or would respond, in particular ways to causal inputs with particular kinds of output. A heart is an organ that circulates blood. (Note that blood, too, is a functional kind. A substance counts as blood, not in virtue of its material makeup, but in virtue of its functional role in a complex system.) An object possesses the property of being a heart provided it occupies this causal–dispositional role. Hearts, like eyes, could differ dramatically across species. And, as the advent of artificial hearts has brought home, a heart need not be a naturally occurring biological entity at all.

Although your heart is a material object, the property of being a heart, is, if you accept the functionalist picture, *not* a material property. It is a property your heart realizes *in virtue of* its particular material constitution, a constitution that suits it for a particular role in the operation of your circulatory system. Your heart's material constitution, an instance of a complex material property, *realizes* the functional property of being a heart. It realizes this functional property because it empowers the object to which it belongs to play the right sort of causal role.

Figure 6.3 represents the relationship between the higher-level property of being a heart and the lower-level property of being a particular kind of biological configuration. The latter property realizes the former. The properties are not identical; being a heart is not 'reducible' to being a particular kind of biological configuration. Something that has the property of being a heart in virtue of possessing the property of being a biological configuration of kind *K*, possesses *both* properties. (As you will discover in subsequent chapters, this technical nicety is, in reality, a particularly momentous consequence of functionalism.) (See Figure 6.3.)

Returning to computing machines, you can see that computational operations are representable by means of boxes or nodes in flow charts. Each box or node represents a function that takes particular kinds of input and yields particular kinds of output. A device that realizes these functions does

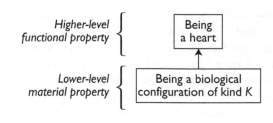

Figure 6.3

so because it possesses the right kind of causal–dispositional structure; it possesses this structure in virtue of the constitution and arrangement of its material parts.

6.9   Mental Properties as Functional Properties

Functionalists take states of mind and mental properties to be functional states and properties. A system is in a functional *state* when it is in a state that answers to a particular job description, that is, when it is in a state that plays a particular kind of causal role in the system. A *property* is a functional property when its possession by an object turns on that object's including a component that plays a particular kind of causal role.

In introducing functionalism I have spoken both of properties and states. I shall reserve detailed discussion of properties for Chapter 12. For the present, I shall rely on an intuitive characterization invoked earlier: properties are ways objects are. A beetroot is red and spherical. The beetroot's redness and sphericity are properties of the beetroot, ways it is. You could think of a state as an object's possessing a property at a time. The beetroot's now being red and the beetroot's now being spherical are distinct *states* of the beetroot. Events or processes involve changes of state. When an object goes into a particular state, it comes to possess a particular property; when an object changes state, it ceases to possess some property and comes to possess some distinct property. A beetroot's becoming red is an event. You could think of processes as sequences of events.

I mention all this simply in order to assuage potential worries about sliding back and forth from talk about properties to talk about states (or processes, or events). A state is not a property, nor a property a state. Nevertheless, in discussing functionalism, it is convenient sometimes to speak of properties, and sometimes to speak of states. (See § 5.5 for further discussion.)

The picture of functionalism on the table incorporates the central idea of multiple realizability (Figure 6.1). Mental properties are realizable by, but not identical with, various material properties. The same mental property, the property of being in pain, for instance, might be realized in one way by a human being and in quite another way by an invertebrate. Imagine that you are now suffering a particular pain, a headache, say. And pretend that a particular neurological state realizes this pain. That neurological state has an identifiable material constitution. This could be studied in a lower-level 'hardware' science, neural anatomy, maybe. What makes the state a realization of pain, however, is not its material makeup, but its playing a particular kind of causal role within your nervous system. Following Ned Block, you could put this by saying that what makes a pain a *pain* is not its being realized by something with a particular material constitution, but its being realized by something that plays, or would play, the right sort of causal role.

A caveat. In characterizing functionalism as I have, I exclude a kind of functionalism advanced by D. M. Armstrong and David Lewis. Armstrong and Lewis take mental properties to be functional properties, but then *identify* these with what most philosophers who call themselves functionalists would regard as their *realizers*. A mental state, on the Armstrong–Lewis view, is the *occupant* of a particular causal role. The functionalism discussed in this chapter – 'mainstream functionalism' – identifies states of mind with the *roles*, not their occupants. (See § 13.4 for more discussion.)

6.10 Functionalism and Behaviorism

Functionalists, embracing the multiple realizability of mental properties, reject the identity theory. Identity theorists are regarded by functionalists as narrow *reductionists*: philosophers who seek to *reduce* the mental (and maybe everything else) to the material. Functionalism is staunchly anti-reductionist, firmly committed to a conception of the universe as containing distinct and irreducible levels of things and properties. This thesis about 'levels' has two central components. First, higher-level items are taken to be 'autonomous' with respect to lower levels: higher levels are not reducible to, identifiable with, or collapsible into lower levels. Second, higher levels are typically said to 'supervene' on (to 'depend on' and/or to be 'determined by') lower levels (Figure 6.4). (I shall have more to say about supervenience and inter-level determination and dependence in Chapter 12.)

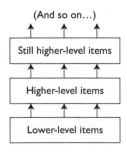

(And so on...)

Still higher-level items

Higher-level items

Lower-level items

Figure 6.4

Functionalists are no less adamant in rejecting behaviorism. According to behaviorists, to be in a particular state of mind is to respond, or be disposed to respond, to stimuli in a particular way. To be in pain is to respond to certain sorts of stimuli in familiar ways, or at least to be disposed so to respond. The notion of a disposition to which behaviorists appeal is notably thin. Some behaviorists deny that dispositions are genuine states of objects. If a vase is fragile, this is not a matter of the vase's being in a particular state. Rather, *all there is* to the vase's being fragile is its being true of the vase that, other things equal, if it is struck it will shatter. All there is to the vase's possession of this disposition is its answering to this (qualified) conditional. The qualification, the 'other things equal' clause, is designed to accommodate 'exceptions'. The vase will not shatter, for instance, were it encased in bubble-wrap, were it s struck by a Styrofoam club, were it quickly heated to the point that it becomes soft and loses its brittleness.

If you find it difficult to understand how an object's having a particular disposition could fail to be a matter of that object's being in a particular state, you are not alone. That issue aside, behaviorist accounts of states of mind apparently fail on their own terms. When you try to say what an agent who possesses a given state of mind is disposed to do, you are invariably compelled to mention *other* states of mind. You will be disposed to eat the Whopper in front of you if you are hungry, for instance, only if you *recognize* it as food, *believe* it is edible, and you do not *accept* assorted vegetarian precepts. (The italicized words denote states of mind.) The lesson here is perfectly general. [Your possessing a given state of mind would dispose you to behave in a particular way *only given other states of mind*. The behaviorist dream of 'analyzing away' the mental is hopeless.]

Functionalists embrace this observation, regarding states of mind as functional states, states characterizable by their place in a structured causal network. Pains, for instance, might be characterized by reference to typical causes (tissue damage, pressure, extremes of temperature), their relations to other states of mind (they give rise to the belief that you are in pain, and a desire to rid yourself of the source of pain), and behavioral outputs (you move your body in particular ways, groan, perspire). Consider your being in pain as a result of your grasping the handle of a cast iron skillet that has been left heating on the stove (Figure 6.5; compare Figure 6.2). Here, your being in pain is a matter of your being in a particular state, one that stands in appropriate causal relations to sensory inputs, to output behavior, and, crucially, to *other* states of mind. These other states of mind are themselves characterizable by reference to *their* respective causal roles. Figure 6.5 provides the barest hint of these relationships.

6.11   Characterizing Functional States

The example illustrates the way in which functional characterizations of states of mind are *interdependent*. Being in a particular functional state is

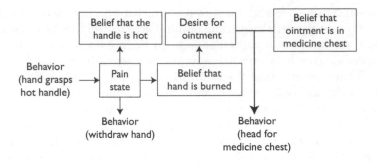

Figure 6.5

a matter of being in a state that bears appropriate relations to *other* states. Thus, a state realizes a given mental property, not in virtue of its intrinsic makeup, but in virtue of relations it bears to other states and to perceptual inputs and behavioral outputs. Recall Wayne's being a vice-president (§ 6.8). Wayne is vice-president, not in virtue of his physical characteristics, his height, or weight, or hair color, but in virtue of his corporate role, a role defined by relations it bears to various other employees who themselves have particular corporate roles.

This might lead you to worry that functional characterizations of states of mind are in danger of succumbing to *circularity*. If behaviorism fails in attempting to provide noncircular reductive accounts of states of mind, accounts that do not themselves require mention of further states of mind, in what sense is functionalism immune to the same difficulty? The functionalist says that your being in pain is a matter of your being in a state that occupies an 'appropriate' causal role in your psychological economy. But can this causal role be characterized informatively? Could you specify it without mention of further states of mind, the characterization of which requires mention of still further states of mind, and so on until you eventually loop back to the original states with which you began?

One preliminary response to this apparent difficulty is to point out that functionalism does not aim to 'analyze away' states of mind. As Figure 6.5 illustrates, the functionalist regards states of mind as perfectly real and irreducible. Indeed, states of mind are identified with roles played by the occupants of nodes in a causal network. Neither pain, nor any other state of mind, could exist in isolation, could exist apart from some such causal network. Minds, unlike stone walls, are not built by putting together self-sufficient elements, but by creating an arrangement of elements that exhibits the right kind of cohesive causal structure. The elements making up the structure – states of mind – owe their identity to relations their realizers bear to other realizers of mental elements. The presence of one state of mind, then, requires the presence of many.

Precisely this feature of the mental encourages worries about circularity, however. If a state of mind owes its character to relations it bears to other states, how could any state have any character? If everyone takes in someone else's washing, how is anything ever washed?

David Lewis, drawing on work by Frank Ramsey (1929) provides an influential line of response to this worry. Functionalists hold that states of mind are characterizable by reference to their place within a network of states. If that is so, it should be possible to characterize this network *as a structure* without mention of any particular component. Imagine that minds are representable by flow charts of the sort depicted in Figure 6.5. Such flow charts would be complex indeed. They might, for instance, include indefinitely many boxes sprouting indefinitely many connections to other boxes.

Imagine that you have managed to specify an entire mental network, imagine that you have constructed a dense flow chart along the lines of Figure 6.5. Now erase the labels inside each box, and replace these with neutral expressions: thus, we might replace 'pain state' with 'F_0', 'belief that the handle is hot' with 'F_1', 'desire for ointment' with 'F_2', 'belief that ointment is in the medicine chest' with 'F_3', and so on (Figure 6.6). Because they involve no mental notions, you can leave the specification of sensory inputs and behavioral outputs as they are. (In fact, as you learned in the course of examining behaviorism in § 4.14, it is doubtful that inputs and outputs *could* be given the sort of neutral specification envisaged. In the interest of simplicity, however, I shall ignore this complication.) Call the resulting flow chart a *total functional description*. A state of pain, then, is a state that occupies the place of F_0 in any system that possesses the causal architecture exhibited by the total functional system.

The idea is that, because the identity of every mental state depends on relations it bears to other states, you cannot characterize such states piecemeal, but only 'holistically' – all at once. Think of chess pieces. Although every piece *has* an intrinsic makeup (and it is customary to use familiar designs for

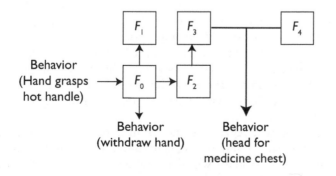

Figure 6.6

particular pieces), a piece is a knight, or a bishop, or a queen, not because it has the intrinsic makeup it has, not because it has a particular shape, or mass, or is made of a particular material, but because of its role in the game. That role cannot be specified without reference to the roles of other pieces. This does not mean that talk of bishops or pawns is objectionably circular, however. It means, rather, that in chess, a piece *is what it is* owing to relations it bears to every other piece.

Suppose this is how it is with states of mind. In that case, your learning to talk about states of mind would be a matter of your mastering a *system* of states. Once you have done this, you would be in a position to single out individual components of that system: individual pains, wants, and beliefs. How might you arrive at such a system? (How do you learn to play chess or tic-tac-toe?) Perhaps you acquire it in learning as a child, to talk of pains, wants, and thoughts. Although you acquire the ability to do this over time, you do not acquire it piecemeal. Rather, 'light dawns gradually over the whole' (Wittgenstein 1969, § 141).

If this seems overly mysterious, reflect on a child's acquisition of a complex skill – riding a bicycle, for instance. Riding a bicycle requires the coordination of myriad component micro-skills. A child does not learn these individually or in isolation, however. The skills are mastered together; the mastery of each depending to some degree on mastery of the others. With enough practice, the child comes to possess the skills as a unit. Once possessed, they can be refined and extended indefinitely.

Functionalists, then, unlike behaviorists, apparently have resources to characterize states of mind without circularity. Of course, behaviorists might make use of the same trick. After all, our total functional system is anchored to behavioral inputs and outputs. Does this mean that functionalism is, at bottom, just a gussied up form of behaviorism?

Not at all. A behaviorist might characterize your being in pain as your responding to a particular kind of input with a particular kind of behavior, and use our specification of a total functional system as a way of spelling out the usual 'other things equal' clause. In taking this route, however, a behaviorist would interpret the nodes in a functional specification, not as designating internal states of agents to whom the specification applied, but as purely notational devices that provide an appropriate pairing of behavioral responses to external stimuli. Thus interpreted, a functional specification would be a complex algorithm, a device for predicting behavioral outputs on the basis of descriptions of inputs. The algorithm would, in effect, provide a characterization of the 'black box' that mediates stimuli (sensory inputs) and outputs (behavioral responses).

Functionalists, in contrast, regard the nodes in a functional specification as 'psychologically real', as designating genuine states of mind, causally efficacious internal states of systems whose causal architecture mirrors the architecture spelled out in a functional specification.

6.12   Functional Systems Generally

Dwell for a moment on the notion of a 'total functional system', and consider just two categories of mental state: *belief* and *desire*. Although we are all alike in many ways – we all have beliefs and desires, for instance – we need not be alike in *what* we believe and desire. Two total functional systems would differ, however, if they differed with respect to any of their beliefs and desires. Indeed, because your own beliefs and desires are constantly changing, the total functional system that constitutes your mind at any given time is bound to differ from the system constituting your mind at earlier or later times. Now, imagine the set – an infinite set, no doubt – consisting of a characterization of every possible total functional system constituting the mind of a mature human being. If functionalism is on the mark, then every possible human mind is exhaustively characterizable by reference to elements in this set.

(For those who care about such things, another way of making the same point would be to allow that the possession of any state of mind is characterizable by a conjunction of conditional – *if–then* – statements; the antecedents – *if*-clauses – that include descriptions of inputs and specifications of total functional architectures; and whose consequents – *then*-clauses – include outputs, behavioral and otherwise.)

This holistic picture suggested by talk of total functional systems needs qualification. You might imagine that adult human beings, by and large, realize broadly similar total functional systems. In contrast, the functional architectures of infants and nonhuman creatures must be decidedly simpler. Does this mean that infants and nonhuman creatures lack minds: that they cannot entertain thoughts, harbor desires, or feel pain?

A functionalist could respond by noting that, although infants and nonhuman creatures do differ functionally from adult human beings, their respective functional architectures overlap those of adult human beings in significant ways. Thus, the total functional systems of infants and nonhuman creatures incorporate states that play the role of pain states (F_0 in Figure 6.6) with respect to inputs and outputs. Their systems are attenuated only with respect to assorted mediating states, those occupying nodes corresponding to beliefs and desires, for instance.

This suggests that there could be borderline cases, cases in which, owing to diminution of complexity, you might not know what to say. Do primitive creatures, earthworms, for instance, or paramecia feel pain? Such creatures draw away from aversive stimuli, and in that regard exhibit their possession of states that bear an important resemblance to our pain states. But the total functional architecture of primitive creatures might be such that it is just not clear what we ought to say about them. In this respect, functionalism mirrors a natural tendency to remain undecided about such cases. Indeed, you might imagine a continuum of total functional systems, ranging from those exhibited by reflective, adult human beings, to those possessed by infants, all the way down to those of single-celled organisms. Drawing a line on this continuum, one that marks a clear-cut boundary between creatures capable of feeling pain, and creatures lacking this capacity, could be largely a matter of decision rather than principle.

6.13   Moving Beyond Analogy

In introducing functionalism, I appealed to a computing machine analogy: minds are analogous to software running on computing machines. Mental states are realized by states of the nervous systems of intelligent creatures in the way computational states are realized by hardware states. Suppose the analogy is apt, suppose mental states *are* analogous to computational states. The question now arises, how do minds actually *work*? What are the principles of operation of mental mechanisms?

One possibility – some would say the only possibility that makes sense – is that mental states are not merely *analogous* to computational states; mental states *are* a species of computational state. We understand computation. You can see how a computer programmed in a particular way does what it does. When you ask how might minds do what they do, the possibility that minds *are* computational devices immediately suggests itself. And really, if mental processes are not computational processes, what *are* they?

Indeed, once you entertain the thought that mental processes could be computational processes, the possibility might strike you as overwhelmingly *obvious*. Computing machines are fed information, process it, and perform various tasks in light of information stored in memory. There is no mystery as to *how* a computing machine could manipulate symbols in accord with principles incorporated in its program. What else *could* thinking be if *not* the processing of symbols in a principled way? Perhaps the computing machine analogy is more than an analogy, perhaps it is a recipe for understanding the nature of the mind. This is the thought to be explored in Chapter 7.

Suggested Reading

Although versions of functionalism have been with us since Aristotle (see Nussbaum and Rorty's *Essays on Aristotle's* De Anima, 1992), the current wave of functionalism could be said to have begun with Hilary Putnam's 'Minds and Machines' (1960). Putnam's subsequent 'Psychological Predicates' (1967) spelled the doctrine out explicitly. Most readers are familiar with this paper under a different title: 'The Nature of Mental States'. This was the title Putnam used when the paper was reprinted, a decision pregnant with philosophical implications (or so I argue in §§ 11.8, 12.12–12.13).

Jerry Fodor's 'The Mind–Body Problem' (1981) provides a succinct, non-technical discussion of functionalism. Fodor's *Psychological Explanation* (1968) comprises more detailed, but still very clear coverage of the same topic. John Haugeland provides an excellent introduction to computers and computation in *Artificial Intelligence: The Very Idea* (1985), and Ned Block's 'What is Functionalism?' (1980b), comprises an indispensable introduction to functionalism. See also Sydney Shoemaker's 'Some Varieties of Functionalism' (1981); and William Lycan's *Consciousness* (1987).

D. M. Armstrong and David Lewis have both advocated versions of functionalism according to which functional properties are identified with their realizers. See Armstrong's *A Materialist Theory of Mind* (1968); and Lewis's 'An Argument for the Identity Theory' (1966), and 'Mad Pain and Martian Pain' (1980). I have not discussed the Armstrong–Lewis brand of functionalism (what Block calls the 'functional specifier' version) in part to keep the discussion as simple as possible, and in part because few functionalists have embraced it. The essays by Block and Shoemaker mentioned above discuss Armstrong–Lewis-style functionalism and argue that it is defective. For a reply, see Lewis's 'Reduction of Mind' (1994). The holistic strategy for characterizing states of mind, to which most functionalists are beholden (and which is illustrated in Figure 7.5) is spelled out by Lewis in 'Psychophysical and Theoretical Identifications' (1972).

Biro and Shahan's *Mind, Brain, and Function* (1982) includes papers on functionalism pro and con. Shoemaker, 'Functionalism and Qualia' (1975), provides a functionalist account of mental qualities (the *qualia*), to which Block's 'Troubles with Functionalism' (1978) is a response. William Lycan's 'Form, Function, and Feel' (1981) affords a functionalist rejoinder.

7 The Representational Theory of Mind

7.1 Mental Representation

Functionalism affords a highly abstract conception of the mind. One especially influential elaboration of this conception depicts minds as symbol processors. To see how this might work, imagine a schematic specification of a functional system resembling the flow chart model deployed in the characterization of organizational hierarchies and computer programs (recall Figures 6.2 and 6.5). Figure 7.1 provides a rough idea of what such a flow chart might look like.

To keep matters simple in the discussion to follow, I propose to focus just on beliefs and desires, omitting the system's other elements. Now, rather than conceiving of beliefs and desires individually, think of the mind as including a 'belief box' and a 'desire box' (Figure 7.2). Occupants of the belief box function as beliefs, occupants of the desire box function as desires. But what are these *occupants*?

Consider your belief that the window is open. More particularly, consider the *content* of this belief: *that the window is open*. A belief with this content can be distinguished from beliefs that have different contents; your belief, for instance, that the room is chilly. You could think of a belief as having two

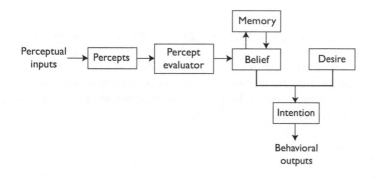

Figure 7.1

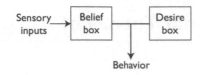

Figure 7.2

'dimensions'. First, there is a 'propositional content', typically expressed in English via a that-clause: *that the window is open, that the room is chilly, that snow is white.* Second, there is an *attitudinal* component: in *believing* that the window is open, you have a particular attitude, an attitude of *acceptance*, toward a particular proposition. Compare *believing* that the window is open, and *desiring* that the window is open: same contents, different attitudes.

Philosophers call beliefs and desires – together with intentions, wishes, hopes, and assorted other 'contentful' states of mind – *propositional attitudes*. In harboring a belief or a desire, you take up an attitude toward a *proposition* – that the window is open, for instance.

What are *propositions*? Propositions are *abstractions* (see § 6.3) When you take an ordinary sentence, 'Snow is white', and consider just its meaning, you are considering the proposition the sentence expresses. You could think of propositions as meanings. When you utter a sentence, you express a particular proposition. As an English speaker, you can say that 'Snow is white' means that snow is white. Here, the sentence and what it means align. But you would not get far without distinguishing sentences and their meanings, distinguishing sentences and propositions those sentences express.

First, distinct sentences in the same language can have the same meaning, can express the same proposition. Thus, the sentences

1   Bachelors procrastinate
2   Unmarried adult males put things off

evidently have the same meaning. Think of the common meaning as a proposition: the two sentences express the same proposition. So, even within a language, there is no simple, one–one mapping between sentences and meanings. (I leave it to the reader to think of examples in which a single sentence could be used to mean different things, to express different propositions.)

Second, and more importantly in the present context, sentences in distinct languages can have the same meaning. The sentences

3   It's raining
4   Il pleut
5   Es regnet

mean the same in English, French, and German, respectively. Each of these sentences could then be said to express the same proposition, the proposition *that it is raining.* Talk of propositions provides a way to talk about meanings independently of sentences used to express those meanings.

Although philosophers regard propositions as indispensable abstractions, we need sentences to express – or, for that matter, to discuss – propositions. Sentences are, so to speak, concrete, here and now propositional vehicles. Sentences stand in for propositions in the material world. This simple point takes on added significance when you start thinking about how the mind works. Thoughts are meaningful. Thoughts express propositions. Beliefs, desires, intentions and the like can be understood as attitudes toward propositions. How might this central feature of our mental lives be fitted into a functionalist framework?

Here is one possibility. Think about states of mind as something like strings of symbols, *sentences.* Sentences can occupy one or another 'box' in a functional system. (Indeed instances of a symbolic string – a sentence – could appear simultaneously in more than one box: you could believe *and* desire that the window is open.) Sentences can be moved into and out of particular boxes in response to what occurs elsewhere in the system.

The idea here is that your forming a belief that the window is open would be a matter of constructing a symbol expressing the proposition that the window is open and inserting it into your 'belief box'. In the same vein, your wanting the window to be open would be your placing such a symbol in your 'desire box'. Your belief box and your desire box are connected in distinctive ways to the rest of the system constituting your mind. If a symbol representing the proposition that the window is closed is in your desire box, for instance, this might – in conjunction with the presence of various other symbols in your belief and desire boxes – lead you to walk across the room and lower the window (Figure 7.3). The presence of the same symbol in your belief box (assuming that it is absent from your desire box) might – and, again, in conjunction with the presence of other symbols in your belief and desire boxes – lead to markedly different behavior.

This way of thinking of functional systems enables us to see more clearly how creatures with very different beliefs and desires might nevertheless be seen as functionally on a par. You, an infant, and Richard Feynman all fit

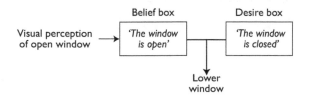

Figure 7.3

the highly simplified models in Figures 7.1 and 7.2. You differ, however, with respect to the symbols that are apt to appear in your respective belief and desire boxes.

This conception of mind, the 'Representational Theory of Mind', has been enthusiastically defended by Jerry Fodor since the 1970s. The Representational Theory of Mind requires the postulation of a system of symbols that function as 'mental representations'. These symbols make up what Fodor calls a 'Language of Thought', a biologically fixed 'code' analogous to the 'machine code' hard-wired into an ordinary computing machine. Your forming a belief that the window is open is a matter of a sentence in the Language of Thought corresponding to the English sentence, 'The window is open', a sentence expressing the proposition that the window is open acquiring an appropriate functional role, a matter of this sentence's being moved into your belief box.

On this model, mental operations are taken to be 'computations over symbols'. [Talk of belief and desire 'boxes' is to be understood as shorthand for talk of specific kinds of computation.] If you thought of the mind as a kind of program running on biological 'hardware', belief and desire boxes would represent subroutines that processes symbols in distinctive ways.

7.2   Semantic Engines

Fodor and his allies have long insisted that the Representational Theory of Mind (and with it the Language of Thought hypothesis) is 'the only game in town'. The Representational Theory of Mind provides a way of understanding how minds, higher-level entities, could systematically affect and be affected by bodily goings-on. Until someone produces a serious competitor, they argue, the theory wins by default.

But how is all this supposed to *work*? What could it mean to speak of sentences in a Language of Thought shunting into and out of belief and desire boxes? Notice first, that the focus here is on sentence *tokens*. [A sentence token – a particular 'inscription' – is a concrete entity, something that could exert causal influence.] A sentence *token* is to be distinguished from a sentence *type*.

To appreciate the distinction, consider the sentences in the box below (Figure 7.4).

How many sentences does the box contain? The box contains two instances, cases, or *tokens* of a single sentence *type*. The answer to the 'how many?'

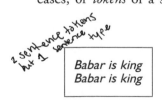

2 sentence tokens but 1 sentence type

> Babar is king
> Babar is king

Figure 7.4

question depends on how you are counting. If you are counting sentence *tokens*, the answer is two: the box contains two sentences. If you are counting sentence *types*, the box contains just one sentence, one sentence type. How many letters are in a Scrabble set? The answer is 26 or 98, depending on whether you are counting letter *types* or letter *tokens*. When proponents of the Representational Theory of Mind speak of sentences occupying belief boxes, or sentences affecting causal processes, they mean to be speaking of sentence tokens, not types: individual entities, not kinds or types of entity.

Because functionalism and the Representational Theory of Mind describe mental operations at a high level of abstraction, it is easy to imagine that you understand them better than you do. It is one thing to describe in a very general way how a system might work, another matter to understand how this description might be implemented in concrete cases. This is so for accounts of physical processes framed in terms of 'information'. And it is so for functionalism and the Representational Theory of Mind. The question is, how is the theory 'implemented'?

Consider the sentences – the *token* sentences – printed on this page. Each one is the result of an ordinary material causal process; and each one produces ordinary material effects: it reflects light in a particular way, for instance, so as to be visible. To see why this is significant, return to the distinction between *sentences* and *propositions* sentences are used to express. When you encounter sentences in your native language, their meanings, the propositions they express, leap out at you. But of course, you can encounter sentences without having any sense of what they mean. This happens whenever you confront sentences in a language you do not understand: you see or hear only marks on paper or sounds.

Now, suppose you set out to build a device capable of manipulating meaningful sentences. How would you begin? When *you* read a sentence you grasp its meaning and respond to that meaning. But what steps would you take to endow the device with a capacity to 'grasp meanings', to *understand*? Opting to include a 'meaning grasping' module, would be to invite the question, how do you do *that*? And this is the original question all over again.

Suppose you constructed a device that:

1   Operated on well-understood mechanical principles, principles the implementation of which poses no insurmountable technical difficulties, but that
2   Its operation was apparently 'intelligent'.

Imagine, for instance, a device that manipulated sentences without regard to their meanings, but did so in a way that coincided with the way those sentences would be manipulated by an agent who grasped their meanings. Such a device – what John Haugeland dubs a 'semantic engine' – would perfectly mimic the performance of a native speaker, but would do so without relying, as a native speaker would, on a grasp of the meanings of sentences it manipulated. Those sentences might express propositions, but the device would 'care' only about their shapes, their 'syntax'. (*Syntax* concerns only *structural* or 'formal' features of sentences; *semantics* concerns their *meanings*.) Such a device, a semantic engine, operates exclusively on syntactic principles and 'formal' relations among sentences, relations definable wholly by reference to sentences' syntactic characteristics.

Yes, but is such a device *possible*?

Not only are semantic engines possible, they exist already, and in large numbers! An ordinary computing machine is a semantic engine. Engineers design and program computing machines so that they manipulate symbols in accord with purely syntactic, purely formal principles. The symbols are meaningful – to us – but the machines that deploy them care nothing about this. They operate on *uninterpreted* symbols, but – and this is the key point – in a manner that honors semantic constraints. (This is just a fancy way of saying that computing machines manipulate symbols in a way that makes sense – to us – in light of their meanings.)

How is this possible? How could syntax 'mirror semantics'? If you have ever studied logic, you have already encountered an important example of systems that make use of purely syntactic or formal principles in the manipulation of symbols, but in a way that honors semantic relations among those symbols. Ordinary rules of inference refer only to *shapes* of symbols. Take the rule commonly known as *modus ponens*:

$$\frac{p \supset q}{q}$$

(In English: 'If p then q' plus 'p', yields 'q'.)

The rule says, in effect, that if you have a particular configuration of symbols (here, '$p \supset q$' and 'p'), you are permitted to write a new symbol (in this case, 'q'). (Think of the $\supset$ as expressing an English conditional – 'if … then … ' – construction.) In formulating the rule, I have used variables (p and q) that range over sentences. The rule, in effect, says that whenever you have a $\supset$ flanked by sentences, together with a sentence that matches the sentence on the left of the $\supset$, you are permitted to 'detach' the sentence to the right of the $\supset$.

For present purposes, what is significant about the *modus ponens* rule is that it is formulated and deployed without regard to semantics, without regard to the meanings of sentences to which it applies. Even so, applications of the rule 'make sense'; they conform to the semantics of inference. If you accept the sentence

1   If it's raining then I'll need an umbrella,

and the sentence

2   It's raining,

Then you can see that the sentence

3   I'll need an umbrella

follows. This is something any English speaker, anyone who understands English, grasps immediately. Systems of formal logic are designed to mirror this kind of semantic knowledge by means of purely syntactic deductive rules the application of which requires no semantic knowledge. In doing derivations or proofs in logic, you care nothing for what the symbols mean, you care only about their shapes and arrangements: you are functioning as a semantic engine!

7.3   Minds as Semantic Engines

Well and good; but what has this to do with *minds*? Suppose your aim were to explain the human mind by assuming that minds manipulate 'mental representations', and that mental representations are 'encoded' by sentences in the Language of Thought.

You might think that there is an obvious objection to such a project. If minds manipulate sentences, symbolic representations, then this would appear to require a sentence *interpreter* or *understander*, some component of the mind that *interprets* the symbols. (Recall the module posited earlier that was supposed to 'grasp meanings'.) This would mean that you would be explaining the mind by positing within it *another* mind, a homunculus, a little intelligent agent whose job requires that he *understand* sentences in the Language of Thought and respond appropriately.

An explanation of this kind is no explanation. The point is perfectly general. You and I are watching a machine that sorts and wraps candy bars. You are impressed, and ask how the machine works. 'Simple', I reply. 'There is a device inside it that controls its operations.' Similarly, explaining that minds are capable of understanding meaningful sentences because minds include a 'sentence understander' is to make no progress.

Against this backdrop it is easier to appreciate the relevance of the notion of a semantic engine. Recall that a semantic engine is a device that performs symbolic operations – manipulates symbols – in a way that reflects semantic (meaningful) relations holding among these symbols, but does so exclusively by means of formal and syntactic – mechanical – principles, that is, without regard to the *meanings* of those symbols. Now suppose you thought that minds processed mental representations. Were *minds* semantic engines, you would not need to assume that minds contain components – little intelligent agents, homunculi – that understand the meanings of those representations. Ordinary computing machines are implementations of semantic engines. Perhaps brains are as well. If so, and if the brain has an appropriate functional organization, then it would seem that we have come a long way toward understanding in a general way how minds could work.

Still, you might think that there is an obvious difficulty. When scientists open up the brain, they see nothing that resembles symbols or sentences in a Language of Thought. What could it be for brains to contain and manipulate *sentences*?

Think of an ordinary computing machine. Engineers regard it as uncontroversial that computing machines 'process symbols'. Yet, were you to inspect the insides of a computing machine while it is engaged in 'symbol manipulations', you would see nothing resembling familiar mathematical or programming symbols. Nor, incidentally, would you see any 0's and 1's, commonly regarded as the basic ingredients of a computing machine's symbolic repertoire. Electronic patterns that play the role of symbols in a computing machine need not resemble your pencil-and-paper representations of those symbols. There is no reason to think that you could 'read off' symbols as they are manipulated by a computing machine any more than you could hope to read off a musical score by closely examining deflections in the groove of a phonograph record or the track on a compact disc. (This is not to say that you could not *learn* to do this. But learning to do it would require learning a complex rule that takes you from electrical events, or patterns of deflections, or magnetic patterns, to more familiar symbols.)

Thus, if the mind were a semantic engine realized by the brain, if mental operations include the manipulation of symbols, sentences in a Language of Thought, the brain's embodiment of those symbols need not resemble the symbols you jot down using pencil and paper or type on a computer monitor. They might involve subtle electrical or chemical processes; they might be embodied in connections among neurons; they might be widely distributed in networks of simpler elements. In any case, there is no reason to imagine that such symbols could be 'read off' the brain in the way you read words off this page. If there is a Language of Thought, its sentences could well be indecipherable from the point of view of an observer examining the microstructure of a brain.

7.4   The Turing Test

The Representational Theory of Mind depicts minds as semantic engines, devices that operate on formally specifiable *syntactic* principles, but in a way that tracks *semantic* – that is, meaningful – relations among symbols, sentences in the Language of Thought. Although mental mechanisms would be indifferent to the significance of symbols on which they operate, operations performed by those mechanisms mirror operations that might be performed by an intelligent agent who understood the symbols and acted on the basis of that understanding.

When you ask a friend to print a document for you, your friend understands your request, and acts on the basis of that understanding. (*How* the friend responds will depend on the friend's current beliefs and desires.) When you 'ask' your desktop computer to print a document by means of a typed or voiced command, the device does not act on the basis of its grasp of the command's meaning. The specific mechanisms that execute your command, care nothing for the command's meaning. Even so, owing to its program, your desktop computer operates *just as though* it understood your command.

Now the punch line. For proponents of the Language of Thought, this is *all there is* to understanding. *You* can be said to understand the sentences on this page. But mental mechanisms responsible for your understanding need not *themselves* understand. On the contrary, if you thought they did, you would be hard-pressed to account for *your* grasp of what the sentences mean. As noted earlier, it would be a bad idea to try to explain the kind of understanding required for meaningful, intelligent thought by positing an internal understander. To avoid trivialization, an explanation must show how meaningful thought could result from the operation of mechanisms that themselves do not need to understand meanings. *Your* entertaining meaningful thoughts might thus be explained by supposing your mind includes an organized collection of components, none of which needs to understand the (meaningful) symbols it processes.

The intimate connection between semantic engines and intelligent thought lies behind an influential discussion of the possibility of 'artificial intelligence' published in 1950 by A. M. Turing (1912–54). Turing was a prominent mathematician whose pioneering work on the theory of computation underlies the development of modern computing machines. Turing was interested in the question whether it might be possible to build an *intelligent* machine. After reviewing failed attempts to define 'intelligence' (and, for that matter 'machine'), Turing proposed to define intelligence 'operationally' and thereby to bypass altogether the vexed question of what exactly constitutes 'real' intelligence.

An operational definition takes the form of a test for determining whether the defined term applies. Thus, you might operationally define 'length' in terms of measurement procedures. Something has length if, for instance, it could be measured using a standard meter stick. Something is a meter long if its ends align with the ends of the meter stick. The Turing test is designed to ensure that whatever passed the test would qualify as intelligent. A computing machine would count as intelligent if it managed to pass the test and not otherwise.

The Turing test is based on a game Turing dubs the 'Imitation Game'. The Imitation Game is played by three ordinary people. One, the interrogator, puts questions to two players, a man and a woman, and tries to work out which is which, which is the man, which the woman. One of the two players must answer truthfully, the other tries to mislead the interrogator. To prevent the interrogator from seeing the players or hearing their voices, the interrogator is stationed in a separate room and communicates with the players by means of a teletype (a primitive form of text messaging). By asking clever questions, the interrogator will sometimes win the game, but will sometimes lose as well. Suppose, over a large number of games, the interrogator wins – that is, correctly discovers which player is which – about half the time.

Now, says Turing, replace one member of the pair being interrogated, the man or the woman, with a computing machine programmed to take the part of the untruthful contestant. If the machine could fool a clever interrogator about as often as a human player could (as we are supposing, about half the time), the machine passes the test: the machine would count as intelligent. (If this seems too easy, you might reflect on the fact that no existing or currently contemplated computing machine comes remotely close to exhibiting the kind of resourcefulness and wit required to fool a moderately competent interrogator.)

Turing's supposition is, in effect, that the machine in question is functioning as a semantic engine. If the machine passes the test, if the machine functions intelligently, then it would seem reasonable to say that the machine *is* intelligent, that the machine *understands* questions put to it by the interrogator, and that the machine *means* just what a human contestant would mean in responding as it does to the interrogator's questions. If *that* is right, it would seem that the Representational Theory of Mind delivers important insights concerning the nature of the mind: minds could be programs running on neurological hardware.

7.5   The Chinese Room

But *is* this right? John Searle contends that it is not. Searle's much discussed argument revolves around a memorable thought experiment. Imagine, Searle says, that you are participating in an experiment in a psychology laboratory. You are seated in a cramped windowless room. At your feet is a basket of plastic Chinese characters, although you have no idea that this is what they are: you are ignorant of Chinese, and for all you can tell the items in the basket could be plastic decorations of an abstract design: *squiggles*. Periodically, a new batch of squiggles appears through a slot in the wall. Although these mean nothing to you, you have been furnished with a manual that instructs you to pass particular sequences of squiggles out through the slot when particular sequences of squiggles are passed in. Suppose you become adept at this. When a sequence of squiggles is input, you can quickly output a sequence called for by the manual. In time, you learn the manual by heart, and so your manipulations of squiggles become virtually automatic.

Meanwhile, outside the room, and completely unbeknown to you, a group of Chinese scientists has gathered. These scientists can read and understand the characters that are passed into and out of the room. They recognize the strings of squiggles they pass into the room as questions framed in Chinese, and the strings of squiggles you pass back out as answers to those questions. (I leave aside the fact that, for the answers to make sense in light of the questions, the manual will need to be very sophisticated indeed.) It appears to the

[Chinese scientists that you understand Chinese. But, says Searle, clearly you do not. You are behaving *as though* you understand, you are operating as a semantic engine, yet you understand no Chinese. At most you are *simulating* a competent Chinese speaker.]

Searle's Chinese Room can be seen as a variant of the Turing test. Think of the Chinese scientists assembled outside the room as taking the role of interrogators in the Imitation Game. You, seated in the room with your manual and basket of plastic squiggles, are standing in for the computing machine. A second player, seated next to you, is fluent in Chinese. The interrogators' task is to work out which of you is the real Chinese speaker. Suppose your performance fools the interrogators about half the time. What would this show?

Searle suggests that it would show only that you have been provided with an ingenious prop – a stunningly clever manual – that enables you to play the part of a Chinese speaker. But you neither speak nor understand Chinese. Your responses to questions are not genuinely intelligent. (Or, to the extent that they are, they reflect, not *your* intelligence, but the intelligence of the authors of the manual.) Because you operate just as a computing machine would (think of the manual as your program), the same would hold for a computing machine that passed Turing's test. A machine that passed the test would manifest, not its own intelligence, but the intelligence of those who programmed it.

Searle hopes to draw a more general conclusion from all this. The Representational Theory of Mind is founded on the idea that the mind is a semantic engine: mental processes consist of operations over uninterpreted symbols (sentences in the Language of Thought). But, Searle insists, the Chinese Room thought experiment makes it clear that there *must* be more to minds than this. A device – a robot, perhaps – whose 'brain' realized a semantic engine and thereby satisfied the requirements of the Representational Theory of Mind and passed the Turing test, could no doubt fool us: an observer might well *think* it intelligent, might regard it as having a mind. But such an observer would be wrong! At best the device would be *simulating* intelligence and understanding, in the way a computing machine might be programmed to simulate a hurricane, or photosynthesis, or the economy of Japan.

The conclusion you are meant to draw is that functionalism, as it is spelled out in the Representational Theory of Mind, does not in fact provide an explanation of what it is to understand the meanings of sentences or to entertain meaningful thoughts. What the Representational Theory regards as a virtue – an explanation of the capacity to understand and to think meaningful thoughts that nowhere appeals to meaning – Searle regards as a fatal error. Semantic engines might be capable of simulating intelligent agents, but [simulated intelligence is not intelligence.]

Searle's opponents have accused him of missing the point. Searle assumes that, in the Chinese Room, there is no genuine understanding. But, the critics argue, this is a misleading appearance that results from the way Searle has set up the thought experiment. Searle invites us to focus on just a single component – *you*, sitting in your chair sorting through a basket of plastic squiggles – rather than the *whole system* of which you are but one component. Thus, while it is undoubtedly true that *you* understand no Chinese, *the system* that includes you and the manual, the room as a whole, *does*.

Searle responds by noting that you might commit the manual to memory, leave the room, and carry on artful conversations with native Chinese speakers. Although anyone would think that you are fluent in Chinese, you still have no idea what Chinese speakers are saying to you, and what you are saying to them: you still do not understand Chinese.

Uncommitted bystanders to this debate might feel pulled in different directions. On the one hand, Searle is evidently onto *something* important. On the other hand, Searle's opponents appear justified in complaining that the appeal of the Chinese Room stems from its tendency to make us focus on a single component – the symbol-processing component – of a system rather than the system as a whole.

I shall leave the debate here, and move to consider the question how sentences in the Language of Thought might come by their semantics, how they could mean what they mean. In due course (in Chapter 13), I shall suggest a way of reconciling these issues. Doing so, however, obliges us to move beyond functionalism and the Representational Theory of Mind, and take a prolonged excursion into metaphysics.

7.6   From Syntax to Semantics

Central to the Representational Theory of Mind, is the idea that minds manipulate mental representations in the form of uninterpreted symbols in the Language of Thought. In this context, 'uninterpreted' means that the processes whereby mental symbols are manipulated operate without regard to the meanings of those symbols. In this respect, mental processes are taken to resemble purely mechanical computational processes. They would resemble as well your bravura performance in the Chinese Room.

Symbols in the Language of Thought, and mental symbols generally, are presumed to *have* meanings. The idea is just that these meanings play no role in the *operation* of devices that process them. If they are, in this sense, uninterpreted, in what does their meaning reside? What gives them their meaning? What 'makes' them mean what they do?

Reflect for a moment on the operation of ordinary computing machines. Suppose someone programs a computing machine to keep inventory in a supermarket. The program keeps track of bananas, cans of soup, and cartons of milk. You could say that the computing machine on which the program runs is storing and processing information about bananas, cans of soup, and cartons of milk. The machine performs operations over symbols that designate these items, however, without regard to what they designate. Indeed, you might imagine that the very same program could be run on a different machine, or on the same machine on a different occasion, to keep track of items in a hardware store. In this case, the device would process and store information about nails, glue, and ant traps. You might even imagine that the very same symbols (the very same pattern of magnetic deflections) that, in the supermarket case, represent bananas, cans of soup, and cartons of milk, represent, in this machine, nails, glue, and ant traps, respectively.

What, then, gives a symbol manipulated by a computing machine its meaning, what makes it designate cartons of milk rather than ant traps? And, you might ask, what gives sentences in the Language of Thought their meaning – for, although it might be controversial whether states of a computing machine are in any sense meaningful, it is surely not controversial that our thoughts have meaning. The entire Language of Thought project is predicated on the assumption that thoughts *are* meaningful, and that this is something that calls for explanation.

Note first, that a devotee of the Representational Theory of Mind follows a long tradition and assumes that the meaning of a given symbol is not *intrinsic* to that symbol. What a symbol signifies is not built into the symbol, but depends rather on how the symbol is put to work by agents (or 'systems') that deploy it. The symbols processed by a computing machine owe their significance to the use to which they are put by agents who program and enter data into the machine for particular purposes. When you type 'bananas' into the machine and this inscription is converted into a pattern of magnetic deflections, this pattern of magnetic deflections, insofar as it functions as a symbol, designates bananas because this is what *you* mean by 'bananas'.

You could say that the meanings of symbols processed by an ordinary computing machine are derivative of the meanings given those symbols by agents making use of the machine and its program. But this could not be how it is with symbols in the Language of Thought. Your thoughts do not mean what they do because you (or anyone else) *assigns* those meanings; your mental concepts do not designate what they designate because you *decide* what they designate. The Language of Thought is supposed to explain how you could have meaningful thoughts in the first place. If the significance of sentences in the Language of Thought depended on your assigning meanings to them, depended on your interpreting them, nothing would have been explained. The assignment of meanings is evidently an activity that *presupposes* meaningful thought. A familiar refrain: it is no good assuming the very thing you hope to explain.

What, then, *is* the source of meaning for the Language of Thought; to what does it owe its semantics? You can exclude the possibility that expressions in the Language of Thought possess intrinsic, built-in significance. And you can exclude the possibility that meanings of those expressions depend on the interpretative activities of thinkers. What options remain?

Perhaps this: expressions in the Language of Thought owe their significance to connections, especially *interactive* connections, those expressions bear to goings-on in a thinker's surroundings. Thus, a particular term in the Language of Thought might designate bananas (and so stand in for the English word 'banana') because it is evoked by the presence of bananas and leads to actions involving bananas. Another term might designate cans of soup (standing in for the English expression 'cans of soup') because instances of it are brought about by agents' interactions with cans of soup.

This sketch is, to be sure, oversimplified. The point, however, is that it is open to a proponent of the Representational Theory of Mind to advance a broadly interactive account of the semantics of the Language of Thought. Such an account would be complex, and would include plenty of *intra*-linguistic interactive elements, interactions among sentences in the Language of Thought. Once the significance of some symbols has been settled, these could be used to define other symbols. And so-called logical terms, those corresponding to the English expressions 'all', 'some', 'and', 'or', 'not', 'if ... then ... ' might be explicable purely by reference to relations sentences in the Language of Thought bear to one another. But the fundamental idea is that the semantics of thought is fixed by the circumstances of thinkers. In this respect, too, ordinary agents would resemble computing machines. The significance of symbols processed by a given computing machine depends in some way or other on the circumstances in which the machine is deployed.

These and related issues will be revisited in subsequent chapters. Meanwhile, it is time to return to an examination of the metaphysics of functionalism.

7.7   Thinking as Computing

In explicating the Representational Theory of Mind, Fodor appeals explicitly to the computer model of the mind. Mental operations are operations performed over symbols, sentences in the Language of Thought. The science of psychology aims to work out algorithms (programs) responsible for intelligent behavior. These could be represented, just as computer programs can be represented, by means of flow charts that specify, albeit 'abstractly', the causal structure of systems they characterize. Psychology, on this model, is a 'higher-level science', one that abstracts from lower-level 'implementation' details.

One advantage of such a view is that it enables us to comprehend how minds might fit into the material world, how minds are related to brains. Minds are related to brains in something like the way computational processes are related to computing machines. Minds are not identifiable with or reducible to brains for just the reasons that programs or computational operations are not identifiable with or reducible to components of the hardware on which they run. Brains realize minds much as computing machines realize particular programs. Just as in describing the operation of a computing machine at the 'program level', you would be describing the machine's causal structure in abstraction from – without regard to – its hardware, so in describing mental operations, psychologists are describing the causal structure of intelligent agents in abstraction from – without regard to – their biological hardware.

All this serves to demystify the mind. You can see why attempts to identify minds with material entities are bound to fail, without thereby embracing dualism, without supposing that minds are immaterial substances. Perhaps, however, the demystification goes too far. You might worry that a computational conception of mental processes threatens to turn us into rigidly programmed robots, beings altogether lacking in creativity, spontaneity, or free will.

The idea, however, is not that you are programmed to follow strict formal routines you are powerless to alter. Intelligent behavior is principled behavior. You could think of the principles you adopt (or cultivate, or learn, or inherit along with your biological constitution) as core ingredients in your mental program. All this is consistent with most conceptions of free will, including conceptions that include elements of spontaneity: causes that are not effects of prior causes. The question of free will – what it is and whether we enjoy it – is independent of the question whether functionalism and the Representational Theory of Mind are true.

7.8   Levels of Description

Return, for a moment, to the thought that the operations of an ordinary computing machine are describable on different *levels*. An electrical engineer or a physicist might describe the operation of a given machine at the hardware level. In so doing, the engineer or physicist employs a characteristic array of hardware concepts. A programmer describing the operations of the very same machine makes use of a very different conceptual repertoire.

Fodor speaks in such cases of distinctive 'taxonomies', distinctive ways of classifying and organizing descriptions and explanations of phenomena. Lower-level and higher-level sciences 'taxonomize' phenomena very differently. The levels here are taxonomic, *classificatory* levels. One level is higher than another if its categories are relatively 'more abstract'. A higher-level science abstracts away from details crucial to a science at a lower level. This is not meant as a precise characterization of levels, but the topic is not one admitting of precision.

Taxonomic categories that specify entities of interest at higher levels need not be, and typically are not, definable in terms of categories found at lower levels. In the computer case, you cannot define computational operations in terms of material transactions in the hardware that realize those operations. One obvious problem with attempts to do so stems from the fact that computational operations are *multiply realizable*: the very same operation could be realized in utterly different sorts of material system. You might think that higher-level operations could be defined by means of a *disjunction* of lower-level goings-on. Thus, the summing operation might be characterizable as *either* a particular kind of brass gear and cog operation (in Babbage's

Analytical Engine), *or* a particular kind of operation in a device made with vacuum tubes, *or* a particular kind of transistor-based operation, *or* ... .

Functionalists are quick to point out that such a strategy faces an obvious and crippling difficulty. The open-ended character of the tentative disjunctive specification above indicates that you would need to add descriptions of further lower-level operations if your aim is to provide an exhaustive lower-level accounting of our higher-level category. It would seem, however, that there are endless lower-level ways of realizing any complex higher-level operation. The prospects of reducing higher-level categories to lower-level categories, even long disjunctions of lower-level categories, are not encouraging.

Even if you allowed a systematic mapping of higher-level categories onto long – perhaps open-ended – disjunctions of lower-level categories, however, the reductive strategy flies in the face of scientific and everyday practice. Suppose you distinguish physics (in particular, *basic* physics), the fundamental lower-level science, from assorted higher-level sciences: the so-called special sciences. (The special sciences include, in addition to psychology, biology, neuroscience, paleontology, meteorology, geology, ecology, sociology, anthropology, economics.) Physics provides us with an inventory of fundamental particles, fields, and forces and laws governing the behavior of those particles, fields and forces. Higher-level sciences deploy higher-level schemes of classification, higher-level taxonomies. While physicists speak of electrons, quarks, and alpha particles, chemists focus on atoms and molecules, and biologists take up complex molecular structures: living organisms. At still higher levels, psychologists, sociologists, and economists ply their trades.

Each of these sciences is distinguished by the way it 'carves up' reality. Categories definitive of a given higher-level taxonomy divide reality in ways that, from the perspective of lower-level sciences, would seem arbitrary. A simple analogy might make the point clear. When you play chess, you move chess pieces in particular ways. Considered from the perspective of chemistry or physics, the range of appropriate moves (those permitted by the rules of chess) would appear entirely unprincipled. Patterns and regularities exhibited in games of chess are visible only at a higher level. Biological categories, seen from the perspective of physics, must appear similarly arbitrary. Biology divides up the universe in ways that, so long as we remain at the level of quarks and electrons, look contrived and unprincipled. Similarly for psychology: psychological concepts – pain and belief, for instance – circumscribe boundaries invisible at lower levels.

The idea in play is that the sciences operate within a hierarchy of levels; fundamental physics operates at the lowest level; biology and neuroscience occupy intermediate levels; and psychology and the social sciences function at still higher levels. This is just to say that each science imposes a system of categories, taxonomy, on the universe. The categories definitive of a given science mark off boundaries that are largely indiscernible within sciences at lower levels. One science's categories are *orthogonal* to another's. This is why there is, in general, no prospect of *reducing* higher-level sciences to sciences at some lower level. Doing so would require a systematic way of drawing higher-level distinctions using lower-level categories. And this is just what would seem to be hopeless.

You might suspect that a conception of this sort goes too far. If physics is the science of everything, then why do we *need* the others? If the special sciences are *not* reducible to physics, why should they be accorded any legitimacy at all?

The answer given by functionalists such as Fodor is that it is precisely because higher-level sciences make use of categories *not* reducible to those of lower-level sciences that the higher-level sciences are vindicated. As you explore the universe, you discover important regularities that are, from the perspective of physics, quite hidden. These regularities hold among objects in virtue of characteristics of those objects that correspond in no principled way to items of interest to the physicist. To ignore such objects and characteristics, however, would require ignoring endless interesting and important regularities.

To see the point, think again of the operation of a computing machine. Suppose you describe the operation of a computing machine at the most basic hardware level, in terms of electron fluctuations inside transistors. If you limited yourself to such descriptions, let alone descriptions framed in terms of fundamental physical categories, you would miss important generalizations that appear only when you begin to consider the machine at the level of its program. You might, for instance, fail to recognize common features in the behavior of two machines with very different material compositions running the same program: both machines are doing sums, for instance, or sending data to a printer. At the ordinary hardware level, or at the level of physics, such commonalities disappear – in the way the pattern formed by arrangements of flowers in a floral clock vanishes when you look just at individual plants.

7.9   From Taxonomy to Ontology

Someone skeptical about this line of reasoning might object that it shows at most that we require higher-level sciences, and the categories they deploy, only as a matter of convenience. Higher-level sciences provide us with what from the perspective of physics or chemistry are hopelessly crude, gappy accounts of goings-on in the world around us. As it happens, these crude accounts are perfectly adequate for certain of our purposes. Moreover, finer-grained accounts would require an investment of time and energy that investigators could ill afford. By keeping to the program level, you can understand, explain, and manipulate the behavior of your desktop computer in a way that is perfectly adequate for most everyday purposes. Those purposes aside, however, the *real* story is to be had only by descending to the hardware level and, ultimately, to the level of micro-physics.

Consider the use of familiar rules of thumb in predicting the weather:

Red sky at night, sailor's delight; red sky in morning, sailor take warning.

Ring around the sun or moon, snow or rain is coming soon.

Rules of thumb are useful, no doubt, perhaps even, as a practical matter, indispensable. Even so, they merely approximate much more complex and fine-grained pronouncements belonging to meteorology and climatology, for instance, and ultimately, of course, in physics. You might see psychology in the same light. Psychology provides us with a stock of rough and ready generalizations that serve our purposes when we interact with one another. But these, at best, approximate truths at lower levels. As you descend from psychology, through neuropsychology, to neurobiology, to chemistry, you refine these approximations until you reach bedrock: fundamental physics.

Fodor speaks for many in arguing forcefully that this way of depicting the relation of higher-level to lower-level sciences is misconceived. Categories embedded in a higher-level science – psychology, for instance – designate perfectly genuine causally efficacious higher-level properties of perfectly genuine higher-level objects. These properties are certainly not reducible to properties found in sciences at lower levels. 'Being in pain' and 'believing that it is raining' designate such higher-level properties. If you cannot find these properties among the properties inventoried by lower-level sciences, you would be wrong to conclude that they are in any way less-than-perfectly-real. On the contrary, this is just what you would expect if psychology is an authentic, 'autonomous', higher-level science.

What makes a property genuine? On the view under consideration, a genuine property is a property that makes a *causal difference* to objects possessing it. If *being red* is a genuine property, then objects possessing this property, red objects, would behave differently than objects lacking it, and the differences would turn on the presence or absence of the property, being red. Many in Fodor's camp would put this in terms of *causal laws*: a genuine property is a property that figures in an established causal law. The special sciences are in the business of formulating causal laws governing the behavior of objects possessing properties figuring in those laws. Genuine properties, then, are revealed by laws uncovered as scientists investigate the universe. If scientists discover causal laws in neurobiology, or psychology, or economics, laws that govern the behavior of higher-level objects, and if these laws range over higher-level properties, then these higher-level properties must be genuine. Of course scientists could be wrong about what the laws are, hence mistaken as to the genuine properties, but that goes without saying. No scientific claim is immune to revision in light of new evidence.

Two features of this view are worth emphasizing.

First, its proponents are committed to a hierarchical, *layered* conception of reality. The world contains levels or layers of objects and properties governed by successive levels of causal laws. Although objects at higher levels are often enough made up of objects at lower levels, it is nevertheless true that higher-level objects and their properties have lives of their own. They are not reducible to, not 'nothing but', arrangements of objects and properties at lower levels (recall Figure 6.4).

(A technical aside you would do well to skip: the 'supervenience' relation is standardly invoked to characterize the relation of higher-level objects and properties to those at lower levels. The idea, roughly, is that, while higher-level objects and properties 'depend on and are determined by' lower-level objects and properties, higher-level objects and properties are nevertheless in some manner *distinct* from lower-level objects and properties. Hearts are made up of cells, and ultimately of quarks and electrons. But, because hearts are multiply realizable, hearts could not *just* be organized assemblages of cells, properties of hearts could not be properties of cells or assemblages of cells. At least this is the story.)

Second, higher-level laws are presumed to be laws that hold only *ceteris paribus*, only 'other things being equal'. In this respect, they differ from laws governing the fundamental entities studied in physics. Laws governing fundamental entities are *exceptionless*. In contrast to these, laws governing entities at higher levels are 'hedged', they apply *ceteris paribus*. Do not confuse *ceteris paribus* laws with probabilistic laws of the sort mentioned in Chapter 2 (§ 2.5). Fundamental laws might turn out to be probabilistic. Their application is nonetheless universal and exceptionless. The laws you might hope to discover in psychology, or economics, or even neurobiology, in contrast, are irreducibly 'hedged'; such laws admit of exceptions, admit of application in strictly limited domains.

I mention this second point because you might be wondering about laws of psychology, laws governing the operation of the mind. Consider a law that you might think governs beliefs and desires:

(L_ψ) If an agent, S, wants x and believes y is needed to obtain x, then S wants y.

If you want to take the subway and believe that, in order to take the subway, you must buy a ticket, then you will want to buy a ticket. Although (L_ψ) governs many instances of desire formation, it is not difficult to imagine exceptions. If you believe, for instance, that you have no money, then your belief that you must buy a token to ride the subway, might lead you to cease to desire to ride the subway – or to desire to panhandle.

More significantly, you could fail to form the desire to buy a token because you are, at the instant it occurs to you that you need to buy a token, knocked unconscious by a slab of falling plaster. Note that, in this case, psychology runs up against a kind of *intervention* that involves entities and processes that fall outside the purview of psychology. Things fail to go right at the psychological level owing to occurrences at the neurobiological level. But psychological laws are necessarily silent about such occurrences: this is what makes psychological laws *psychological* laws.

The moral could be extended to the laws of every special science. According to Fodor, each special science carves up the world in a particular way and endeavors to discover laws governing the entities falling under its special categories. These entities are made up of lower-level entities. Goings-on affecting these lower-level entities can have higher-level consequences. Changes in the molecules of your brain, for instance, can have dramatic repercussions for your brain and for your state of mind as well. But the laws of each special science concern only entities at the level appropriate to that science. Psychological laws contain no mention of molecules, although molecular events in the nervous system can and certainly do affect psychological processes. So long as you regard the laws of a special science such as psychology to be *autonomous*, so long as you take them to be irreducible to laws governing lower-level entities, you can rest assured that the laws must fail to be exceptionless.

7.10   Layers of Reality

Where does all this leave functionalism and the Representational Theory of Mind? I have taken you on a rather lengthy detour though issues in the philosophy of science in order to motivate the metaphysical conception of mind that has been most influential in functionalist circles. Although not all functionalists subscribe to this picture, many do. The picture has been prominent, both in philosophy, and in allied disciplines in the cognitive sciences, so it is worth spelling out. The picture provides a rationale for the popular view that the world is *layered*, that minds are higher-level entities, and that mental properties are higher-level properties. This is a central tenet of virtually all versions of functionalism (an exception is the Armstrong–Lewis brand of functionalism mentioned in § 6.9).

You could sum up the metaphysical picture implicit in mainstream functionalism by noting that functionalists take mental terms or predicates – 'being in pain', 'believing that bears are furry' – to designate functional properties of entities to which they are ascribed. Functional properties are ultimately realized in material systems by nonfunctional properties of those systems. When you are in a particular mental state, when you are in pain, for instance, that state is realized in you by some material state of your brain. In another kind of creature, an octopus, say, or in an Alpha Centaurian, the very same mental state – pain – would be realized by a completely different kind of material state. You, an octopus, and an Alpha Centaurian are all in pain, you all possess the property of being in pain. In you, pain is realized by a particular kind of neurological process; in an octopus it is realized by a very different sort of neurological episode; in an Alpha Centaurian it is realized by a non-neurological, silicon-based process.

Functional properties, quite generally, are multiply realizable. It is anyone's guess as to what the limits might be on realizers for pain. Might a computing machine be programmed to feel pain? If a computing machine could be given the right sort of functional organization, then, according to the functionalist, it could indeed feel pain: the property of being in pain would be realized by transfers of electrons across transistors – or, in the case of Babbage's Analytical Engine, by some sequence of rotations of brass cogs and cylinders.

In all this the notion of multiple realizability is left unspecified. When a given mental state, ψ, is realized by a given physical state, ϕ, then ψ, though *distinct* from ϕ, in some way *depends* on ϕ. Spelling out this dependence relation – the realizing relation – turns out to be surprisingly difficult.

Multiple realizability and the associated idea that the world consists of levels of entities and properties resurfaces in Chapters 11 and 12. Meanwhile, it is time to consider a somewhat different approach to the mind, one that regards minds as *social constructs*, products of the interpretive practices of language users. In Chapter 10, functionalism reappears as the target of an important line of criticism that focuses on an aspect of the mind functionalists are often accused of ignoring: the *qualitative* aspect, which comes to the fore when you reflect on the nature of *conscious experiences*.

Suggested Reading

The most prominent proponent of the Representational Theory of Mind (and the Language of Thought) is Jerry Fodor. See *The Language of Thought* (1975). Kim Sterelny's *The Representational Theory of Mind: An Introduction* (1990) provides a good introduction to the Representational Theory. See Robert Cummins's *The Nature of Psychological Explanation* (1983) and Gilbert Harman's *Thought* (1973) for early statements of the view. Susan Schneider (*The Language of Thought: A New Philosophical Direction*, 2011) raises doubts about Fodor's conception of the Language of Thought and sketches an alternative.

John Haugeland elaborates the notion of a semantic engine in 'Semantic Engines: An Introduction to Mind Design' (1981b). John Searle's discussion of the Chinese Room, 'Minds, Brains, and Programs' (1980), originally appeared as a target article in *Behavioral and Brain Sciences*. The paper was accompanied by critical responses and a rejoinder by Searle. Alan Turing's appeal to the Imitation Game to explicate the concept of intelligence can be found in 'Computing Machinery and Intelligence' (1950). Haugeland's *Artificial Intelligence: The Very Idea.* (1985, 6–9) includes a convenient summary of the Turing test. See also, Gualtiero Piccinini's 'Computational Modeling vs. Computational Explanation: Is Everything a Turing Machine, and Does It Matter to the Philosophy of Mind?' (2007) and 'The Mind as

Neural Software? Understanding Functionalism, Computationalism, and Computational Functionalism' (2010).

Fodor sketches a reasonably accessible account of the semantics of the Language of Thought in his *Psychosemantics* (1988). A more recent version of the same story is told in *The Elm and the Expert: Mentalese and its Semantics* (1994). These same volumes are a good source for anyone interested in Fodor's ideas on laws, properties, and the special sciences.

Accounts of the semantics of interior states that attempt the same thing in different ways can be found in Fred Dretske, *Explaining Behavior: Reasons in a World of Causes* (1988); and in Ruth Millikan, *Language, Thought, and Other Biological Categories: New Foundations for Realism* (1984). Millikan's position is nicely summarized and defended in her 'Biosemantics' (1989). See also *Varieties of Meaning* (2004) and *Language: A Biological Model* (2005).

8 The Intentional Stance

8.1 Minds as Constructs

Approaches to the mind considered thus far are 'realist' in character. All assume that minds and their contents are bona fide features of the world, features taking their place alongside stones, tables, trees, electrons, and fields. But perhaps this is a mistake. Perhaps our unfailing realism has been the source of errors and confusions that characterize much of our theorizing about the mind. Might we do better to regard minds as *constructs*? Might the ascription of thoughts and feelings to agents resemble the ascription of a latitude and longitude to a locale on the surface of the Earth? Latitudes and longitudes are not kinds of entity, not components of the planet alongside rivers, canyons, and mountain ranges. A child who, looking at a globe, mistook the equator for a feature on the Earth's surface would be confusing a characteristic of our descriptive apparatus with a characteristic of the planet. Maybe this is how it is with us when we attempt to situate minds in a world of material bodies.

You might boggle at the thought that anyone could be tempted to suppose that minds are on a par with coordinate systems. After all, we are all intimately acquainted with our own minds, and this acquaintance appears not to be a matter of our imposing any coordinate-like system on ourselves. Further, and more to the point, it is hard to see how any such theory could possibly succeed. Pretend for a moment that ascribing states of mind resembles the application of a coordinate system on a spatial region. This application of a coordinate system is something you *do*, something that evidently depends on your having thoughts, intentions, and a broad range of distinct states of mind. In this regard coordinate systems are 'mind dependent'; their existence depends on the existence of intelligent minds. How could this model possibly apply to *minds*? How could *minds* be mind dependent?

To see the problem, pretend for a moment that minds depended on the imposition of a coordinate-like system. Suppose, for instance, that Smith's having a mind is a matter of your imposing a coordinate system on Smith. Your doing this evidently requires that *you* have a mind; however, something would seem to require another agent, Jones, to impose a system on *you*. But now the same is going to hold for Jones; Jones's having a mind depends on Jones's being interpreted by Brown. You are in this way led to a regress of minds, each depending on the prior existence of some distinct mind. If having a mind requires another mind, it is hard to see how *anything* could have a mind.

I propose to bracket this regress worry for the moment, and look in more detail at one attempt to articulate 'interpretive' accounts of the mind. Once you are clear on what such an account amounts to, you will be in a position to evaluate the seriousness of the envisaged regress. My plan is to look at the work of Daniel Dennett, an influential proponent of an interpretive conception of mind. You will see that the issues are less straightforward than a quick sketch of the regress problem above might suggest.

8.2   Taking a Stance

As you are discovering, thinking about the mind systematically can be a frustrating exercise. You are immediately aware of goings-on in your own mind, but this closeness provides little in the way of illumination. Your mind, you might think, is just your brain going about its business. But salient characteristics of minds seem alien to brains. The attraction of dualism is muted by a suspicion that, in bifurcating the world into material and nonmaterial domains, dualism places minds outside the scope of objective scientific inquiry. Materialism leaves open the possibility of inquiry, but offers no guidance as to how to proceed. We find ourselves faced with a dilemma. On the one hand, it seems right to think of minds as belonging to the natural order. On the other hand, it is hard to see how the natural order could accommodate important aspects of mentality.

Philosophical frustration, unrelieved, encourages the reexamination of presuppositions. Ryle, for instance, challenges the Cartesian picture of the 'ghost in the machine', the idea that minds are *things*, substances that animate bodies. Substituting brains for ghosts, Ryle holds, merely repackages the Cartesian folly. Once you abandon the idea that minds are things, organs responsible for intelligent action, you are in a position to recognize that, to say that a creature has a mind, is just to say that the creature is capable of intelligent, 'mindful' behavior.

Dennett, a student of Ryle's, is concerned, as his teacher was not, to advance a scientifically informed account of minds and their operation. Like Ryle, Dennett insists on distinguishing ordinary practices of mental state ascription from systematic attempts to understand mechanisms responsible for intelligent behavior. Dennett argues that the ascription of propositional attitudes – beliefs, desires, intentions – is constrained only by a weak requirement of 'rationality'. You can correctly and legitimately ascribe propositional attitudes to any system – animal, vegetable, or mineral – the behavior of which could be construed as rational in light of the system's 'ends'. The result is a deliberately 'instrumentalist' approach to the mind: a creature's *having* a mind is strictly a matter of our usefully *regarding* the creature as having a mind. This amounts, in practice, to our treating the creature as 'one of us': a being with various (mostly true) beliefs about the world and desires for particular states of affairs; a creature that acts reasonably in light of those beliefs and desires.

You observe a robin hunting worms in the garden. You explain – that is, make sense of – the robin's behavior by supposing that the robin is hungry and so seeking food. The robin *believes* that worms are food, *believes* that worms are to be found in the garden, and in consequence *desires* to hunt worms in the garden. The robin, in sum, acts reasonably in light of its beliefs and desires.

In explaining the robin's behavior by reference to beliefs and desires, you are adopting what Dennett calls the 'intentional stance'. This 'stance' is one we take up in order to *make sense of* and predict the behavior of virtually any organism. Why is that octopus emitting a black inky substance? Because the octopus believes it has been spotted by a predator, wants to protect itself, believes it can do so by placing a dark cloud between it and the predator, and believes that by emitting an inky fluid, it will cause a dark cloud to come between it and the predator. Why is this white blood cell enveloping that microbe? Because the cell wants to destroy invaders, believes the microbe is an invader, and so wants to destroy it. For its own part, the microbe wants to invade a red blood cell, believes that it is likely to find a red blood cell by swimming about randomly in the bloodstream, and so swims randomly.

Do robins, octopodes, and white blood cells *really* have the beliefs and desires you ascribe to them? Do such organisms *really* behave rationally? Or do they merely behave *as if* they had beliefs and desires (and acted reasonably in light of these)? In ascribing beliefs and desires in such cases do we really mean it, or are we speaking metaphorically or perhaps engaging in a measure of harmless anthropomorphizing?

Questions of this sort are, on Dennett's view, completely wrong-headed. A creature's having beliefs and desires *just is* a matter of the creature's behavior being describable and explicable via the intentional stance. If you can make sense of the behavior of a microbe by taking up the intentional stance toward its activities, then the microbe does indeed have beliefs and desires, hence reasons for what it does. There is no more to having beliefs and acting on reasons than this, there is no *further* question whether the beliefs and reasons are really there.

You might object. If this is all having beliefs, desires, and reasons amounts to, then plants must have beliefs, desires, and reasons, too! This elm sinks its roots deep into the soil because it wants to find water and believes that water is likely to be found at greater depths. More shockingly, on a view of this sort what would prevent *artifacts* – your laptop computer, or even a lowly thermostat from having beliefs and desires? Your laptop computer is displaying a 'printer is out of paper' alert because it believes that the printer is out of paper, and wants you to refill the paper tray. The thermostat turns on the furnace because it believes that the room temperature has dropped below 20° C, and it wants to increase the temperature to at least 20° C.

You might concede that, although we – all of us, really – *talk* this way on occasion, we do so merely as a matter of convenience. You can see single-celled organisms, plants, and artifacts as loosely *analogous* to rational agents in certain ways. Thus there is no harm in speaking of them *as if* they were like us in those ways. But of course they are not *really* like us. Their behavior is governed by far simpler mechanisms. To imagine that they have – *really have* – beliefs and desires, to suppose that they have – *really have* – reasons for what they do, is to mistake the metaphorical for the literal.

Dennett insists, however, that ascriptions of beliefs and desires to single-celled organisms, plants, and artifacts are no more metaphorical than is the ascription of beliefs and desires to our fellow human beings. *All there is* to an entity's having beliefs and desires, *all there is* to an entity's acting on reasons, is the entity's *behaving as if* it had beliefs and desires and acted on reasons. In ascribing beliefs, desires, and reasons to organisms or objects, you adopt the intentional stance. The intentional stance enables you to make sense of, predict, and cope with the behavior of whatever falls under it. But it will do this quite independently of whether those entities have an internal makeup resembling ours.

As noted earlier, a doctrine of this kind construes the propositional attitudes 'instrumentally'. That is, the correctness of an attribution of beliefs, desires, and reasons for action lies, not in its corresponding to some independent fact or state of affairs, but to its serviceability. To the extent that the practice of ascribing propositional attitudes serves our interests, to the extent that it enables us to make sense of and predict the behavior of objects with which we interact, it is fully justified. To expect anything more, to take a baldly 'realist' line on beliefs, desires, and reasons for action is to miss the point of the practice.

Return for a moment to an example mentioned at the start of this chapter: a child who mistakes the equator on a globe for a geological feature of the planet. Imagine that the child is on a ship that crosses the equator. The child is assured that the ship is indeed crossing the equator, but all the child sees is open water. A child of philosophical bent might reason that, if the equator is not a visible something it must be an invisible something, a visually undetectable *immaterial* entity. Compare the child to a philosopher who mistakes beliefs and desires for features – inner features – of intelligent creatures. When these fail to be found among the material features of such creatures, the philosopher concludes that they must be immaterial (or perhaps 'higher-level') entities. In both cases, the mistake is to imagine that components of a scheme we use to describe aspects of the world designate features of the world.

8.3   From Intentional Stance to Design Stance

An entity's having beliefs, desires, and reasons for action, then, is simply a matter of that entity's being susceptible to descriptions framed in terms of beliefs, desires, and reasons. In deploying such descriptions, you take up the intentional stance. You find this unavoidable in the case of your fellow human beings, and equally unavoidable in attempting to come to terms with the exploits of nonhuman creatures. In the case of simple organisms, plants, and inanimate objects, you find that you can, in most cases, dispense with the intentional stance and explain their behavior by working out their *design*. In so doing, you descend to what Dennett calls the *design stance*. You make sense of the behavior of objects by regarding them as having been designed or engineered in a particular way to achieve a particular end.

You can describe the behavior of your desktop computer by attributing various beliefs and desires to it. But a programmer is in a position to make sense of the device's behavior by reference to its program. In the same way, a biologist is in a position to explain the behavior of a white blood cell, by reflecting on its design from an evolutionary perspective. The design of a desktop computer has a human origin. The design of a white blood cell, or the circulatory system of a frog, or the mechanism that controls the growth of a plant reflects the hand of Mother Nature. Evolutionary pressures ensure that badly engineered mechanisms, those that prove maladaptive, are weeded out.

The design stance does not *replace* the intentional stance. When you arrive at a 'design-level' understanding of a white blood cell or the behavior of a bird protecting her nestlings by feigning injury, you do not *falsify* claims made from the intentional standpoint. On the contrary, you merely offer a different kind of explanation as to why such claims might hold. Such explanations in many ways resemble functional explanations. But your capacity to deploy the design stance in particular instances does not, according to Dennett, mean that beliefs, desires, and reasons for action are, at bottom, functional states.

You adopt the intentional stance when your interest in understanding or explaining the behavior of some entity is largely action-oriented – when you have an interest in predicting, quickly and without expending much effort, how that entity is likely to behave. If this is your aim, the intentional stance is brilliantly cost-effective. You resort to the design stance only when your interests change and when circumstances make it possible (or desirable) to examine more carefully and systematically mechanisms controlling a creature's activities. An ethologist adopts the design stance in explaining the behavior of a particular species of bird, but a hunter need not, and typically will not.

Psychologists, psychobiologists, sociobiologists, and, in general, cognitive scientists adopt in their various ways the design stance toward human beings. Once again, this is not a matter of rejecting or negating the intentional stance we take up in order to make sense of one another's behavior by appealing to beliefs, desires, and reasons. Nor, on Dennett's view, is it a matter of discovering that beliefs, desires, and reasons are at bottom functional states responsible for behavior. Beliefs, desires, and reasons for action ascribable to you are so ascribable, perhaps, because you have the functional architecture you have. But beliefs, desires, and reasons are not causally potent components of that architecture. A move to talk of causes and mechanisms of behavior is a move to the design stance.

What, then, would a design-level description of a human being look like? You can get some idea by reflecting on what scientific investigators tell us about, for instance, the mechanisms of vision, or memory, or language-processing. Explanations of such things involve appeals to details of our nervous system – components of the retina and optic nerve, for instance – in a way that regards these as subserving particular systemic ends. Examples of the design stance taken toward human and nonhuman creatures' capacities abound in psychology and biology textbooks.

In adopting the design stance you, in effect, take up the intentional stance toward mechanisms you regard as underlying creatures' behavior. You see these mechanisms (as opposed to the creature as a whole) as having ends, and working to achieve them. You might worry that this imports an unwarranted anthropomorphic element into our fine-grained accounts of creatures' inner workings. You might worry as well that the strategy bogs down in a kind of circularity: complex states of mind are explained by positing mechanisms that possess the very features we had hoped to explain. To what extent are these worries well-founded?

8.4   From Design Stance to Physical Stance

Dennett's idea is that you might account for mental phenomena by, for instance, finding neural mechanisms capable of a design-level description, one that, true enough, involves seeing those mechanisms as working to achieve certain goals. The explanatory process need not stop there, however. You move to explain *these* mechanisms by uncovering simpler mechanisms that make them up, sub-mechanisms. The retina is taken to perform a particular intelligent function, and this is explained by discovering that the retina consists of rods, cones, and assorted other cells that themselves perform intelligent, but much more limited, narrowly-directed functions. As you analyze systems into their component subsystems in this way, you eventually arrive at a level at which the constituent mechanisms are acutely focused, obsessively 'single-minded'. At this level of analysis, you might expect to find, for instance, individual cells that do nothing more than detect the presence or absence of a particular chemical substance and notify neighboring cells accordingly.

When you reach this level, you have in effect 'discharged' the design stance, and thereby moved to the *physical stance*. You can see *how* the imagined cell performs its function by examining its chemistry, its material makeup. In this way your investigations are grounded in the nonmental, non-intentional, and the threat of circularity is deflected. Intentionality, that feature of thoughts in virtue of which they are *of* or *about* one thing or another, is seen to stem from the biochemistry of organisms enjoying it.

8.5   The Emerging Picture

Functionalists regard it as a significant empirical question whether creatures – or artifacts – to which we commonly and unhesitatingly ascribe beliefs, desires, and reasons for action – do in fact harbor beliefs, desires, and reasons. The question is one that might be resolved for a given creature by discovering whether that creature sufficiently resembled us functionally. Dennett regards the picture implicit in this approach as a red herring. The *having* of beliefs and desires is wholly a matter of being so describable. When you regard it as more than that, when you imagine that in ascribing beliefs, desires, and reasons you are identifying components of mechanisms causally responsible for behavior, you run the risk of anthropomorphizing and thereby missing important discontinuities between the minds of human beings and the minds of other creatures.

This way of putting it might seem surprising. After all, the near universal applicability of the intentional stance could easily strike you as heavily anthropomorphic. Dennett's idea is straightforward, however. In taking up the intentional stance – in ascribing beliefs, desires, and reasons for action – you deploy a system of categories that enables you to sort out and predict the behavior of creatures, artifacts, and natural systems. The justification of this practice depends, not on its successfully cataloging cogs and levers responsible for the operation of whatever it is you hope to explain, but on its utility. For a great many purposes, this is all you need. You explain to a companion what your laptop computer is doing by noting that it *wants* to print a document, *discovers* that the printer is out of paper, and *hopes* to attract your attention with a bouncing icon.

The italicized words in the preceding sentence are not, if Dennett is right, used metaphorically: they hold literally of your laptop computer; you are using them in exactly the sense you would use them in describing the behavior of a fellow human being. You would err, however, if you imagined that what goes on *inside* your laptop computer resembles – functionally or otherwise – what goes on inside a human being. Understanding what makes *us* tick requires a descent to the design stance. And when you descend, you begin to notice vast differences between laptop computers, human beings, and various nonhuman creatures, differences that are invisible so long as you remain at the intentional level.

As noted earlier, in taking up the design stance you, in effect, extend the intentional stance to mechanisms responsible for the behavior of intelligent systems. The project is saved from circularity or a bottomless regress by the fact that it is premised on the possibility that you could successively analyze intelligent systems into subsystems until you arrive at a systemic level, the operation of which is, although perhaps physically complex, trivial from a design perspective. Here you move to the physical stance and 'discharge' your higher-level talk of beliefs, desires, and reasons for action. Your arriving at this level, your taking up the physical stance, does not falsify or replace your higher-level intentional stance and design stance assessments, however. To imagine that it does, is to lose sight of the utility and economy afforded by the intentional and design stances. This utility and economy provide all the justification anyone could need for deploying them. So says Dennett.

8.6   Thought and Language

In common with most theorists who regard themselves as cognitive scientists, Dennett accepts the idea that human beings and nonhuman creatures process information and internally manipulate *representations* of their surroundings. It is one thing for a creature's behavior to be guided by representations, however, and quite another matter for a creature to *appreciate* that this is what it is doing. There is, Dennett contends, not merely a difference in *degree*, but a difference in *kind* between a capacity for representation (a capacity, according to Dennett, possessed by single-celled organisms and thermostats) and a capacity for *higher-order representation*: representation *of representations* – or representation of oneself as representing. Only creatures capable of surveying their own representations (and recognizing these representations as theirs), only creatures capable of taking up the intentional stance toward *themselves*, deserve to be described as 'thinking'.

The behavior of sea slugs and single-celled creatures suggests that they are guided by representations of aspects of their limited horizons, but you need not regard such creatures as capable of thought in the strictest sense. What of beagles, or dolphins, or chimpanzees? Again, a case can be made for saying that such creatures represent their surroundings. Do they think? They do so, Dennett contends, only if they represent self-consciously, only if they possess a capacity for second-order representation, a capacity to appreciate, hence represent, representations *as* representations.

This latter capacity, Dennett believes, emerges with the advent of language. If you accept Dennett's suggestion that thinking includes an ability to manipulate representations self-consciously, then it would follow that thought and language go hand in hand. This is not because language is required as a *medium* or *vehicle* for thought. (This is the view of proponents of the Language of Thought.) Thinking need not be linguistic or language-like; thought could be non-sentential, or 'pictorial'.

The connection between thought and language is less direct. Evolutionary pressures for self-conscious representation are absent until the birth of cooperative communication. Communication provides a mechanism for the sharing of information. More importantly (from an evolutionary perspective), communication provides a way for creatures to turn the possession of information not possessed by others to their own advantage. If I know something you do not know and are unlikely to know unless I tell you, I can trade my information for some benefit, or, if it serves my interests, *mislead* you.

If you look at the evolutionary paths of nonhuman species, you will see that members of those species typically inhabit surroundings in which information obtained by one individual is likely to be obtainable by every other individual. When this is not so, practices of deception can emerge (as when chimpanzees take steps to prevent fellow chimpanzees from discovering a hidden morsel of food). Such practices mandate a degree of representational sophistication that constitutes what might be called 'proto-thought', a stage on the evolutionary road to fully fledged thinking.

Infants and young children probably lack the kind of reflective capacities that Dennett considers necessary for genuine thought. In one much discussed experiment, a child watches a puppet hide a toy in a particular place. The puppet goes away and, during its absence, the experimenter, in full view of the child, moves the toy to a *new* hiding place. The child is then asked where the puppet will look for the toy when it returns. Three-year-olds typically say that the puppet will look in the *new* hiding place; older children reply that the puppet will look where the toy was originally hidden.

One possible explanation for this disparity is that, although younger children represent the world, they are as yet unable to represent *representations* of the world. In that case the children would be in no position to represent the puppet's imagined representations of the world, and thus unable to regard the puppet as falsely representing the toy's location. Predicting that the puppet will look in the new hiding place would not, or so it is claimed, require the child to represent the puppet as having a true representation, hence does not require the child to represent the puppet as representing anything. Think of these representations as *beliefs*. Younger children, it appears, have a capacity for belief, but not a capacity for second-order belief, a capacity for beliefs about beliefs.

The argument implicit in Dennett's line of reasoning is founded, not on purely philosophical a priori considerations concerning what suffices for thought. It is rather that, when you look below the surface at how other creatures do what they do, you are not tempted in the slightest to imagine that they engage in self-conscious thinking in anything like the sense in which you and I do. A philosopher or a devoted pet owner might point out that it is still possible that infants, or chimpanzees, or dolphins, or beagles engage in elaborate, but secret cogitations. This impression, Dennett suggests, is just the result of deploying the intentional stance over-zealously.

Once you realize this, once you descend to the design stance, you discover that nature has provided surprisingly elegant solutions to problems posed by the environment. Were you to set out to build a nest, you would no doubt first plan a course of action and keep this plan in mind – modifying it as necessary – as you proceeded with the task. Encouraged by the intentional stance, you might imagine that a bird building a nest operates in much the same way. When you begin to study the behavior of birds more carefully, however, you learn that their elaborate, and in many cases ingenious, solutions to the 'nest-building problem' are not the result of elaborate and ingenious thoughts but are products of simpler mechanisms shaped by evolution. The mechanisms are ingenious certainly, but the ingenuity is Mother Nature's, not the birds'.

Do not be misled by reference to creatures' being guided by representations or by representations of representations. Dennett's talk of representations is not talk of entities inside the head that have distinctive causal roles analogous to sentences in the Language of Thought postulated by the Representational Theory of Mind. For Dennett, the only question is whether you can make sense of a creature's behavior at the design level without having to introduce second-order representations, representations of representations, that is, without having to suppose the creature in question is capable of taking up the intentional stance toward other creatures.

8.7   Kinds of Mind

Although you are within your rights to describe infants, chimpanzees, dolphins, beagles, sea slugs, even thermostats as having beliefs, desires, and reasons for what they do, Dennett contends that you would do well to reserve the notion of *thought* for creatures who, like yourself, have evolved with a capacity for self-conscious representation, a capacity to entertain representations of representations. Does this mean that only creatures resembling us have minds? Not according to Dennett. Having a mind is a matter of being guided by representations, that is, of behaving in ways that can be explained by appeal to representations. And we have ample evidence that the activities of infants, chimpanzees, dolphins, beagles, and sea slugs are governed by representations of their goals and circumstances. Perhaps this is so even for the lowly thermostat.

Conceding that sea slugs and thermostats have minds, however, is not to concede very much – at least not if Dennett is right about minds. You can still identify vast qualitative disparities among *kinds* of mind. Dennett envisages a hierarchy. At the basic level, are primitive 'Darwinian' minds, minds hard-wired to respond in optimal, albeit relatively fixed, ways to a relatively stable environment. Darwinian minds are possessed by the simplest creatures, those that have evolved adaptive solutions to problems posed by their circumstances. In the case of Darwinian creatures, the steps from the intentional stance to the design stance, and from the design stance to the physical stance, can be relatively direct.

At a rung above Darwinian creatures are creatures endowed with 'Skinnerian minds' (named in honor of the behaviorist psychologist, B. F. Skinner). Skinnerian minds are possessed by creatures capable of learning via operant conditioning – trial and error. A creature possessing a Skinnerian mind exhibits a degree of mental 'plasticity' not possessed by simpler Darwinian creatures. A Skinnerian creature can adapt its behavior to changes in its circumstances. In this way creatures endowed with Skinnerian minds have a hand in shaping themselves to fit their environmental niche. For Darwinian creatures, this role is played exclusively by Mother Nature: Darwinian minds are shaped wholly by evolutionary pressures. For such creatures, adapting to changing circumstances is not an option.

'Popperian minds' belong to creatures who have managed the trick of representing their environment in a way that enables them to test likely outcomes of distinct courses of action 'in their heads', and so to learn without the attendant risk of potentially lethal errors.

Why 'Popperian'? Popperian minds operate on principles reminiscent of those the philosopher Karl Popper takes to lie at the heart of scientific rationality. According to Popper, the success of science as a rational enterprise hinges on scientists' willingness to engage in 'conjecture and refutation'. Theories are conjectured and tested against the evidence. A theory is accepted to the extent that it survives rigorous testing.

A Skinnerian learns from experience, trial and error; a Popperian can learn by anticipating experience. Rats are evidently Popperian. A rat allowed to explore a maze can later put its knowledge of the maze to use in attaining a particular reward. The rat does so (according to psychologist E. C. Tolman) by constructing a 'cognitive map' of the maze. Once constructed, this 'map' can be used to the rat's advantage in negotiating the maze to obtain a food pellet.

> Skinnerian creatures ask themselves, 'What should I do next?' and haven't a clue how to answer until they have taken some hard knocks. Popperian creatures make a big advance by asking themselves, 'What should I think about next?' before they ask themselves, 'What should I do next?' (It should be emphasized that neither Skinnerian nor Popperian creatures actually need to talk to themselves or think these thoughts. They are simply designed to operate *as if* they had asked themselves these questions.)
>
> (Dennet 1996, 100)

At the top of Dennett's hierarchy are creatures endowed with 'Gregorian minds' (so named, not for the Pope, but for the psychologist, Richard Gregory). A creature possessing a Gregorian mind, like its Popperian counterparts, is capable of testing hypotheses in its head. The difference is that Gregorian minds are capable of representing *self-consciously*. This opens up new horizons and possibilities, not available to Popperians.

Human beings, endowed as we are with language, possess Gregorian minds. We are also, in some measure, Darwinian, Skinnerian, and Popperian. The human nervous system bears the marks of its evolutionary history, exhibiting Darwinian, Skinnerian, Popperian, and Gregorian aspects. Any complex action requires the coordination of all of these elements. You must not, then, conflate kinds of mind with kinds of creature. The brain of a Skinnerian creature, for instance, a creature capable of learning, incorporates Darwinian – hard-wired – mechanisms, as do sophisticated mammalian brains. A Gregorian creature, one capable of self-reflection, is not *non*-Darwinian, or *non*-Skinnerian, or *non*-Popperian. Rather, Gregorian creatures – among terrestrial species, human beings – have evolved additional capacities that distinguish their minds from the minds of creatures lacking self-consciousness, capacities bound up with a capacity for linguistic communication.

Important differences between Gregorian and other sorts of creature are largely invisible so long as you rest content with the intentional stance. You ascribe beliefs, desires, and reasons for action in a way that, wrongly interpreted, can make minds of non-Gregorian creatures appear Gregorian. So long as your interest is merely in interacting with and predicting the behavior of such creatures, this attitude is perfectly justified. But when you pursue a deeper understanding of what makes creatures tick, when you seek to refine your understanding and increase your prospects of predicting and manipulating creatures' behavior, you are bound to look below the surface. When you do, when you descend to the design stance, you discover that differences swamp similarities.

Most notably you discover that the intelligence of nonhuman creatures is, in comparison to our own, rigid and 'gappy'. Spot, whose behavior exhibits considerable intelligence in many domains, is unable to arrive at a solution to the problem of how to unwind his leash from a lamp post. It seems not to occur to dolphins (regarded by some enthusiasts as our intellectual peers) to try to escape tuna nets by leaping over them, although this is something any dolphin might easily do.

These gaps in intelligence appear puzzling only so long as you imagine that other creatures think as you do. The results of careful experimental work suggest otherwise. Thus, impressive as they are, tool-using chimpanzees and ants that engage in 'farming' fungus harvested for food all fall well short of the Gregorian plateau. Reports of chimpanzees (and other apes) engaging in apparently deceptive practices might suggest that this assessment is overly pessimistic: perhaps chimpanzees have a 'theory of mind' that they put to use in deciding how to interact with their fellows. Dennett discourages this interpretation. The intelligence displayed by chimpanzees and other nonhuman creatures does not call for the Gregorian solution. Indeed, if you interpret chimpanzees as thinking as you would about matters that concern them, then their inability to generalize this thinking in obvious ways appears baffling.

8.8   Consciousness

What of conscious experiences? Many philosophers of mind regard consciousness as the stumbling block for naturalistic, scientifically inspired accounts of the mind. According to Dennett, however, the 'problem of consciousness'

– what David Chalmers calls 'the hard problem' – is a problem of our own making. An obsession with the qualitative aspect of experience, its 'feel', its 'what-it's-like-ness', has prevented philosophers from appreciating a solution to the alleged mystery of consciousness that is ready to hand.

Dennett's idea is implicit in his discussion of higher-order representation. Representations play an important role in the production of behavior in even the simplest creatures. Consciousness, however, emerges only with the capacity to reflect on these representations, and this capacity, according to Dennett, is linked to the ability to deploy language. Strictly speaking, thought and consciousness are possible only for linguistically endowed creatures. For such creatures, conscious states of mind are not those exhibiting distinctive *qualitative* or 'phenomenological' features, or those located in some private chamber of the mind, but those that, in competition with other representational elements, assume control of behavior.

Why should this feature be thought to suffice for consciousness? Surely more is required for representational states to take on the characteristics of a conscious experience.

> Such questions betray a deep confusion, for they presuppose that what *you* are is something *else*, some Cartesian *res cogitans* in addition to all this brain and body activity. What you are, however, just *is* this organization of all the competitive activity between a host of competencies that your body has developed.
>
> (Dennett 1996, 155–6)

Does this mean that other creatures – chimpanzees, dolphins, beagles – are 'zombies', that they do not feel pain, for instance? No. Such creatures have pains and assorted other sensory states. What they lack is an additional capacity to reflect on these states. And this lack, Dennett suggests, means that, although they may be said to feel pain, they do not 'suffer'. Attempts to model their pains on ours are invariably misleading.

Dennett is aware that, in advancing such a view, he is opening himself to attack from pet owners and animal rights activists. He argues, however, that our moral obligation to refrain from needlessly harming other creatures stems, not from their possession of a capacity to suffer as we do, but merely from the fact that they, like us, can *experience* pain. A capacity for pain, however, is to be distinguished from a higher-level capacity, your capacity to reflect that you are in pain. A creature lacking this capacity cannot dwell on its pain, or dread its onset, or be haunted by painful memories. And, says Dennett, a capacity for such things underlies the capacity for suffering.

How could one's possession of the capacity for self-reflection affect the *feeling* of pain, the *qualitative* dimension of an experience of pain? Dennett thinks this is the wrong question to ask. Experiential qualities – *qualia* – are dubious entities, artifacts of an outmoded and discredited Cartesian conception of the mind. You can account for the apparent prominence of these qualities by recognizing that when you are in pain, for instance, you are in a particular kind of state, one that, among other things, leads you to believe that you are in a state with particular qualities. Creatures lacking language lack a capacity for higher-order, reflective thought, hence for thoughts of this sort. Such creatures can be in states functionally resembling your pain states, but they lack the wherewithal to reflect on those states.

Does this imply that such creatures *feel nothing* when they are in pain? The question, for Dennett, presupposes what is false, namely that pain states or episodes possess intrinsic qualitative 'phenomenal' features. They do not. This does not mean that nonhuman creatures do not undergo pain, or that their pains are less intense or distressing than ours. To think that would be to assume – again, falsely – that pains are what they are – *pains* – in virtue of their intrinsic qualitative 'phenomenal character'. *Nothing* possesses an intrinsic qualitative 'phenomenal character', however! The fact, if it is a fact, that pain states lack it, then, is entirely unremarkable. Functionalists might agree (§ 6.11). (See Chapters 10 and 13 for more on experiential qualities.)

If you find this view puzzling or implausible, you are not alone. To his credit, Dennett takes seriously the problem of reconciling the apparent qualitative nature of conscious experience with the character of the material states and episodes that seem to 'underlie' such experiences. As many philosophers like to point out, it is hard to see how these could be reconciled without accepting some form of dualism.

One way to see what Dennett is up to is to compare the qualitative dimension of a pain with the qualitative aspect of an after-image. (An after-image is what occurs when, for instance, you 'see spots' after a camera flash has gone off in your face.) When you experience a round yellowy-orange after-image, nothing material in your vicinity – and certainly nothing in your brain – need be round and yellowy-orange (see §§ 5.9–5.10, 10.8, 13.8). Similarly, when you experience a pain as dull and throbbing, nothing need be dull or throbbing. Perhaps this is no more mysterious than our entertaining thoughts of dragons or mermaids when there are no dragons or mermaids.

8.9   Searle's Objection

One response to such attempts to analyze away the qualities of conscious experience is to argue, as John Searle has, that the move merely represses a problem without solving it. Searle's argument is straightforward. Suppose you hallucinate a tangerine-colored geranium on the table in front of you. There need be nothing tangerine-colored or geranium-shaped in your vicinity. But now consider your hallucination itself. We seem to have removed a tangerine-colored or geranium-shaped item from the public material world, and placed it inside your mind. The qualities you seem to find in the 'external world' exist, perhaps, but 'only in your mind'. Nevertheless, they indisputably exist there: *in your mind*. And this is no help at all if our aim is to advance a fully materialist conception of mind.

Recalling a point encountered in Chapter 1, we commonly distinguish appearance from reality. When it comes to the mind, however, appearance *is* reality. Suppose you agree that something's merely *appearing* pink is a matter, not of its *being* pink, but of your being in a particular kind of mental state. You banish the perceived pinkness – the *appearance* of pinkness – to the mind. Searle takes Dennett to be attempting a similar move with respect to *experienced* pinkness. But how, Searle asks, is this supposed to work? Perhaps experienced pinkness is 'merely apparent'. This means that your experience of pinkness is just a matter of your taking yourself to be experiencing pinkness. And this just seems only to move the troublesome 'phenomenal quality' from a first-order perceptual experience to a second-order experience, an experience of an experience (just as the quality was originally moved from the external world into the mind). This does not remove the troublesome quality, however. It merely shifts it from one venue to another.

From this it seems to follow that attempts to dispense with qualities of conscious experiences by attaching them to higher-order mental states – your beliefs about the pain you now feel, for instance – are bound to fail. You eliminate the problematic qualities from pain states only by depositing them in *representations* of pain states.

These issues have arisen in earlier chapters (see especially § 5.10). There you saw that it is vital to distinguish qualities of objects experienced from qualities of experiences. Your visual experience of a red tomato in bright sunlight has a distinctive qualitative character. You can designate these qualities by mentioning their causes: experiential qualities of the sort attendant on looking at brightly illuminated ripe tomatoes. But it would be a mistake to confuse qualities of the cause with qualities of the effect. An *experience* of a red tomato – what you might naturally call a 'red experience' – need not *itself* be red. In fact, an experience, unlike a ripe tomato, is not the sort of thing that *could* be red. When you hallucinate a red tomato, or for that matter experience a vivid reddish after-image, you undergo an experience something like the experience you undergo when you see a red tomato in bright sunlight. And again, although your experience is *of* a reddish, round object, your experience is not itself round or reddish.

The point of all this is to suggest that Searle's contention that, when it comes to the mind, appearance *is* reality, is scarcely uncontentious. If Searle means that when you undergo a reddish after-image, when something appears reddish to you, then something *is* reddish – if not something outside you, then a mental something, a 'red appearance' – the contention seems unwarranted. If, however, you interpret Searle as saying something weaker, namely that when you experience something your experience has a distinctive character, then it is not clear how deeply it cuts against Dennett.

It would be odd to deny that experiences have any qualitative character whatever. If tomatoes have qualities, so do the nervous systems of human beings. Suppose you interpret Dennett – charitably – to be denying only that experiences have the qualities of experienced objects. A vivid visual experience of a brightly illuminated red tomato need not itself be bright red. Then Searle's complaint that Dennett cannot account for the appearances looks misguided.

Searle's attack is on the right track in one respect, however. If you distinguish carefully qualities of objects (hallucinatory or otherwise) from the qualities of our experiences of those objects, then there is no particular incentive to introduce higher-order states of mind – beliefs about one's pains, for instance – to account for the qualities of conscious experience. If your having a conscious experience is a matter of your being in a particular state, a particular *qualitative* state, no fancy philosophical footwork is required to accommodate conscious qualities.

In any case, the move to higher-order states to account for conscious experiences ought immediately to arouse suspicion. Suppose you believe that France is roughly hexagonal. Your having this belief, on most views, Dennett's included, need not be a matter of your undergoing a conscious experience. Now imagine that, on reflection, you come to believe that you believe that France is roughly hexagonal. Your having this belief is a matter of your being in a particular second-order state, your having a belief about a belief. But if your original belief was not itself conscious, why should the addition of a second-order belief-about-a-belief render it conscious? The second-order belief is on a par with its first-order counterpart. Why should a pair of nonconscious states occurring in tandem add up to consciousness?

It would not be to the point to note that self-reflective thoughts are often conscious. The question is whether consciousness is brought about by second-order thought. Surely you are conscious of many things – your surroundings, for instance, or the disposition of your limbs – without being aware that you are aware of these things. Second-order states of mind, although undoubtedly important, seem ill-suited to marking off the boundary between 'conscious' and 'nonconscious'.

Perhaps this is too quick. Many philosophers side with Dennett in thinking that the key to consciousness lies in higher-order thought, thoughts about thoughts. The topic is one you will encounter again in Chapters 10 and 13.

Suggested Reading

A good place to start for readers seeking an introduction to Daniel Dennett's work is *Kinds of Minds: Toward an Understanding of Consciousness* (1996). Anyone wanting more details should consult *The Intentional Stance* (1987), and *Consciousness Explained* (1991a); see also 'Real Patterns' (1991b). In *The Nature of True Minds* (Heil 1992, chapter 6), I discuss and embellish an argument – very different from Dennett's – deployed by Davidson to establish that thought requires language. Davidson's own account of the relation of language and thought can be found in 'Thought and Talk' (1975) and in 'Rational Animals' (1982). I also discuss at length Davidson's influential approach to minds and their contents in chapter 9, second edition of *Philosophy of Mind: A Contemporary Introduction* (Heil 2004).

E. C. Tolman's discussion of rats' use of 'cognitive maps' to negotiate mazes can be found in his 'Cognitive Maps in Rats and Men' (1948). My depiction of an experiment designed to show that very young children lack a capacity for representing self-consciously is an amalgam of a number of experiments. See Heinz Wimmer and Josef Perner, 'Beliefs about Beliefs: Representation and Constraining Function of Wrong Beliefs in Young Children's Understanding of Deception' (1983). See also Perner's *Understanding the Representational Mind* (1991). Related experimental work can be found in Alison Gopnik and J. W. Astington, 'Children's Understanding of Representational Change and its Relation to the Understanding of False Belief and the Appearance–Reality Distinction' (1988), and Louis J. Moses and J. H. Flavell, 'Inferring False Beliefs from Actions and Reactions' (1990). (I am grateful to Eric Schwitzgebel for these references.)

Jonathan Bennett's succinct *Rationality* (1964) comprises a fascinating thought experiment involving honeybees designed to illuminate the relation of the capacity for language and the capacity for rational thought. Bennett's follow-up, *Linguistic Behaviour* (1976), is more challenging. José Bermúdez's *Thinking Without Words* (2003) provides an interesting treatment of the question whether language is required for thought. What makes the book especially valuable is Bermúdez's discussion of empirical work on the topic.

The line of argument I attribute to Searle against Dennett's notion that consciousness could be understood as a kind of second-order representation can be found in *The Rediscovery of the Mind* (1992, chapter 5, esp. 121–2). See also Searle's review of Chalmers' *The Conscious Mind: In Search of a Fundamental Theory* (1996) in 'Consciousness and the Philosophers' (1997). Chalmers' reply to Searle, and Searle's response, appears in 'Consciousness and the Philosophers: An Exchange' (1997).

9 Eliminativism

9.1 From Instrumentalism to Eliminativism

Dennett defends an avowedly 'instrumentalist' conception of minds: the utility of talk about minds and their contents – beliefs, desires, and the like – depends on the usefulness of such talk in description and explanation. A doctrine of this kind could be contrasted with 'realist' conceptions of the mind. Realists take talk of minds, their states, and their contents to be on a par with talk of planets, rocks, and trees. Beliefs, desires, pains, and emotions are genuine constituents of the world, constituents that figure in real mechanisms responsible for the production of intelligent behavior.

If you are attracted to an instrumentalist conception of the mind, you might want to consider a dark cousin of this conception: *eliminative materialism*. Eliminativists hold that really there *are* no intentional states: no beliefs, no desires, no intentions, no reasons for actions. Eliminative materialism has been promoted by Richard Rorty, Patricia and Paul Churchland, and by Stephen Stich, among others.

Eliminativism is worth a look for two reasons. First, it represents what could seem a perfectly natural extension of Dennett's thoughts on the intentional stance. Dennett holds that the ascription of familiar psychological states – beliefs, desires, and reasons for action, for instance – is just a way of coping with complex systems. If, however, you want to understand exactly how those systems operate, you must abandon the intentional stance, move to the design stance, and eventually to the physical stance. This makes it appear that conventional talk of minds and their contents represents, at bottom, a kind of pretense, one that, were our concern solely an accurate plumbing of reality, we could all live without.

A second reason for taking eliminativism seriously is that someone might be tempted to describe the identity theory or the sort of position discussed in § 11.8 as eliminativist. Understanding why that is not so requires understanding what 'realism about minds' requires. Having a clear view of what exactly eliminativism amounts to will put you in a position to distinguish realism from its denial.

9.2 Ontological Commitment

What exactly do eliminative materialists hope to eliminate? The quick answer is that eliminativists eliminate minds. This conjures an image of jack-booted troopers scouring the countryside on a mission to eradicate minds, perhaps with the aim of turning a terrified populace into zombies.

You will be heartened (or maybe disappointed) to learn that this is not what eliminativists are about. Indeed, the label 'eliminative materialism' is inherently misleading. Eliminativists deny that anything in the world answers to our talk about minds, mental states, and mental processes. You cannot 'eliminate' what never existed, so the idea that eliminativists want to do away with minds is confused. Rather, eliminativists argue that reference to minds and states of mind could – and ought to be – eliminated from descriptions and explanations of the nature and behavior of sentient creatures.

Why should anyone care? Why should the possible elimination of a way of talking, a way of describing the world, have any interesting implications for how things stand in the world?

You have much to say about the world. Some of what you say is intended to describe features of the world that you regard as 'really existing'. When you mention the moon or DNA molecules, you mean to be endorsing the idea that such things are *out there*, that they exist and affect us in various ways. But what about talk of the income of the average taxpayer, or the remarkable team spirit exhibited by the Australian XI against England? Is there an average taxpayer? Is there, in addition to the enthusiastic play of the Australian XI, a team spirit?

Eliminativists (and legions of philosophers with little sympathy for eliminativism) would answer such questions by appealing to W. V. Quine's 'criterion of ontological commitment' (Quine 1948). If, says Quine, you want to know the kinds of entity to which you are 'committed', what entities you take to be genuine, mind-independent denizens of the universe, consider what you ineliminably 'quantify over' in scientific theories you accept.

To understand Quine's principle, first consider what it means to 'quantify over' something. Start with the idea that you could take any theory and express it in a canonical notation: Quine's preference is for a first-order logic (the logic you study when you study elementary logic). Suppose you have a theory that tells you among other things, that there are electrons and that electrons are negatively charged. These assertions would be expressed in a first-order logic as

1    $\exists x E x$
2    $\forall x (E x \supset N x)$

In English, 'there is at least one thing, x, such that x is an electron' and 'if anything, x, is an electron, x is negatively charged'. The first sentence features an *existential quantifier*, '$\exists x$', read as 'some', or 'at least one'; the second sentence includes a *universal quantifier*, '∀x', that expresses the sense of 'all' or 'any'. In deploying these sentences, you are 'quantifying over' electrons, and things that are negatively charged. This means, if Quine is right, that, in accepting these sentences, or their natural language equivalents, as true, you are 'committed to the existence' of electrons and negative charge.

What of team spirit and the income of the average taxpayer? Quine's suggestion is that such terms function as a kind of shorthand for more complex expressions concerning the comportment of particular cricket players and the sum of the incomes of all the taxpayers divided by the number of individual taxpayers. In this way reference to team spirit and average taxpayers can be 'paraphrased away' – *eliminated* – from your overall theory of the world. Because 'quantification over' average taxpayers or team spirit is eliminable, you are not committed to the existence of either.

What is eliminated here are not *entities*, but *terms* purporting to refer to entities. There are at least two ways of doing this. First, as with the average taxpayer, you might recognize a term as abbreviation for some less elegant phrase, or as a *façon de parler*, a figurative expression. Second, you might discover that a term you once thought referred to some real feature of the world, does not. In the seventeenth and eighteenth centuries chemists explained combustion by reference to an element they called *phlogiston*. When combustion occurs, when you burn a log in the fireplace, phlogiston is driven out, and you are left with a 'dephlogisticated' residue, the original substance 'purified'. Chemists, in effect, 'quantified over' phlogiston in their theories, they manifested an ontological commitment to phlogiston. Experimental anomalies associated with oxidation eventually discredited phlogiston theories. Phlogiston ceased to figure in generally accepted theories, chemists ceased to 'quantify over' phlogiston.

Eliminativists about minds have taken both these routes. Some, Rorty, for instance, suggest that talk of minds could be a remnant of a superstitious past when the behavior of animate objects was explained by reference to animating spirits. Talk of minds resembles talk of spirits or phlogiston: we habitually appeal to them in explanations of the behavior of sentient creatures, but better explanations are available, explanations that do not mention minds. (Recall the dismissive attitude of psychological behaviorists (§ 4.12) toward the use traditional mental categories in explanations of behavior.)

Others regard talk of minds as a mere figure of speech, one we could do without. (You might recognize this as a close relative of Dennett's view.) The advance of neuroscience suggests to many that we are on a trajectory to phase out serious scientific talk of minds: we are on our way to replacing mention of states of mind in explanations of the behavior of sentient creatures with references to those creatures' neurological makeup. Were this to happen, we would have effectively eliminated references to minds and states of mind in our best theories, cease to 'quantify over' psychological states and properties.

Do not imagine that eliminativists are out to abolish talk of thoughts and feelings. Eliminativism foresees the demise of mental categories in scientific endeavors to explain behavior. Even if this happened, however, it is a safe bet that reference to minds and states of mind would continue unabated in ordinary discourse. Nowadays no one thinks that the Sun goes around the Earth, but we persist in speaking of the Sun rising and setting.

Bearing all this in mind, let us turn our attention to particular eliminativist arguments. I begin with a discussion of considerations favoring eliminativism advanced by Patricia and Paul Churchland, then turn to a distinct line of reasoning developed by Stephen Stich. I conclude with a discussion of a charge sometimes leveled against eliminativist doctrines, namely that they are self-refuting.

9.3   Theories and Theory Reduction

The Churchlands, Patricia and Paul, regard talk of minds as little more than a time-honored, but highly fallible technique for coming to grips with the vagaries of intelligent behavior. When you look at what makes sentient creatures (including human beings) tick, when you look beneath the hood, you discover intricate neural mechanisms. The principles on which these mechanisms operate bear scant resemblance to the platitudes of 'folk psychology', the commonsense theory of mind encoded in our language, enshrined in societal and legal institutions, and infesting the social and behavioral sciences.

If you are genuinely interested in understanding and explaining the behavior of sentient creatures, then, you face a choice. On the one hand, you could try to find a way of reading folk psychological categories into neurophysiological categories. On the other hand, should that fail, you could simply reject folk psychology as a false theory. If folk psychology goes, psychology goes as well, and with it the various social sciences. Thus, psychological categories and modes of explanation are either 'reducible' to more fundamental neurobiological categories, or psychological categories and modes of explanation apply to nothing: beliefs, desires, and the lot are, like phlogiston or witches, non-existent. In either case, psychological categories would no longer figure in serious science. Once this happens, once you no longer 'quantify over' psychological categories in serious explanations of behavior, you would no longer be ontologically committed to mental entities.

Psychology provides us with a modestly serviceable theory founded on 'intentional' categories, categories including belief, desire, motive, intention. As is the case for *any* empirical theory, however, this one could turn out to be inadequate in light of the emergence of a new and better theory. Suppose, as seems likely, neuroscientists develop theories that do a significantly better job of predicting and explaining the activities of sentient creatures than do conventional psychological theories. Suppose, further, that neuroscience does so without recourse to familiar mental categories: beliefs, desires, images, and the like. Imagine that, in the new theory, such things are never mentioned, only neurons, synapses, ganglia, and neurotransmitters.

When you turn to the history of science, you discover that when a new theory threatens to replace an existing theory, two outcomes are possible.

1   An old theory might be shown to be 'reducible to', that is to be a special case of, the new theory.
2   The new theory could wholly displace or overturn the older theory.

Consider, first, theory reduction. Reduction occurs when categories of the old theory are mirrored by categories in the new theory. In that case, terms for the older categories could be said to designate 'nothing but' what terms for the new categories designate. Temperature, for instance, turns out to designate the mean molecular kinetic energy of molecules. Theories in which the concept of temperature figures, then, are reducible to more fundamental physical and chemical theories. This is why reduced theories can be seen as special cases of the theories to which they are reduced. Indeed, you might be inclined to regard entities and properties included in the reduced theory as being *explained* by the reducing theory. Temperature, you now see, turns out to *be* mean molecular kinetic energy of molecules; this is the deep story about temperature. In the same way scientists discovered that lightning *is* a stream of electrons; this is the deep story about lightning.

Although the history of science includes stunning examples of theory reduction, it is perhaps more common for a new theory simply to *replace* an older theory. Heat was once explained by postulating an impalpable fluid, *caloric*, that was thought to flow from heated bodies to adjacent cooler bodies. (Caloric replaced phlogiston in the explanatory schemes of eighteenth century chemists.) Caloric, although weightless, was taken to occupy space and, importantly, to be conserved as mass–energy is conserved. The passage of caloric into a cold body caused the body to swell, thus accounting for heat expansion – without an accompanying gain in weight – observed in bodies when they were heated. With the coming of the chemical revolution, belief in caloric was abandoned, replaced with the notion that heat was, not a substance, but a kind of energy. Unlike the concept of temperature, caloric was not *reduced* to anything more fundamental, but simply *eliminated*.

According to the Churchlands, it is this latter, eliminative fate that awaits our ordinary intentional mental concepts. Neuroscience promises not to *illuminate* our mental categories but to *replace* them. Thoughts, beliefs, imagery, and the like will turn out not to *be* complex neural goings-on, but, as with caloric, to be non-existent: theoretical posits to which nothing in the world corresponds.

An eliminativist who takes this line will admit that it is unlikely anyone would give up talk of beliefs and desires in everyday life. You continue to speak of the Sun's rising and setting, even though you know full well that the apparent motion of the Sun is due to the rotation of the Earth. Someone who failed to be tolerant of such talk would be a tedious companion. Similarly, when it comes to minds and their contents, you could 'think with the learned and speak with the vulgar', as Bishop Berkeley put it in defending idealism (§ 3.4).

Anyone whose aim is an accurate view of matters would be obliged to admit that, just as it is strictly false that the Sun rises and sets, it is false that anyone *really* has beliefs, desires, or reasons for action; false that any creature is *really* guided by imagery; and false that anyone has ever *really* thought of anything. Psychologists and social scientists who persevere in the quest for a refined scientific grip on states of mind as traditionally conceived are barking up the wrong tree. They resemble alchemists who persisted in operating with alchemical categories long after alchemical categories had been discredited.

9.4   Stich's Argument

Stephen Stich arrives at a similar conclusion, but from an altogether different starting point. As in the case of the Churchlands, Stich regards folk psychology as a fallible theory of intelligent behavior. Unlike the Churchlands, however, Stich's focus is on what he takes to be the most promising (or perhaps the *only* promising) articulation of folk psychology, namely that provided by the Representational Theory of Mind (the centerpiece of Chapter 7).

Recall that, according to the Representational Theory of Mind, states of mind of intelligent creatures are embodied by sentences in a built-in Language of Thought, the brain's 'machine code'. Mental processes consist in the manipulation of these sentences to produce outputs in response to sensory inputs, themselves encoded as sentences in the Language of Thought. The model here is a general purpose computing machine. Inputs are 'transduced' into a sequence of symbols the machine processes in accord with symbol-processing rules to yield symbolic outputs that, in turn, trigger mechanical outputs.

The idea that mental operations are computations over symbols does not imply that the mind is a blind, mechanical device, but only that mental mechanisms are biological counterparts of mechanisms appealed to by computer programmers. Thoughts – sentences in the Language of Thought – correspond to strings of symbols processed by a computing machine. Just as there is nothing mysterious about a computing machine's processing symbols, so there is nothing mysterious about the mind's entertaining and manipulating thoughts. Minds are programs running on the brain's hardware.

Stich is happy to accept all this, but he takes it to promote an eliminativist agenda. How so? Think first of all of defining features of states of mind: beliefs, desires, and intentions. Such states of mind have *intentionality*: they are *of* or *about* various things. Intentionality is not a mere incidental *accompaniment* of states of mind. The very identity of a particular state of mind (or, at any rate, a particular propositional attitude) depends on its intentional *content*: what it is of or about. Chicken Little's belief that the sky is falling concerns the sky and its falling, and differs from her belief that the sky is blue. These beliefs differ in their *content*; and this difference in content is taken to make a difference in how Chicken Little behaves or would behave.

All this might appear to be belaboring the obvious but, Stich argues, the consequences of embracing the Representational Theory of Mind are profound. Sentences in the Language of Thought, in common with strings of symbols processed by a computing machine, doubtless *have* meanings, but these meanings play no role at all in the operation of mechanisms that process them. This feature of the Representative Theory of Mind (a feature made salient by Searle's 'Chinese Room', § 7.5) is regularly touted as an important *virtue* of the theory. In fact, the theory is thought by its proponents to provide an *explanation* of the basis of intentionality. Any such explanation would have to show how the intentional could emerge from combinations of non-intentional elements. You might recall the point from Chapter 7. If you set out to explain how agents *understand* meaningful utterances, it would be a bad idea to posit an internal 'understander' – a homunculus. Your explanation would be appealing to just what it purported to explain!

The Representational Theory of Mind avoids the 'homunculus problem' by supposing that the *semantic* features of a system – those features pertaining to meaning and intentional content – could be implemented by purely *syntactic* mechanisms – mechanisms that manipulate symbols without regard to their significance. This makes it possible to understand how a purely mechanical system – a computing machine or a brain, for instance – could operate 'meaningfully' without having to posit homunculi whose job is to interpret symbols coursing through the system and act appropriately in light of the meanings of those symbols.

This is the good news. The bad news? According to Stich, the model afforded by the Representational Theory of Mind effectively strips the categories of folk psychology of explanatory significance. Our application of these categories is grounded on the presumption that intelligent agents do what they do because of what they believe, want, fear, and value. But the deep story turns out to be wholly *syntactic*. *What* you believe, want, fear, or value – the *contents* of these states of mind – plays no role whatever in mechanisms that produce your behavior. Intentional categories – belief, desire, emotion, and the like – classify states of mind by reference to what they concern, their *content*, however. It follows that appeals to beliefs, desires, and emotions are explanatorily empty. You do not do what you do because of what you believe or what you desire. You do what you do because your psychological states have the syntactic forms they have. They could have these forms even if their content were utterly different, even if they had no content at all.

Recall the computing machine used to keep inventory in a supermarket (§ 7.6). Its states were said to represent bananas, cans of soup, and cartons of milk. However, the same machine, running the same program, might keep track of nails, glue, and ant traps were it deployed in a hardware store. The machine is indifferent to the significance of the symbols it processes, just as you would be indifferent to the significance of the A's and B's in inferring 'B', from 'if A then B' plus 'A':

$$A \supset B$$
$$\frac{A}{B}$$

In such cases, although the symbols might *have* meanings, these meanings play no role in the operation of the devices in which they occur. The conclusion: their meanings are causally and explanatorily irrelevant to what those devices do.

You can appreciate the force of Stich's argument by recalling Searle's Chinese Room (§ 7.5). Searle notes that *understanding* plays no role in operations performed in the room – but those operations perfectly mimic mental operations as conceived of by the Representational Theory of Mind. Searle's point is that external observers who explain processes undertaken in the room by invoking intentional categories like understanding, belief, and desire are deluded. Such things have *no* part to play in the operation of the symbol-processing system that includes a basket of symbols, Searle, and his book of symbol-manipulation rules. Searle takes this to show that there must be more to the mind than symbol processing and, on this basis, rejects the Representational Theory of Mind.

Stich, reasons in the opposite direction. There are, he contends, excellent reasons to accept the Representational Theory. Indeed, Stich sides with Jerry Fodor in regarding the Representational Theory as 'the only game in town'. But Searle has the right idea: if you accept the theory you must accept, as well, that appeals to belief, desire, meaning, understanding, and the like have no place in scientific explanations of intelligent behavior. Minds operate on purely syntactic principles.

Again, Stich is not claiming that symbols processed by mental mechanisms – or, for that matter, symbols processed by computing machines – *lack* meaning. The Chinese symbols Searle manipulates are not meaningless. They are, after all, strings of *Chinese* characters. Rather, the claim is that any meaning they might have is irrelevant to their causal role in the mechanism that processes them. It is false that we do what we do because of what we believe and want, just as it is false that the Sun rises and sets; folk psychology, together with any more refined 'scientific' psychology is a false theory. The Representational Theory of Mind, long regarded as the theoretical vanguard, has turned out to be a Trojan Horse!

Might you respond to Stich by noting that, although symbolic representations cause what they do by virtue of their formal, syntactic features (and not by virtue of what they mean), the significance of symbols 'piggybacks' on their form. Imagine a symbol, CAT, that means cat. The system that processes this symbol does so in virtue of its non-semantic, syntactic properties – its shape. But wherever the symbol goes its meaning goes. This is the force of regarding minds as 'semantic engines'. The intimate connection between syntax and semantics might be enough to secure the 'causal relevance' of intentional states.

The residual worry with such a response is that it appears to make intentionality – meaning – *epiphenomenal*. Causally efficacious symbols *have* meanings, but they do what they do owing to their non-intentional features. This is exactly the epiphenomenalist's picture (§ 3.6). If the significance of intentional states plays no role in what those states do or would do, then it would lack explanatory value.

This is a serious problem for the Representational Theory of Mind, a problem that will resurface in Chapter 11 as a difficulty for any account of mind that distinguishes sharply between mental properties, intentional or otherwise, and material properties.

9.5 Prospects for Reduction or Elimination

Eliminativism stakes its case on the conviction that explanations of the activities of sentient creatures framed by reference to states of mind are 'ripe for replacement'. Is this so?

Consider a conception of scientific explanation advanced by Jerry Fodor in an influential defense of the 'special sciences', including psychology. Suppose the universe consists of fundamental particles in dynamic arrangements governed by fundamental laws of nature. Physics – not physics generally but basic, *fundamental* physics – is in the business of providing explanations of particle behavior. These explanations would make use of fundamental categories (electron, quark, charge, force, energy, field) in the formulation of fundamental laws. Physics (and henceforth I shall mean by 'physics', fundamental physics) has a claim on being the 'science of everything'.

This is not to say, however, that physics is the *only* science that *all* science is, at bottom, 'really physics'. The world – the world described by physics – admits of many different categorical systems, many different 'taxonomies'. Different taxonomies 'divide' or 'carve up' the world differently. Taxonomies, and the categories making them up, do not *create* divisions in the world. Rather, they recognize divisions that physics ignores. For instance, categories deployed by geologists or meteorologists count as similar states of the world that, from the perspective of physics, differ dramatically. The same holds for biology, psychology, anthropology, economics. Each of these special sciences operates with a distinctive taxonomy, a distinctive collection of concepts or categories.

There is no reason to believe that categories in the special sciences could be replaced by categories at home in physics. Recall the example of chess in § 7.8. You can describe and explain a particular chess game using chess categories. All of the motions of players and pieces, all of the states leading to these motions, *could*, at least in principle, be described and explained in terms of fundamental physics. The descriptions and explanations, however, would leave out all that the original chess descriptions and explanations illuminated – similarities between this game and other games, for instance. The effect would resemble attempting to tell time by redescribing Big Ben in terms of its constituent particles.

Eliminativists might contend that such points reflect, at most, purely *practical* limitations on observers; they cut no explanatory ice. If that were right, it would seem to follow that the *only* science would be fundamental physics. Arguments that would show that psychological categories are 'in principle' dispensable, would show the same for biology (every plant, every organism, is, after all, a physical system made up of particles obeying fundamental laws), meteorology, and every other special science. The problems facing an attempt to eliminate biology are not merely practical problems lacking theoretical interest. Denied resources supplied by biological categories, there would be many generalizations you could not appreciate, many truths you could not express.

Might this be so for biology, meteorology, and geology, but not for psychology? Might psychological categories fail, as biological categories do not fail, to 'carve the world at its joints'? Might psychology have *distinctive* liabilities? That is certainly an abstract possibility. Psychology could prove to be especially inept at identifying interesting, 'projectable' characteristics of sentient creatures that could play illuminating explanatory roles. Is the future of psychology cloudy or bright? Rather than tell you what I think about psychology's prospects, I shall leave the matter in your hands, at least for now.

Without wanting to prejudice your reflections, let me add that you are unlikely to develop a satisfying resolution to these issues without first addressing a host of issues residing at the interface of metaphysics and epistemology. What, for instance, does realism about a given subject matter – psychology, for instance – require? (Many philosophers would appeal here to Quine's criterion of 'ontological commitment', discussed above in § 9.2.) If you think that minds are real, self-standing features of the world, what relation must minds bear to the world's other features? For that matter, if you think that trees, or white blood cells, or neurons are real features of the world, what relation must *these* entities bear to other features, in particular, what relation do they bear to particles and fields? Finally, are there distinctively psychological truths, truths about the mind expressible only in a psychological vocabulary? If there are such truths, what features of the world make them true, and what relation do these features bear to features of the world that make truths of biology, or physics true?

9.6   Is Eliminativism Self-Refuting?

I have dwelt on the viability of eliminativism as a philosophical theory concerning how things might stand with minds and states of mind, the pros and cons of the thesis that there might be no minds. Some philosophers have argued that eliminativism cannot so much as get off the ground.

Eliminativism, they claim, is *self-refuting*. If no one believed anything, then how could anyone believe the eliminativist thesis? If no one thought, if no one had reasons for action or belief, how could eliminativists expect us to accept their arguments? Accepting an argument is a matter of accepting various statements as providing good reasons for belief in particular conclusions. But none of this could make any sense if eliminativism were correct. The eliminativist resembles the obnoxious philosopher who buttonholes you and offers tiresome arguments to the conclusion that he – the obnoxious philosopher – does not exist.

You need not be a fan of eliminativism to have doubts as to the cogency of the suggestion that eliminativism is self-refuting. A hypothesis could, it seems, be such that its truth is inconsistent with its being asserted – or even believed – to be true, yet for all that nevertheless *be true*. Consider the hypothesis that all assertions are false. Pretend for a moment that the hypothesis is true: every assertion is false. Were this so, the hypothesis could not be truly asserted! There would be something self-defeating, then, about someone's pounding the table and insisting that every assertion is false. But it does not follow from this that every assertion is *not* false.

You might think of eliminativists as indicating a possibility by using terminology that would be empty were that possibility actual. From this, however, it seems not to follow that the possibility in question is not a genuine possibility. It does follow that, in 'asserting' the thesis, the eliminativist asserts nothing. But that is a consequence of the theory, not an objection to it!

In this context, it might be useful to cite a famous passage from Wittgenstein's *Tractatus Logico-Philosophicus* (1922), § 6.54. The *Tractatus* concerns (among many other things) the conditions required for thoughts to 'picture' the world. For complicated reasons I shall ignore here, the position Wittgenstein takes would, if true, make it impossible for anyone to entertain thoughts concerning the relation thoughts bear to the world. Yet this is apparently a central topic in the *Tractatus*! Does this mean that Wittgenstein's thesis is self-refuting? Not according to its author:

> My propositions serve as elucidations in the following way: anyone who understands me eventually recognizes them as nonsensical, when he has used them – as steps – to climb beyond them. (He must, so to speak, throw away the ladder after he has climbed up it.)
>
> He must transcend these propositions, and then he will see the world aright.
>
> (Wittgenstein 1922)

The sentences used to formulate the thesis succeed indirectly: by 'showing' the reader what is intended, rather than by 'saying' it outright.

Were eliminativism correct, this might be all a committed eliminativist could do. But whether eliminativism is correct or not, whether eliminativism could be regarded as a reasonable hypothesis without thereby assuming its falsehood, it would be hasty to imagine this shows that eliminativism is false. Pushing matters to an extreme, suppose that, if eliminativism were true, nothing anyone says makes any sense. Does it follow that eliminativism is *not* true, that the world is not as the eliminativist apparently describes it? Think about it – if you can!

These comments should not be taken as an endorsement of eliminativism. As will become evident in Chapter 13, there might be no compelling reason to accept the eliminativist's conclusions – even if you embrace the idea that neuroscience or a syntactic theory of mind might one day supplant psychology.

Suggested Reading

Eliminative materialism was conceived as a response to, or extension of, the mind–brain identity theory (Chapter 5). Early influential exponents included Paul Feyerabend ('Materialism and the Mind–Body Problem', 1963) and Richard Rorty ('Mind–Body Identity, Privacy, and Categories', 1965; 'In Defense of Eliminative Materialism', 1970). More recently, eliminativism has been defended by Paul Churchland in *Scientific Realism and the Plasticity of Mind* (1979); and in 'Eliminative Materialism and the Propositional Attitudes' (1981). See also Patricia Churchland's *Neurophilosophy* (1986).

Quine's influential discussion of 'ontological commitment' occurs in 'On What There Is' (1948). A discussion of the doctrine, see Heil, *The Universe as We Find It* (2012), chapter 8.

Stephen Stich defends his own brand of eliminativism in *From Folk Psychology to Cognitive Science: The Case Against Belief* (1983). Lynne Rudder Baker (responding to Stich, among others) has argued that eliminativism is self-refuting; see her *Saving Belief* (1987), chapter 7, 'The Threat of Cognitive Suicide'. For an extended discussion of the question whether eliminativism is self-refuting, see my *The Nature of True Minds* (1992), 5–11.

Ramsey *et al.* ('Connectionism, Eliminativism, and the Future of Folk Psychology', 1991) argue that 'connectionist' models of the mind imply eliminativism. For a response see Heil, 'Being Indiscrete' (1991). Horgan and Woodward, in 'Folk Psychology is Here to Stay' (1985), and Jackson and Pettit, in 'In Defense of Folk Psychology' (1990) defend 'folk psychology' against the menace of elimination. See also O'Leary-Hawthorne's 'On the Threat of Elimination' (1994). Christensen and Turner's *Folk Psychology and the Philosophy of Mind* (1993) is a collection of papers devoted to arguments for and against eliminativism.

10 Consciousness

10.1 The Status of 'Raw Feels'

Psychologist E. C. Tolman, after offering a detailed account of what he took to be mechanisms underlying 'purposive behavior in animals and men', turns to the topic of 'raw feels', Tolman's term for purely sensory conscious experiences. Tolman, in common with his twenty-first century counterparts, sees psychology as in the business of explaining intelligent behavior by reference to various cognitive states and processes, states and processes involving 'mental representations', 'cognitive maps', and propositional attitudes: beliefs, desires, intentions, and the like. In so doing, psychology would seem to be ignoring the sensory side of our mental lives. This, Tolman notes, leaves us with a mildly embarrassing residue of familiar mental phenomena that fall outside psychology's explanatory net.

Tolman's attitude is that of a scientist intent on policing the boundaries between science and superstition. Yes, we are certainly aware of undergoing sensory experiences, but these evidently fall outside the purview of science. He envisions three 'scrap heaps' into which 'raw feels' might be 'chucked'.

> First, it may be contended that 'raw feels' just have to be ignored. They are mere scientific will-of-the-wisps. They are subject matter for poetry and esthetics and religion, not for science. And hence the only thing a scientist can say in answer to one who insists on raising a final question concerning them, is to retort in the language of the street, 'Aw, forget it'.
> (Tolman 1932, 426)

Tolman cites philosopher C. I. Lewis as a proponent of such a view. Lewis speaks of 'immediate experience'.

> The supposition of a difference in immediate experience which is not to be detected through divergence in discrimination and relation, is a notion very difficult to handle. Because such a difference would, *ex hypothesi*, be ineffable. We can have no language for discussing what no language or behavior could discriminate. And a difference which no

language or behavior could convey is, for purposes of communication, as good as non-existent.

(Lewis 1929, 112n)

Lewis's idea is that a phenomenon that is 'ineffable' (not fully and objectively describable) and not publicly accessible is, so far as science is concerned, 'as good as non-existent'. Science must, of necessity, ignore such a phenomenon. Consciousness might be a big deal for all of us conscious agents, but conscious experiences, even if they exist, make up a vanishingly small collection of phenomena when you consider the diversity present in the universe as a whole. Obsession over such things is an expression of hubris, an unwarranted injection of parochial human concerns into the business of science.

Still, 'as good as non-existent' implies 'existent but elusive'. Can, or must, science turn its back on such phenomena? This is an odd prospect. Why should a phenomenon's 'ineffability' or relative uniqueness place it out of bounds to science? If something is a feature of the world, however elusive, it would seem to be a candidate for systematic scientific inquiry. If not, then we should need some reason other than the phenomenon's alleged 'ineffability' to exclude it from consideration. One reason might be that Descartes was right: minds are nonmaterial substances not susceptible to description or explanation of the sort applicable to material phenomena. This would insulate minds from conventional empirical inquiry.

Does acceptance of conscious sensory experiences bring with it a commitment to Cartesian dualism? It would seem incredible that scientific scruples could force us to accept a doctrine that bifurcates the world into material and nonmaterial domains. The idea smacks of defeatism: conscious experiences pose a problem for scientific explanation, so the advice is to ignore them. In any case, you have by now learned enough to recognize that such conceptions of mind stem, at bottom, not from the laboratory, but from philosophical reflection. (Remember: philosophers are not the only philosophers.) Dualism did not fall from the sky. It results from philosophical attempts to 'locate' mental phenomena. Surely, the lesson to draw from the apparent recalcitrance of mental – specifically, conscious – phenomena to scientific investigation is that we need to reconsider philosophical presuppositions that encourage such a view.

What to do? Tolman suggests two further 'scrap heaps' to which you might consign conscious experiences or 'raw feels'.

Second, it may be answered that a more reasonable assumption is to assume some sort of consistent correlation between raw feels and correlated immanent determinants – so that, in so far as the determinants operating in one individual seem to *approximate* those in another individual, the raw feels of the first may be said at least to approximate those of the second.

(Tolman 1932, 427)

So another way to justify science's turning its back on purely sensory conscious phenomena is to suppose those phenomena are either correlates or epiphenomenal accompaniments of material processes. This would amount to a slightly less reprehensible approach to the problem. The world is still bifurcated into the material and the nonmaterial, but nonmaterial items either are impotent by-products of material processes or somehow shadow material processes without getting in their way.

> A third answer has been suggested. Raw feels may be the way physical realities are intrinsically, i.e., in and for themselves. Bertrand Russell believes that experienced qualities are the intrinsic nature of a nervous process. E. B. Holt, on the other hand, argues that qualities are the intrinsic nature of those environmental objects to which the organism responds. The former position is near to that which is traditionally called 'pan-psychism', the latter is the claim of neorealism.
>
> (Tolman 1932, 427)

One possibility, then, is that qualities of conscious experience permeate reality: even electrons exhibit minute 'sparks' of consciousness. Were consciousness pervasive in this way, it might operate as a 'constant' that could be safely ignored in accounts of different phenomena: consciousness, although perfectly real, would 'cancel out' in scientific explanation. Alternatively, what you might think of as qualities of conscious experiences, could, in reality, be qualities of experienced objects 'out there' in the world: the division between the mental and the material is illusory.

I shall discuss these last two options in §§ 10.8 and 10.9. You have already encountered versions of Tolman's first and second options. Behaviorists (philosophical and psychological) and eliminativists might be understood as uninterested in – indeed disdainful of – conscious experiences, Tolman's 'raw feels'. Proponents of the identity theory hope to *identify* conscious experiences with goings-on in the nervous system. But if consciousness is, as U. T. Place puts it, *nothing but* a 'brain process', conscious qualities are effectively 'reduced' to material features of brains. Dennett's account of consciousness is similarly deflationary: consciousness is the prerogative of linguistically endowed creatures who have a capacity to reflect on their own thoughts. Functionalists and proponents of the Representational Theory of Mind have downplayed consciousness, preferring to focus on computationally tractable states of mind. (To be fair, some functionalists, Sydney Shoemaker, for instance, have tried to provide functionalist accounts of consciousness, but the results have been disappointing; see § 10.3.)

If eliminativists, behaviorists, identity theorists, and functionalists could be understood as tossing consciousness onto Tolman's first scrap heap, parallelists, occasionalists, and epiphenomenalists might be seen as consigning conscious experiences to his second heap. Parallelists, occasionalists, and epiphenomenalists all subscribe to the idea that mental events 'shadow', but

have no effect on, make no difference to, physical occurrences. Such theorists admit conscious experiences, but gainsay their status in explanations of
behavior.

One question you should keep in the back of your mind is whether
Tolman's list is exhaustive. Are there options Tolman does not consider? Are
there ways of taking conscious experiences – 'raw feels' – seriously without
shunting them off to one explanatory 'scrap heap' or other?

10.2 The Mystery of Consciousness

What is it about consciousness that leads so many philosophers and scientists to regard it as mysterious? You know you are conscious, and it would
not occur to you to doubt that others are conscious as well. Most people
accept that dogs and cats are conscious. How far down the chain of being
does consciousness extend? Are mice conscious? Snakes? Spiders? Sea
anemones? You might suspect that consciousness is not an all-or-nothing
affair: consciousness comes in degrees. Human beings are fully conscious,
other creatures less so. Snakes and spiders are barely conscious if they are
conscious at all.

If you understood which features of our material makeup were responsible
for consciousness, you could hope for a decisive empirical answer to such
questions. The trouble is, anyone investigating consciousness empirically
comes face to face with what Joseph Levine has called the *explanatory gap*
(introduced in § 4.3). Thus, even if you knew *which* neural occurrences were
'responsible' for consciousness, it is hard to see how this knowledge could
lead to an understanding of *why* a mechanism with a particular material
character should 'underlie' or 'give rise to' conscious states with a particular
qualitative character. (And what is it to 'underlie' or 'give rise to' a conscious
experience, anyway?)

Before looking more carefully at these difficulties, it would be useful to
distinguish two ways in which consciousness is commonly discussed, two
'senses' of consciousness:

1 *Creature consciousness*
2 *Mental state consciousness*

We say that a creature – a *sentient* creature – is conscious when the creature is awake, alert, and responding to goings-on in its environment. A dog
scratching fleas or chasing a squirrel is conscious in this sense. The same dog
asleep in the kitchen is not conscious. That sentient creatures are conscious
in this regard is uncontroversial.

Mental state consciousness is another matter. If you are reading
these words, you are undergoing a conscious perceptual experience. It
would seem, however, that, although *you* are conscious, many of your
current mental *states* are not conscious. As you have discovered already,

philosophers find it difficult to say exactly what it is for a state of mind to be conscious. (If the earlier quotation from C. I. Lewis is correct, if consciousness truly is 'ineffable', this would scarcely be surprising.) One approach would be to appeal to distinctive conscious *qualities*. A conscious mental state has a *phenomenology*: there is *something it is like* to be in that state, something you might have difficulty articulating, but something you recognize immediately: you know it when you experience it. Philosophers like to speak of 'phenomenal qualities'. A conscious state would be a state exhibiting such qualities. 'Phenomenal qualities', 'qualities of conscious experiences', 'raw feels', *'qualia'* are all terms meant to designate whatever it is that you are 'directly' or 'immediately' aware of when you are aware of how things *seem* to you.

The mystery of consciousness concerns mental state consciousness. On the one hand your conscious experiences are what you are most familiar with, they are intermediaries between you and the world (in perception), what is most immediately before your mind when anything is before your mind. In this regard consciousness is not all mysterious. It is, in some respects, what you know best. What *is* mysterious is the apparent 'gap' between what you recognize, or think you recognize, to be the case concerning your conscious experiences and what science and common sense tell us about the material world, including your brain. Tolman's comments reflect frustration with this gap, and Tolman's 'scrap heaps' represent attempts to bridge it – or, in the 'Aw, forget it' case, to paper over it.

Researchers regularly claim to have overcome the explanatory gap in finding that brain states and conscious states can exhibit a common 'structure'. You might find, for instance, a region of the brain apparently responsible for color judgments. Experienced colors have a three-dimensional character (hue, saturation, brightness). A color you experience has a location in a three-dimensional 'color space'. It could easily turn out that brain mechanisms that produce color judgments vary along three dimensions, so the 'computational space' has a three-dimensional structure corresponding to your experienced, 'phenomenal color space'.

If something like this turned out to be the case, it might explain why conscious experiences of color are representable in a three-dimensional space. But this would not be to bridge the explanatory gap. That gap concerns *experienced* qualities. Color experiences might have a structure, but there is more to them than this, a *qualitative* more. Why should creatures with brains resembling ours have experiences with *these* qualities? For that matter, why should *we* experience colors in *this* way? Presumably, endless qualities could be represented by means of a three-dimensional 'quality space'. Why are your color experiences *qualitatively* as they are and not some other way? (Imagine a creature whose color experiences resemble your sound or taste experiences. While you are at it, reflect on the 'beetle in the box', § 4.4.) There seems to be no principled answer. The connection between features of goings-on in your brain and the qualitative character, the *phenomenology*, of your conscious experiences seems, at best, a 'brute', unexplained feature of the world.

10.3   Qualities of Conscious Experiences

In Chapter 7, I suggested that functionalism probably deserves to be thought of as the default conception among theorists in psychology and cognitive science. Whatever its standing, functionalism provides a convenient platform from which to examine various accounts of consciousness.

Pretend, then, that you were attracted to the functionalist's depiction of states of mind as functional states. Functionalists hold that you would be in a given state of mind, you would be in pain, for instance, just in case you were in a state that satisfies a particular 'job description', a state that plays a particular kind of causal role: the pain role. Among other things, you would be in a state brought about by tissue damage, or pressure, or extremes of temperature, and one that itself brings about a range of characteristic 'pain responses', behavioral and mental: you cringe, you form the belief that you are in pain, and you acquire a desire to take steps to alleviate the pain.

All this seems perfectly satisfactory, as far as it goes. The trouble is, it appears not to go nearly far *enough*. When you are in pain you are undoubtedly in a kind of state that has a distinctive causal profile. But could this be *all there is* to your being in pain? Surely, when you experience pain, your experience has a characteristic qualitative *feel*. As noted earlier (see also § 4.10), philosophers sometimes call attention to this feel by noting that there is 'something it is like' to be in pain – to have a blinding headache, for instance. And this 'what it is like', the *qualitative dimension* of pain, seems oddly missing from the functionalist's story.

You might not have noticed this because you might have assumed that pain states have the role they have *owing* to their qualitative character. The reason a state of pain leads you to whimper and cast about relief is that it is *painful!* But functionalists reverse the order of explanation. A pain state is not a pain because it is painful; the state is painful because it plays the right sort of causal role. The state does not do what it does because it is painful; it is painful because it does what it does.

This appears to leave qualities of conscious experiences in limbo. We need somehow to accommodate the evident fact that in having a headache, you undergo a kind of conscious experience, an experience with certain especially salient qualities. Philosophers often refer to these qualities as *qualia* (see § 8.8). ('*Qualia*' is plural; the singular form is '*quale*'.) *Qualia* are Tolman's 'raw feels', qualitative features of our conscious mental life that we attend to when we contemplate what it feels like to be in pain, or view a sunrise at Uluru, or bite into a jalapeño pepper.

A functionalist need not deny that when you are in pain, your being in pain has a characteristic feel, although functionalists sometimes *do* deny this, apparently because they can find no place in the universe for experiential qualities. What a functionalist must deny, however, is that the qualitative dimension of pains is what makes pains *pains*. (Again, reflect on the 'beetle in the box' argument discussed in § 4.4.) A functionalist *might* grant that pains are invariably *accompanied by* feelings of certain sorts, just as pop stars are invariably accompanied by teenagers clamoring for mementos. What makes a given state a state of pain, however, is not what it is like for a creature in the state, but the state's role in the creature's psychological economy.

This means, among other things, that when you react to being in pain, when you complain, seek relief, find your thoughts distracted, and the like, you are responding, not to the *feel* of the pain, not to its distinctive qualities. Your response is just one manifestation of the realizer, the state, *whatever* it is, that plays the pain role. The qualities – if indeed there are such – you find so unpleasant have nothing to do with the state's being a pain, nor with the state's causing what it does, including its causing you to believe that you are in pain.

10.4 Zombies

One apparent consequence of a conception of this sort is that it opens up the possibility that a creature could be in pain, yet experience *none* of the qualitative 'feels' that preoccupy us when we are in pain. Let us be clear about the case. In imagining a creature that satisfies the functionalist's conception of pain, yet lacks 'raw feels', you would not be imagining a creature anesthetized. An anesthetized creature is not in pain by anyone's lights. Rather, you would be imagining a creature who thinks and behaves exactly as you do when you are in pain. The creature complains, takes steps to alleviate the pain, and appears to be suffering just as you would. The causal connections, hence appropriate pain behavior, are all present. What is missing is the 'inner' aspect of pain, the qualitative aspect.

You might doubt that there could be such creatures. The idea, however, is not that creatures of the kind in question – 'zombies' (introduced in § 4.3) – are possible given prevailing laws of nature. Is it possible that pigs could fly? No, not given the physical makeup of pigs and laws governing the universe. But (it is said) laws of nature are *contingent*: the laws could have been different. And if you allow that the laws of nature could have been different, then, you can allow that the world could have been such that pigs fly. Similarly, those who regard the zombie possibility as a live one declare that zombies would be possible given differences in the fundamental laws of nature.

If talk of laws of nature being different strikes you as wholly idle, consider the possibility of building a functional duplicate of a creature capable of feeling pain – a cat, for instance – from brass rods, springs, and gears. When the device goes into a state functionally equivalent to the state the cat is in when it undergoes a painful experience, the device must *be* in pain. (This is the functionalist hypothesis.) But it seems crazy to imagine that the device *feels* anything at all. If this possibility is a live one, then scientists would have manufactured what amounts to a zombie, in this case a zombie cat.

Where is this line of thought leading? Well, the mere conceivability of zombies appears to imply that, if functionalism is correct, conscious qualities are not 'essential' to minds. Zombies satisfy all the functionalist criteria for possessing a full complement of states of mind. Yet zombies lack anything like the qualitative 'feel' that permeates our conscious experiences; zombies lack an 'inner life'. It seems to follow that we all could have been just as we are now with our full complement of psychological states – including the firm conviction that we are not zombies – while altogether lacking qualitatively imbued conscious experiences. Were that so, we would inhabit a universe not detectably different from our actual universe from the *outside*, but, from the *inside*, dramatically different – a universe *without* an 'inside'!

Some critics of functionalism regard the zombie possibility as sufficient grounds for rejecting the functionalist conception of mind. Such critics take the qualitative aspect of the mental lives of sentient creatures to be central and essential to mentality. How, they ask, could functionalists seriously contend that a creature could be in pain, yet utterly lack anything resembling what we regard as the conscious *feeling* of pain?

One functionalist response to the zombie story would be simply to contend that, despite appearances, zombies are not, as a matter of fact, conceivable. The kind of complex functional organization required for a creature to be in pain, would not be possible unless the creature underwent conscious experiences with the kinds of experiential qualities that are salient to creatures in pain. To be in pain, is not merely to produce appropriate pain behavior under the right circumstances. It is, as well, to form beliefs that one is in pain, that the pain has certain qualities (it is dull, or sharp, or stinging). A creature capable of experiencing pain is capable as well of 'picturing' pain and empathizing with other creatures. And all these activities – reflecting on one's pain, picturing the pain of another – would seem to be out of reach for zombies. If that is so, then zombies *would* differ from us functionally in important respects, and there would be no compulsion to regard them as possessing minds, or at any rate, possessing minds similar to *our* minds.

Other functionalists have thought that a response of this sort is out of keeping with the spirit of functionalism. Functionalism identifies mental properties with causal powers. If *qualia* – 'raw feels', the qualitative dimension of conscious experiences – resist this identification, you are faced with a choice. Either you reject functionalism, or you bite the bullet and accept that conscious qualities are not, after all, essential to conscious states of mind. Conscious qualities, at best, contingently *accompany* states of mind: experiences are relegated to Tolman's second 'scrap heap'.

I have been focusing on functionalism here, and I shall continue to do so in the next section, but it is important to recognize that points I have been making about functionalism and qualities of conscious experiences apply to a wide spectrum of -isms in the philosophy of mind. Any account of the mind that characterizes states of mind causally, or by relations they bear to other states, any account of the mind that does not build qualities into states of mind, is, for better or worse, going to have similar consequences.

10.5 Biting the Bullet

Let us return to the thought that consciousness, in all its qualitative splendor, is a natural, albeit strictly inessential, *accompaniment* of mental goings-on. The laws of nature operative in the universe might ensure that any creature, resembling us in material composition and organization, would also resemble us with respect to conscious experience. (David Chalmers goes further, contending that fundamental laws of nature holding in our universe guarantee that anything resembling us *functionally*, regardless of its material composition, must resemble us with respect to conscious qualities: no zombies allowed!) But there is no deeper necessity in the connection between qualities of conscious experience and properties of material systems. There *could* be a universe, precisely resembling ours in every material detail, but entirely devoid of consciousness. A universe of this sort, a zombie universe, would, were functionalism correct, be a universe in which agents have a full repertoire of beliefs, desires, feelings, and emotions. It is just that, in the zombie universe, these familiar states of mind would lack the inner, qualitative dimension they exhibit in our universe.

What if it were possible in the universe just as it is – *our* universe – to construct a functional duplicate of a conscious agent that lacked conscious experiences?

To set the stage, reflect on the fact that, according to functionalists, minds are complex *structures* comprising states that bear the right kinds of causal relation to one another and to inputs and outputs. You could depict the mind as a network, each node of which represents a mental state. States are defined, not by their intrinsic natures, but by their place in the network, by relations they bear to other states. This means that it would be possible – and indeed functionalists insist that it *is* possible – to replace occupants of particular nodes with utterly different kinds of entity, provided only that the *relations* the occupant bears to other occupants are preserved.

The possibility of a zombie cat was intended to suggest that you could, in principle at least, concoct a system that satisfied this requirement, and so, on functionalist criteria, possessed a mind, while altogether lacking conscious experiences. If you thought that conscious experiencing was a central feature of mentality, this would be bad news for functionalism. The cat example proved inconclusive. Consider, however, another thought experiment developed by Ned Block designed to highlight the inability of functionalism to provide a plausible overall account of the mind.

Imagine the population of China linked together and to the outside world by mobile telephones, and organized in a way that corresponds to the way that, according to functionalists, a human mind is organized. Each member of the Chinese population is a node connected to other nodes in a network modeled after the human mind. A functionalist is obliged to admit that this system *is* a mind: that it perceives, has beliefs and pains, that the system is *conscious*. This strikes most impartial observers as wildly implausible. The individuals making up the system have beliefs and desires, form intentions, suffer pains, and become depressed; certainly, the individual 'nodes' are conscious, but not the system as a whole. If functionalism implies – absurdly – that the Chinese population duly organized *is* conscious, then functionalism must be rejected.

A functionalist might try denying that the population of China *could* be organized in a way that mirrors the organization of the human mind. If, however, *all there is* to the mind is an appropriate functional arrangement, then it is hard to see what could motivate such a denial. If the population of China is inadequate, include the population of the entire planet, or the insect population, or the cells making up your digestive tract. Providing these are organized in the right way, providing they satisfy a system of the sort illustrated in Figure 6.6, they must count as minds (presumably *conscious* minds).

Fanciful examples might not be required to make this point. It would not be especially surprising if the so-called brain in the gut, or even the autonomic nervous system (that portion of the nervous system dedicated to the control of non-voluntary bodily functions: respiration, heart rate, and body temperature), matched a significant portion of the functional organization of a conscious mind – if not the mind of an adult human being, then the mind of an infant or the mind of some 'lower' sentient creature.

Functionalists would seem to have two options here. First, they could bite the bullet here, and simply accept this consequence as a discovery, one surprising result of an independently plausible theory. Consciousness is at best an accidental accompaniment of states of mind. Second, functionalists could follow Chalmers and insist that, appropriately organized, the Chinese population (as a whole) *does* undergo conscious experiences. If you are not already committed to functionalism, however, and you find neither option appealing, you would have a compelling reason to conclude that functionalists have missed the boat.

10.6 Mary, Mary, Quite Contrary

Functionalism focuses on *structure*. A state of mind is what is – a pain, for instance – if it bears the right relations to other states of mind and to inputs and outputs. Those other states of mind are what *they* are owing to *their* place in this structure. If you think of a structure as an arrangement of nodes and connections (recall Figures 6.5 and 6.6), then you could think of functionalism as concentrating on the connections. It does not matter *what* occupies particular nodes. What matters is that you have the right *connections*: nodes would be 'realizers' of particular kinds of state, and intrinsic qualities of nodes are irrelevant. (Once again, recall the 'beetle in the box', § 4.4.) Thus, on the official functionalist view, what makes a pain a pain is not its intrinsic character but relations it, or its realizer, bears to other states. (And, again, what makes these other states the states *they* are would be the relations they bear to all the rest.) Structure rules!

Can functionalists – or, for that matter, philosophers or scientists of any theoretical persuasion – get away with downgrading the intrinsic qualitative character of conscious experiences, or is qualitative character the 800-pound gorilla that no one can afford to ignore?

Many philosophers have emphasized the central place conscious experiences have in our commerce with the world. Often this is done by lovingly describing particular experiences in vivid detail and challenging nay-sayers to deny the obvious. The difficulty with this approach is that it amounts to little more than a forceful restating of a position its proponents hope to defend. Frank Jackson has argued that there is a much more satisfying way to establish the fundamental status of conscious experiences. Jackson's argument takes the form of another simple, but memorable thought experiment.

Mary (invariably described as a 'brilliant scientist') specializes in the physics and psychophysics of color and color perception. She has learned 'all there is to learn' about these topics, she has mastered 'all the physical facts'. Mary's accomplishment is especially impressive owing to her circumstances: Mary was raised and educated in an exclusively black and white environment. Nothing in her laboratory is colored. Mary has had no direct access to colored objects, or colored lights, or colored anything. Her black and white computer monitor is her only means of communication with the outside world. Everything she knows about color she has read in books and articles displayed on her computer monitor and experiments she has performed remotely on subjects outside the room. You can get a feel for Mary's situation by imagining what it would be like to live the life of someone in a black and white movie.

One day Mary is released from the room. As she steps outside, she experiences first hand a Technicolor world. She sees a ripe tomato illuminated by bright sunlight. She sees something red. Mary is smart enough to recognize the tomato as a tomato (just as you might recognize Gene Autry's sorrel, Champion, in the flesh even though you had only seen the horse in black and white films). She knew already that ripe tomatoes were red and that they looked red when illuminated in bright sunlight. She is stunned, however, to discover *what it is like* for something to look red. Although Mary could discourse for hours on the physiology and psychology of color experiences, she is completely unprepared for her first conscious visual *experience* of something red, her first 'red experience'. Jackson sums all this up by saying that, in experiencing red for the first time, Mary learns a new fact. Mary already had command of all the *physical* facts concerning color, so this new fact must be a *nonphysical* fact, a *mental* fact concerning the experience of red.

The title of the paper in which Jackson unleashed Mary on the philosophical world is 'Epiphenomenal *Qualia*'. Jackson's idea is that, experiencing red is a matter of being in a qualitatively imbued conscious state. Qualities of this state are invisible from the 'outside'. Only you could be aware of the qualities of your conscious experiences. These qualities evidently have no effect on the operation of physical systems, however; they are *epiphenomenal*. So long as she remained in her black and white environment, Mary had only indirect access to such qualities. She knew, from the testimony of others, that experiences were qualitatively rich and variegated. She could predict how people would describe their experiences of ripe tomatoes. What she could not know, however, was *what it is like* to have a 'red experience'.

This last claim needs to be understood in the right way. In one sense Mary already knew what it was like to see a ripe tomato: she knew that experiencing a tomato was similar to experiencing a red billiard ball and dissimilar to experiencing a Granny Smith. She had a thorough understanding of 'color space'. In another sense, however, Mary did *not* know what it was like. Knowing that requires *undergoing* the experience and thereby becoming aware of, encountering 'directly', its qualitative nature.

What Mary discovered about color experiences is meant to apply to conscious experiences generally. The lesson Jackson wants you to take away is that being consciously aware of something is to be in a state of mind with a particular sort of qualitative character, a character utterly unlike the character of material bodies – including the brain. Your only access to conscious qualities is through your experiencing them first hand. This feature of conscious qualities places them outside the physical domain.

Taking Jackson seriously means taking dualism seriously. One possibility, the possibility Jackson himself favors (or favored; he subsequently recanted), is that qualities of conscious experiences, *qualia*, are epiphenomenal by-products of processes in the brains of sentient creatures. Consciousness, as Chalmers puts it, 'arises from' material systems of the right kind. This makes consciousness *dependent on* matter. The nature of this dependence relation is mysterious, however. I shall say more about that in a moment, but first it would be worth spelling out why Jackson thinks *qualia* must be *epiphenomenal*.

Suppose *qualia* could influence material events. In that case, Mary, who knows 'all the physical facts', would have stumbled on endless causal 'gaps' in the material world. Various events in the brains of sentient creatures would be inexplicable or only partly explicable physically. But there is no reason to think that this is how it is. True, quantum physics allows for spontaneous events, and doubtless such events occur in the brains of sentient creatures and affect their operations. A spontaneous event is an *uncaused* event, however, not an event with an unknown or unknowable cause. Thus, if it seems to you that the qualities of your experiences make a difference in the material world, if you think these qualities make a difference in what you do or say, that is only because material brain events responsible for your experiences *also* produce material effects. The situation would be one in which a material cause has two effects: a material effect and an immaterial (and epiphenomenal) effect.

What about the idea that consciousness *depends* on material goings-on? I mentioned Chalmers as someone who holds such a view. In fact, what Chalmers contends is that the basis of consciousness is not the material (biological or chemical) makeup of creatures that are conscious. Rather, consciousness 'arises from' functional organization, which in turn is realized by various material states and processes. If you undergo a particular sort of conscious experience, this is because you are in a particular sort of *functional* state. If you are in the pain state, you will undergo a painful experience with all its aversive qualitative character. Any being, whatever its material makeup, in the same functional state would undergo a qualitatively similar experience. Chalmers thinks that laws governing the blossoming of consciousness are *fundamental* laws of nature, laws on a par with those governing the fundamental particles. Because these laws are fundamental, they cannot be explained in terms of, or derived from, other laws.

One consequence of such a view is that, if you *could* organize the Chinese nation in a way that mimicked the functional state underlying pain, the Chinese nation *would* undergo a painful experience. Any doubts you might have about this possibility would have to be tied to doubts that you could organize the Chinese nation so as to match the functional organization of a sentient creature in pain.

Another challenging feature of Chalmers's position comes into view when you combine the following claims.

1   Laws governing the emergence of consciousness tie conscious states to functional states.
2   These laws are fundamental.

Functional states are multiply realizable. The realizers of pain, for instance, make up a heterogeneous, possibly open-ended, collection of material states. Because the laws are fundamental, they would have to connect each kind of conscious state with heterogeneous arrangements of particles. It is not easy to think of examples of fundamental laws that have this many-to-one character, especially given that each of the many is a monstrously complicated interconnected arrangement of particles.

If Chalmers does not suit, however, what options are left? To be a viable candidate, a theory would need to take qualities of conscious experiences seriously, but in a way that reconciles consciousness with what science reveals about the natural world. What are the prospects?

10.7   Emergence and Panpsychism

The discussion of Chalmers' brand of dualism has brought into focus the difficulty of understanding what it could mean for consciousness to 'arise' or 'emerge' from organized collections of particles. You can understand how, by arranging stones in the right way, you get a cathedral. You can understand how, by putting together molecules in the right way, you get a liquid. But how could you get consciousness from arrangements of nonconscious material particles? How could anything wholly devoid of conscious qualities contain 'seeds' of consciousness?

Galen Strawson suggests that the difficulty in understanding how consciousness could result from combinations of nonconscious material particles (or fields, or whatever the fundamental things turn out to be) is analogous to the difficulty in understanding how you could get something with spatial characteristics, a spherical shape, for instance, by assembling a collection of nonspatial entities. Spatial wholes need spatial parts. Perhaps, then, conscious wholes need parts that are conscious. If the parts – the fundamental parts – are conscious, you have *panpsychism*, a candidate for Tolman's third 'scrap heap' for conscious qualities.

Panpsychism has a checkered history. Mystics, nature-worshipers, and proponents of a 'world soul' have promoted panpsychism. But it is also possible to imagine a more modest, empirically motivated panpsychism. The idea would not be that electrons and quarks have minds, but that qualities of conscious experiences are included among the qualities possessed by the fundamental things. On the version of panpsychism endorsed by Strawson, electrons would not be mini-souls, but merely contain experiential ingredients of consciousness, a kind of primitive *awareness*. Only fully developed sentient creatures would undergo recognizably conscious experiences. You can make a triangle or a sphere by organizing non-triangular or non-spherical elements in the right way, but the elements must have *some* spatial characteristics. Similarly, you can make a conscious mind by arranging elements that are not themselves minds, but the elements must have *some* conscious characteristics.

The alternative, according to Strawson, is to imagine that conscious qualities are *emergent* phenomena: when you organize particles in the right way, conscious qualities put in an appearance for the first time, conscious qualities *arise*. Although talk of emergence comes easy, it is not at all easy to provide an informative characterization of the notion. Emergence appears to have something to do with properties of *parts* and properties of *wholes*. Indeed, wholes *can* possess properties not possessed by any of their parts. Suppose you have three matchsticks. You arrange these so as to form a triangle. Now the whole is triangular, although none of its parts is triangular.

The triangle just *is* the three matchsticks duly arranged, however. Triangularity is not something additional, not an add-on, not something that pops into existence; triangularity is what you have when you have the parts arranged in the right way. If this were all there were to emergence, the phenomenon would be completely unmysterious. The trouble is that, according to Strawson, the model does not to apply in the case of conscious experiences and the material parts of sentient creatures. It is hard to see how, just by arranging the particles in a particular way, you could produce something with conscious qualities – unless the qualities were present in the particles already. In fact, it was just this difficulty that led to thoughts of emergence in the first place.

Maybe the example is flawed. Maybe triangularity is a poor candidate for emergence. Consider arranging the particles so as to produce a collection of H_2O molecules. Although none of the particles, none of the molecules that are made up of the particles, is transparent or liquid, the resulting collection is. Although this example appears more promising, Strawson thinks it differs importantly from the case of consciousness. Once you understand molecular structures, you can understand *how it is* that collections of H_2O molecules would be transparent and liquid. You have nothing like this in the case of consciousness. No one has the faintest understanding of how the particles or the organic molecules they make up, when arranged brain-wise, could result in conscious experiences. And, again, this is what leads philosophers and others to suppose that consciousness, or qualities of conscious experiences, are, unlike liquidity and transparency, and certainly unlike triangularity, distinctively *emergent*.

Whatever emergence is supposed to be, then, it is not at all like what happens in cases of triangularity or liquidity. So what *is* emergence? Sometimes emergence is characterized *epistemologically*: an emergent property of a whole is one that could not be *predicted* just on the basis of knowledge of the parts. This is certainly true in the case of consciousness.

The trouble is that it is probably true as well of triangularity and liquidity. Could you predict, in advance, that matchsticks placed in the right relations to one another would yield a triangle? (If you think this would be easy, remember that it would not be fair describing the 'right relations' as triangular.) When you consider liquidity, it becomes clear that you could not predict that a particular arrangement of particles would produce something liquid and transparent given only information about the particles and nothing more. Once you understand *liquids*, you might be in a position to predict correctly. But the same could be said for consciousness: you know that the right combinations of particles yield consciousness. The difficulty is in seeing *why* this should be so. Describing consciousness as emergent seems merely to be appending a label to a mystery.

Strawson provides an example. Suppose someone claimed that spatial qualities are emergent: when you put together nonspatial entities in the right way, the result is something triangular, or spherical, or three meters across. How could this possibly work? It would be no help to say that, as a matter of 'brute fact', spatial qualities emerge. The idea that spatiality 'arises' from entities that are themselves nonspatial looks implausible on the face of it. But this, says Strawson, is how proponents of the emergence of consciousness seem to be thinking of it.

Strawson's suggestion is that, just as you could not get spatial things from nonspatial things, so you could not get conscious qualities from ingredients that lack such qualities. Indeed, the need to appeal to emergence stems from theorists assuming from the outset that the pertinent qualities are completely absent in the fundamental things, then wondering how they could occur in the experiences of sentient creatures. The mistake is to start with the gratuitous assumption that the qualities *are* absent in the fundamental things. Compare someone who begins with the assumption that the fundamental things must be nonspatial, then finds it deeply mysterious how triangularity or sphericity emerges, how spatiality arises from assemblages of nonspatial entities.

The point is perfectly general. If you start with the supposition that mental qualities are utterly different from qualities of material things, if you start with the supposition that the world is bifurcated into the mental and the material, you are bound to have difficulty reconciling the two, showing how the mental could in some fashion arise from the material. Appealing to emergence would, in that case, be an appeal to mystery: the mental *just does* arise from the material, but there is no saying how this could be possible.

By Strawson's lights, then, the concept of emergence at play in discussions of consciousness is incoherent; emergence is nothing more than a label for an unintelligible relation invented to solve a problem of our own making. Strawson's preferred alternative, *panpsychism*, begins with a rejection of the assumption that the fundamental things are devoid of conscious qualities, devoid of *awareness*. Strawson argues that the rejection of this assumption is in fact entirely *consistent* with what physics tells us about the fundamental things. Physics describes these things wholly by reference to what they do or would do, leaving open their 'intrinsic nature'. In this Strawson echoes physicist Arthur Eddington.

> Science has nothing to say as to the intrinsic nature of the atom. The physical atom is, like everything else in physics, a schedule of pointer readings. The schedule is, we agree, attached to some unknown background. Why not then attach it to something of a spiritual nature of which a prominent characteristic is *thought*. It seems rather silly to attach it to something of a so-called 'concrete' nature inconsistent with thought, and then to wonder where the thought comes from. We have dismissed all preconception as to the background of our pointer readings, and for the most part we can discover nothing of its nature. But in one case – namely for the pointer readings of my own brain – I have an insight which is not limited to the evidence of the pointer readings. That insight shows that they are attached to a background of consciousness. Although I may expect that the background of other pointer readings in physics is of a nature continuous with that revealed to me in this particular case, I do not suppose that it always has the more specialized attributes of consciousness. *There is nothing to prevent the assemblage of atoms constituting a brain from being of itself a thinking object in virtue of that nature which physics leaves undetermined and undeterminable.*
>
> (Eddington 1928, 259–60; emphasis in original)

Strawson's brand of panpsychism, then, is apparently consistent with what physics tells us about the fundamental things. Qualities of conscious experiences are not immaterial, nonphysical qualities. The sharp material–immaterial, physical–mental dichotomy with which we began is misguided. What you might regard as nonphysical qualities are in fact characteristic of physical things. (The conscious facts *are* physical facts; Mary, as it happens, does *not* know 'all the physical facts'!) Mind permeates nature, at least in the sense that mental qualities, the elements of consciousness are everywhere present. The mind–body problem, the problem of consciousness arises only when you under-describe the physical world, when you leave out its 'intrinsic qualitative nature'. You are apt to do this when you interpret physicists' silence on the intrinsic nature of the fundamental things as a denial that they have an intrinsic qualitative nature. But silence is not denial.

10.8 Representationalism

Panpsychism hopes to solve the problem of consciousness by supposing that consciousness is in at the ground level. Qualities of conscious experiences are already present in the fundamental things, so there is no mystery in their being present in sentient creatures.

Panpsychism, however, is but one of *two* possibilities making up Tolman's third 'scrap heap'. The second possibility is what Tolman calls *neorealism*. Neorealists hold that qualities you might regard as belonging to conscious experiences are in reality qualities of objects experienced. Such qualities seem mysterious only when you try to locate them in the heads of sentient creatures. This line of thought is the complement of panpsychism. Whereas panpsychism takes qualities of conscious experiences and spreads them on the world, neorealism takes qualities of conscious experiences to *be* material qualities of perceived material things.

Imagine that you are now looking at a stately gum tree. You are, let us suppose, undergoing a conscious visual experience of the tree. Now ask yourself, what are the qualities of this conscious experience? As noted in Chapter 5, it would be a mistake to confuse qualities of an object you perceive with qualities of your experience of the object. The tree you happen to be looking at is 15 meters tall and green. Your perceptual experience of the tree is neither. Indeed, as you would have discovered already, it is difficult to say with any precision *what* the qualities of your perceptual experience of the tree – as opposed to the qualities of what you are experiencing (the tree) – might be.

To run together qualities of what you experience with qualities of your experience is to commit the 'phenomenological fallacy' (§ 5.9–5.10). The ease with which this fallacy is committed is arguably what lies behind the widespread belief that conscious qualities are profoundly mysterious. You describe your perceptual experience by describing what you are experiencing – what else could you do! You are experiencing something leafy and green.

But nothing in your brain is leafy and green. So how could your perceptual experience be an occurrence in your brain?

This line of reasoning is evidently fallacious. But now, in considering a perceptual experience, if you subtract the qualities of whatever is experienced (in this case, qualities of the tree) what is left? Whatever qualities remain would be qualities of the experience itself. And it is most unclear what these might be. Maybe experiences themselves altogether lack qualities. Or maybe, as the neorealists have it, what we *call* qualities of experiences are just qualities of what we are experiencing: when you 'subtract the qualities of whatever is experienced', *nothing* remains. Experiences of things collapse into the things experienced. Or, if, as identity theorists would have it, experiences are occurrences in the brains of sentient creatures, experiences have whatever qualities neurological occurrences have. These would be qualities to which you have no ready conscious access.

This way of approaching what you might think of as the problem of consciousness is characteristic of *representationalism*. Representationalists are fond of citing the philosopher, G. E. Moore, who describes experiences as transparent or 'diaphanous'. Your having a perceptual experience of the stately gum tree is a matter of your becoming aware of the tree's qualities. If you are asked to describe your experience, you will describe the tree, the 'object' of your experience.

Seizing on the point, a representationalist might contend that experiences themselves lack qualities of their own, qualities identifiable independently of the qualities of objects experienced: experiences are 'transparent'. Or, more cautiously, although experiences could have qualities, these are not qualities you would be in any sense aware of in undergoing the experience.

Representationalists hold that your consciously experiencing something is a matter of representing that thing: to be conscious is to represent. Although not all representations, not even all *mental* representations, are conscious (see §§ 8.8 and 10.9), all conscious states are representational. Consciousness is always consciousness *of* something. And to be conscious of something is to represent that something. When philosophers speak of intentionality, they have in mind the *ofness* of representational states.

You might dispute this. Compare dreading an upcoming examination with experiencing undirected dread – *angst*. Your dreading an examination is apparently representational: your dread has an object, the examination. But *angst*, unfocused dread, appears not to be representational, not to have an object. Rather it is a *mood*, it 'colors' experiences of things and events. Ask yourself whether this is a serious stumbling block for representationalism or a mere detail that a representationalist might easily accommodate.

Let us suppose that moods are not a big deal, that qualities available to you in conscious experiences – *qualia*, so-called – are just those qualities you *represent* experienced objects and events as having. And, again, these are to be distinguished from qualities of representations themselves. My earlier representation of a gum tree is a representation of something leafy and green, but the *representation* is neither leafy nor green. The representation has qualities, all right, just not *these* qualities. Representations of the very same object – representations of something leafy and green – could have endless different qualities depending on the medium of representation. You might represent the tree by using a pen to inscribe sentences on white paper with blue ink. A painter might represent the tree by means of colored paints on canvas. And an electronically inclined designer might represent the tree by creating a pattern of colored pixels on a computer screen. Although each of these representations represents a tree, each differs in its intrinsic qualities from the others – and from the tree.

So suppose that you agree with the representationalist: experiencing a tree is in part a matter of representing the tree mentally. In visually experiencing a tree, you represent the tree as having various visually detectable qualities. Your representation would seem to have, as well, assorted intrinsic qualities of its own, perhaps qualities of the neurological processes in which your representation is encoded. It is a safe bet that you know little or nothing of these qualities. Certainly you know nothing of them solely on the basis of your visual experience of the tree.

Now consider the qualities you represent the tree as having. Perhaps these qualities – or rather our representations of them – are enough to satisfy those who harp on *qualia*, self-proclaimed '*qualia* freaks'. If so, we would have uncovered a way of reconciling what are misleadingly called 'qualities of conscious experience' and materialism. A functionalist, for instance, could contend that qualities of *experiences themselves* are not present in ordinary awareness. But that is no loss, that poses no problem for functionalism. Your becoming aware of the qualities of an experience would require that you experience your experience – by observing the operation of your surgically exposed brain in a mirror, for instance.

What of those qualities that might strike you as *purely* mental, qualities that appear to have *no* place in the material world? What about qualities exhibited in dreams and hallucinations? How could representationalism deal with these? Not by locating them in objects experienced. Neither dream objects, nor objects hallucinated, exist.

Perhaps your dreaming that you are fleeing a greenish alien or your hallucinating a greenish alien is just a matter of your representing the presence of a greenish alien. Your representation itself need not be greenish – any more than the words on this page that represent the alien are greenish. Indeed, in these cases, nothing at all need be greenish. Greenishness drops out of the picture. Compare this with your experience of a throbbing pain in your left big toe. Your having such an experience is, as may be, a matter of your representing a throbbing, aversive occurrence in your big toe. As noted in Chapter 2, the experience – as we are now supposing, the representing – need not itself be in your big toe. If you are tempted by materialism, you would locate it (or, if you are a functionalist, locate its 'realizer') in your brain. Further, although in the normal case, your experience of a pain in your toe will be an experience of an actual physiological occurrence in your toe, it need not be. This would be so if your experience were hallucinatory, or if you were suffering a 'phantom' or 'referred' pain.

What of the throbbing quality? It seems unlikely that *this* is a quality of anything in your toe. When you examine the toe closely, you do not discover anything throbbing. Is the throbbing a quality of your experience, then? This too seems unlikely. Were a scientist to delve into your brain, the scientist would be unlikely to stumble on throbbing aggregations of neurons. Perhaps the throbbing is like the greenishness you represent the alien as having: it is not a quality possessed by anything. You represent certain occurrences as throbbing, but nothing in fact throbs. (Or, at any rate, nothing possesses a distinctively mental quality identifiable as a throbbing. Lights and music uncontroversially throb.)

The idea is that if a materialist or functionalist account of consciousness dispenses with such qualities, it would not be dispensing with anything you could possibly miss. You *represent* objects as having such qualities, but it does not follow that anything actually *has* the qualities – any more than, from the fact that you can represent mermaids, it follows that mermaids exist. In some cases, then, cases of hallucination, for instance, or in dreams – what opponents of functionalism describe as qualities of conscious experiences, *qualia* – might be qualities of nothing at all! What you naturally think of as qualities of conscious experiences are qualities you, correctly or mistakenly, represent objects and occurrences as having. Alternatively, to say that your experience possesses such qualities is just to say that you are, at the time, representing something as having them.

Opponents of representationalism regard this line of argument as a kind of sleight of hand. All parties to the discussion can accept a distinction between qualities of experiences and qualities experienced objects are represented as having. It is much less obvious, however, that real qualities of your experiences are not available to you except in the indirect way envisaged earlier – via observations of your own brain.

Accepting for the moment that experiences are inevitably representational, a veridical visual experience of a tomato, a visual hallucination of a tomato, and a 'mental image' of a tomato are alike representationally: they all represent a tomato. But they surely seem to be alike qualitatively as well. Hallucinating a tomato, for instance, resembles – qualitatively! – visually perceiving a tomato. And the qualitatively similarity between imagining and perceiving a tomato is what gives imagery its point.

A representationalist would insist that the similarities in question are all purely representational. Your visual perception of a tomato, your hallucination of a tomato, and your tomato imagery all include similar representational elements – representations of features of a tomato. But is this enough? A painting and a detailed written description of a tomato both represent a tomato. They do so in very different *ways*, however; they involve qualitatively different representational *modes*. In contrast, hallucination and imagery apparently resemble ordinary perception not merely representation-ally but also, and crucially, in the *way* they represent. If ways of representing concern representational 'vehicles', then qualities of these would seem to qualify as qualities of the corresponding experiences. Or is this just more mystery-mongering?

10.9   Consciousness as Higher-Order Representation

Descartes regarded all states of mind as fully conscious. The notion that a mental state or process might be *non*conscious would have been, for Descartes, unintelligible. Nowadays, researchers routinely appeal to noncon-scious mental states and processes to explain the behavior of sentient crea-tures. Your visually apprehending a complex scene, for instance, might involve many layers of processing of sensory inputs. You engage in routine activities 'unthinkingly', without attending to what you are doing.

You can undoubtedly think of many examples of mental activities that elude awareness. But if not all mental states and processes are conscious, what distinguishes those that *are* from those that *are not* conscious? One possibility (introduced in § 8.6 in the course of a discussion of Daniel Dennett's treatment of consciousness) is that consciousness occurs only with the occurrence of 'higher-order' mental states.

To see what this means, think about representationalism. The discussion of representationalism in the previous section was aimed at illuminating a particular sort of response to the puzzle of consciousness. According to the representationalist, a conscious state is a representational state. But nothing in representationalism requires that *every* mental representation be conscious. Suppose that not all mental representations are conscious, suppose that sentient creatures can represent states of the world and states of their own bodies *nonconsciously*. What distinguishes conscious representational states from nonconscious representational states?

Perhaps being conscious is a matter of representing a representational state. Imagine that you perceptually encounter a tree. In so doing you 'register' the presence of the tree and various of its qualities. But you could do this without being fully conscious of the tree. (Think of walking through the woods in pursuit of a kind of butterfly. You negotiate a tree-filled environ-ment more or less automatically, rarely turning your attention to individual trees.) Your *consciously* experiencing the tree might be a matter of your being in a representational state, the object of which is not the *tree* but your *repre-sentation* of the tree. A sentient creature's behavior is mediated by its repre-sentations of the world. These representations *become* conscious when the creature becomes aware of *them*, when the creature *represents* them.

One worry about such a view is that it seems unlikely that all sentient creatures, all creatures you might be inclined to regard as conscious, are capable of higher-order states of mind. (If Dennett is right – see Chapter 8 – only linguistically endowed creatures, only creatures adept at the use of language, would be capable of thoughts about thoughts.) You might doubt, then, that a capacity for higher-order states of mind is a *necessary* condition for consciousness.

At this point a proponent of the view that conscious thoughts are higher-order representations could appeal to a distinction (made in § 10.2) between 'creature consciousness' and 'mental state consciousness'. To say that a creature, a squirrel, for instance, is conscious is to say that the squirrel is awake, alert, and responding to its environment. No doubt much of what the squirrel does is guided by the squirrel's mental representations of its circumstances. The squirrel is conscious. It is another matter, however, to suppose that the squirrel's mental states are conscious. The higher-order theorist holds that there is no reason to think that they are: the hypothesis that they are is not required to account for the squirrel's behavior. So the fact that a higher-order theorist does not count the squirrel's states of mind as conscious need not be a mark against the theory.

Still, you might think that when the squirrel is in pain or thirsty the squirrel's states of mind are themselves fully conscious: the squirrel is undergoing conscious experiences. This would mean that, in the squirrel's case, creature consciousness apparently involves mental state consciousness: the squirrel's behavior would not be fully explainable otherwise. It is not obvious, then, that higher-order representation is necessary for mental state consciousness.

You might wonder, as well, whether higher-order representation is *sufficient* for consciousness. If representational states can be nonconscious, it would seem that you could have cases in which a nonconscious state is nonconsciously represented by a higher-order state. But then it is hard to see how adding a higher-order representation could *itself* render a state consciousness.

Needless to say, higher-order theorists are equipped with responses to these worries. The question is whether this is the best we can do; whether, more broadly, all of the qualities of conscious experience can be accommodated representationally. Return to the Chinese nation worry about functionalism (§ 10.5). Suppose the Chinese nation could be organized so as to reflect the functional organization of a representing agent. And suppose that some of the resulting representations were representations of representations. Would this tempt you to regard the Chinese nation as conscious, or the nation's represented representations as conscious? Or is the worry here simply a manifestation of inchoate 'intuitions' about consciousness?

10.10 Explaining Consciousness

One catch-all response to worries of this kind is to point out that consciousness is deeply mysterious on anyone's view. No one has any clear idea how to accommodate consciousness to the material world, no clear idea how to explain the phenomenon of consciousness. That being the case, we are in no position to tar functionalism, or representationalism, or higher-order theories with what appear to be their implausible consequences. *Every* attempt to resolve the problem of consciousness has its implausible aspects. Dualism is satisfying when you focus on your own case, but dualism is hard to reconcile with a plausible scientific picture of the world. Theories that play nicely with science inevitably run afoul of subjective experience.

You might, in the end, have to accept this sad possibility; you might have to allow that the nature of consciousness is such that a fully satisfying account of conscious experience is not in the cards. If you hope to venture an informed opinion on such topics, you will need a firmer grip on the meta-physical issues that underlie the debate. Chapter 11 opens the discussion with an examination of *non-reductive physicalism*, a currently influential approach to the nature of the mind growing out of attempts to reconcile distinctive features of the mind with the preeminent status of physics and the physical sciences generally.

Suggested Reading

The best known discussion of the ineliminability of the 'what it's like' question is Thomas Nagel's much-cited 'What is it Like to be a Bat?' (1974). Nagel's concerns applied to functionalism have yielded complex debates over the status of *qualia*, the qualities of conscious experiences. See also Frank Jackson's 'Epiphenomenal Qualia' (1982). For another perspective, see Janet Levin's 'Could Love be like a Heatwave?' (1986). A survey of contemporary accounts of consciousness can be found in Robert Van Gulick's 'Consciousness' (2011) in the online *Stanford Encyclopedia of Philosophy*.

Ned Block's Chinese nation case appears in his 'Troubles with Functionalism' (1978). Sydney Shoemaker defends functionalism from the '*qualia*' threat in 'Functionalism and *Qualia*' (1975). See also 'Absent *Qualia* are Impossible – A Reply to Block' (1984b). A different line of response to Block can be found in William Lycan's *Consciousness* (1987), chapters 4 and 5; see also Lycan's *Consciousness and Experience* (1996).

Zombies, in the special sense associated with functionalism, are the invention of Robert Kirk. See his 'Zombies vs. Materialists' (1974). Kirk's more recent views on the subject are spelled out in *Raw Feeling* (1996, chapter 3), and *Zombies and Consciousness* (2005). The philosopher most impressed by zombies is David Chalmers. Chalmers, in a widely discussed book, argues that zombies, though 'nomologically impossible', are logically possible, and so make consciousness deeply mysterious; see *The Conscious Mind* (1996), especially, § ii, 'The Irreducibility of Consciousness'.

Thomas Nagel discusses panpsychism sympathetically in 'Panpsychism', chapter 8 of *Mortal Questions* (1979). Galen Strawson's more recent defense of panpsychism can be found in 'Realistic Monism: Why Physicalism Entails Panpsychism' (2006) and *Real Materialism and Other Essays* (2008). On the topic of emergence, see Cynthia and Graham Macdonald's introductory essay of their anthology, *Emergence in Mind* (2010), and other papers in the same volume.

The representationalist account of *qualia* discussed in this chapter is a hybrid of views advanced by Gilbert Harman, 'The Intrinsic Quality of Experience' (1990); Fred Dretske, *Naturalizing the Mind* (1995, chapter 3); and Michael Tye, *Ten Problems of Consciousness: A Representational Theory of the Phenomenal Mind* (1995). Lycan's 'In Defense of the Representational Theory of Qualia (Replies to Neander, Rey, and Tye)' (1998) anchors a symposium on representational theories with discussion by Karen Neander, Georges Rey, and Michael Tye. John McDowell's 'The Content of Perceptual Experience' (1994) initiates a more unsettling approach to representation and conscious experience.

Readers skeptical of the idea that consciousness is wholly representational might look at Block's 'Mental Paint' (2003) and Colin McGinn's *The Problem of Consciousness: Essays Toward a Resolution* (1991).

Versions of higher-order theories of consciousness have been defended by David Rosenthal in 'Two Concepts of Consciousness' (1986) and *Consciousness and Mind* (2005); by Peter Carruthers in *Phenomenal Consciousness* (2000) (see also Carruthers' earlier 'Brute Experience' (1989); and by Uriah Kriegel, 'The Same-Order Monitoring Theory of Consciousness' (2006). Critics of this approach include William Seager, 'A Cold Look at HOT Theory' (2004), Charles Siewert, *The Significance of Consciousness* (1998), and Mark Rowlands, 'Consciousness and Higher-Order Thoughts' (2001).

For an accessible account of the 'brain in the gut' by a journalist, see Sandra Blakeslee's 'The Brain in the Gut' (1996). The live possibility that the autonomic nervous system satisfies functionalist criteria for the mental is eloquently defended in T. D. Ryder's 'Evaluating Theories of Consciousness Using the Autonomic Nervous System for Comparison' (1996).

11 Non-Reductive Physicalism

11.1 From Substances to Properties

Chapters 2 and 3 were devoted to a discussion of Descartes's *substance dualism* and its historical successors. Nowadays substance dualism has few proponents. Nevertheless dualism survives in the form of a widespread acceptance of a dualism of properties: *property dualism*. Functionalists, for instance, embrace a kind of property dualism in arguing that mental characteristics, although *realized by* or *grounded in* agents' material makeup, are not *reducible to* material characteristics. More generally, philosophers calling themselves *non-reductive physicalists* hold that mental states and properties are *dependent on*, yet *distinct from*, material states and properties. A view of this sort has struck many philosophers as not merely attractive, but *inevitable*.

You have already encountered two important varieties of non-reductive physicalism: functionalism and the Representational Theory of Mind. Anyone who regards qualities of conscious experiences to be distinctively nonmaterial but in some way dependent on physical characteristics of sentient creatures falls into this camp as well. It would not be much of an exaggeration to describe non-reductive physicalism as today's orthodoxy in the philosophy of mind. You might wonder what lies behind this remarkable philosophical convergence.

As with so much in philosophy today, it starts with Descartes. Descartes begins with the thought that there are two fundamental kinds of substance: mental substances and material substances. Each kind of substance has a unique definitive *attribute*. A material substance is an *extended* substance, a substance with spatial characteristics, a substance that has some definite size, shape, and spatial location. Properties of material substances are *modes of extension*: ways of being extended. Mental substances, in contrast, *think*. Properties of mental substances are *modes of thought*. Bear in mind Descartes's wide-ranging conception of thinking, which is meant to include doubting, understanding, affirming, denying, willing, refusing, sensing, dreaming, and having mental images.

So: mental substances think; material substances are extended; no extended substance thinks; no thinking substance is extended. The attributes of thought and extension *exclude* one another in something like the way being spherical and being cube-shaped exclude one another in a particular object at a particular time.

Spinoza (1632–77), who succeeded Descartes as the preeminent 'rationalist' philosopher, advanced a somewhat different picture. Given the traditional characterization of substance as something absolutely independent of any other thing, Spinoza argued that there could be, at most, *one* substance – the universe itself. Dependent entities – attributes and modes, for instance – could exist only if a substance exists for them to be attributes of or to modify. If something exists, then, it must be either the one substance or an attribute or mode of this one substance. Spinoza regards thought and extension as two fundamental attributes of the one substance: one and the same substance thinks and is extended.

So, whereas Descartes has extended substances and thinking substances, Spinoza has just the one substance. For Spinoza, ordinary objects, animals, and people are modes, not substances; ways the one all-encompassing substance is in a particular region at a particular time. The motion of material bodies is a kind of wave motion analogous to the motion of a football across a television screen.

Spinoza extends this idea to individual selves. You and I are modes of the one substance, which Spinoza called *deus sive natura*: God or nature. Think of Spinoza's one substance as space–time or the unified field. What we regard as the material universe is this one substance under the attribute of extension. Thought and extension permeate the one substance in the way gravity permeates space. This makes Spinoza both a pantheist and a kind of *panpsychist* (see § 10.7), a combination that proved especially unappealing to religious authorities.

11.2 Substance Monism, Property Dualism

Reflect a moment on the implications of Spinoza's view of the material universe for our commonsense conception of the world. Were Spinoza right, for instance, were the motion of objects through space analogous to the 'motion' of a football across your television screen, would motion be only an illusion? For that matter, would ordinary objects be merely apparent, not proper *objects* at all any more than a wave in the ocean is an object. (A wave presumably is not an object, not a substance, but a way a substance is dynamically organized in a particular spatio-temporal region at a particular time.) If this strikes you as far-fetched or wacky consider that, on current physical theory, it is a live possibility that what we think of objects – planets, trees, electrons – could turn out to be Spinoza-like disturbances in space–time or the quantum field.

Spinoza differs importantly with Descartes in contending that one and the same substance could possess *both* mental and physical attributes: extended things could think; thinking things are extended. (Indeed, if there is just one substance and this substance is extended, then if any substance thinks, this extended substance thinks.) The idea that one substance could possess both mental and physical attributes did not originate with Spinoza, however. In a letter (1697) to Stillingfleet, the Bishop of Worcester, Locke, discussed what he called 'thinking matter', the idea that one and the same substance could possess both material and mental properties.

Such a view was championed at length by Joseph Priestley (1733–1804). Locke and Priestley embraced corpuscularism, the doctrine that the material world comprises particles dynamically situated in space. Neither had an interest in the idea, central to Spinoza's view, that there could be at most one substance. (Although Locke did briefly flirt with a variant of this thesis, namely that the fundamental material substance was space itself.)

This chapter focuses on a version of *property dualism*, according to which:

1 Mental and material properties are distinct kinds of property; and
2 A substance can possess both mental and material properties.

A third precept is often added to these:

3 Mental properties depend on material properties.

Property dualism can be contrasted to substance dualism, on the one hand, and, on the other hand, to the kind of property monism favored by Spinoza (and by Donald Davidson; see § 13.9). Both Spinoza and Davidson regard the distinction between mental and physical attributes as a *distinction in conception only*, not what Descartes called a *real distinction*. Both Spinoza and Davidson contend that anything at all that answers to a description framed in a mental vocabulary could be designated using a material vocabulary (and vice versa). For them, the mental–material distinction is a distinction among concepts or terms, not a distinction in reality.

Property dualists insist that the mental–material distinction *is* a distinction in reality, not merely a difference in ways of representing or classifying reality. I have characterized property dualism in terms of *material* and mental properties. Elsewhere I speak of *physical* and mental properties. In general, I prefer 'material' to 'physical' in discussing issues in the philosophy of mind. Material is to be contrasted with nonmaterial. As I see it, the nature of what we regard as physical reality is an open question. If Galen Strawson's panpsychism is right, for instance, then 'physical properties', the properties of the fundamental physical things, would *include* 'mental properties'. In the remainder of this chapter, however, in deference to the ways property dualists characterize their own positions, I shall use 'material' and 'physical' interchangeably.

Property dualism of the kind under consideration here, allows for the possibility that ordinary objects – trees, boulders, grains of salt – are substances in their own right and not merely modes of a single, all-encompassing substance. There are, or could be, endless substances. Some of these, stones, for instance, or electrons, will have physical properties, but no mental properties; some, for instance terrestrial creatures with minds, will have *both* physical properties *and* mental properties. Might a substance have mental properties, but no physical properties? 'Physicalist' proponents of property dualism deny this possibility thereby denying the possibility of immaterial entities: spirits or angels. Others leave the possibility open in principle.

Non-reductive physicalists begin with the conviction that some properties are 'irreducibly mental'. These philosophers reject the identity theory (Chapter 5), according to which mental properties *are* physical properties, accepting a weaker 'token identity' claim: every token (that is, every particular) mental substance is identical with some physical substance. You can make sense of this contention if you bear in mind that a 'mental substance' is a substance possessing a mental property and a 'physical substance' is a substance possessing a physical property. So every substance is a physical substance, every substance has physical properties, and some physical substances are mental substances as well, bearers of mental properties.

Few property dualists today would be content to leave it at this. The idea is not just that mental properties are inevitably accompanied by physical properties. Although mental properties are perfectly respectable properties in their own right, mental properties are in some way dependent on – 'grounded in' or 'realized by' – physical properties. You yourself have the mental properties you have *because* you have certain physical properties, presumably certain biological and chemical properties. Your mental makeup is a consequence of your physical makeup. Even so, your mental characteristics are distinct from, not 'reducible to', your physical characteristics. A view of this kind is meant to allow psychologists, neuroscientists, and philosophers to take mental properties seriously without incurring the liabilities of traditional forms of dualism.

11.3 Mental Causation: Background Issues

Substance dualists find it difficult to make sense of the apparent fact that minds and bodies affect one another causally. When you drop a lump of coal on your toe (a physical event), you feel pain (a mental event). When you form an intention to rub your throbbing toe (a mental event) you rub the toe (a physical event). Each case calls for causal interaction between mental and physical substances. But if, as Descartes insists, mental and physical substances are utterly different – physical substances are extended, mental substances are not – how *could* such causal interaction occur? How *could* an unextended substance find purchase in an extended world? How *could* an extended entity affect a nonspatial, unextended entity?

Non-reductive physicalists reject the Cartesian picture. They accept that a physical substance is a substance possessing physical properties. These properties include modes of extension, but they could also include other properties not reducible to extension: having a particular mass and a particular charge, for instance. Non-reductivists accept, as well, that a mental substance is a substance possessing mental properties, Cartesian modes of thought. All this is consistent with an orthodox substance dualism. What is *not* consistent with substance dualism is the further claim that a mental substance must be a physical substance. One and the same substance could be both mental and physical, could possess both mental properties and physical properties: a thinking substance could be extended.

A view of this kind might seem a perfectly natural emendation to Cartesian dualism. Indeed, many of Descartes's contemporaries questioned his insistence that no substance could be both conscious and extended. Cartesian metaphysics guaranteed this result, but why accept that metaphysics uncritically – particularly when it seems to guarantee the unintelligibility of mental–physical causal interaction?

Note, incidentally, that the intractability of the Cartesian mind–body problem stems, not from Descartes's insistence that minds and bodies are distinct substances. A familiar instance of causation is the interaction between two billiard balls when one strikes the other causing it to roll across the table. Descartes's problem, rather, stems from his commitment to the idea that minds and bodies are radically distinct *kinds* of substance. This is the idea rejected by non-reductive physicalists. Mental properties are anchored in the physical universe.

The mind–body problem is solved! Paradise awaits! Before steaming ahead, however, two matters of detail need to be addressed.

First, property dualism arises in large measure as a response to worries as to how minds and bodies could interact causally. The hope is that, by permitting bearers of mental properties to be bearers of physical properties as well, you could avoid these worries.

Second, I have been speaking glibly of causal interaction among *substances*: between minds and bodies, for instance. Most philosophers, however, regard causation as primarily a relation among *events*, and as a relation among substances only derivatively. Imagine trying to retrieve a can of paint on a high shelf you can barely reach. As you coax the can toward the edge of the shelf with your fingertips, it topples off, striking you on the head causing a painful lump. You might naturally think of the can as causing the lump. 'Strictly speaking', however, speaking with the philosophers, it was not the can, a *substance*, that caused the lump, but the can's striking your head, an *event*. Similarly, the *effect* of the can's striking your head is not the lump, but your coming to have a lump, another event. These events 'involve' substances (a can and a head), but they are not themselves substances.

What is an event? One possibility is that an event is a substance's coming to have (or lose) a property (at a particular time). The can's falling (an event) is the can's acquiring a particular momentum; your coming to have a painful lump on your head (another event) is your acquiring the property of having a painful lump. Much more could be said about events; whole books have been written on the topic. This brief sketch should provide all you need to assess the prospects for property dualism.

11.4   Mental–Physical Supervenience

The table is set. There are *substances*, objects or things in the ordinary sense, and there are *properties*, ways substances are. There are, in addition, *events*: substances gaining (or losing) properties at particular times. Property dualism permits mental and physical properties to be properties of one and the same substance. The physicalist version of property dualism requires, in addition, that every mental substance – every substance possessing mental properties – is also a physical substance – a substance possessing physical properties. A substance, a lump of granite, for instance, might possess only physical properties, but no substance could possess exclusively mental properties.

The physicalist idea is that mental and physical properties exhibit an important *asymmetry*: a substance's possession of a mental property *depends on* the substance's possession of the appropriate physical properties. This is sometimes put in terms of a *supervenience* principle:

(S) The mental supervenes on the physical.

If mental–physical supervenience holds, there could be no mental difference without a physical difference; substances alike with respect to their physical properties must be alike with respect to their mental properties. (A caveat. As you would soon discover were you to delve into the matter – something I strongly advise you not to do – there are various ways of formulating the supervenience principle, each of these ways yielding subtly different doctrines. My informal formulation expresses what is usually called 'strong supervenience'. I ignore subtleties here because they do nothing to illuminate the topic.)

Suppose supervenience holds: objects differing mentally must differ in some way physically. This leaves open the possibility that objects could be the same mentally, but differ physically. Proponents of supervenience regard this, not as a puzzle, but as a point in favor of the doctrine. By allowing that mental properties supervene on physical properties, but not vice versa, you can accommodate the phenomenon of 'multiple realizability' beloved by functionalists (§ 6.6). You, an octopus, and an Alpha Centaurian, despite differing dramatically in your respective physical properties, could all experience pain. Pain, it is said, is 'multiply realizable'. To say that pain, and other mental characteristics, supervene on physical characteristics of objects is to say that you could not change in some mental way – you could not be in pain then cease to be in pain – unless you changed in some physical way; and if you and I differ mentally – you are thinking of Alice Springs, I am thinking of porcupines – you and I must differ in some physical way.

We are edging towards the idea that mental properties in some way depend on, are 'grounded in', or 'arise from' physical properties. It is not just that every substance possessing mental properties *happens* to possess physical properties as well. The mental properties a substance possesses *depend on* its complement of physical properties. Differently put, mental properties are possessed by sentient creatures *in virtue of* their physical properties. This is to go beyond the supervenience principle (S). That principle specifies a kind of correlation between physical and mental properties. Real-world dependence is another matter.

Perhaps the dependence in question stems from laws of nature (§ 10.4–10.5). Given the laws of nature, a creature with a particular kind of physical makeup *must* thereby possess particular mental properties. If mental properties are 'multiply realizable', then this relation would be many–one: different kinds of physical property could yield the same mental property. Laws of nature (or perhaps deeper metaphysical 'laws') *guarantee* that your being in a particular kind of neurological state *necessitates* your being in pain; those same laws ensure that an octopus's being in a somewhat different kind of physical state necessitates the octopus's being in pain.

This could be illustrated by Figure 11.1 (borrowed from Chapter 6's discussion of functionalism).

Here M_1 represents a mental property, P_1, P_2, P_3, and P_4 stand for M_1's physical 'realizers'. By now it should be clear why functionalism is usually interpreted as a form of property dualism. A functionalist sees mental properties as 'irreducible' – mental properties are distinct from physical properties – but mental properties are regarded as belonging to physical objects by virtue of those objects' possession of the right kinds of physical property: mental properties have physical 'realizers'.

Philosophers attracted to this kind of picture disagree over the status of the envisioned mental–physical dependence relation. Some, as suggested above, regard it as grounded in laws of nature. Others insist that the relation is more fundamental. How could that be? What could be more fundamental than laws of nature? Imagine a universe with different laws of nature. That seems easy enough to do. In our universe objects attract each other with a force proportional to the squares of their distances. Imagine a universe in which objects attract each other with a force proportional to the *cubes* of their distances. Could you imagine a universe in which mental–physical dependencies were different?

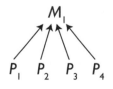

Figure 11.1

Suppose that your being in a certain neurological state, P_1, necessitates your being in pain, M_1: your being in pain, M_1, is 'grounded' in your brain's being in P_1. Could there be a universe in which beings like us could be in the very same neurological state, P_1, but did not feel pain, did not possess M_1? (A universe featuring 'zombies' would be an example of such a universe; see § 10.4.) Or is such a world flatly impossible – just as it is flatly impossible that there could be a world in which triangles had four sides or $2 + 3 \neq 5$? Philosophers attracted to property dualism differ on these issues. Happily, although the issues are important in some contexts, this is not one of them.

11.5 Causal Relevance

Suppose you accept the property dualist's picture as sketched above. Sentient creatures possess assorted physical properties. In virtue of their possession of these physical properties, sentient creatures possess various mental properties. Mental properties possessed by such creatures are 'grounded in', 'realized by', or 'arise from' their physical properties.

You could think of a mental property on this account as a 'higher-level' property. A 'higher-level' property is a property possessed by a substance in virtue of its possession of some distinct, 'lower-level' 'realizing' property. The situation can be depicted via a diagram (Figure 11.2).

Here, M represents a mental property, P some physical property (a brain property, perhaps), and the vertical arrow stands for the 'grounding' or 'realizing' relation.

I shall continue to play along with the common philosophical supposition that causation is a relation among events: one event, the cause, brings about another event, the effect. I shall continue, as well, to regard events as objects' coming into possession of (or losing) properties (at particular times). In the diagram below, 'M' and 'P' represent properties not events. Given the recommended gloss on 'event', you cannot say that M and P – properties – might be causes or effects. You can say, however, that events in which these properties figure, might be causes or effects (or both: causes are typically effects of prior causes, effects bring about further effects). Your coming to possess P (your brain's coming to be in a particular state) is an event, and so is your coming to possess M (your coming to be in a particular mental state).

$$M$$
$$\Uparrow$$
$$P$$

Figure 11.2

You could say that a property is *causally relevant* to the production of some effect just in case an object's coming to possess the property (an event) causes the effect (another event), an object's coming to possess a distinct property. More concretely, suppose your coming to possess M (your experiencing a pain in your toe, for instance) causes you to rub your toe. In that case, M would be *causally relevant* to this bodily effect. To see the point of talk about causal relevance, return to the unfortunate incident of the plummeting can of paint. The can slips from the shelf and strikes your head, producing a painful lump. The can has many properties: it is cylindrical, made of tin, has a certain mass, and, at the moment of impact, a particular velocity. The can has other characteristics as well. It contains yellow paint; the can itself is green; it was manufactured in Little Rock in December 2012; it is your only can of yellow paint.

Some of these characteristics of the can of paint are causally relevant to the production of the lump on your head, some are not. It would seem that only those features in the first list – the can's mass, shape, physical composition, and velocity – are relevant to the production of the lump. The can has a multitude of other characteristics, but these seem irrelevant to the production of *this* effect. (Although not irrelevant *tout court*: the falling can produces a green reflection in a nearby window pane. The can's color – but not its mass – *is* causally relevant to the production of *this* effect.)

The example makes clear that objects involved in causal sequences can have properties that play no role in the production of certain outcomes of those sequences; certain of the objects' properties are *causally irrelevant* to the production of those outcomes. The properties are on hand, but they have no role in the production of a particular effect.

11.6   The Causal Relevance of Mental Properties

You are at last in a position to understand what might be called the 'new mind–body problem', the new problem of mental causation. Property dualism coupled with substance monism was supposed to resolve the Cartesian problem of mind–body causal interaction. Mental substances (substances with mental properties) *are* physical substances. One and the same substance can possess *both* mental and physical properties, so there is no mystery in mental substances having effects on physical substances, no mystery in the causal interaction of physical and mental substances.

Sadly, a difficulty remains. Although mental events – events involving substances featuring mental properties – can have effects on the physical world, mental *properties* appear to be causally irrelevant to the production of those effects. Just as the paint can's color or place of manufacture are irrelevant to its effect on your head, so the mental properties of a mental episode appear to be irrelevant to the production of any physical effects that episode might have.

How could this be so? Suppose mental properties are, as non-reductive physicalists think they are, 'higher-level' properties – where a higher-level property is a property possessed by an object in virtue of that object's possession of some lower-level, 'grounding' or 'realizing' property. In cases in which you might unthinkingly regard some higher-level property as relevant to the production of some outcome, a closer look suggests that it is the property's lower-level 'realizer' that is doing the causal work.

Suppose that, having been struck on the head by a falling paint can, you form the intention to place an ice pack on the wound. As a result, you walk to the refrigerator looking for ice. So stated, it appears that your forming the intention – a mental event – has a definite physical effect – your walking to the refrigerator. But is this right? We are imagining that your forming an intention is a higher-level episode; something 'realized' by some lower-level occurrence (probably an occurrence in your brain). The situation is as depicted in Figure 11.3 (see opposite); I represents your intention and B_1 some neurological occurrence responsible for I.

When you move toward the refrigerator, is this motion, B_2, produced by I or by B_1? There are excellent reasons to think that any physical effects in this case are produced by B_1, *not* by I (as in Figure 11.4).

Quite generally, it is hard to see *how* higher-level phenomena could exercise any influence over lower-level processes. Lower-level processes are governed by lower-level laws. At the most fundamental level, these laws are presumed to be 'strict' or exceptionless. The behavior of an electron is affected only by goings-on at the fundamental physical–chemical level. The fact that an electron is one component in a vast system – the system making up your body, for instance – is neither here nor there so far as the electron is concerned.

Consider the apparent causal relation holding between B_1 and B_2. It is hard to make sense of the idea that the higher-level mental event, I, might play a role in the production of B_2. I's causing (or contributing to the causing of) B_2 would require a kind of 'downward causation' (Figure 11.5).

It appears, however, that B_1 is, by itself, causally sufficient for the production of B_2, so I's contribution would be superfluous. (Philosophers speak here of 'causal overdetermination'.)

Perhaps the mistake is to assume that causation can 'cross' levels. Perhaps I's effects are other *higher-level* goings-on. Suppose, for instance, your forming the intention to move toward the refrigerator leads to your forming the further intention, I', to open the refrigerator door (Figure 11.6).

The problem is that, your acquiring this new intention is, on the model we are provisionally accepting, a matter of your acquiring a new higher-level property, a property 'grounded in' or 'realized by' some lower-level property (Figure 11.7).

Now it looks as though the higher-level property, I', is on the scene, *not* because it was caused by I, but because *its* 'realizer', B_2, is on the scene. Because B_2 was caused by B_1, it is hard to see how I could make *any* causal contribution whatever to the occurrence of I'. All this yields the picture opposite (Figure 11.8).

I and I' appear to be *epiphenomenal*, mere by-products of causal processes.

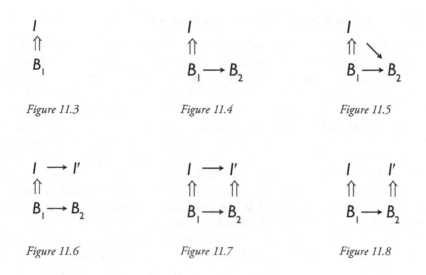

Figure 11.3   Figure 11.4   Figure 11.5

Figure 11.6   Figure 11.7   Figure 11.8

An analogy introduced in the discussion of epiphenomenalism (§ 3.6) might help make these inordinately abstract points clear. Think of a sequence of images on a movie screen. Movie images follow one another in orderly succession. No image is causally responsible for any succeeding image, however. Each image is produced, not by the image that preceded it, but by a movie projector that includes a lens, a source of illumination, and a reel of film. Each image is as it is, not because preceding images were as they were, but because the projector is as it is. Here, projected images are meant as analogues of higher-level mental properties. Features of the projector, including the film that winds through it, are analogues of lower-level physical 'realizing' properties. Higher-level properties (images) are present only because of properties of lower-level events (properties of events in the projector).

If this is how it is with mental properties, then mental properties would be causally irrelevant to the production of bodily behavior. Mental properties would be irrelevant, as well, to the production of subsequent higher-level mental events. The problem here is not that the properties in question are *mental*, but that they are *higher-level* properties. Such properties are causally 'preempted' or 'screened off' by their lower-level 'realizers'.

Ironically, the move that involved taking mental properties to be higher-level properties 'grounded in' lower-level physical realizing properties was the very move that was supposed to accommodate mentality to the physical world. Instead, by relegating mental properties to higher levels, non-reductive physicalists appear only to have reintroduced the mind–body problem in a new, but no less virulent, form. If mental properties are higher-level properties, mental properties are, to all appearances, epiphenomenal.

11.7   The Challenge of Causal Relevance

You could challenge this conclusion in a number of ways. One popular response is to appeal to the undoubted explanatory success of psychology and the special sciences (meteorology, geology, mineralogy, paleontology, and the like). These sciences deal exclusively with what are standardly identified as 'higher-level phenomena'. Nevertheless, they offer what are apparently genuine causal explanations. The collision of two cold fronts causes a line of thunder showers across central Europe; the stream's contour caused erosion on its southern bank; bad money drives out good (Gresham's Law). The success of causal explanations in the special sciences – including psychology – could be taken as excellent evidence that higher-level states and properties are indeed causally implicated in the production of significant higher- and lower-level effects. Who are philosophers to question scientific success?

Imagine Descartes responding to his critics by noting that we have excellent evidence for mental–physical causal interaction, so who are the critics to call such interaction into question. Such a response would not have occurred to Descartes because he was well aware that the problem was to make sense of the possibility of mental–physical causal interaction *given* his conception of the mental and the physical.

Sauce for the goose is sauce for the gander. The question the non-reductive physicalist must answer is not *whether* causal explanations that appeal to higher-level items are successful; clearly they are. The question, rather, is what could account for the success of these explanations *given* the picture advanced by non-reductive physicalists. One possibility is that such explanations identify properties that, despite their higher-level status, manage somehow to 'make a causal difference' to their possessors. The problem is, given the property dualist's picture, it is hard to see how this possibility is supposed to *work*.

Advocates of non-reductive physicalism have filled philosophy journals with attempts to respond in this way, attempts to reconcile their conception of the mental and its relation to the physical with mental–physical causal interaction. These include:

1   Weakening the requirements for causation so as to allow that C's cause E's provided only that the E's exhibit the right sort of 'counterfactual dependence' on the C's (roughly: had this C not occurred, this E would not have occurred) (Loewer 2002a, 2002b, 2007).
2   Distinguishing 'good' from 'bad' causal overdetermination, so that higher-level properties and their lower-level 'realizing' properties could *both* be regarded as causally relevant to production of various effects (Bennett 2003, 2008).
3   Explicating the realizing relation as one in which causal powers of instances of higher-level realized properties make up a subset of causal powers of instances of realized properties, so that higher-level properties could make themselves felt via their realizers (Pereboom 2002, Shoemaker 2007).

I shall forbear discussion of these attempts because they involve difficult, often excessively technical, arguments and the deployment of controversial theses that would take us well beyond the purview of an introduction to the topic. Instead, I shall sketch, very briefly, a non-technical, flat-footed reinterpretation of considerations that have most often been offered in support of non-reductive physicalism.

11.8   Jettisoning Higher-Level Properties

Suppose for a moment that higher-level terms we deploy in the special sciences including psychology and in ordinary life, do not function as names of definite *properties* at all. Rather, such terms apply to objects or events by virtue of those objects' or events' possessing any of a range of more or less *similar* lower-level properties. On a conception of this kind, there are no higher-level *properties*. There are, if you like, higher-level *terms* and higher-level *explanations* in which these terms figure. These higher-level terms apply to objects by virtue of 'basic level' properties; and higher-level explanations hold in virtue of basic level causal goings-on.

Confused? The idea is simple. Consider a concrete case, your being in pain. The non-reductive physicalist holds that your being in pain is a higher-level property: a property you possess in virtue of your possession of some lower-level 'realizing' property. Because these 'realizing' properties can vary across species, being in pain is presumed to be 'multiply realizable'. Suppose, however, there were *only* the lower-level 'realizing' properties. The term 'is in pain' applies indifferently to a creature possessing any of these lower-level properties. Rather than a single higher-level, multiply realized *property*, M, (Figure 11.9) there is a single *term*, '*M*', that applies to creatures in virtue of their possession of a range of distinct, but *similar* properties, B_1, B_2, B_3, ... (Figure 11.10).

Would a view of this kind 'eliminate' pains and other higher-level items? Not obviously (see § 9.1). Pains, cold fronts, and other allegedly higher-level phenomena, turn out to be perfectly real. What makes it true that you and an octopus are in pain, however, is not your and the octopus's sharing a single higher-level property, but your being in complex state that is relevantly similar to a state of the octopus, a state similar enough to fall under a single pain concept.

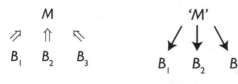

Figure 11.9   Figure 11.10

One way to think of this suggestion might be to see it as recommending the adoption of Armstrong–Lewis-style functionalism over 'mainstream' functionalism (see § 6.9). According to the two Davids, Armstrong and Lewis, functionalism is not a metaphysical thesis, but a thesis about the meaning of mental terms. Mental terms pick out features of the world by reference to causal roles played by those features. Your being in pain, for instance, is your being in a state that has the right sorts of causes and effects. Your being in pain *is* your being in that state. An octopus's being in pain *is* the octopus's being in a state with a broadly similar causal profile.

This is in contrast to the thesis that your being in pain is a matter of your possessing a particular higher-level property, the pain property, that super-venes on, or arises from, or is realized by, a particular physical property. Armstrong–Lewis functionalism, in effect, identifies pains with their 'real-izers'. What unifies talk of pains is not that such talk latches onto a *single property* shared by diverse creatures, but that it applies to diverse creatures by virtue of broad *similarities* among those creatures' physical conditions.

Where does this leave 'causal relevance'? You have seen that there is every reason to doubt that higher-level properties beloved by non-reductive physi-calists could figure in causal transactions. On the view under consideration, however, mental properties are not higher-level properties. Mental *terms* ('is in pain', for instance) apply to sentient creatures by virtue of those creatures' physical makeup. There is no unique property, the pain property, shared by creatures in pain. There are, rather, many distinct but similar properties answering to the 'pain predicate': 'is in pain'. Each of these properties figures uncontroversially in bodily causal sequences. Thus, a sentence of the form 'Gus's pain caused him to weep and rub his head,' could be literally true. It would be true if Gus were in a state answering to 'is in pain' and if this state had a causal role in the production of Gus's weeping and rubbing his head.

11.9 The Upshot

Philosophers with strong attachments to non-reductive physicalism, and its attendant property dualism, would balk at this sort of approach to the problem of the causal relevance of the mental. These philosophers are convinced that mental properties, and indeed many other kinds of property, occupy higher levels of reality (see §§ 7.9 and 7.10). If you take such a view seriously, you will see the world as stratified into *layers*: higher strata super-vening on – that is, depending on, without being reducible to – lower strata. Physics and chemistry are concerned with what we take to be the lowest, most basic stratum. Classical materialism failed in attempting to *reduce* the mental to the physical, to *identify* minds and their contents with phenomena in lower strata. You can have a kind of attenuated materialism, however, by supposing that minds and their contents, while irreducible, are grounded in or realized by more basic physical structures, higher levels supervene on lower levels.

If you find this picture attractive, bear in mind that you will need to provide some account of the grounding or realizing relation, and you will need to account somehow for the apparent causal efficacy of higher-level phenomena. Philosophers have expended much ingenuity on these topics. The results, to date, have not been encouraging. If, in contrast, you are dissatisfied with conceptions of the mind and its relation to the physical world that have occupied previous chapters, if you remain open-minded, you might find the next two chapters useful. Those chapters develop and extend the position sketched above.

Suggested Reading

Benedictus de Spinoza (1632–77) could be considered the progenitor of modern property dualism. (Although I describe Spinoza as a progenitor of property dualism, I do not regard Spinoza himself as a dualist about properties. Spinoza's position is in fact close to Davidson's – see below.) In *The Ethics* (1677) Spinoza argues for the thesis that there is a single substance with infinite attributes, two of which are available to the human intellect: mentality and materiality (roughly, Descartes's thought and extension). These are two 'aspects' of a single, unified whole: *deus sive natura* (God or nature).

Take this idea, reformulate it as a thesis about descriptions (mental and physical descriptions might be at bottom distinct ways of describing a single thing), subtract its pantheist trappings, and the result is the position, 'anomalous monism', defended by Davidson in 'Mental Events' (1970). This paper introduces the thesis that the mental *supervenes* on the physical: objects alike physically must be alike mentally; no mental change without a physical change. Davidson, who is agnostic about properties, formulates supervenience as a thesis about *descriptions* or *predicates*. Other philosophers, most notably Jaegwon Kim, have transformed the thesis into a thesis about *properties*: mental properties supervene on physical properties. See Kim's 'Supervenience and Nomological Incommensurables' (1978), 'Causality, Identity and Supervenience' (1979), and 'Supervenience as a Philosophical Concept' (1990). I suggest, here and in Chapter 14, that philosophers have erred in moving too quickly from talk of descriptions and predicates to talk of properties, a move neatly reflected in Putnam's decision to re-title 'Psychological Predicates' (1967) as 'The Nature of Mental States'.

In retrospect it is easy to see philosophers' infatuation with supervenience as an unfortunate distraction, but at the time appeals to supervenience seemed to provide a way of making sense of the ontology implied by functionalism (Chapter 7). For critical discussion of philosophical applications of the concept of supervenience, see Terence Horgan's 'From Supervenience to Superdupervenience: Meeting the Demands of a Material World' (1993), and my 'Supervenience Deconstructed' (1998).

Property dualism has reinvented itself as 'non-reductive physicalism', a view concerning which Kim has expressed strong reservations. See his 'The

Non-Reductivist's Troubles with Mental Causation' (1993b), *Mind in a Physical World* (1998), and *Physicalism, or Something Near Enough* (2005). Heil and Mele's *Mental Causation* (1993) includes the aforementioned Kim paper as well as other useful papers on mental causation and the problem of the 'causal relevance' of mental properties. Jeffrey Poland, in *Physicalism: The Philosophical Foundations* (1994) and John Post, in *The Faces of Existence* (1987), provide detailed, often technical, arguments for versions of non-reductive materialism of the kind Kim challenges. In the same vein, see Derk Pereboom and Hilary Kornblith's 'The Metaphysics of Irreducibility' (1991), a response to Kim's arguments, Pereboom's 'Robust Nonreductive Materialism' (2002), and Sydney Shoemaker's *Physical Realization* (2007). Fodor's views on the irreducible status of the special sciences can be found in his 'Special Sciences: Still Autonomous after All These Years' (1997).

In explaining why philosophers have doubts about the causal impact of 'higher-level' properties, I introduce a movie analogy (§ 13.6). Kim deploys an interesting example originating with Jonathan Edwards (1703–58), the New England divine. Edwards appeals to successive images in a mirror. See Kim's 'Blocking Causal Drainage, and Other Maintenance Chores with Mental Causation' (2003).

12 Metaphysics and Mind

12.1 The Status of Philosophies of Mind

In the eleven preceding chapters, you have been subjected to a number of diverse perspectives on the mind. Each of these perspectives originally crystallized in response to puzzles seen at the time to be especially challenging. Descartes, for instance, was struck by apparent differences between properties of minds and properties of material objects. That focus led him to regard mental properties and the material properties as properties of utterly different kinds of substance. Psychological behaviorists, in contrast, were bent on making minds scientifically respectable subjects of empirical inquiry. Given their conception of scientific respectability, this meant showing that truths about minds and their contents ought to be replaced by descriptions of observable bodily motions and propensities for such motions.

Although it is easy to see where each of the conceptions of mind we have examined goes off the rails, you would miss something important if you did not recognize that each can be seen as at least partly successful: each provides answers to questions considered pressing by its proponents, each offers plausible solutions to high-profile problems. At the same time, each provokes new difficulties while leaving unresolved a host of residual problems. This is unsurprising. Theories of mind are developed in the course of coping with issues that are, at the time of their introduction, regarded as central. To the extent that a theory is successful, the problems it solves recede into the background, and those it leaves unresolved become salient.

In the next chapter I sketch an account of the mind that endeavors to make sense of what I like to think would strike you as plausible in each of the views discussed thus far, while dodging their attendant difficulties. I regard it as an important point in favor of the account that it encompass core insights of a variety of distinct, even incompatible, theories. In philosophy there is a tendency to take doctrines with which we disagree and dismiss them out of hand. But a view can be wrong, even mostly wrong, without being *altogether* wrong. When you consider the historical development of theories in the philosophy of mind, you can see that the same difficulties cycle into focus again and again. One generation addresses the qualitative aspect of mentality, the next focuses on its scientific standing, its successor takes up the problem of mental content. The cycle then starts over, each generation rediscovering what had been largely invisible to its immediate predecessor.

Under the circumstances, it would be disingenuous to claim originality for any view. Virtually every point I make in this chapter and the one to follow has been made before by other, more inventive philosophers. Chief among these are Descartes, Locke, Spinoza, and Locke's twenty-first century philosophical counterpart, C. B. Martin (1924–2008). Although these philosophers provide the chief inspiration for the position I shall advance here, I borrow freely from Russell, from Davidson, and from Wittgenstein – and from their assorted fellow travelers.

Throughout this volume, I have emphasized the importance of metaphysics and in particular, ontology – our best systematic assessment of what there is – for the philosophy of mind. I shall now endeavor to make good on this line. Certain important conclusions concerning minds and their place in nature follow from what I take to be an independently plausible ontology. I outline these in the sections that follow, although I do not try to defend them in depth (for that see Heil 2003a and 2012). Many of these conclusions fall outside currently popular conceptions of mind. That, I submit, is all to the good.

Ill-considered metaphysical commitments lead to problems in the philosophy of mind that are largely of our own making. It would scarcely be an exaggeration to say that the philosophy of mind today is a repository of bad metaphysical choices. We can hope for an improvement, not through the invention of ever more intricate epicycles, but by our coming to recognize that so many of our assumptions did not fall from the sky but are optional. If this is all you take away from this chapter, I will consider it entirely successful.

12.2 Metaphysical Preliminaries

Increasing numbers of philosophers of mind see themselves as 'cognitive scientists' and make a point of distancing their pursuits from those of a philosophical temperament that distinguishes sharply between science and philosophy. The hope is that we can replace unconstrained armchair metaphysical speculation with hard-nosed, empirically informed theorizing. The idea is not so much that we should seek empirical answers to long-standing philosophical questions, but that we should *replace* the questions and embark on a scientifically respectable investigation of the territory.

Although it would be foolish not to take seriously the fruits of empirical labors, it would be no less foolish to imagine that the deep problems that beset the philosophy of mind would yield uncontentious solutions if only we replaced philosophy of mind with psychology and neuroscience. As matters now stand, even if we possessed a fully adequate empirical theory of consciousness, we should be in no position to recognize it as such.

The problem is not so much a lack of detailed information as a lack of an adequate metaphysical framework in which to make sense of whatever information we might obtain. We have learned much and we have much to learn about the brain. But, to take one currently prominent example, it is hard to see how any conceivable neurobiological discovery could account for the qualities of conscious experience. Working psychologists and neuroscientists do occasionally worry about the ontological status of consciousness. When we philosophers turn our backs on ontology, we turn our backs on pressing questions of a kind that our training was supposed to equip us to address. The philosopher who, posing as a friend of science, forgoes philosophy is a pathetic figure.

My belief is that anyone who might hope to advance an empirical theory of the mind must have a clear conception of the underlying ontology. This would afford, not an axiomatic system within which to deduce truths about the mind, but a suitable structure within which to locate empirical truths. The test of an ontology is its power: its capacity to provide a sensible overall account of how things stand. This account should comport, at least broadly, with commonsense observation constrained by the sciences. The sciences do not speak with a single voice, however. Ontology goes beyond the sciences in providing a unifying framework within which claims issuing from the several sciences can be plotted.

Enough of this! The time has come to get down to brass tacks.

12.3   Substances and Properties

A good place to start is at the beginning. At a first approximation, the universe comprises substances possessing properties and standing in spatial and temporal relations to one another. Substances are simple: a substance lacks parts that are themselves substances. You can have a complex *object* – trees, neurons, and atoms are complex objects – but not a complex *substance*. Wholes depend on their parts. Complex objects depend for their existence on their substantial parts, the substances that make them up. In that case, there must be simple substances, substances lacking parts that are themselves substances. Were every object made up of other complex objects, there would be nothing to anchor the existence of any object.

Substances are property bearers, where properties are particular ways particular substances are. Properties are what were traditionally called *individual accidents* and what Descartes, Locke, and Spinoza called modes, *ways*. (Philosophers nowadays follow D. C. Williams and call accidents or modes *tropes*.) Every substance must be some way or other, or, as is more likely, many ways. Every way must be a way some substance is. Pretend for a moment that a particular billiard ball is a substance. Then the billiard ball's shape is one way it is, its color is another way it is, and its mass is a third way.

I have described the universe as comprising substances. I take it to be an empirical question – a question for science, for fundamental physics – what the substances are and what they are like, *how* they are. Substances might be corpuscular, particle-like, in the mold of the atoms envisaged by the ancient Greeks, quarks and leptons, perhaps. Substances might, in contrast, be fields, or a single unified field, or space–time itself, or dancing superstrings, or something stranger still.

Likewise, it is an empirical question what the properties are. If electrons are substances, then the charge, mass, and spin of a particular electron are particular ways that electron is, properties of the electron. If the substances turn out to be fields, then ways the fields are would be the properties.

It might seem crazy to insist that substances must be simple: a substance cannot be made up of parts that are themselves substances. In so insisting, I follow Descartes, Locke, Leibniz, Spinoza, and a host of other philosophers. Descartes has two kinds of substance: extended and thinking. There might be but one extended substance, space itself, or there might be many extended corpuscular substances. In either case, Cartesian substances – extended or thinking – are simple. Locke's substances are the material corpuscles – part-less atoms – and perhaps souls, mental corpuscles. Leibniz's substances are mental atoms, 'monads'. Spinoza has a single extended, thinking substance, the universe itself.

But *why* demand simplicity? *Why* no complex substances? I can think of at least two reasons. First, on the traditional conception, a substance is a non-dependent entity, something the existence of which depends on the existence of no other entity, something that could exist in the absence of any other entity. A complex object, an object comprising parts that are themselves substances, would depend for its existence on parts that make it up – a dependence that disqualifies it as a substance.

Second, substances are propertied; every substance is some way or ways. If properties are ways substances are, however, I cannot see how a complex object, something made up of particular substances bearing particular relations to one another *could* be a bearer of properties. At the very least, the sense in which a simple substance bears a property would differ dramatically from the sense in which a complex (consisting of substances standing in relations) could be said to bear a property. Imagine a complex consisting of three substances, *A*, *B*, and *C*, standing in particular relations (Figure 12.1).

Could this complex bear a property, *P*? To what does *P* belong? Not to *A*, *B*, or *C*. *P* is meant to be borne by the complex, by *A*, *B*, and *C*'s standing in the *R* relation (Figure 12.2).

So? Why should *that* be a problem? Why doubt that the *A-B-C* complex could bear a property, why doubt that the complex is a propertied substance?

Start with the idea that properties are ways substances are. What would a way that *A-B-C* is be? Well, *A*, *B*, and *C* are *arranged* in a particular way, *A*, *B*, and *C*, bear certain relations to one another. But the 'way' here is not the way a thing is, it is a way things are arranged: the *A-B-C* arrangement. You do not have the arrangement *plus* ways that arrangement is. What you might informally regard as properties of complex objects – the

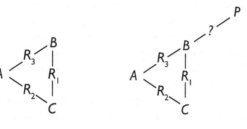

Figure 12.1   *Figure 12.2*

object's shape or color, for instance – are just the arrangements of its constituents.

You might reasonably wonder where all this is going. Am I setting you up to accept some outrageous thesis down the road? Am I sneaking a rabbit into the hat? Relax. The position I am developing here is meant to provide a basis for truths held dear by psychologists, neuroscientists, and, as seems likely, by you. Bear with me.

Before moving on, however, two points are worth noting. First, in declaring that substances must be simple, I am not suggesting that substances are infinitesimal 'point particles'. A simple substance could be spatially extended, a simple substance could have endless *spatial* parts. (A simple substance could be temporally extended, as well, although I shall spare you discussion of 'temporal parts'.) Further, a simple substance could have many properties, it could be many ways. A simple substance lacks *substantial* parts, parts that are themselves substances.

An object, a tree for instance, made up of substances depends on those substances for its existence. A spatially extended thing is not made up of its *spatial* parts, however. An extended thing does not depend for its existence on its spatial parts. Those parts, rather, depend on *it*. Because objects' substantial parts could coincide with their spatial parts, we sometimes refer to an object's substantial parts using spatial terms. You might slice a tomato in half, presenting its right half to a companion. In so doing, you detach a substantial part of the tomato coincident with its right half.

Second, earlier I used as an example of a substance a billiard ball and as examples of properties the ball's shape, mass, and color. But billiard balls are not in fact simple. Billiard balls have substantial parts, or at least they do if the substances are particles: electrons, quarks. In metaphysics, however, you start with simple illustrative examples that include the seeds of their own revision. You get the idea of what substances and properties are by treating the billiard ball as a simple and its color, shape, and mass as properties. As Keith Campbell as suggested, you could say the billiard ball is a 'substance-by-courtesy', a quasi-substance, its color, shape, and mass are 'properties-by-courtesy', quasi-properties.

Why *not* think of the billiard ball's color, shape, and mass as properties? As noted already, if you start with the idea that properties are modes – particular ways particular substances are – it is hard to see how a complex object, a complex consisting of substances related in particular ways, *could* have properties. Suppose the billiard ball is a complex of substances analogous to the complex depicted in Figure 12.1. Properties of this complex would be ways it is. But ways it is are just ways its constituent substances are and ways these are arranged. There is nothing more to the billiard ball's sphericity than its constituents being as they are, arranged as they are. You do not have the constituents (as they are) arranged as they are *and* the ball. You do not have the constituents (as they are) arranged as they are *and* the ball's color.

There are of course many true things you could say about the billiard ball, many ways you could describe the billiard ball or any other complex object. Many predicates hold true of it. The mistake is to imagine that each of these predicates designates a *property* of the ball. Rather, they hold true because the ball's constituents are as they are, arranged as they are and related as they are to endless other substances. To imagine that to every significant predicate there corresponds a property, is to let language call the shots ontologically. It is true that there is a billiard ball and that the billiard ball is spherical, red, and has a particular mass. But what makes these truths true – their *truthmakers* – is a particular arrangement of substances of particular kinds. At least this would be so if the substances are particles. If there is just one substance, the unified field, for instance, then the truthmakers for claims about the billiard ball are going to be ways this field is, particular local eddies or fluctuations.

Please do not imagine that any of this in any way denigrates billiard balls, their colors, shapes, and masses. It is an effort, rather, to get at the deep story about such things. The deep story about the billiard ball is that it is not a substance. It is a complex arrangement of substances, perhaps, or a thickening in a region of space–time, or a disturbance in a field. I shall continue to use the billiard ball as an example, however, pretending that it is a 'simple' and that its color, shape, and mass are properties.

In practice, billiard balls *are* treated as substances, simples, and their shapes, colors, and masses are treated as properties. Indeed, 'property' has a relaxed use reflected in the practice of taking any predicate that holds true of an object to designate a property. The *Book of Common Prayer* describes God as a being 'whose property is always to have mercy'. And you might, in this Episcopalian sense, be said to have the property of being two miles from a red barn, or the property of being a secret admirer of Joyce Kilmer. But these are just ways of saying that God is always merciful, that you are two miles from a red barn, and that you secretly admire Joyce Kilmer. Suppose it is true of you that you are two miles from a red barn. The predicate 'is two miles from a red barn' applies (truly) to you in virtue of some complex of appropriately arranged substances (maybe billions of them) standing in the right sorts of relation. So you can have a predicate's truly applying to a complex without its being the case that the predicate names a property.

If substances are simple and properties – genuine properties – are ways substances are, then the substances and properties are going to be discoverable, not by analyzing language or engaging in philosophical reflection, but by going to fundamental physics. Episcopalian properties, quasi-properties, are just what you get when you arrange particular kinds of fundamental substances in the right ways.

Whether particles, or fields, or something stranger yet, substances are bearers of properties. When you turn your attention to a substance, you can consider it as a bearer of properties, *and* you can consider its properties, ways it is. The billiard ball can be considered as something red, as something spherical, as something having a particular mass. In so doing, you are treating the ball as a substance, a bearer of properties, something that is various ways. But you can also consider the ball's properties: its redness, its sphericity, its mass. When you do this, you turn your mind to ways the ball is. A substance's properties are not *parts* of the substance. The ball's redness, sphericity, and mass do not make up the ball in the way its constituent particles do.

When you consider the ball as a substance, you are 'abstracting', engaging in what Locke called 'partial consideration', you are considering the ball as a property bearer. In considering the ball's redness or its shape, you are abstracting as well, considering ways the ball is. The ball and ways it is are equally *abstractions*. The ball and ways it is can be separated in thought, but not in reality.

Putting all this together: a substance is a bearer of properties, properties are particular ways particular substances are. Every substance is some way or other, every substance has properties. Every property is a way some substance is. Substances and properties are not components of a complex entity. Although you can distinguish substances as property bearers from properties they bear, these are separable only in thought, not in reality. Substances cannot exist apart from properties, nor properties apart from substances. A substance can gain or lose properties, but this is not a matter of its properties coming and going. There is nothing more to a property than a substance's being a particular way. A substance can cease to be one way and come to be some other way, but these *ways* could not migrate to other substances or 'float free'. Nor could a substance exist, lacking properties, as a 'bare particular', being no way at all.

12.4   Universals

In describing properties of substances as I have, I mean to be distancing myself from the idea that properties are *universals*. Some proponents of universals hold that universals are 'transcendent' entities residing 'outside' or independently of space and time. Particular substances 'participate in' or 'instantiate' universals. Particular spherical substances might be thought to instantiate the universal *sphericity*. This conception of universals is loosely associated with Plato. Another conception, perhaps stemming from Aristotle, but more recently ably defended by D. M. Armstrong, locates universals in their instances. The universal sphericity is taken to be wholly present in each of its spatially and temporally distinct instances (and nowhere else). A universal is, in a certain sense, made up of its instances, although these instances are not its parts: the universal, remember, is regarded as *wholly present* in each of its instances.

Philosophers who favor treating properties as universals hold that such a conception serves up a solution to Plato's 'one-over-many' problem. Consider a red billiard ball and a railway warning flag. The billiard ball and the flag are *the same* in one respect and *different* in other respects. You might put this by saying that the ball and the flag *share a property*; that they possess *the same property*; or, if properties are ways, they are the *same way* colorwise. A proponent of universals focuses on the italicized phrases in the preceding sentence. If the billiard ball and the flag *share* a property, then there is *some one thing*, a property, common to both. This property, redness, is common to *all* red objects. Similarities among objects are thus grounded in their shared properties. These are the 'one' in the 'one-over-many'. Differences are determined by properties being possessed or 'instantiated' by distinct substances. These are the 'many'. 'Identical twins' are *the same* in sharing properties, *different* in being distinct substances, distinct instances of their shared properties.

You might find talk of universals mysterious. The mystery would be lessened slightly if focused on the thought that universals are meant to differ in kind from particular 'concrete' objects such as warning flags and billiard balls. What holds for a particular need not hold for a universal. This helps only a little, however. It remains difficult to see what could be involved in an object's instantiating a universal (on the 'Platonic' view) or what it could be for a universal to be (as Armstrong says) wholly present in each of its instances. I hope to bypass such puzzles by recommending an account of properties that takes properties seriously but without embracing universals.

12.5   Properties as Particularized Ways

Before looking more closely at the nature of properties, it might be worth asking why exactly anyone would imagine that the world contains such entities. Some philosophers have thought that properties are creatures of philosophers' imaginations. Talk of properties, they contend, should be replaced by talk of objects or classes of objects. A red object is not an object that possesses the property of being red, but merely an object that answers to the predicate 'is red', one that resembles other objects or belongs to a particular class: the class of red objects. Objects belong to this class, perhaps, because they are similar, but this similarity is an irreducible feature of the objects. Objects are what they are, *holus-bolus*.

This is not the place to discuss such doctrines in detail. Instead I shall merely call attention to a flat-footed worry about attempts to dispense with properties. Consider two red objects. Is the redness of the objects solely a matter of the objects' resembling one another or the objects' being members of a class of objects: the class of red objects? This seems to have the order of explanation the wrong way round. The objects are not red *because they resemble one another*, they resemble one another *because they are red*; the objects are not red *because they belong to a class*, the class of red objects; they belong to the class *because they are red*. (Class membership must be earned!) Think of the red flag and the red billiard ball. These differ in shape, size, and mass, but are similar *in color*. This natural perspective on similarity pushes us back to *ways objects are*: the flag and the billiard ball resemble one another and fall into the class of red objects because they are similar *in some respect*. And it is hard not to think that talk of 'respects' here is talk of properties of objects, ways objects are.

I do not imagine that a staunch opponent of properties will be much moved by these observations. In such matters it is unrealistic to expect knock down arguments. The most you can hope for is an ontology that squares with our overall assessment of how things stand. In this context, we do well to remind ourselves of a simple point. (I borrow here from C. B. Martin's 1980). Consider the sentences below:

1   The ball is spherical.
2   The ball is red.

Suppose that these sentences hold true of a particular billiard ball. Now it would seem on the face of it that the sentences do not hold true of the object *as a whole*. Rather, there is *something about* the ball in virtue of which it is true to say of it that it is spherical; and something *else* about the ball in virtue of which it is true to say of it that it is red. In speaking of 'something about the ball' you are, or surely seem to be, speaking about a way the ball is. And this is just to speak about what I have been calling a property.

I have distinguished this notion of a property – a particularized way an object is – from notions of properties as universals. In recent years, philosophers have used the term 'trope' as a label for what I am calling particularized ways. I resist this designation because proponents of tropes are often keen to replace substances with 'bundles' of tropes. Tropes, they think, are literally *parts* of the objects they make up. But the ball's redness or sphericity do not seem to *make up* the ball, an electron's mass and charge do not seem to be *parts* of the electron.

On the view I am recommending, objects are not made up of properties in anything like the way a billiard ball is made up of atoms or molecules. To repeat an earlier suggestion: when you consider an object you can consider it as a bearer of properties – a substance – or you can consider properties it bears. Substances are not collections or bundles of properties; a substance is a bearer of properties.

A simple substance is various ways (the spherical way, the red way), and these ways are its properties. Complex objects – billiard balls, molecules, and (what we now call) atoms – are substances in a relaxed Episcopalian sense: substances-by-courtesy, quasi-substances. In just the same way characteristics of complex objects are properties only in a relaxed sense: properties-by-courtesy, quasi-properties. A complex object is made up of simple substances possessing particular properties and standing in particular relations to one another. Characteristics of a complex object are just what you have when you have *these* substances, possessing *these* properties, arranged in *this* way. There is nothing more to the characteristics of a complex object than this. Characteristics of complex objects do not 'emerge'; they are nothing in addition to, nothing 'over and above', particular arrangements of the propertied substances that make them up. (I shall have more to say about the notion of 'emergence' presently.)

I might note in passing that the conception of properties I favor can accommodate at least one aspect of the motivation for positing universals. Proponents of universals appeal to 'one-over-many' considerations: distinct objects can be *the same* in various respects. I say properties are particularized ways objects are. Now consider classes of exactly resembling properties. These classes will perfectly coincide with the universals as conceived of by Armstrong.

As David Robb, has pointed out, the temptation to regard properties as universals could be thought to stem from a desire to have a single entity do 'double duty'. If you start by thinking of properties as *ways objects are*, you can connect these ways with *types* of object. A universal is simultaneously a type of object and a way particular objects are. But suppose you let the properties be the ways, and the types be collections or classes of exactly similar ways. Then two objects fall under a single type (both are the *same* color, both are red), not because they share a constituent – a universal redness – but because they possess exactly similar properties that, owing to their similarity, fall into the same class. These classes could be thought of as *ersatz universals*.

On this conception, things that might be thought to 'share a universal' share, instead, membership in a class of things possessing exactly resembling properties. The relation of resemblance these properties bear to one another is a primitive, 'internal' relation. *Objects* resemble one another in virtue of their properties; *properties* – the basis of resemblance – resemble one another (when they do) *tout court*. Suppose properties α and β are exactly resembling. Then this resemblance is intrinsic, 'built into' the properties. One consequence of this is that, if property χ exactly resembles α, then χ exactly resembles β as well.

Let me say a word about a matter that might worry some readers. I have described properties as ways substances are. This gives the impression that the properties are exhausted by the ways actual, existing substances are.

There are, however, ways substances could be but no substance is – or, for that matter, no substance ever will be. Two kinds of particle could be such that, *were* they to collide, the collision would yield a third kind of particle possessing unique properties. (I discuss a case of this kind below.) This could be so, even if the requisite collisions never took place. So: there are ways substances could be but no substance is (or ever will be). Thus put, ways might appear mysterious. The mystery can be avoided by noting that non-actual possible ways are prefigured in ways actual substances are. Properties of substances are dispositional *for* (they are 'directed to' and 'selective for') particular kinds of manifestation – themselves properties, ways substances could be – that need never occur. The intrinsic 'readinesses' of whatever properties there are ground claims concerning non-actual, possible ways.

12.6 Powerful Qualities

Properties are ways substances are. I regard this view as close to the common-sense conception. Reverting to commonsense examples, you distinguish the red of a billiard ball and the red of a railroad warning flag, even though these two objects might be precisely the same shade of red. You have two 'instances' of red, one belonging to the ball, the other to the flag. Now it is time to look more closely at the nature of properties.

Properties are qualities that empower their possessors in particular ways. Properties are *powerful qualities*. Consider the sphericity of this billiard ball. The ball's sphericity is a *quality* of the ball, but not an inert quality. In virtue of being spherical the ball would roll. So the ball's sphericity is a power or disposition of the ball. In virtue of being spherical, the ball is disposed to roll when it is placed on an inclined surface. But this is not all. In virtue of being spherical the ball is disposed to make a circular concave impression in the carpet, to reflect light so as to look spherical, and to feel spherical to the touch.

The qualities and dispositionalities of any complex object considered as a whole result from interrelations among properties of its constituent substances. A ball would roll, for instance, only if it is spherical *and* solid. But every property contributes in a distinctive way to the qualities and dispositionalities of objects possessing it. The ball would roll (rather than tumble) down an inclined plane owing to its sphericity; it would make a circular (rather than square) impression in the carpet and look or feel spherical (rather than cubical) in virtue of its sphericity.

A reminder. Throughout the chapter, I treat familiar objects such as billiard balls as examples of substances and features of these objects as properties. In so doing I am following a long tradition in philosophy and science in which everyday features of the universe are used to illustrate theses pertaining to the fundamental things. Billiard balls are not substances and a billiard ball's redness and sphericity are not properties. A billiard ball is a quasi-substance and its redness is a quasi-property. (Which is not at all to say that there are no billiard balls or that nothing is red or spherical!) Nevertheless billiard balls serve well enough as illustrations. They have the advantage of keeping the discussion from becoming hopelessly abstract. In any case, my use of such examples here does not affect the central argument of the chapter.

The thesis that properties have a dual nature is to be distinguished from the thesis that there are two kinds of property: dispositional properties and qualitative or 'categorical' properties. On the latter view, it makes no sense to suppose that a property could be *both* dispositional and qualitative. Every property is exclusively one or the other. A dispositional property, the property of solubility possessed by a salt crystal, for instance, or the property of being fragile possessed by a delicate vase, is to be distinguished from categorical (that is, non-dispositional, purely qualitative) properties such as being blue or being warm. In virtue of their possession of dispositional properties, objects behave, or would behave, in particular ways under the right conditions. In virtue of their possession of categorical properties, objects exhibit particular qualities.

Under the assumption that dispositions and qualities are associated with distinct kinds of property, philosophers have been moved to advance a variety of theories. For some, the two kinds of property are irreducibly distinct. Others, however, noting that a non-dispositional property could make no difference at all in the world, have doubted the existence of non-dispositional, categorical properties. Such properties would be, for instance, undetectable – assuming that the detection of a property requires that its possession by an object contribute in some way to the object's causally affecting observers.

Further, as these philosophers point out, the usual examples of allegedly categorical properties are unconvincing. Take being blue or being warm. Surely, an object's being blue is what disposes it to reflect light in a particular way, and an object's being warm disposes it to affect the surrounding air differentially. When you consider properties ascribed to objects by the sciences, these seem invariably dispositional: having mass, for instance, or having negative charge, are characterized by reference to ways in which possession of these properties affects or would affect the behavior of their possessors. Considerations of this sort have convinced some philosophers that every genuine property is a dispositional property, a *power*.

Another contingent of philosophers, however, appeals to the strangeness of the idea every property is a disposition, a power for some manifestation: a power to dissolve in water, a power to break if dropped. A world consisting exclusively of powers would seem to be a world in which objects would be forever poised to act, but never act. An object's acting would be a matter of its dispositions' being manifested. But if a manifestation were itself nothing more than a 'pure disposition', a disposition to be manifested in a particular way under the right circumstances, then the situation would resemble one in which a bank check is backed by a check, which itself is backed by a check, and so on indefinitely. Unless a check is ultimately backed by something other than a check, it is worthless; and, similarly, unless a disposition issues in something other than a pure disposition, something *qualitative*, nothing occurs.

This point might be expressed slightly differently. A disposition is itself a manifestation of some disposition. (I shall say more about the manifestation of dispositions presently.) If every manifestation were *nothing more than* a disposition for some further manifestation, the result would be an unwelcome regress. The universe evidently contains actualities as well as potentialities. But pure dispositionalities appear to be pure potentialities. Imagine a row of dominoes lined up so that, were the first to fall it would topple the second domino, which would topple the third domino, which would topple. ... Now imagine that *all there is* to the dominoes is their power to topple and be toppled. It is hard to see how any toppling occurs; there are no *things* to topple or be toppled.

(For devotees of possible worlds, Simon Blackburn (1990, 64), puts the point this way:

> To conceive of *all* the truths about a world as dispositional is to suppose that a world is entirely described by what is true at *neighboring* worlds. And since our argument was a priori, these truths in turn vanish into truths about yet other neighboring worlds, and the result is that there is no truth anywhere.)

Aware of these difficulties, some theorists have suggested that dispositional properties must be 'grounded in' non-dispositional properties. A dispositional property, on this view, might be a 'higher-level' property, a property had by an object in virtue of its possession of some 'lower-level' non-dispositional property. (You encountered higher-level properties in Chapter 7's discussion of functionalism and in Chapter 11. Functionalists think that mental properties are higher-level properties realized by lower-level properties that play the right functional role.)

Consider the dispositional property of being fragile. This is a property an object – this delicate vase, for instance – might have in virtue of having a particular molecular structure. Having this structure is held to be a lower-level non-dispositional property that grounds the higher-level dispositional property of being fragile; the vase is fragile, the vase possesses the dispositional property of being fragile, *in virtue of* possessing some non-dispositional structural property.

If properties are not powers, their possession would seem to make no difference to their bearers. If they are powers, powers to produce other powers, they seem to be elusive pure potentialities. Does it help to suppose that powers are in some way grounded in properties that are not powers?

In the first place, you might wonder what more there is to an object's possessing a given higher-level property beyond the object's possessing its lower-level 'grounding' property. Reflect on the fragility of this vase, and suppose that fragility is a higher-level property had by the vase 'in virtue of' its having a particular lower-level property, maybe a certain crystalline structure. In what sense exactly does the vase possess two distinct properties here: a non-dispositional structural property *and* a dispositional property? For that matter, in what sense is the vase's *structure* non-dispositional? Surely, it is its molecular structure that *itself* disposes the vase to reflect light in a particular way, to remain rigid at moderate temperatures, to make a particular ringing noise when tapped by a spoon, and, yes, to shatter when struck by a hard object. If having a certain structure is a property, then it would seem to be as dispositional as any other property you could imagine!

Proponents of the idea that dispositions are higher-level properties point to the fact objects with very different molecular structures could turn out to be fragile: being fragile is 'multiply realizable'. This, however, ought not incline you to doubt that the property of being fragile possessed by *this* vase – *this* vase's fragility – is a perfectly ordinary ('lower-level') property of the vase, perhaps the very property mentioned already: having a particular molecular structure.

That would fit nicely with the view I am advocating. Properties have a dual nature: every property is at once qualitative and dispositional, every property contributes in a distinctive way to the qualities *and* dispositionalities of objects possessing it. So the vase's structure is a 'categorical', here and now, qualitative feature of the vase. But in having this structure the vase is fragile: it would shatter were you to drop it. You can separate these natures only in thought – just as you can mentally separate a triangle's triangularity from its trilaterality – by 'abstracting', by considering the one without considering the other.

Locke's partial consideration or abstraction is the activity of mental separation. It is what enables you to consider an object's color without considering its shape, or its shape without considering its color, even if every object with a shape must be an object with a color.

What relation does the dispositionality of a property bear to its qualitative nature? These are not merely correlated, not merely 'necessarily connected' as are triangularity and trilaterality. They are, rather, the selfsame property, differently considered. A relationship of this sort resembles that found in ambiguous figures. Figure 12.3 depicts the face of an old lady and the profile of a young woman. The same lines make up both figures. You can distinguish the figures by shifting your attention. But neither figure could be present without the other. In the same way, a property's intrinsic dispositionality and qualitative nature are separable only in thought.

The ambiguous figure is designed to illustrate the thesis that a property's dispositionality and qualitativity are not 'aspects' or 'sides' of the property: they are the property itself, differently considered. A property's dispositionality *is* its qualitativity and these *are* the property itself. Properties are powerful qualities.

Figure 12.3

Earlier I observed that the idea that objects' dispositional features are 'grounded' in their structure appears to be a non-starter. Structures themselves are evidently dispositional as well as qualitative. More importantly, if you can so much as conceive of simple objects, objects that lack parts – hence lack structure in the relevant sense – you must conceive of those objects as possessing dispositionalities. They are not, at any given moment, doing all they could do, all they are capable of doing. If there are elementary particles, these particles are certainly capable of endless interactions beyond those in which they are actually engaged at any given time. Everything points to dispositionality's being a fundamental feature of our world.

Why have so many philosophers found it natural to distinguish two classes of property: categorical and dispositional? The distinction is traceable to Ryle (see § 4.6). On the one hand, there are categorical properties, properties had by objects 'categorically' properties taken to be possessed by objects flat-out, here and now. On the other hand there are non-categorical, merely if–then properties: dispositional properties. An object's 'having' one of these properties is for the object to have the potential, under the right circumstances, to behave a certain way – to dissolve, for instance, or to shatter. By my lights the distinction is merely a projection onto the world of our own habits of selective attention. Once you adopt the perspective I am recommending, once you recognize powers or dispositions as here and now features of objects, this kind of distinction lapses. In no sense are dispositional properties merely 'if–thens'. Dispositional properties are fully 'categorical', fully present here and now.

The philosophical debate over whether properties are dispositional or categorical has had the following form. One side points out that the notion of a non-dispositional property is the notion of a property that would make no difference to what its possessor does or would do. It is concluded that no genuine property is categorical – in my terminology, no property is qualitative – or that the qualitative side of things is derived somehow from their dispositionalities. The opposing side focuses on the elusiveness of pure

dispositionality, and concludes that dispositionality must have a non-dispositional, purely qualitative, 'ground'.

As is common in cases of intractable philosophical disagreement, both-
sides arguments are right in one respect and wrong in another. Suppose a
property is dispositional. It does not follow that that the property is *not*
qualitative. Similarly, if a property is qualitative, it does not follow that the
property is *not* dispositional. Arguments favoring a conception of properties
as powers or dispositions do not show that properties are not qualities, and
arguments to the conclusion that properties are qualities do not show that
properties are not dispositions. Both sorts of argument are consistent with
the position advanced here: every property is *both* dispositional and qualitative, properties are powerful qualities.

Before moving on, I might point out the utter naturalness of this conception of properties. Consider the property of being square, *squareness*.
Squareness is an excellent example of what have standardly been regarded as
categorical or qualitative properties. Suppose, then, that squareness endows
its possessors with a certain quality – the quality that comes to mind when
you think of something's being square. It is no less true, however, that
squareness endows objects with certain powers or dispositions. A square peg
would make a square impression in soft clay; a square peg would reflect light
differently than a round peg; a square peg would feel different to the touch
than a round peg. It is hard not to conclude that being square – squareness –
is simultaneously dispositional and qualitative. In this squareness resembles
other properties. In this regard, squareness is representative of properties
generally.

12.7 Manifestations of Dispositions

Taking dispositionality seriously requires distinguishing dispositions from
their *manifestations*. A disposition can be perfectly real, wholly present here
and now, yet remain unmanifested. A vase can be fragile without ever shattering, a chemical substance can be soluble without ever dissolving.

Dispositions typically require for their manifestation suitable *reciprocal
disposition partners*. If salt is soluble in water, then the dissolving of this
crystal of salt is the *mutual manifestation* of the salt's solubility and the
surrounding water's complementary disposition to dissolve salt. A property's
dispositionality is intrinsic to it, built in. Its *manifestations* typically depend
on the presence of reciprocal disposition partners. (Typically. The disposition
of a radium atom to decay is manifested spontaneously.)

The reciprocity of dispositions means that a single kind of disposition can
manifest itself differently with different kinds of reciprocal partner. Litmus
paper turns pink when immersed in acid, blue when dipped into a base.
The microstructure of a metal makes it opaque and electrically conductive
– different kinds of manifestation with different kinds of reciprocal partner
(ambient light radiation in one case and electrical charge in the other).

Owing to its sphericity, a billiard ball would roll (rather than bounce) down an inclined plane, make a round (rather than square) impression in the sand, and reflect light so as to make a round image on a photographic plate.

One further element is required to complete the picture. I have said that particular manifestations of dispositions depend on the presence of appropriate reciprocal disposition partners. But they can depend, as well, on the *absence* of disposition partners that could block the manifestations in question. Salt dissolves in water, but not if an inhibitory agent is present; exposure to sunlight results in skin lesions, but not if a suitable 'sunblock' is used.

12.8 Causality and Dispositionality

Causal truths are ultimately grounded in the mutual manifestations of reciprocal disposition partners. Consider a simple causal sequence, a key's opening a lock. The effect, the lock's being open, is a mutual manifestation of dispositions possessed by the lock and the key. The cause, the key's turning, is itself the mutual manifestation of reciprocal disposition partners that include the key and the hand holding the key.

The dispositional model allows for the replacement of the image of linear causal sequences or chains, with a conception of the universe as an inclusive dispositional *network*. Consider what the cause of a particular effect might include. A match ignites when it is struck. It is customary to think of the cause as the striking and the effect as the igniting. But the match would not ignite in the absence of oxygen. Is the presence of oxygen, then, a part of the cause? The presence of oxygen is not obviously part of the event – the striking – identified earlier as the cause. Might the presence of oxygen be a 'background' condition required for the cause to have the effect it has?

This way of looking at the matter requires a distinction between causes and background conditions in a way that appears metaphysically arbitrary. If, in contrast, you were to regard the match's igniting as the mutual manifestation of reciprocal disposition partners that include the surface on which the match is struck, the surrounding oxygen, and the chemical makeup of the match tip, you would want to assign equal credit to each of these contributing factors. Distinguishing causes from background conditions is to mistake a feature of our explanatory practices (in identifying causes, we omit elements our audience would take for granted) for a feature of the universe.

Another potential source of embarrassment for the prevailing view of event causation concerns the relative *timing* of causes and effects. A cause must precede its effects. But, as Hume noted, if a cause *precedes* its effect, there would seem to be a temporal gap or boundary between the occurrence of the cause and the onset of the effect. The causing event would be over before its effect begins. But how can an event that has run its course influence a subsequent event? If, in contrast, the causing event and its effect temporally overlap, it would seem that the portion of the causing event that occurs before the onset of the effect could not be implicated in the occurrence of the effect.

Suppose you cause your car to move by pushing it with a particular force. Do you first push the car and then the car moves? Your pushing (with a particular force) and the car's moving are apparently *simultaneous*. Of course you *set about* pushing the car prior to pushing it and prior to its moving. The car is not moved by your setting about pushing it, however, but by your pushing it.

If you replace the traditional conception of event causation and causal chains with a conception of causal–dispositional networks, such worries recede. Events are mutual manifestings of reciprocal disposition partners. Reciprocal disposition partners do not stand in relations of succession to one another. The appropriate model is not that of links in a chain, but of playing cards remaining upright by mutually supporting one another on a table top. (And note: the table top and the gravitational field are fully fledged reciprocal partners, not 'background conditions'.)

What of 'probabilistic' causation: causal relations in which causes apparently yield effects only with a certain probability? The quantum theory seems to tell us that probabilistic causation is the rule rather than the exception. Philosophers who favor accounts of causation based on causal laws explain probabilistic causation by building probabilities into the laws. What might the analogue be for a disposition-based account?

Start with the idea that every property bestows a definite dispositionality on its possessor. This dispositionality manifests itself in a definite way given particular kinds of reciprocal disposition partner (and in the absence of 'blockers'). How dispositions manifest themselves, and their manifesting themselves as they do on a particular occasion, are both perfectly definite, perfectly 'deterministic'. How could probabilities enter the picture?

Here is one possibility. Probabilistic causation stems from *spontaneity*. When a radium atom decays, it does so spontaneously. Nothing makes the atom decay. In decaying, the atom goes into a particular state. Its going into that state is a matter of its (spontaneously) coming to possess a particular disposition. The atom is now, as it was not previously, disposed to various manifestations with various kinds of disposition partner. *These* manifestations are perfectly 'deterministic'. Probabilities enter, not in the manifesting of dispositions, but in whether dispositions are on hand to be manifested.

It is time to move on. I do not imagine that these brief remarks provide anything approaching a decisive rebuttal of the prevailing conception of causation as a sequential asymmetrical relation among particular events. I want only to indicate that the appealing simplicity of that view requires complicating the metaphysics in various unattractive ways. These complexities are nicely resolved within the dispositional model. To that extent, at least, the model appears viable.

12.9   Complex Objects

The universe comprises a dynamic arrangement of fundamental substances. The substances might be elementary particles, they might be superstrings, they might be fields; there might be a single, seamless substance: space–time, the unified field, or the universe itself. What the substances are is an empirical question to be answered, if at all, by fundamental physics. Substances are simple, substances lack parts that are themselves substances. Complex objects are made up of substances standing in various relations to one another and to other substances. A complex object includes substances as parts. Substances, although simple, have a kind of structure – substances have properties – but no substantial parts.

If there is but one substance – perhaps the universe itself – then what we commonly regard as complex objects such as trees, molecules, and planets, are properties of this substance, *modes*, local ways it is. Think of Spinoza's conception of material bodies as 'thickenings' of space. Although I take seriously the possibility that there is but one substance – in fact, if I had to bet, this is where I would put my money – I shall couch the discussion here in terms of fundamental particles. I leave it to you, the reader, to apply the lessons to the case of a single substance.

Complex objects have objects as parts. These parts could themselves be complex, but you might hope eventually to arrive at simple objects, substances, objects not made up of objects. Complex objects are constituted by their constituent substances. Is there any more to complex objects than this? Many philosophers have thought so.

Think of a statue and the particles that make it up. Is the statue *just* the collection of particles? It would seem not. The collection of particles could change, and the statue remain. You could repair the statue and replace a piece that has broken off. When you do so, the result is a new collection of particles, but 'the same' statue. More dramatically, you could destroy the statue without destroying the collection of particles by rearranging its particles so as to form a cube, for instance, or by grinding the statue to dust. The statue and the collection of particles have distinct *identity* and *persistence conditions*: the statue could continue to exist when the collection of particles does not, and the collection of particles could survive when the statue is destroyed.

Maybe the statue is the collection of particles *arranged in a particular way*: the statue is the particles plus their arrangement. If the statue is ground to dust, its particles remain, but their arrangement is lost. However, it looks as though, so long as you preserved the arrangement, you could replace particles and the statue, but not the collection, would remain. Carve off a small piece of the statue and the statue remains, but the collection is diminished.

Considerations along these lines have led philosophers to the view that statues, and indeed complex objects generally, are distinct from arrangements of their constituent parts. True, they are, at any given time, *made up* of a collection of parts. But this just shows there is more to an object's identity than the objects that make it up and the relations these bear to one another. In the case of the statue, you might imagine two spatially overlapping objects: the statue (characterized by its identity conditions over time) and a collection of particles (characterized by its very different identity conditions over time).

The resulting picture is of a universe consisting of 'layers' of objects and properties. Statues are 'higher-level' objects; particles that make up statues, and perhaps certain collections of these particles, are objects at a lower level. Now it seems possible to explain the role of the special sciences. Physics is the science of objects at the basic level. Each special science – biology, for instance, or meteorology, or psychology – deals with some domain of higher-level objects. The world comprises, then, not just objects, but a *hierarchy* of objects at distinct levels.

This layered conception of reality is widely accepted. I believe it is mistaken. Appeals to levels of reality, ontological hierarchies, lead to a distorted picture of how things stand and to a multitude of philosophical puzzles and mysteries.

Consider again the idea that the statue is not to be *identified* with the collection of particles that make it up, nor even with the collection of particles arranged in a particular way. The plausibility of this idea requires taking 'collection' in an especially rigid sense. In this sense, a collection is destroyed when it loses a single member, when a member is replaced by a duplicate, or when a new member is added. Now consider a more relaxed notion of a collection. This relaxed notion is the notion you deploy when you think of a stamp collection, or a collection of buttons or paintings. In this relaxed sense, a collection can gain or lose members, and yet remain the same collection. How many members can a collection gain or lose, how much can a collection change and still remain the same collection? This could be partly a matter of decision.

When you consider the statue as a collection of particles in this relaxed sense, it is rather more plausible to say that the statue, here and now, is 'nothing over and above', 'nothing other than', *is just* this collection of particles arranged as they are. Still, this might not be not quite right. Arguably, statues are artifacts, produced by intelligent creatures with particular ends in mind. An appropriately arranged collection of particles that 'fell from the sky' or was produced by the random action of waves on a rocky outcropping would not be a statue – although of course you could easily mistake it for one. A statue, then, is not merely an appropriately shaped collection of particles. In order to constitute a statue, a collection of particles must have the right kind of 'causal history'. This history must include intelligent creatures and their states of mind.

Now suppose you build all this into the picture, suppose you take the collection of particles (in the relaxed sense of collection) and add to it, not merely relations these particles bear to one another, but also relations they bear to other particles, themselves members of collections of particles. The relations will be complex indeed, they will very likely exceed anything that could be grasped by a finite human mind. Moreover, once 'collection' and 'appropriate arrangement' are deployed in a relaxed sense, the possibilities for variation will be endless.

This is merely to say that there is no prospect of providing a definition, or even an illuminating set of 'necessary and sufficient conditions' for something's being a statue appealing only the vocabulary of particles and relations among these. To regard this as an impediment to a serious ontology of complex objects, however, is to miss the point. The thought here is not that talk of statues is translatable into, or analyzable in terms of, talk of particles and their relations. The idea, rather, is that, at any given time, this is all there is to the statue; a statue, here and now, nothing other than, distinct from, or 'over and above' a particular collection of particles, where 'collection' is taken in the relaxed sense and includes relations these particles bear to one another and to other particles belonging to other collections.

Imagine that God sets out to create a world containing statues. God could do so by creating the particles and ensuring that they bear the right relations to one another. The creation of a single statue could well require the creation of a dynamic arrangement extending over time and taking in an impressive spatial region. If a statue requires the existence of intelligent creatures with particular thoughts, then other collections of simple objects with similarly dynamic and extended spatial and temporal relations will need to be included as well.

Again, the thesis is not that 'statue' can be defined or analyzed in terms of atoms or molecules and their relations. There is no hope of spelling out detailed conditions of identity or persistence in terms of constituent objects and their relations. Rather, the *truthmakers* for claims about statues are ultimately arrangements of simple substances: something is a statue in virtue of its being a collection (in the relaxed sense) of substances bearing appropriate relations to one another and to other collections of substances. There is no question of specifying these collections independently of the statue concept, nor is this required. The suggestion is not that you could replace talk of statues or reduce such talk to talk of leptons and quarks. The picture I am offering is an ontological picture, not a reductive account of concepts or word meanings.

You might worry that such a picture is hopelessly austere. It might appear to deny reality to anything but the simple substances and relations these bear to one another. In the words of the ancient Greek atomist, Democritus (§ 4.1): only the atoms and the void are real. But this is to caricature the view I am endorsing. Statues exist, all right; it is true that there are statues (we 'quantify over statues', § 9.2); it is just that statues are nothing in addition to dynamic arrangements of simpler things. Statues are not higher-level entities – except in the ontologically innocuous sense that they are complex entities made up of simpler constituents in complex dynamic arrangements. And this is so, as well, for every putatively higher-level entity, including ourselves, our social institutions, and the products of these.

A reminder. The example of a statue and particles that make it up encourages the idea that the universe is grainy: complex objects are assemblages of simple particles. Although I admit this as a possibility, it is not the only possibility and, if physics is to be believed, it is not even an especially likely possibility. Imagine, for a moment, that objects are modes of space–time or the quantum field, ways these things are. Such objects would not be particle-like, although we could well experience them as particle-like.

As noted earlier, none of this would affect what I have said here. I have, to be sure, spoken of statues and their constituent particles, but this could be regarded as nothing more than a way of speaking about fluctuations or disturbances in space–time or the quantum field. As it happens, the universe is such that these disturbances are rarely isolated affairs. They 'clump together' in particular ways. This 'clumping' gives rise to what we describe (to my mind, quite correctly) as statues and the particles making them up. Their 'clumping' is explained by the dispositionalities of the fundamental entities (or, in the case that there is but one of them, the fundamental entity).

Although I remain officially agnostic on the question whether substances are ultimately particles, or fields, or something else – this is not, after all, a question for a philosopher to decide – I shall continue to treat substances as particles moving about in space, interacting, and persisting over time. This is solely a matter of expository convenience. I am supposing that truthmakers for claims about objects populating the universe could turn out to be something that does not match our ordinary conception of particles as persisting, mobile, self-contained entities.

12.10   Emergence

This compositional picture is meant to apply to properties as well as objects. Substances are various ways. These ways are properties, or, to invoke traditional terminology, modes. Complex objects, substances-by-courtesy, quasi-substances, have assorted characteristics, Episcopalian properties, properties-by-courtesy, quasi-properties. Quasi-properties are nothing more than particular interacting arrangements of propertied substances. A billiard ball's redness and sphericity result from a particular arrangement of substances of the right kinds. The ball's redness and sphericity are ways this arrangement is.

This conception stands in marked contrast to the view that properties of wholes are 'emergent'. The universe consists of simple substances. Properties are ways these substances are, modes. It could turn out, and indeed it appears altogether likely, that there are, in fact, very few kinds of property. Properties are, in the words of David Lewis, 'sparse'. But from a small number of different kinds of substance, you get many combinatorial possibilities, many kinds of complex object that are many ways, that possess many quasi-properties. Quasi-properties are nothing in addition to, nothing 'over and above' ways the fundamental substances are arranged.

Does this mean that emergence, genuine emergence, the emergence of genuinely new *properties* (as distinct from new kinds of arrangement of familiar substances), is impossible? Not at all. But if emergence occurs – and I believe it does occur – it occurs at the basic level, at the level of fundamental substances. At the basic level what is emergent cannot be a way more basic things are arranged.

Think of it this way. Suppose you accept that substances must be simple and properties are modes, ways substances are. Getting a new property on the scene requires getting a new kind of substance on the scene: property emergence requires substance emergence. Is this crazy?

Not only is it not crazy, it is a straightforward consequence of current conceptions of the behavior of elementary particles. Imagine that the universe contained just two kinds of elementary particle, α-particles and β-particles. Prior to some particular time, these particles never interact – owing, perhaps, to their occupying non-overlapping spatial regions. Eventually, however, an α-particle encounters a β-particle. As a result, the particles 'annihilate' and a new kind of elementary particle, a χ particle, emerges. Something like this was evidently widespread during, or immediately after, the Big Bang. It occurs routinely in particle accelerators.

This is one kind of emergence. A second kind of emergence might be thought to occur when particles in a quantum state become 'entangled'. When this happens, the particles are said to 'lose their identity'. This is not the place to discuss quantum physics, but my suggestion is that when this happens, a new substance comes into being. This substance is not *made up* of the entangled particles. The entangled particles are ways the substance is, modes. If, as some physicists and philosophers have suggested, the universe as a whole is one mass of entangled particles, then the universe is a single substance, what appear to observers to be particles are in fact modes of this substance, ways it is.

The compositional picture requires a distinction between substances and complex objects, arrangements of substances. It requires, as well, a distinction between properties, on the one hand, *genuine* properties, properties of the fundamental substances and, on the other hand, Episcopalian quasi-properties, characteristics of complex objects. These characteristics are particular ways particular substances are arranged. Such characteristics are not emergent in any interesting sense. Genuine emergence is the emergence of a substance, a new kind of fundamental particle or, as in the case of 'entangled' particles, a substance, the modes of which are what we had previously regarded as particles.

12.11   Levels of Being

Does the ontology I am recommending fly in the face of everyday experience or our ordinary take on reality? It does, certainly, fly in the face of a popular philosophical refrain according to which the world is *layered*: the world incorporates *levels* of objects and properties arranged hierarchically. However, such levels are *philosophical* posits introduced as ingredients of *philosophical* theories. Such theories are designed to reconcile everyday experience with the picture of the world we develop in the course of pursuing finer-grained scientific ends. In rejecting a philosophical posit and the theory in which it is embedded, however, I am by no means recommending that you turn your back on everyday experience. On the contrary, I am offering a competing account of the basis of that experience, one that, with luck, meshes as well with what the sciences tell us about the universe.

At this point, someone could dig in. The layered view of the world, it might be argued, comes not from everyday experience, not from philosophy, but from *science*. The special sciences concern objects and properties occupying distinct ontological strata. Each level is autonomous with respect to those below it, in the sense that it cannot be 'reduced' to lower levels. Laws governing higher-level objects are not replaceable by or derivable from lower-level laws. Nevertheless, objects and properties at higher levels are in some way 'grounded in' objects and properties occupying lower levels.

The favored account of 'grounding' is thought to be captured by the notion of 'supervenience': higher-level items 'supervene' on those at lower levels (see § 11.4). This means, roughly, that higher-level differences require differences at lower levels; lower-level objects and properties suffice for higher-level objects and properties, but that the higher-level supervening objects and properties are distinct from their lower-level grounds. (I should note that supervenience, as it is usually characterized, is consistent with, but does not imply, the second conjunct. I include it merely to make explicit one prominent motive for appeals to supervenience.) The distinctness of higher-level items is reflected in (or perhaps is constituted by) their being governed by distinct laws of nature.

An evaluation of this approach requires a brief detour through the philosophy of language.

12.12   Predicates and Properties

Properties, as I have characterized them, are genuine features of the world: modes, particularized ways substances are. Properties are to be distinguished from predicates. The *property* of sphericity – being spherical – is one thing, the *predicate* 'is spherical', is something else again. The predicate is a linguistic expression the role of which is to name or designate a property. Does every property have a linguistic designation? That seems unlikely. As scientists learn more and more about the universe, they uncover new, as yet unnamed, properties. Laboratories and particle accelerators are designed to facilitate the creation of new properties, properties not previously encountered. When this happens, scientists are obliged to invent a new name or devise a descriptive predicate.

This much seems obvious. What is less obvious, however, is whether every predicate designates a property. To be sure, some predicates apparently designate nothing at all: 'is a square circle', for instance. The predicate 'is a cure for the common cold', although perfectly meaningful, apparently fails to designate a property of anything. Scientists could, of course, discover that it does, or, more likely, learn how to manufacture a drug possessing characteristics that answer to the predicate.

Other predicates present different challenges. Consider the predicate 'is good'. It is a matter of some controversy whether this predicate designates a property of objects, or whether it serves merely to express a speaker's approval of things to which it is applied. When you tell me that Brussels sprouts are good, are you saying that Brussels sprouts, in addition to being leafy, green, and pungent, possess the property of being good? Or are you rather *commending* Brussels sprouts (perhaps *because* they are leafy, green, and pungent)? I shall not try to answer this question here. It is enough to recognize that it is at least a matter of dispute whether 'is good' designates a genuine property.

What of a predicate like 'is a stone'? Does this predicate designate a property possessed by particular objects, those qualifying as stones? There are stones, undeniably. But is there *a* property, *the property of being a stone*, possessed by every stone and in virtue of which it is true that it is a stone? This might strike you as an odd question, but bear with me. Perhaps we can see our way through at least one philosophical thicket, and begin to pull some of the lessons of this chapter together.

12.13 Properties, Realism, and Anti-Realism

Philosophers sometimes argue as follows.

(R) Take a predicate, 'ϕ'. Either 'ϕ' designates a property or it does not. If 'ϕ' designates a property, then to say that something, α, is ϕ is to say something true (if α has ϕ) or false (if α lacks ϕ). You are a *realist* about ϕ's just in case you take 'ϕ' to express a property. Otherwise you are an *anti-realist* about ϕ's.

Anti-realists about a given domain hold that entities in the domain are either non-existent or in some way language or mind dependent. Most of us are anti-realists in the first sense about ghosts and unicorns. We deny that such things exist. Putting this into the philosophers' linguistic mode: we believe that the predicate 'is a ghost' and the predicate 'is a unicorn' designate nothing at all. (One qualification: any consistent predicate can apply to agents' beliefs. It might be true of you that you *believe* there are ghosts or unicorns.) Relative to believers in such things, we could be described as 'eliminativists' about ghosts and unicorns. Where ϕ's are unicorns, we declare that there are no ϕ's (Chapter 9).

Other anti-realists are more subtle – or devious. They hold that sentences apparently ascribing ϕ's to objects, need to be understood, not as straightforward *ascriptions* of ϕ, but as something else. 'Expressivist' views in ethics are a familiar example. To say that α is good, for instance, is taken not to ascribe a property, goodness, to α, but to express the speaker's approval of α.

All this is good fun, but what of thesis (R)? My suggestion is that (R) mischaracterizes realism. One source of this mischaracterization is a failure to take seriously the distinction between predicates and properties. And one result of a tacit allegiance to (R), or something like (R), is what encourages an ontology of levels of being, an unwieldy hierarchical conception of reality.

To see what is wrong with (R), consider how a predicate might be thought to hold true of an object. The predicate 'is spherical', we might say, holds true of a billiard ball in virtue of the ball's possessing the property of *being spherical*. (And the deep story here is going to be that the ball's sphericity is a particular way its constituents are arranged.)

Now consider the predicate 'is a stone'. English speakers agree that this predicate holds true of many objects: many objects are stones. Does 'is a stone' name or designate a *property* of objects, a property (1) shared by all stones, and (2) in virtue of which each of those objects answers to the predicate 'is a stone'? Do not say: 'well of course! Stones, by virtue of being stones, share the property: *being a stone*. If the predicate did not designate a property, then it would be false that it is applicable to objects we call stones. But that is absurd – surely there are stones!' This kind of response amounts to little more than a reaffirmation of (R).

Take a moment to reflect on the nature of properties. If, against my recommendation, you regard properties as universals, then every object possessing this property must be, in some respect, identical with every other object possessing it. If you agree with me that a property is a particular way an object is, then you will agree that the sense in which two objects 'share' a property, the sense in which they have 'the same' property, is just that the two objects are exactly similar in some way. Although the sphericity of this billiard ball is numerically distinct from the sphericity of another billiard ball, the sphericity of the two balls might be exactly similar. None of this implies that, if being spherical is a property, every spherical object must be exactly like every other. Spherical objects can differ in all sorts of ways. It does, however, imply that every spherical object must be exactly like every other spherical object in one way: the shape way.

In the case of sphericity, you might think this condition is often met. Many different objects, many different kinds of object, are identical (or exactly similar) with respect to their sphericity. (If you are worried that no two objects could be exactly similar with respect to their sphericity, then replace sphericity with the mass of an electron. I use the example of sphericity to illustrate the point, not to make it.) What of being a stone? Again, many different things, many different kinds of thing, answer to the predicate 'is a stone'. But do these things share a *single* property, are they identical (or exactly similar) in some one respect, a respect in virtue of which the predicate 'is a stone' holds true of them? Suppose, as seems likely, they do not. Suppose there are many ways of being a stone. Does it follow that stones do not exist? Must we be anti-realists about stones, 'stone eliminativists'?

No, not unless we cling to principle (R). The predicate 'is a stone', like *most* predicates, is intended to apply indifferently to a wide range of objects with a wide range of characteristics. It does so, not because these objects are identical (or exactly similar) in some one respect. It does so because the objects are *similar enough*. How similar objects must be to fall under a predicate depends on the predicate and its deployment. This is something you learn when you learn to apply particular predicates to the world.

I do not think that there is anything new or startling about this idea. It has been advanced at various times by many different philosophers. Wittgenstein is the most celebrated recent example of a philosopher who has harped on the point. But I do not think the idea includes much in the way of substantive philosophy. Every language user appreciates it quite directly and unselfconsciously.

The really important point here is that a predicate that does not *express*, *name*, or *designate* a property could nevertheless hold true (or fail to hold true) of an object such as a stone, and hold true of the object in virtue of genuine features of the object. In the case of complex, everyday objects and objects that make up the subject matter of a special science, these features will be ways interrelated propertied substances are arranged. An object is spherical, perhaps, in virtue of possessing the property of sphericity or, if the object is complex, in virtue of being made up of substances arranged in the right way. An object is a stone, however, not in virtue of possessing the property of being a stone, but in virtue of being made up of substances possessing various other properties. It could well be the case that kinds of arrangements of propertied substances, sufficing for the application of the predicate 'is a stone', form an open-ended class. If this is so, then stones need have nothing in common beyond a certain 'family resemblance'. Only a philosopher with an agenda would conclude from this that there are no stones, or that nothing really is a stone.

Let me summarize. Some predicates *hold true* of objects in virtue of properties possessed by those objects or by their constituent substances. Of these predicates, some, perhaps only a very few, designate properties possessed by the objects to which they apply. Others do not. (In putting the point this way, I am using expressions of the form '"ϕ" designates [or "expresses"] a property' to characterize cases in which 'ϕ' functions as the *name* of a property – if properties are universals – or as the name of a collection or class of exactly similar properties – if properties are particularized ways substances are, modes.) Realism about a given predicate, 'ϕ', realism about ϕ's, requires that 'ϕ' applies truly to objects in virtue of properties possessed by those objects or in virtue of ways their constituent substances are organized. If you take these particles and arrange them in this way, the result is a statue. Differently arranged, the result might be a carburetor or a geranium.

'Realism about the ϕ's', then, does *not* require that 'ϕ' *designate* a property. If 'ϕ' does designate a property, objects answering to or 'satisfying' 'ϕ' must be identical (or exactly similar) in some one respect, a respect in virtue of which 'ϕ' holds true of them. And, I might add, objects that do not satisfy 'ϕ' differ from objects that do satisfy 'ϕ' in this respect.

Although there are stones – stones exist – being a stone is not a property possessed by all and only stones. I have been harping on the idea that 'is a stone' applies truly to objects, not by virtue of those objects' sharing a single property, but by virtue of their being pertinently similar. Of course, if my earlier contention that properties are borne by substances and substances are simple is accepted, then being a stone could not be a property – at least not if stones are complex objects. None of this, I contend, denigrates the reality of stones and their characteristics. It is merely an accounting of the ontology of such things.

All this is just to take properties seriously. It is unlikely that properties could be 'read off' from the predicates contained in ordinary language or in vocabularies of the special sciences. Moreover, unless you regard (R) as unassailable, you should be happy to allow that predicates need not name properties in order to hold true of objects, and indeed to hold true of those objects in virtue of properties possessed by their constituent substances.

I see this line of reasoning as a natural extension of the line taken on objects earlier. You could allow that statues exist – you could be a 'realist about statues' – without supposing that 'being a statue' designates a single property shared by all statues. This fits comfortably with the compositional picture. A statue is nothing more than a particular collection of simpler objects bearing appropriate relations to one another and to other collections of objects. This in no way jeopardizes the standing of ordinary objects such as statues, nor, I believe, would anyone other than a philosopher imagine that it does.

Suggested Reading

I discuss the position sketched in this chapter in more detail in *From an Ontological Point of View* (2003a) and *The Universe as We Find It* (2012).

C. B. Martin defends aspects of the approach in 'Substance Substantiated' (1980), 'Power for Realists' (1992), 'The Need for Ontology: Some Choices' (1993), 'On the Need for Properties: The Road to Pythagoreanism and Back' (1997). Many of these themes are developed in *The Mind in Nature* (2008). See also 'The Ontological Turn' (1999), a Martin and Heil joint effort.

Keith Campbell's *Metaphysics: An Introduction* (1976) is to my mind the best *ontologically serious* introduction to the topic. The book has long been out of print, but is available in most university libraries. E. J. Lowe's *A Survey of Metaphysics* (2002) is excellent, as is his more challenging *The Possibility of Metaphysics* (1998). Another very useful text is Michael Loux's *Metaphysics:*

A Contemporary Introduction, 3rd ed. (2006), a companion volume in the Routledge series to which this book belongs.

The thesis that, if there are objects, there are simple objects is discussed by E. J. Lowe in 'Primitive Substances' (1994), and by me in *The Universe as We Find It* (2012, chapters 2 and 3). For an account of objects as fields, see Steven Weinberg, 'Before the Big Bang' (1997). According to Weinberg, 'in the modern theory of elementary particles known as the Standard Model, a theory that has been well-verified experimentally, the fundamental components of nature are a few dozen different kinds of field' (Weinberg 1997, 17). (I owe the citation to Michael Lockwood.) See also Keith Campbell's excellent *Abstract Particulars* (1990).

Locke's conception of substance is spelled out in *An Essay Concerning Human Understanding*, ed. P. H. Nidditch, (1690), bk. ii, chapter 23. See also Martin's aforementioned 'Substance Substantiated' and E. J. Lowe's 'Locke, Martin, and Substance' (2000b); see also Lowe's *Locke on Human Understanding* (1995, chapter 4).

Plato discusses universals – the Forms – in various places, including the *Phaedo*, the *Republic* (books 6 and 7), and, in a more critical mode, in the *Parmenides*. David Armstrong provides a deft introduction to the topic in *Universals: An Opinionated Introduction* (1989). Armstrong's *A World of States of Affairs* (1997) brings Armstrong-style immanent universals up to date. Tropes – what I call modes – are discussed sympathetically in Keith Campbell's 'The Metaphysics of Abstract Particulars' (1981) and, at more depth, in *Abstract Particulars*, cited above. See also Peter Simons's 'Particulars in Particular Clothing' (1994). Anna-Sofia Maurin's *If Tropes* (2003) is a good recent book-length discussion of tropes.

Hugh Mellor, Sydney Shoemaker, and Chris Swoyer depict properties as fundamentally dispositional. See Mellor's 'In Defense of Dispositions' (1974), Shoemaker's 'Causality and Properties' (1980), and Swoyer's 'The Nature of Natural Laws' (1982). George Molnar's posthumously published *Powers* (2003) comprises an excellent discussion of dispositionality. Alexander Bird's *Nature's Metaphysics: Laws and Properties* (2007) tackles powers from the vantage point of the philosophy of science.

The notion that dispositions are categorically grounded is defended by D. M. Armstrong in many places, including *A Materialist Theory of the Mind* (1968, 85–8). See also, Prior, Pargetter, and Jackson's 'Three Theses about Dispositions' (1982), and Frank Jackson's 'Mental Causation' (1996). I call this view into question, although it is widely regarded as so obvious as not to require defense – and, on that basis, deserves to be called the default view. See my 'Dispositions' (2005) for a reasonably accessible discussion.

Jeffrey Poland's *Physicalism: The Philosophical Foundations* (1994) provides a detailed defense of a layered ontology of the kind attacked in this chapter. See also John Post's *The Faces of Existence* (1987), and my *The Nature of True Minds* (1992), esp. chapter 3 where I discuss (far too uncritically, as I now think) the layered picture.

Readers seeking an example of an argument in which realism about predicates is linked to those predicates' designating properties might consult Paul A. Boghossian, 'The Status of Content' (1990). In explicating 'non-factualist' (that is, anti-realist) accounts of a predicate, '*P*', Boghossian says that what such conceptions have in common is '(1) [t]he claim that the predicate "*P*" does not denote a property, and (hence) (2) the claim that the overall (atomic) declarative sentence in which it appears does not express a truth condition' (161). Note the parenthetical 'hence'.

Poland (in *Physicalism: The Philosophical Foundations*, chapter 4) advances an account of the realizing relation according to which realizing properties (1) suffice ('nomologically', that is, as a matter of natural law) for realized properties, and (2) instances of realizing properties constitute instances of realized properties. I discuss a similar conception in *The Nature of True Minds*, 135–9. See also Sydney Shoemaker's *Physical Realization* (2007).

Emergence is discussed by Timothy O'Connor in a number of co-authored papers, including 'The Metaphysics of Emergence' (2005) and 'Emergent Individuals' (2003). Cynthia and Graham Macdonald's collection, *Emergence in Mind* (2010), includes papers discussing the emergence if minds and their properties. Paul Teller provides an account of emergence in quantum physics in his 'Relational Holism and Quantum Mechanics' (1986) and *An Interpretive Introduction to Quantum Field Theory* (1995).

For an enthusiastic discussion of *ceteris paribus* laws, and their significance for the special sciences, see Jerry Fodor's 'You Can Fool Some of the People All of the Time, Everything Else Being Equal: Hedged Laws and Psychological Explanation' (1991). See also Fodor's 'Special Sciences: Still Autonomous after All These Years' (1997). An application of this kind of view to the problem of mental causation can be found in Ernest Lepore and Barry Loewer, 'Mind Matters' (1987).

Readers seeking more information on supervenience should consult Jaegwon Kim's 'Supervenience as a Philosophical Concept' (1990) and Terence Horgan's 'From Supervenience to Superdupervenience' (1993). I provide an overview of the topic and discuss its implications for the philosophy of mind in *The Nature of True Minds* (chapter 3), and a more critical look in 'Supervenience Deconstructed' (1998).

13 The Mind's Place in Nature

13.1 Applied Metaphysics

The previous chapter gestured toward a basic ontology according to which the universe comprises simple substances standing in various relations to one another. Simple substances, although lacking parts that are themselves substances, exhibit a kind of structure: substances are property bearers, substances are various ways. You can consider a substance as a bearer of properties, as being particular ways, and you can consider its properties, ways it is. Complex objects are made up of dynamic, interrelated collections of simple substances. What you might regard as properties of complex objects, 'properties-by-courtesy', Episcopalian quasi-properties, are ways the object's simple constituents are arranged. When distinct substances 'share' a property, there is some way in which the objects are exactly similar.

You need not agree with the details of this ontological blueprint to appreciate the lessons for the philosophy of mind I now hope to extract from it. An adequate defense of those details would require an extended excursion into hard-core metaphysics not appropriate in a volume of this kind. The same could be said for most of what follows. My intent is not to offer air-tight proofs or dis-proofs, however, but merely to illustrate the benefits of a comprehensive ontology for the kinds of issue in the philosophy of mind that have taken center stage in the preceding chapters.

In this context it is important to recognize that competing conceptions of mind presuppose particular ontologies. These remain largely hidden in the background, most often because they are widely accepted, hence taken to require no defense. Ontology calls the shots in the philosophy of mind, however. Problems become salient only in the context of a particular ontology. But ontologies are not philosophically innocent. If the ontology developed in the previous chapter is implausible, it is so relative to its competitors. Once you look closely at the competitors, you might warm to the position I am recommending.

In taking the measure of an ontology you will want to look at its explanatory power. In this regard, issues arising in the philosophy of mind are especially useful. Locating minds in the world poses severe challenges to any ontological scheme that distinguishes appearance and reality. In what follows, I spell out ways in which topics addressed throughout this book might be addressed from the perspective afforded by Chapter 12.

13.2   Multiple Realizability

Philosophers of mind, particularly those of a functionalist bent, are fond of the idea that mental properties are 'multiply realizable'. I know of no clear characterization of multiple realizability, but the idea is roughly this:

> (MR) A property, ϕ, is multiply realizable, when an object, α's, having ϕ depends on and is determined by α's possessing some distinct property, σ, from a (possibly open-ended) class of properties, Σ. (Σ includes at least two members.) For any object, α, when a member of Σ, is possessed by α, α realizes ϕ.

I do not put much weight on the details of this characterization. What I have to say, however, depends only on the idea that, when a property is multiply realizable, objects possessing it are taken to possess *both* that property and its realizer. In Figure 13.1, M represents a multiply realized mental property (ϕ in the characterization above), P_1, P_2, P_3, P_4, ... , P_n represent physical realizers of M (the members of Σ). This, I think, is a central feature of the notion of multiple realizability as most philosophers conceive it.

Pretend that being in pain is, as M is, a multiply realized property: the 'pain property' is capable of being possessed by many very different kinds of creature. If the pain property is multiply realizable, then any creature possessing the pain property – any creature in pain – would do so – would be in pain – in virtue of possessing some distinct realizing property: P_1, or P_2, or P_3, or ... . This property would be the 'pain realizer' in that creature. The guiding idea is that a property such as being in pain could have endless and varied realizers. The neurological property that realizes your pain differs from the property that realizes pain in an octopus. If Alpha Centaurians experience pain, and if Alpha Centaurians have silicon-based nervous systems, then some utterly different property realizes pain in Alpha Centaurians.

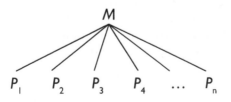

Figure 13.1

A brief reminder. Readers who have taken to heart my contention in Chapter 12 that properties must be possessed by simple substances, will recognize that the 'properties' in question here are Episcopalian properties-by-courtesy, quasi-properties. The distinction is not one that proponents of multiple realizability make, however. To keep the discussion as simple as possible, I intend to play along with this practice, hoping you will bear in mind that the properties that occupy center stage are in fact what you have when you organize particular fundamental substances in a particular way. Sometimes it is best to follow Bishop Berkeley's advice and 'think with the learned and speak with the vulgar' (§ 9.3).

One much discussed problem facing anyone who regards mental properties generally as multiply realizable, is the problem of *mental causation*. If a mental property is realized by a material property, then it looks as though its material realizer pre-empts any causal contribution on the part of the realized mental property.

The matter, addressed in § 11.6, bears reiterating. The apparent difficulty is illustrated in Figure 13.2 (where M_1 and M_2 are mental properties, P_1 and P_2 are nonmental realizers, ⇑ represents the realizing relation, and → indicates the causal relation.) In this case, mental properties, M_1 and M_2, appear to be 'epiphenomenal': M_1 has no causal part in bringing about either P_2 or M_2.

If you insist that mental properties make a causal difference, then you are obliged to say how this might work. Suppose, for instance, M_1 is the property of being in pain, P_1 is its neurological realizer, M_2 is the property of intending to take aspirin, and P_2 is M_2's realizer. Now, it is natural to suppose that M_1 brings about M_2 (Figure 13.3).

Given the relation of M_2 to P_2, however, it looks as though M_2 is on the scene owing to P_2's being on the scene.

Recall the analogy developed in § 11.6. The succession of images on a movie screen is explained by goings-on in the movie projector responsible for their appearance on the screen: a causal sequence in the projector gives rise to a sequence of images on the screen. Although the images occur in intelligible patterns, no image is causally responsible for images succeeding it. Similarly, the dependence of higher-level, realized properties on their lower-level

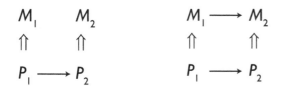

Figure 13.2   Figure 13.3

realizers, although not causal, apparently undercuts the possibility of higher-level causal relations in the way causal relations among successive images on a movie screen would be undercut by their dependence on goings-on in the projector. (If you let M_1 and M_2 in Figures 13.2 and 13.3 stand for images and P_1 and P_2 stand for occurrences in the projector responsible for the occurrence of those images, you can see that 13.3 misrepresents the true causal story, which is more accurately captured by 13.2.)

Suppose you accept the functionalist idea that mental properties (or states or events) are higher-level items with lower-level physical realizers. Now it will be hard to see how these higher-level items could causally influence other higher-level occurrences unless they somehow play a role in producing the lower-level realizers of those occurrences. Reverting to our diagrams, M_1's bringing about M_2 would require M_1's causing P_2 (Figure 13.4). However, what makes it the case – or so it would seem – that M_2 is on the scene, is not M_1, but P_2's being on the scene.

The difficulty now is that P_2 appears to be 'causally over-determined'. P_1, by itself, provides sufficient causal grounds for P_2. (Compare the occurrence of an image causally influencing an occurrence in the movie projector responsible for the appearance of a succeeding image.)

Worse, perhaps, in imagining that M_1 could play a role in the production of P_2, you would seem to be flying in the face of a widely held belief that the physical order is 'causally closed' or autonomous. Causal generalizations ranging over higher-level phenomena are *defeasible*. Such generalizations hold only *ceteris paribus*, only 'other things being equal'. A rational agent who judges it best, all things considered, to perform a given action, will perform the action – *ceteris paribus*. An agent's failure to perform the action need not mean the generalization is defective. An agent could be foiled by some 'outside factor': the agent might be struck by a falling tree limb, for instance, and knocked silly. When it comes to the fundamental physical things, however, there *is* no 'outside'. Laws governing these things are 'exceptionless'. The particles (or particle systems) involved in the sequence of events that includes the agent's deliberations and the falling limb are all marching in step with the fundamental laws.

'Downward causation' would require abandonment of the idea that the physical realm is causally autonomous. Whether this is a serious difficulty, or

Figure 13.4

merely a prejudice that could be discarded without jeopardizing the standing of physics, is debatable. I shall argue, in any case, that you need not choose between epiphenomenalism (illustrated by Figure 13.2), on the one hand, and, on the other hand, 'downward causation' (Figure 13.4).

13.3   An Alternative Approach

Suppose, first, you accept the idea defended in Chapter 12 that properties are *powerful qualities*: an object has the dispositions (or 'causal powers') and qualities it has in virtue of the properties it possesses. Now imagine that being in pain is realized in you by your undergoing a particular complicated neurological process. When you consider your wiring from a functionalist perspective, it looks as though it is this neurological process – the putative realizer of pain – and not the 'pain itself' that brings about bodily changes associated with pain.

In spite of all that has been said concerning the higher-level status of mental properties, you might still find this last thought baffling. If a property realizes the property of being in pain, why not say that pain is *identifiable* with its realizer? If the realizing property makes a causal contribution, then, so does the putatively realized property, being in pain. The difficulty (or rather one of the difficulties) with this suggestion is that proponents of multiple realizability regard the distinction between realized, higher-level properties and their lower-level realizers as non-negotiable. Thus, when a higher-level property is realized by a lower-level property *both* properties must somehow be on hand. The realized property, or its instance, cannot be absorbed by the realizing property, or its instance.

Attempts to reconcile multiple realizability and causal efficacy have included the invocation of purely counterfactual accounts of causation; appeals to the idea that any property figuring in a causal law (even a 'hedged' *ceteris paribus* law) thereby possesses causal efficacy; and reversion to one or another variety of 'reductionism': mental properties are identified with their realizers or with disjunctions of their realizers. I encourage you to be suspicious of all these strategies. Rather than arguing the point here, however, I shall present an alternative picture of multiple realizability. This alternative picture takes seriously the ontology of properties, and applies my earlier observations about predicates and properties.

Suppose, if you will, that the predicate 'is in pain', like the predicate 'is a stone', does not designate a property. The predicate 'is in pain' holds true of objects, and it holds true of those objects in virtue of their properties. But the property in virtue of which an object satisfies the predicate 'is in pain' is not a generic pain property: *being in pain*. There *is* no such property.

I hope I have said enough to make it clear that I am not advocating a form of eliminativism or anti-realism about pain. I am not denying that it is often – all too often – true of creatures that they are in pain. The idea, rather, is that 'is in pain' applies to creatures in states that are *similar* in certain important respects: similar enough to merit application of the predicate. These similarities stem from creatures' possession of certain properties. The important point is that the properties need not be the same properties in every case: creatures are neither identical nor exactly similar in those respects in virtue of which it is true of them that they answer to the pain predicate. Your pain and an octopus's pain are similar, but not exactly alike, just as your headache yesterday is broadly similar, but not exactly similar, to your backache today.

This result would seem to offer us all anyone could reasonably want. On the one hand, it allows for 'realism' about pain: pains are genuine features of the world. Being in pain just *is* to be in one of the states a functionalist would regard as a realizer of pain. On the other hand, it does not lead to worries about pain's being causally insignificant, 'epiphenomenal'. The account accommodates the notion that what it is, in virtue of which a creature is in pain, could vary widely across species or even individuals.

Imagine, for a moment, that pain is, at least in part, a functional notion. That is, a creature satisfies the predicate 'is in pain' partly, if defeasibly, in virtue of being in a state that plays a particular sort of complex causal role. (This could be so even if pain has, as I believe it must have, an essential qualitative dimension.) As functionalists never tire of pointing out, many different kinds of state could fill this role. (This is especially clear because any specification of the role will, of necessity, incorporate a measure of vagueness.) Very different kinds of creature, then, could be in pain. They are all in pain, however, not because they share (in whatever sense) a property – the putatively higher-level property of being in pain – but because they are similar in relevant ways. The ways are relevant, because they are accounted so by wielders of the 'pain predicate'. Their similarities stem from distinct but similar properties possessed by creatures answering to this predicate.

13.4   Higher-Level Properties

Mainstream functionalists contend that, by virtue of being functional properties, mental properties are higher-level properties. This is sometimes put by saying that mental properties are higher-*order* properties. A higher-order property would be a property of a property, however, and that is not what functionalists have in mind. Mental properties are not properties of their realizers. They are properties possessed by sentient creatures 'in virtue of' those creatures' possession of distinct, realizing properties. Being in pain is, on this view, the higher-level property of possessing some property (being in some state) that fills a particular functional role. Differently put: pain is the role, not its occupant. Pretend for the moment that *all there is* to a creature's being pain is for the creature to possess an appropriate functional organization. Does it follow that being in pain is a higher-level property?

First, an admission. I find it not at all clear what there could be to an object's possessing a higher-level property beyond its possessing some lower-level realizing property. Suppose, as I have been supposing, that the predicate 'is in pain' applies to creatures possessing a range of distinct, though similar properties, properties *similar* with respect to the dispositionalities they bestow on their possessors. There is no obvious reason to postulate an *additional* higher-level property to accompany each of these diverse lower-level properties – and good reasons *not* to do so. If there is a higher-level unifying element in the picture, it is supplied by our use of the predicate.

If I am right about this, then multiple realizability is not, as it is standardly thought to be, a determination relation among properties. It is simply the commonplace phenomenon of predicates applying to objects in virtue of distinct, although pertinently similar, dispositionalities possessed by those objects. And it would seem that this is something that holds of the bulk of the predicates deployed in everyday life and in the various sciences.

Here is the picture. Suppose you satisfy the predicate 'is in pain' in virtue of being in a certain complex neurological state, ϕ. Might creatures very different from you, creatures belonging to other species satisfy the predicate 'is in pain' in virtue of being in ϕ? That would seem unlikely. Remember: distinct objects that share a property must be, with respect to that property, *exactly similar* or, if properties are universals, *identical* (where 'identical' here means not exactly similar but 'one and the same'). If you take seriously familiar functionalists' arguments for multiple realizability, however, you will be strongly inclined to doubt that the requisite exact similarities (or identities) are on the cards.

What follows is *not* that being in pain is to be in a higher-level state realized by lower-level states that have similar functional profiles. What follows is that being in pain *is* to be in one of these 'lower-level' states. A state counts as a pain state in virtue of being a state with the right kind of functional profile – the pain profile. And, if the functionalists are to be believed, many *different* kinds of state could have the same functional profile. What more could you want?

13.5   Causality and *Ceteris Paribus* Laws

A view of the kind I have sketched makes sense of the significance of so-called *ceteris paribus* laws in the special sciences, including psychology (see Chapters 6 and 7). *Ceteris paribus* laws are taken to differ from 'strict' exceptionless laws associated with fundamental physics. The behavior of every physical object is governed by the laws of fundamental physics. Putatively higher-level objects, however, in virtue of putative higher-level properties, are thought to be governed by 'less strict', *ceteris paribus* laws – laws that admit of 'exceptions'. Indeed, a predicate's figuring in formulations of such laws is sometimes taken as a criterion of its designating a genuine higher-level property. This is thought to account for the 'projectability' of certain predicates. (A predicate is projectable when it could, for instance, be deployed successfully in inductive contexts – in reasoning, for instance, from '*heretofore observed α's are β's*' to '*all α's are β's*'.)

On the view I am recommending, there are no higher-level objects or properties. There are, to be sure, complex objects; objects made up of parts that are themselves objects. Properties of complex objects – quasi-properties – are ways their constituent objects are arranged. An object's dispositional nature is bestowed on it by its properties, and those properties are distinguished, in part, by dispositionalities they bestow. Objects possessing *similar* properties can be counted on to behave similarly, then, at least to the extent that their behavior is affected by their possession of those properties. This, I submit, is enough to ground lawlike generalizations holding – *ceteris paribus*, other things equal – of those objects.

This way of looking at matters locates causal powers squarely in the world among the substances and properties, and downplays the idea that a causal law is a distinct *external* factor – an invisible hand – governing interactions among material objects. Causal laws are typically expressed by formulae, or equations, or principles that hold of the universe in virtue of properties present in the universe. Any imaginable universe exactly like our universe with respect to its properties would, of necessity, be exactly like our universe with respect to its causal laws. Laws are contingent – *if* they are contingent, a big *if* – not because you could imagine holding the objects and properties fixed and varying the laws, but because you could imagine universes containing different kinds of substance and property.

13.6   Levels of Reality vs. Levels of Description

Philosophers would do well to dispense with the voguish 'layered' conception of the world. It is one thing to accept the platitude that reality can be variously categorized and described, then to notice that our categories can be ordered in a loose hierarchy. It is another matter to reify the hierarchy, imagining that it maps autonomous ontological strata.

I suspect that the tendency to read our descriptive practices into the world is abetted by our sometimes excessive reliance on formal techniques in addressing substantive metaphysical concerns. Abstract reasoning requires ontological grounding, however. This is easy to lose sight of so long as philosophers persist in conceptualizing substantive issues by invoking purely modal inventions such as 'supervenience' (a detailed discussion of which you have been mercifully spared) and relying on appeals to counterfactual and subjunctive conditional analyses to capture substantive features of the world – dispositionality and its cousin causality, for instance. You need not follow me and commit yourself to a detailed ontological scheme, but you should at least have a grasp of the options and their implications. And this is a matter of taking up an attitude of what the Australians call *ontological seriousness*.

13.7   Zombies (Again)

In § 10.4 you were introduced to the distinctively philosophical notion of a zombie. A zombie, you might recall, is a being exactly like you or me with respect to its micro-physical constitution, but altogether lacking in conscious experience. Because a zombie's nervous systems is no different from yours, zombies would not be empirically detectable. A zombie's behavior perfectly mirrors the behavior of a conscious agent. When a zombie sits on a tack, its neural circuits are activated just as yours would be had you sat on a tack, so it leaps up, yelping. What the zombie lacks is any conscious sensation of pain.

How could a zombie fail to notice this remarkable deficit, you ask. Well, functionalism holds that mental properties are functional properties. Functional properties are possessed by objects in virtue of their causal–dispositional makeup. And (it is assumed) a zombie's dispositional makeup is, as yours and mine is, grounded in its nervous system. The zombie, then, would *behave* as you or I behave, *believe* what you or I believe, *want* what you or I want. The zombie would, just as you or I would, scoff at the suggestion that it lacked conscious experiences. Because a zombie believes that it has conscious experiences; its denial, although false, is perfectly sincere.

You would be forgiven for finding all this quite beyond the pale. The thought that there could be a creature who is a molecule-for-molecule duplicate of you, a perfect twin, yet who altogether lacks conscious experiences is one only a philosopher could take seriously – or even *entertain*. The guiding idea, however, is that there is nothing in the intrinsic nature of our material constitution that could be taken to guarantee consciousness in the way three-sidedness, for instance, guarantees triangularity. This is sometimes expressed by saying that zombies are 'logically (or 'conceptually') possible'. Of course (the thought continues), *as a matter of fact* the laws of nature ensure that any creature with your physical constitution (indeed, if David Chalmers is right, *any* system with the right kind of functional organization) would be conscious. In the same way, although there is no *logical* impossibility in the thought that pigs can fly, pigs cannot fly. The difference in these cases is that it is easy to understand why pigs cannot fly, but not at all easy to understand how brains 'give rise to' conscious experiences.

The zombie possibility rests on the assumption that laws of nature are contingent; they hold in our universe, but, theological considerations aside, there is no further reason why they should hold: they just *do*. The connection between your material nature and the distinctive qualitative nature of your conscious experiences is, in the final analysis, imponderable, an inexplicable 'brute fact'. You can understand a phenomenon such as photosynthesis or lactation by looking closely at the operation of biological mechanisms responsible for photosynthesis and lactation. But there is nothing comparable in the case of consciousness. By looking closely at goings-on in the brain, you could isolate important mechanisms and, perhaps eventually, arrive at a thorough-going account of the causal–dispositional structure of the brain. This would include knowledge of which kinds of neural structure were responsible for which kinds of conscious experience. None of this, however, would shed any light at all on the question, why conscious experiences with *these* qualities should accompany *these* neurological configurations. This is the deep mystery, what Chalmers dubs the 'hard problem', of consciousness.

The first thing to notice about a view that takes zombies seriously is that it presumes a particular ontology of properties. Properties are taken to be wholly dispositional, vehicles of causal powers: the way an object behaves or would behave depends on its complement of properties. A property's causal powers are not intrinsic to it, however, not a part of its nature. It is at least 'logically possible' that there could be a universe consisting of objects bearing the same properties as objects in our universe (and no others), yet in that universe, owing to differences in fundamental laws of nature, the properties would bestow entirely different dispositionalities on their bearers. *One* implication of such a view is that powers and qualities vary independently; the relation between qualities and dispositions is presumed contingent. It is a matter of contingent natural law that objects possessing particular qualities possess particular dispositionalities.

Chapter 12 introduced an independently motivated alternative to this conception of properties. Properties are *powerful qualities*. Every property is at once dispositional and qualitative. Every property contributes in a distinctive way to its possessor's qualities and to its possessor's dispositionalities. These contributions belong to the nature of the property. It would be impossible, flat-out impossible, for there to be a universe containing the same properties as our universe (and no more), but differing in respect to objects' causal powers or qualities.

Philosophers occasionally speak as though qualities were unique to conscious experiences. Qualities – *qualia*, so-called – are regarded as a special problem for the philosophy of mind. But, it would seem, there is ample reason to think that *every* object, by virtue of being as it is, by virtue of being a property bearer, has qualities. It is easy to lose sight of this seemingly obvious point if you follow the functionalists and fixate on 'causal powers'. When you do that, qualities appear not to matter. If qualities do not matter, if they are 'epiphenomenal', they lack scientific standing. And, sure enough, when you look at science, you find that qualities are, on the whole, ignored. In physics, for instance, laws and principles are formulated as ranging over numerical magnitudes that presumably hold true owing to the dispositionalities of the fundamental constituents and states. The mistake, however, is to interpret physicists' *silence* about qualities as an outright *denial* that objects, even fundamental substances – quarks and electrons – have qualities.

Suppose I am right. Suppose every property contributes in a distinctive way to its possessor's dispositionalities and qualities; and suppose that this is built into the nature of properties. Suppose, as well, that you are at bottom a complex object wholly constituted by simpler objects bearing appropriate relations to one another and to other objects that make up the universe. Your experiences are states of, and events involving, this complex object. These states and events are manifestations and manifestings of finely-tuned dispositionalities, expressions of your dispositional nature. But you have, as well, a *qualitative* nature, one inseparable (except in thought, via 'abstraction') from your dispositional nature. Your experiences have the qualities they have, not because these are tacked on by idiosyncratic laws of nature, but because they are built into the properties that constitute your mental life. *Whatever* exists has qualities, so it is no surprise that states of mind have qualities.

If this is so, then functionalism could be seen in a new light. Functionalists hold that a given state is a pain state, because it has the right sort of causal profile, the pain profile. If the state is correlated with a particular quality (painfulness, a distinctive *feeling*), this could only be because it plays the right sort of causal role *and* there is a law of nature that connects states playing this role with painfulness. This kind of account is odd on the face of it because it would seem to have the order of explanation backwards. It is natural to suppose that a state plays the pain role because it is *painful*, because it is as it is *qualitatively*, not the other way round. If properties are powerful qualities, if every dispositional state is qualitative, this is exactly what you *can* say. Functionalism is right to regard states of mind as being characterizable by reference to roles they play in our mental lives, but wrong to suppose that this makes qualities irrelevant. Dispositional states *are* qualitative states, their dispositionality *is* their qualitativity.

13.8 Qualities of Conscious Experience

Now a new problem arises, however. Qualities of conscious experiences appear to differ dramatically from qualities you would discover were you to inspect the nervous systems of a conscious agent. How *could* the qualities of a conscious experience turn out to be the qualities of a brain? How could anyone imagine that the feeling of nausea, or the smell of a rose, or the taste of Vegemite, or the sound of a train whistle, or the look of a winter sunset could possibly be identified with anything going on in the spongy, gray material making up a brain?

Imagine that you are looking at a ripe tomato illuminated by bright sunlight and having the kind of conscious experience you would characterize as that of seeing a ripe tomato in bright sunlight (Figure 13.5). Simultaneously, a neuroscientist scans your brain. The neuroscientist observes nothing at all resembling the qualities of your experience. The neuroscientist's observations reveal only boring neurological qualities and processes that bear no similarity to your vivid Technicolor experience. Indeed, qualities of your experiences appear unique to those experiences. They are imbued with qualities of a kind that could not conceivably exist outside consciousness. Any attempt to reduce experiences and their qualities to neurological goings-on must certainly fail.

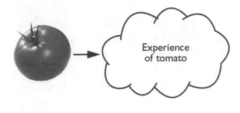

Figure 13.5

This way of formulating the problem, however, is founded on a confusion, one discussed at some length in Chapters 5 and 10. Two important distinctions emerged in those discussions. First, qualities of your visual *experience* of a tomato must be distinguished from qualities of the *tomato*. It should come as no surprise that nothing red and spherical occurs inside your cranium when you look at a spherical red object such as a tomato. To be sure, you are apt to *describe* your experience by reference to its *object*, by reference to what it is an experience *of*: an experience *of* a spherical red object. It is the tomato that is spherical and red, however, not your experience. So the first distinction to be made here is that between qualities of experiences and qualities of objects experienced.

A second distinction is related to the first. When a neuroscientist observes your brain (visually, let us suppose), the neuroscientist undergoes experiences with certain intrinsic qualities (Figure 13.6). Suppose that your visual experience of the tomato *is* a complex occurrence in your brain, and that this occurrence is observed by the neuroscientist. There is no reason to think that qualities of the neuroscientist's experiences ought in any way to resemble qualities of an experience of a tomato. Indeed there is every reason to think that they ought *not* to resemble those qualities. The tomato is spherical and red, but your experience of the tomato is neither. Why should an experience of your experience, then, be anything like your original tomato experience? There is, it would seem, no mystery in the fact that the neuroscientist's experience (of your experience) differs qualitatively from your experience (of a tomato).

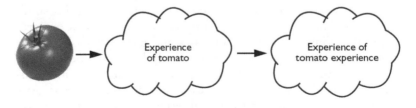

Figure 13.6

13.9   Neutral Monism

Now, however, a new difficulty appears on the scene. Qualities of your experiences, *whatever* they are, appear to differ utterly from the qualities of *any* imaginable material object. How then could anyone seriously entertain the hypothesis that conscious agents are nothing more than complex material systems, conscious experiences nothing more than manifestations of complex material dispositions?

The worry here is twofold. First, the qualities of conscious experience seem utterly different – qualitatively, if you like – from the qualities of material objects. Second, the qualities of conscious experience appear to be ineluctably tied to subjects of experience: *experiencers*. Without experiencers, these qualities could not exist. They are in this respect deeply *mind dependent*; their being experienced is *all there is* to them. As Hume put it, they 'are what they seem and seem what they are'. This means that your 'access' to these qualities is direct and privileged in a way that does not hold for your access to qualities of any material object. The qualities of a conscious experience are necessarily 'private', available only to the agent undergoing the experience; the qualities of material objects, in contrast, are 'public', and necessarily so.

I have been promoting what most philosophers would describe as a 'materialist' or 'physicalist' conception of mind. I reject this description for reasons that will soon become clear. But, for the moment, let us suppose that the position I am advocating is a form of materialism: every object, property, state, and event is a material object, property, state, or event.

As you read these words, you are undergoing a particular visual experience, you are experiencing, visually, the print on this page (and perhaps much else besides). Direct your attention to the qualities of this experience. This will require a shift of attention from the words on the page to your awareness of the words on the page. The qualities you encounter when you do so are not ones you could easily describe. Maybe you could not describe them at all; maybe they are 'ineffable'. This need not be because these qualities are unfamiliar or elusive. They are the most familiar qualities of all. Their seeming difficult to describe stems from your having learned to ignore them, your having grown accustomed to treating them as 'transparent' indicators of the qualities of perceived objects. Your description of them, then, would unavoidably be framed in terms of the objects of your experience. Roughly, the qualities of your current visual experience are qualities of the sort you have when you look at a book in conditions like those under which you are now looking at this book.

In becoming aware of the qualities of your experience, then (still assuming materialism), you become aware of material qualities, presumably qualities of your brain. Qualities of your experiences are the only material qualities with which you are acquainted in this immediate way. Your acquaintance with qualities of this book is causally indirect. (It is causally indirect even if it is not *epistemically* indirect, even if it does not require an inference on your part.) It is a matter of your undergoing an experience as a result of your perceptual contact with the book. This experience is a mutual manifestation of neurological dispositions and those of the book, the intervening light radiation, and your visual system.

Your visual awareness of the print on this page is a matter of your having experiences imbued with particular qualities. A neuroscientist's simultaneous visual awareness of goings-on in your brain is a matter of the neuroscientist's having experiences imbued with particular qualities. In each case, the qualities are qualities of neurological activities. I hope I have convinced you that it is wholly unsurprising that the character of the neuroscientist's awareness differs from the character of your awareness. This is not because the qualities of your respective awareness belong to radically distinct kinds of substance or occupy distinct realms – yours belonging to a mental realm, the neuroscientist's to a material realm. On the contrary the qualities of both experiences belong to brains!

It would seem, then, that you have a direct line to some material qualities – qualities of your brain. The puzzle (presupposed by philosophers who regard *qualia* as deeply mysterious) of how the qualities of conscious experiences could possibly be qualities of material objects is displaced. If you are a serious materialist, it is hard to see how this result could be avoided.

Right, but I have denied that the view sketched in this chapter is materialist. Am I a 'property dualist', or some sort of idealist? Not at all. I reject the 'materialist' label only because it carries with it the implication that there is an *asymmetry* in the identification of mental qualities with material qualities: the mental is supplanted by the material. On the view I am recommending, there is no such asymmetry. If you insist on a label, I prefer one used by Bertrand Russell – and, more recently, by Michael Lockwood – in making many of the points I have been making here: 'neutral monism'. Neutral monism includes the denial that there is a mental–material chasm to be bridged. The mental–material distinction is, as Spinoza and Donald Davidson contend, a distinction of conception only, not a *real* distinction, not a distinction in reality.

One advantage of such a position is that it sidesteps questions as to what exactly counts as a material – as distinct from mental – object, property, state, or event. These are questions that a conventional materialist – or, for that matter, a property dualist – cannot avoid, questions notoriously difficult to answer in a satisfying way.

Are we left with a deep mystery? Does what I have said threaten to burden physics and neuroscience with a range of unexpected qualities, 'flickers of consciousness' among the neurons? Not at all. Physics and neuroscience are advised to proceed exactly as they now do. I am simply indicating how it would be possible for neurological goings-on to possess the kinds of quality associated with conscious experience. Bear in mind that any neuroscientist who denies that qualities of conscious experience could be neurological qualities must first convince us that this denial is not based on the kind of confusion discussed earlier: a confusion between qualities of different kinds of experience. A visual experience of a brain would be qualitatively different from a visual experience of a ripe tomato. The experience had by a neuroscientist observing your experiencing a ripe tomato need be nothing at all like the neuroscientist's experience of a ripe tomato.

13.10 'Privileged Access'

What a relief! We can dispense with the idea that *qualia*, qualities of conscious experience, are an embarrassment, or that such things are artifacts of outmoded philosophical theories to be banished with those theories. Such ideas are founded on ontologies with features we need not embrace.

Even if this kind of optimism is warranted, however, we are left with a formidable problem as regards conscious qualities. Your experiences evidently depend on *you* for their existence; an experience is always some conscious agent's experience. Further, you are conscious of your experiences (and their qualities) – to the extent that you *can* be conscious of them – in a way that would seem to preclude error. You can misdescribe or mislabel an experience, but it is hard to see how you could be *mistaken* about your experiences – how you might, for instance, take yourself to be in pain when you are not in pain. According to a long tradition that includes Hume (and, more recently, John Searle), when it comes to your own experiences, there can be no distinction between appearance and reality: the appearance *is* the reality. If experiences are neurological goings-on, however, if the qualities of your experiences are neurological qualities, what explains the intimate relation you evidently bear to them?

In this context it is vital to recognize that the awareness you have of your own conscious experience is not a matter of your having *two* experiences (1) the original experience, and (2) an experience *of* the original experience. Your awareness of your experience is constituted by your having it. For this reason, talk of 'access' to the character of conscious experiences is potentially misleading. It conjures an inappropriate model, that of observer and object. Your sensation of pain is not an object that you inwardly experience – or sense. Your having it *is* your sensing it.

I have emphasized (here and in Chapters 5 and 11) the importance of distinguishing (1) your undergoing some process or being in some state, and (2) observations of your undergoing a process or being in a state. To hearken back to an example deployed in § 5.11, your refrigerator's defrosting differs unproblematically from your observing its defrosting. In just the same way, your undergoing a pain is altogether different from my observing your undergoing it. Now, if 'directly observing a pain' is a matter of *having* a pain, it is unsurprising that *only you* can 'directly observe' your pains. This is just to say that only you can *have* your pains. And that is no more mysterious than the thought that only your refrigerator – and no other refrigerator – could undergo *its* defrosting.

None of this implies that you could not be wrong about your sensory states. Error resembles truth in presupposing *judgment*. Judgments you make about your conscious states *are* distinct from those states. This leaves room for error.

But wait! Common experience, buttressed by philosophical tradition, suggests that, when it comes to your own conscious states of mind, your judgments are 'incorrigible': error about such things is impossible. Is there some way to honor this conviction – or what lies behind it – without assuming incorrigibility? I think so.

Focus for a moment on ordinary perceptual error. You mistake a stick in your path for a snake. Sticks, after all, can look alarmingly snake-like. Expectation can have an important role here. You are more likely to mistake a stick for a snake when you are on the lookout for snakes. It is less easy to see how you could mistake a stick for a billiard ball or a coffee cup, a hawk for a handsaw. This does not mean that such mistakes are impossible. But to make sense of them, you would need to tell a complicated story. (In desperation, you might appeal to the philosopher's catch-all error-producer, the evil scientist who interferes directly with your brain.)

When it comes to your own sensory states, it is relatively easy to see how you could err in judging a state to be of a particular sort when it is in fact a state of a different, though similar, sort. Is that unsettled feeling in the pit of your stomach hunger or nausea? On a particular occasion you might find it difficult to say. As in cases of ordinary perceptual error, expectation can lead you astray. Further, neurological disorder, or a hypnotist (or an evil scientist) might bring it about that you err more egregiously: you judge that you are in pain, when you are not, or that you are not in pain, when you are.

One source of the conviction that you could not be wrong about your own conscious sensory states, then, is the difficulty in imagining how a sensory episode of a particular sort *could* be mistaken for something else. A second source stems from a recognition that error in judgment is unlikely when, to paraphrase Locke, the content or object of a judgment (or a belief) and the proximal cause of the judgment (or belief) are one and the same. Your being in pain leads you 'directly' to judge that you are in pain (or to form the belief that you are in pain); (Figure 13.7).

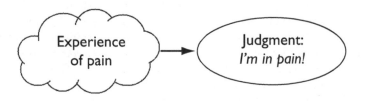

Figure 13.7

In contrast, the proximal cause of your judgment that a billiard ball lies in your path is not the billiard ball, but your *experience* of the billiard ball (Figure 13.8). You can imagine cases in which a billiard-ball-like experience occurs, and so leads you to judge that a billiard ball is present, when no billiard ball is present. Hallucination, perceptual illusion, dreaming, and of course the machinations of an evil scientist could result in such non-veridical experiences. Perhaps post-hypnotic suggestion or neurological disorder could result in your judging that a billiard ball is present when neither a billiard ball, nor a billiard-ball experience, is present.

You can make sense, then, of the impression that you could not be wrong about your own conscious experiences without supposing that judgments about such things are incorrigible. You can see, as well, how it might seem to you that, although you could be wrong about the presence of billiard balls, you could not be wrong about the occurrence of billiard-ball-like experiences. In all such cases, error is possible, albeit improbable.

What of the ego – the 'I' – the subject of experiences? Where are *subjects* located on my conception? Not, I think, in anything like an inner observer or spectator, a self that monitors experiential goings-on. You do not observe your experiences, you undergo them. You are, it would seem, partly constituted by those experiences. As Kant noted, every conscious experience includes an implicit 'I-am-undergoing-this-experience' judgment. Think of the *I* as made up of what all these experiences, thoughts, judgments, and the like point to; a kind of 'virtual entity'. The self need not be a substance – a conception I share with Locke.

I conclude that the approach to mind that I am recommending provides an appealing account of conscious experience. Much of its attraction stems from its being grounded in an independently motivated ontology. That ontology was introduced, not *ad hoc*, not because it promised to solve particular problems in the philosophy of mind, but because it offered a plausible self-standing picture of the universe.

Although I am partial to this ontology, I admit that many of the conclusions I have drawn out of it are individually consistent with various other ontological schemes. The question is whether competitors can comfortably accommodate the range of phenomena discussed here. An ontology cannot

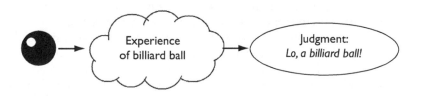

Figure 13.8

be assessed piecemeal. Nor is it advisable to pursue ontology by looking at problems in isolation. As noted earlier, the measure of an ontology is its power, its capacity to make sense of a broad assortment of disparate puzzles, and to do so in a natural way. On this measure, the ontology sketched in Chapter 12 has a lot to be said for it.

13.11   Imagery and Intentionality

Thus far I have ignored a topic that, until recently, dominated mainstream work in the philosophy of mind: *intentionality*. Intentional states of mind are those that are in some respect *representational*. Your thinking of a Whopper is a matter of your having a thought with a particular *content*. Your thought *concerns*, it is of, or *about*, a Whopper.

Chapters 7 and 8 took up two influential approaches to the 'propositional attitudes' (beliefs, desires, intentions, and the like). The propositional attitudes form an important class of intentional states of mind. Do they exhaust the class? Some philosophers and psychologists appear to have thought so, but such thoughts manifest something like a lack of imagination, or, at any rate, a lack of appreciation for the central role of imagination in our mental lives. Consider the phenomenon of mental imagery. On the face of it, imagery represents an important species of 'non-propositional' intentionality. Your believing that Whoppers are nutritionally challenged is perhaps not imagistic. But I would wager that the bulk of your Whopper-related thoughts are exclusively imagistic. (You *do* have Whopper-related thoughts, don't you?)

At the dawn of the twentieth century psychologists engaged in a lively debate over the possibility of 'imageless thought'. At the time, the radicals were those who contended that thought is *not* invariably 'imagistic'. Now, a hundred years later, the roles are reversed: the radicals are those who are skeptical of the received doctrine that thought could be wholly *non*-imagistic.

Why should anyone doubt the occurrence of mental imagery? In part, perhaps, because of an ongoing aversion to *qualia*, qualities of conscious experiences, an aversion stoked by discussions of imagery. If you are a card-carrying functionalist, there appears to be no room for such things. As a result, functionalists and materialists who fancy that qualities, generally, are metaphysically (or scientifically) dodgy, have deployed various analytical techniques designed to boil qualities down into something non-qualitative. I have argued that there is no need to do this, however, no need to fear that the qualities of conscious experience are scientifically proscribed.

A second worry about imagery stems from a tendency to suppose that having a mental image is a matter of observing (with the mind's eye, if the image is visual) a picture inside the head. A fierce debate has raged between proponents of 'pictorial' conceptions of imagery (Stephen Kosslyn, for instance) and those who insist that imagery must be 'propositional' (Zenon Pylyshyn). My belief is that both parties to the debate misconceive the nature of imagery. Having an image (a visual image, let us suppose) of a red squirrel is not a matter of observing a picture of a red squirrel in your head – or in your pocket, or anywhere else. Having an image of a red squirrel resembles *perceiving* a red squirrel. And perceiving, even perceiving a picture, is not picture-like. The entities – and qualities – involved in imagery are no more (nor less) remarkable than those implicated in ordinary perception.

Perceiving a squirrel has two components: (1) the squirrel, and (2) your perceptual state, brought about, presumably, by the squirrel. In contrast, imagining a squirrel is a matter of going into a state resembling the state you go into when you perceive a squirrel, but in the absence of the squirrel. The absence of the squirrel means that the state you are in was not caused by a squirrel, but by something else, most likely something internal. Once you are clear on the nature of imagery, you are free to admit, what should be obvious anyway, that mental imagery plays a central role in our intelligent commerce with the universe.

How central a role? Philosophers are perhaps by nature inclined to play down the significance of imagery. This is probably due, in part, to philosophers' occupational fixation on arguments and theses spelled out in sentences. When we philosophers turn our minds to such things, we typically do so in a linguistic mode. We rehearse arguments, try out theses, and formulate replies, all in language – how else? I suspect this long-standing practice has contributed to the widespread belief that the mind is largely – even exclusively – a consumer of propositional attitudes.

A moment's reflection, however, reveals that nothing of the sort follows. When you rehearse an argument in your head, you are engaged in an important form of imagery: *verbal* imagery. You hear words in your head, or, more likely, you both feel and hear yourself uttering words. This is, if anything is, a robust species of imagery. Conscious thoughts, even 'propositional' thoughts, are imagistic.

How exactly is imagery to fit into the picture of mind that has emerged in this chapter? Recall the earlier discussion of your visually apprehending a ripe tomato in bright sunlight. The visual experience you undergo when this happens exhibits certain qualities. Now, *imagine* what a ripe tomato in bright sunlight looks like: form a visual image of the tomato. When you do this successfully, you pass into a state that *resembles* the state you are in when you actually see the tomato. Your imagining the tomato *resembles* your visually perceiving the tomato – and it goes without saying that neither resembles the tomato. This is just to say that the qualities of the two states are similar. Talking silently to yourself yields the same kind of phenomenon. In talking to yourself, your experience resembles, qualitatively, the experience you have when you speak aloud.

These points seem to me so obvious I scarcely know how to argue for them. Even so, they are often denied. In discussions of mental imagery, it is common for discussants to proclaim that their own imagery is dramatically attenuated, or even altogether absent. (In some quarters a professed lack of imagery is worn as a badge of honor.) My suspicion is that these assertions are founded on what psychologists call a *criterion difference*, a difference in what individuals take to constitute imagery.

I have said that imagining a ripe tomato illuminated in bright sunlight resembles perceiving a ripe tomato illuminated in bright sunlight. Bear in mind that the qualities of your perceptual experience are manifestly not the qualities of the tomato. The tomato is red and round, but your visual experience is neither red nor round. Bear in mind, as well, that the occurrence of visual imagery of this kind is not a matter of scrutinizing (with an inward-looking mind's eye) a private interior object, a picture on an internal television screen, or a brain-generated holographic tomato. If you ask yourself whether you encounter such objects and suppose that a negative answer implies that you lack imagery (or that your imagery is severely attenuated), you are misconstruing the nature of imagery. Absent special circumstances, you have no reason to believe anyone who claims never to deploy imagery. (Try this. Ask the skeptic about imagery to say, 'I never have images'. Now ask the skeptic to say this silently, to *think* it. Skeptics who can do this undermine their own skepticism. Talking to yourself is a matter of making use of verbal imagery.)

13.12   Putting Imagery to Work

What is the *point* of mental imagery? The suggestion thus far has been that *any* conscious thinking must be imagistic. (Here I align myself with the early twentieth century foes of imageless thought.) If you are like me, then much of the pertinent imagery will be verbal imagery. Much of it, but not all of it.

We all rely endlessly on imagery of other sorts in negotiating our surroundings. Imagery is an integral ingredient in our capacity for anticipatory action. Intelligent creatures do not merely react to stimuli from the outside. Intelligence – mindfulness – includes the ability to anticipate environmental vicissitudes and the effects of prospective actions. You can 'see' that you have room to pass the car ahead of you on a narrow road, that the cereal box is too tall to be placed upright on the shelf. Carpenters employ images in framing houses, and athletes rely on imagery to anticipate the trajectories of moving objects or to maneuver past opponents. Imagery unquestionably plays a fundamental, and almost certainly ineliminable, role in the exercise of such abilities.

Owing to the abiding influence of the computer paradigm in cognitive psychology, imagistic (conscious) thinking has not received the attention it deserves. Attempts to study imagery using computational models too often miss the point altogether by seeking to reduce images to *descriptions* expressible in lines of code. Neither imagery nor perception can be so reduced, however – and indeed, as I have suggested, imagery and perception are intimately connected. Qualities of perceptual experiences are what survive in imagery. When you engage in functional abstraction, however, it is all too easy to lose sight of these qualities. Indeed, the point of functionalism (and its close relative, the computational model of mind) is to settle on a level of description that factors out qualities of states of mind altogether. (Remember, a functional state is what it is owing to its causal profile, not its qualities.) Against this background, it is no wonder that imagery has languished largely unappreciated.

Suppose I am right about the importance of imagery. Suppose imagery is fundamental to minds regarded as systems capable of manipulating representations. And suppose imagery is a matter of our undergoing experiences qualitatively resembling perceptual experiences. You could see why purely computational models of the mind would be so unpromising. Imagining an object is akin to perceiving an object, not to describing it. The aim of computational models, however, is, often enough, the production of descriptions. Thus modeling perceiving or imagining would require envisioning a device that, in response to appropriate inputs, produces descriptions of objects and events seen or imagined. (Recall the Representational Theory of Mind discussed in Chapter 7 according to which our commerce with the world is mediated by sentences in a Language of Thought.)

That psychologists – egged on by philosophers, it has to be said – have taken such models as their guiding inspiration does much to explain the disappointing one-dimensional character of so much mainstream cognitive psychology. Ironically, although thought is indeed often linguistic in character, it is no less imagistic for that. Describing your surroundings to yourself is not a replacement for imagery, but a deployment of it.

13.13 Twin-Earth

Even if these ideas are on the right track, we are still a long way from anything approximating an account of intentionality – the 'ofness' and 'aboutness' of thought. The prevailing 'externalist' line on intentionality regards the 'content' of intentional states (what these states are *of* or *about*) as being determined by particular causal relations' agents bear to the world. The inspiration for this view stems chiefly from a handful of influential thought experiments. Here is one example made famous by Hilary Putnam.

The term 'water', as English speakers use it, designates a particular kind of colorless liquid that, as we now know, is H_2O. When you entertain thoughts that you would express (in English) by utterances including the word 'water', those thoughts concern this substance. Now imagine a distant planet, Twin-Earth, a planet that is, in all ways save one, a precise ('molecule-for-molecule') duplicate of Earth, populated by intelligent creatures that are (except in one respect) precise duplicates of intelligent creatures inhabiting Earth. Inhabitants of Twin-Earth that speak what they call 'English' call their planet 'Earth'. Twin-English-speakers live in and visit countries they call 'New Zealand', 'the United Kingdom', 'Canada', 'the United States', 'Australia'; and they venerate historical figures named 'Plato',

'Napoleon', 'Princess Di', and 'Ned Kelly'. Despite these stunning similarities, there is one important difference between Earth and Twin-Earth. The colorless, tasteless, transparent stuff that fills rivers, lakes, and oceans, is used in making tea, falls from the sky, and is called (by Twin-English speakers) 'water', is not H_2O, but a different chemical compound, XYZ.

Now, while the English word 'water' means *water* (that is, H_2O), and thoughts we should express using the word 'water' are thoughts about *water*, the Twin-English word 'water' does not mean *water* (does not mean what 'water' in English means). Nor do inhabitants of Twin-Earth who think thoughts they would express (in Twin-English) using the word 'water' entertain thoughts of water. No, the meanings and thoughts associated with your twin's utterances of 'water' mean, not water, but XYZ, *twin*-water.

Of course, I am describing the case from the perspective of an English speaker here on Earth. My Twin-Earth counterpart would use words indistinguishable from mine. But we on Earth would translate that twin's references to (what *he* calls) 'water' as references to *twin-water*, his references to (what he calls) 'Earth' as references to Twin-Earth, and so on. Similarly, the twin would describe *my* references to (what I call) 'water' as references to (what *he* calls) 'twin-water', and – well, you get the idea.

The moral Putnam invites us to draw from Twin-Earth is that 'meanings just ain't in the head'. What words mean, and what thoughts those words express, depends on whatever it is with which speakers and thinkers causally interact. 'Water' in your mouth means water (and not twin-water) because you causally interact with *water* (and not twin-water). The same sounds produced by your twin mean *twin-water* (not water) because your twin interacts causally with twin-water (XYZ), not water (H_2O).

Applying this theme more broadly, it appears to follow that the meanings of the words you use and the contents of your thoughts (what your thoughts are thoughts *of*) depend on causal relations you bear to our surroundings. Still more broadly, intentionality depends on agents' *context*. Context must include appropriate causal relations, but it could include assorted social relations as well. The meanings of your utterances might depend, for instance, on the role they play within a particular community of speakers, a community that acts in accord with various linguistic norms and standards.

Focus briefly on the causal requirement. The idea, in its simplest terms, is that thoughts concern their causes. A causal view, such as Putnam's, competes with views that try to explain intentionality 'from the inside out'. The Twin-Earth case might be taken to show that no inside out account of thoughts *could* work. After all, you and your twin are identical (at least in the relevant ways) on the inside; yet your thoughts differ in content: yours concern water, your twin's concern twin-water.

Do Twin-Earth cases support a causal account of intentionality as against an inside out account? To answer this question, you would need some idea of what a competing inside out account might look like.

13.14   Intentionality Delivered

Think for a moment about the 'directedness' involved in dart tossing. Gravitational influences aside, the direction a dart takes depends wholly on agent-centered factors: how you grip the dart, the character of your arm motion, the timing of the release, and the like. Although a dart's trajectory depends wholly on the agent, what the dart *hits* depends on features of the world, features over which an agent might have no control. When you toss a dart perfectly aimed at the center of a target, it will not hit the center if I move the target while the dart is in flight. You might sum this up by saying that what a dart hits depends on two factors: how it is tossed – its agent-determined trajectory – and how the world is.

Now, suppose that the directedness of thoughts resembled the aiming of a tossed dart. Suppose that a thought's 'aim' were a wholly internal affair. (Never mind for the moment what it would be for a thought to be 'aimed'.) This is the kind of view that Twin-Earth cases and their cousins are designed to contest. But consider: your thought of water on Earth 'hits' H_2O; your twin's intrinsically indiscernible thought on Twin-Earth 'hits' XYZ. You could accept that what your thought is about differs from what your twin's thought is about, without supposing that the explanation of this difference is to be found in an incoming causal chain. So? Well, if both the 'inside out' model and the causal model yield comparable judgments in Twin-Earth cases, these cases can scarcely be used to support causal accounts of intentionality against 'internalist', inside out competitors.

Your thoughts take you *to* the world. What is *in* the world, what the deep story is concerning what your thoughts are about, is another matter. The sciences, in particular fundamental physics, are in the business of providing this deep story. To the extent that you and your Twin-Earth counterpart are ignorant of the deep story as to the nature of what you each call 'water', the contents of your thoughts are the same. Only when you learn that water has the nature it has, could your thought contents be said to differ from your counterpart's on Twin-Earth.

You are probably skeptical of the hokey inside out, dart-tossing model to which I have appealed. How, you might reasonably ask, are thoughts supposed to project outward – as darts do?

Think first of dispositionality. I argued in Chapter 12 that properties are powerful qualities: every property contributes in a distinctive way to the qualities and dispositionalities of objects possessing it. A disposition is intrinsically 'projective'; it is *for* a particular kind of manifestation with particular kinds of reciprocal disposition partner. A disposition might fail ever to be manifested – if, for instance, an appropriate reciprocal partner is missing or non-existent. Nevertheless, the disposition *is* projective for this manifestation with this kind of reciprocal partner.

My first suggestion, then, is that a central ingredient of intentionality, projectability, is built into every property! I do not mean that electrons or cabbages think, or are endowed with, intentionality. I mean only that every object, electrons and cabbages included, possesses projective disposition-alities. And these, I submit, are apt building blocks of genuine intentional states.

Second, consider an intelligent creature navigating its environment. The creature entertains imagistic thoughts. These enable the creature to test 'hypotheses' and, in general, serve to guide its actions in a way that you could describe as intelligent. What accounts for the *contents* of the creature's imagistic thoughts? What makes a creature's image of a tree branch an image of a tree branch? The creature is in causal contact with its surroundings, to be sure. But is it this causal contact that is responsible for the creature's thoughts' projective, intentional character? Maybe not. Maybe the projectivity of thought comes from the distinctive anticipatory and reflective role thoughts would have in the life of the creature. This role is founded in complex, focused dispositionalities that constitute the creature's states of mind.

Suppose, for instance, that your visually perceiving a ripe tomato in bright sunlight is a matter of your undergoing a particular sort of conscious experience. This conscious experience is the mutual manifesting of a complex disposition intrinsic to your visual system and dispositions of the tomato and the intervening light radiation. What makes this manifesting a visual perceiving of the *tomato* is its being a mutual manifesting with dispositions of the tomato. (This is simply to acknowledge the causal requirement included in our concept of perception.) But, I contend, what makes the experience projective for the tomato (what gives it its intentional 'trajectory') is intrinsic to *you*.

Imagine hallucinating a tomato. Here, your dispositional condition is manifested, not (as in the first case) in concert with a tomato, but with other reciprocal partners – internal partners, presumably. The result is an experience that qualitatively resembles the experience you would have were you to apprehend a tomato visually. The intentionality of this experience, what makes it a hallucination of a *tomato*, is not grounded in causal connections you might bear to tomatoes. Nor, incidentally, is it based on the resemblance of your experience to a tomato: experiences of tomatoes do not resemble tomatoes. The 'ofness' of your experience is grounded rather in the fact that it is a manifesting of a disposition apt for visual experiences of tomatoes. This aptness, like any dispositional aptness, is built-in, intrinsic to your visual system. It does not depend on your being in causal contact with tomatoes, nor, for that matter, on there being any tomatoes at all. In this respect it is no different from the disposition of a salt crystal to dissolve in water. The salt possesses this disposition even in circumstances (or imagined universes) in which there is no water.

Context plays a role in such cases, but not the role ascribed to it by the causal theorist. Your 'tomato thoughts' are, as I have put it, 'apt' for tomatoes because your environment includes tomatoes and not twin-tomatoes. But this is no more than a reflection of a point made earlier. What a thought concerns depends on two factors:

1. How the thought projects, its 'aim'.
2. The character of the region of the universe on which it projects, its 'target'.

13.15 Functionalism Adieu

You might think I am endorsing a paradigmatically *functionalist* conception of intentionality; I am not. It is essential to an imagistic thought that the thought possesses definite *qualities*. These qualities are what equip it to play the role it plays. Functionalism 'abstracts' from qualities possessed by whatever items play particular functional roles. These items *have* qualities perhaps (although even this is doubted in some quarters), but the qualities are incidental to the items' roles in the system. (Recall the 'beetle in the box, § 4.4.) I disagree. The *qualitative* similarity of imagistic thought to perceptual experience fits that thought for its role in the life of the creature.

Although perceptual experience undoubtedly precedes (and has a causal bearing on) subsequent reflective imagistic thought, it is not this causal linkage that accounts for thoughts' projective character. Projectivity is *built into* the thought. A thought 'targets' a state of affairs by virtue of endowing its possessor with a capacity to anticipate and interact with states of affairs of that kind. To be sure, *which* state of affairs a creature interacts with depends on the creature's circumstances. You and I interact with H_2O; our counterparts on Twin-Earth interact with XYZ.

This is not to deny that some mental concepts are 'causally loaded'. What you *remember* or *perceive*, for instance, depends in part on the causal source of your thoughts about the past or your current perceptual state. Nor am I denying that all of us rely heavily on observations of causal connections in ascribing thoughts to others. What I *am* denying is that any of this explains the projectivity, the ground floor intentionality, of states of mind. The projectivity of thought is dispositionally ordered, and the pertinent dispositions, even those with external causes, are intrinsic to thinkers.

Nor am I suggesting that a thought's hitting a particular target – a thought's being about a particular individual, for instance – is explicable solely on the basis of the intrinsic features of the agent. *What* target a thought hits depends on factors that are, in most cases, outside the thinker's control. Your thoughts are about H_2O, in part because of their intrinsic character, and in part because of your circumstances. Your twin's thoughts, on Twin-Earth, concern what turns out to be XYZ because your twin's circumstances differ from yours.

These sketchy remarks are not meant to encompass a complete theory of intentionality. I intend them only as antidotes to prevailing doctrines. This could seem thin stuff. I might feel more guilty were it the case that those wedded to causal accounts of intentionality themselves possessed detailed theories; but they do not. They offer examples designed to convince their audience that intentionality requires an incoming causal component of some kind. I admit that there is often an incoming causal component, but I deny that this is the *basis* of intentionality.

13.16   Dénouement

At the outset of this chapter, I suggested that an advantage of the conception of mind to be discussed was that it accommodates a range of plausible ingredients of its competitors without incurring their liabilities. Competing views need not be wholly wrong; most include important insights. These should be reflected in any promising overall view. I have said enough now to make the recommended conception of mind clear, at least in its broad outlines. It is time to look again at the competition.

Dualism

Mind–body dualism focuses on what are presumed to be dramatic differences between the mental and the material: states of mind are private, our 'access' to them privileged; the mental realm exhibits a range of distinctive qualities seemingly absent from the material domain. In contrast, material states of affairs are public, our access to them is indirect and fallible; and material states – brain states, for instance – are apparently bereft of anything like qualities exhibited in conscious experience. On some theories, material objects lack qualities altogether; material properties are exclusively dispositional, 'pure powers'.

Consider, first, the essentially 'subjective' character of states of mind. The dualists' mistake is to imagine that this is to be explained by taking minds to be windowless containers housing objects only observable from the inside: images on an internal television monitor purporting to represent the 'external world'. Those of us on the outside can only guess at your mind's contents.

I am not alone in contending that this is a faulty model. My suggestion is that the privacy and privilege apparently enjoyed by states of mind is to be explained, in part, by reference to a distinction between *being in* a particular state and *observing* that state. Your awareness of your conscious states of mind is constituted by your being in those states. Judgments you form about those states, while not incorrigible, are nevertheless eminently trustworthy. I am aware of your conscious states of mind, if at all, not by being in those states, but by being in a distinct state, one that constitutes my awareness of you and your antics. This, I might add, is not a comment on neurological mechanisms, but a reflection on the basis of a much discussed epistemological asymmetry.

What of distinctive mental *qualities*? I have argued that, despite their elevated status in some circles, it is by no means always clear what these qualities are supposed to be. When you savor the aroma of a Whopper, your enjoyment is founded on qualities of your olfactory experience. Before you deny that these qualities could conceivably be qualities of your brain, you should be clear on their precise nature. And, I have suggested, this is not something anyone has an especially good grip on.

If you take seriously the kind of compositional ontology sketched in Chapter 14, and if you honor the minimal requirements of a causal account of perception, then you should be prepared to grant that the qualities of your conscious experiences could in fact be qualities of your brain. If you think of a brain as a material object, then these qualities would be material qualities. Moreover, these would be material qualities with which you would have what could be called direct acquaintance. You have no such direct acquaintance with the qualities of material objects you observe in the universe around you, or in the laboratory.

I am not suggesting that there is an unbridgeable epistemological chasm between the universe and us or that we are imprisoned behind an immutable 'veil of perception'. I am only pointing out one consequence of a position that takes the denial of dualism seriously. Theorists who oppose dualism, while harping on vast differences between mental and material qualities seem to have hold of the wrong end of the stick.

All this leads me to characterize the account of the mind set out in this chapter as a kind of 'neutral monism'. Mental and material properties are not distinctive kinds of property. Certainly, some properties can be labeled mental, some, perhaps the very same properties, material. But the idea that this practice has momentous ontological significance is largely a prejudice inherited from dualism. One symptom of this is the difficulty philosophers have in making the mental–material distinction precise. This is just what you would expect if the distinction is, as I have suggested, one *of conception only*, not a *real distinction*. If you want to make progress in understanding the place of minds in the universe, my advice is to abandon the distinction and turn instead to serious ontology.

The Identity Theory

The identity theory holds that mental properties *are* material properties. In one respect, the thesis I have defended in this chapter is in agreement: there are no mental properties distinct from material properties. In another respect, however, the identity theory evidently misfires. Identity theorists identify being in pain, for instance, with a particular kind of neural condition. In so doing, they tacitly suppose that being in pain is a *property*: being in pain is a property that, as it happens, is identical with some definite neurological property.

I have insisted, however, that it is a mistake of a fundamental sort to imagine that predicates used truly to ascribe a state of mind to a creature must designate a property possessed by that creature and by any other creature (or entity) to which it applies. The predicate holds of assorted creatures, and it holds of them in virtue of properties they possess, but it does not follow that it holds of them in virtue of their possessing the very same (or an exactly resembling) property.

This is the lesson taught by functionalism. The functionalist critique of the identity theory makes it clear that it is at least unlikely that there is a single neurological property answering to the predicate 'is in pain'. The appropriate response, however, is not to suppose that 'is in pain' must therefore designate a *higher-level* property shared by creatures in pain. Rather, you must simply recognize that properties in virtue of which it is true that very different kinds of creature are in pain are just different – although similar – properties.

If you eliminate this confusion, however, I should be happy to call the thesis sketched in this chapter a *kind* of identity theory.

Functionalism

One way to understand functionalism is to recognize that functionalists fixate on the dispositional nature of states that give minds their distinctive character. This is perfectly appropriate. What is *not* appropriate is the further thought that *qualities* of these states are irrelevant to their functional roles. A pain state is a state that plays the pain role, but the state is not on *that* account painful. Rather, the state plays the pain role because it is *painful*. Minds are dispositional systems, but this does not imply that minds lack qualitative natures or that qualities play no role in their operation.

There are excellent independent grounds for the belief that every property (every intrinsic property of a concrete object) is *both* dispositional and qualitative. The *dispositionality* and (if I may) *qualitativity* of a property are inseparable – except in thought. Properties are powerful qualities. States of mind are, at once, qualitative and dispositional. But there is no grand mystery here: *every* state is simultaneously qualitative and dispositional. If you regard the mind as a broadly functional system, then you can still say that some components in this system occupy the roles they occupy, in part, *because* they are as they are qualitatively. But as soon as you say this, you have turned your back on a central tenet of mainstream functionalism.

By and large the most basic sciences are in the business of exposing the dispositional structure of the world. It would be a mistake to infer from the silence of physics as to the world's qualitative nature that physics establishes that the world lacks such a nature. This mistake – the mistake of the functionalist – becomes crippling when you set out to understand the mind and its operations. A scientist can pass the buck on qualities by relegating them to minds. The current crisis over consciousness, the so-called 'hard problem' of consciousness, stems from an implicit recognition that the buck stops here. As is often the case in philosophy, the crisis is of our own making. If *everything* is qualitatively saturated, then it cannot be a mystery that states of mind are qualitatively saturated. This is the grain of truth to be found in panpsychism. If your states of mind are states of your brain, then the qualities of those states *are* qualities of brain states. I hope that I have done enough in Chapters 10 and 12 to make this conclusion less counter-intuitive than it is customarily taken to be.

The Intentional Stance

Dennett's 'instrumentalism' about the mind has it that talk of minds is not aimed at identifying underlying mechanisms governing intelligent actions, but at providing a convenient predictive scheme applicable to adaptive systems, biological or otherwise. Although it is hard to drum up enthusiasm for this kind of anti-realism about the mind, it seems right in at least one respect. Dennett's arguments call attention to difficulties with the idea that every mental predicate corresponds to a unique mental property and the related idea that there is a well-understood distinction between mental and material properties.

Mental predicates – 'is in pain', 'is thinking of Alice Springs' – apply to agents owing to properties possessed by those agents, but this does not mean that there is a one–one predicate–property correspondence. Mental predicates apply to agents owing to those agents' possession of any of a family of similar properties. In every case, the question is what are the truthmakers for an application of a given predicate. And when you look at the truthmakers, the utility of the mental–material distinction fades. Ultimately, the distinction is one of conception only, not what Descartes called a real distinction.

13.17   Concluding Note

Perhaps I have said enough to provide an inkling of a way of approaching minds and their place in nature that addresses long-standing puzzles in the philosophy of mind. I believe that the approach promises to solve problems its competitors purport to solve, and that it does so without their attendant liabilities. This is a large claim. It would be immodest were it not for the fact that I do not represent the view as original: I trace it to Locke, to Descartes, to Spinoza, and to the work of Keith Campbell, D. M. Armstrong, and C. B. Martin.

I do not pretend that this sketch is enough to persuade confirmed proponents of alternative views. I hope, however, that I have said enough to lend plausibility to the approach, and thereby to attract fence-sitters and neutral bystanders. Readers wanting more are invited to consult the readings set out in the section that follows.

Suggested Reading

Topics discussed in this chapter are given a fuller treatment in *From an Ontological Point of View* (2003a, chapters 17–20), and *The Universe as We Find It* (2012). See also C. B. Martin's *The Mind in Nature* (2008).

Michael Lockwood, *Mind, Brain, and Quantum* (1989), chapter 10, advances a conception of mental qualities – *qualia* – with similarities to the conception sketched in this chapter; see also 'The Grain Problem' (1993). Lockwood draws on Bertrand Russell's *Analysis of Matter* (1927), and in an historical appendix cites Schopenhauer, W. K. Clifford, Wilhelm Wundt, and Immanuel Kant as promoting related views. The position I advance, however, differs from Lockwood's in a number of important respects. Lockwood takes dispositions to be 'grounded in' what he calls 'intrinsic qualities'; I regard every property as intrinsically dispositional *and* qualitative. Lockwood distinguishes qualities of conscious experiences from our awareness of those qualities; I take conscious experiences to be manifestations of neurological dispositions. The qualities of these are conscious qualities. Awareness of these qualities is not a matter of inwardly observing an experience. In having an experience you are aware of its qualities.

Daniel Dennett is one philosopher who argues for the replacement of metaphysics by empirical science when it comes to questions about the nature of mind. For a readable introduction to Dennett's views, see *Kinds of Minds: Toward an Understanding of Consciousness* (1996).

Zombies were the invention of Robert Kirk in his 'Zombies vs. Materialists' (1974); see Kirk's *Raw Feeling* (1996) for some reservations. David Chalmers discusses at great length (and defends the possibility of) zombies in his *The Conscious Mind: In Search of a Fundamental Theory* (1996, chapter 3).

Nigel J. T. Thomas's 'Are Theories of Imagery Theories of Imagination' (1999) contains an excellent historical and philosophical discussion of theories of imagery. Thomas's 'Experience and Theory as Determinants of Attitudes toward Mental Representation: The Case of Knight Dunlap and the Vanishing Images of J. B. Watson' (1989) contains a fascinating discussion of what I call 'criterion differences' in reports of imagery – or the lack of it. Michael Tye discusses the dreary debate between proponents of 'pictorial' conceptions of imagery and their 'propositional' opponents in *The Imagery Debate* (1991). The 'imageless thought' controversy raged early in the twentieth century. For a useful summary and discussion, see Kurt Danziger, 'The History of Introspection Reconsidered' (1980).

Causal theories of content in the philosophy of mind and the philosophy of language (roughly, the view that meaning or content depends on agents' causal histories) are all the rage. Without endorsing them, I attempt to motivate such views in *The Nature of True Minds* (1992, chapter 2). Important primary sources include Hilary Putnam, 'The Meaning of "Meaning"' (1975a), and *Reason, Truth, and History* (1981), chapters 1 and 2; and Donald Davidson, 'Radical Interpretation' (1973). Some authors emphasize social context as a factor in the determination of meaning. See, for instance, Wittgenstein, *Philosophical Investigations* (1953); Tyler Burge, 'Individualism and the Mental' (1979), and 'Individualism and Psychology' (1986); and Lynne Rudder Baker, *Saving Belief: A Critique of Physicalism* (1987).

Dispositional accounts of intentionality are defended by C. B. Martin and Karl Pfeifer in 'Intentionality and the Non-Psychological' (1986); Martin and Heil, in 'Rules and Powers' (1998); and by George Molnar, in *Powers* (2003). Martin's 'Proto-Language' (1987) provides a defense of imagistic thought and an important critique of the idea that thought requires language.

References

Anderson, A. R., ed. (1964) *Minds and Machines*. Englewood Cliffs, NJ: Prentice Hall.

Armstrong, D. M. (1961) *Perception and the Physical World*. London: Routledge and Kegan Paul.

Armstrong, D. M. (1968) *A Materialist Theory of the Mind*. London: Routledge and Kegan Paul.

Armstrong, D. M. (1989) *Universals: An Opinionated Introduction*. Boulder, CO: Westview Press.

Armstrong, D. M. (1997) *A World of States of Affairs*. Cambridge: Cambridge University Press.

Armstrong, D. M. (1999) *The Mind–Body Problem: An Opinionated Introduction*. Boulder, CO: Westview Press.

Averill, E. and B. F. Keating. (1981) 'Does Interactionism Violate a Law of Classical Physics?' *Mind* 90: 102–7.

Bacon, J., K. Campbell, and L. Reinhardt, eds. (1992) *Ontology, Causality, and Mind*. Cambridge: Cambridge University Press.

Baker, L. R. (1987) *Saving Belief: A Critique of Physicalism*. Princeton, NJ: Princeton University Press.

Barnes, J. (1987) *Early Greek Philosophy*. London: Penguin.

Beakley, B., and P. Ludlow, eds. (1992) *The Philosophy of Mind: Classical Problems, Contemporary Issues*. Cambridge, MA: MIT Press.

Bechtel, W., G. Graham, and D. A. Balota, eds. (1998) *A Companion to Cognitive Science*. Oxford: Blackwell.

Bennett, J. (1964) *Rationality*. London: Routledge and Kegan Paul. Reprint. Indianapolis: Hackett (1989).

Bennett, J. (1976) *Linguistic Behaviour*. Cambridge: Cambridge University Press.

Bennett, K. (2003) 'Why the Exclusion Problem Seems Intractable, and How, Just Maybe, to Tract It'. *Noûs* 37: 471–97.

Bennett, K. (2008) 'Exclusion Again'. In Hohwy and Kallestrup (2008): 280–305.

Berkeley, G. (1710/1979) *Three Dialogues between Hylas and Philonous*. R. M. Adams, ed. Indianapolis: Hackett.

Berkeley, G. (1713/1983) *Treatise Concerning the Principles of Human Knowledge*. K. Winkler, ed. Indianapolis: Hackett.

Bermúdez, J. L. (2003) *Thinking Without Words*. Oxford: Oxford University Press.

Bird, A. (2007) *Nature's Metaphysics: Laws and Properties*. Oxford: Clarendon Press.

Biro, J. I. and R. W. Shahan, eds. (1982) *Mind, Brain, and Function*. Norman, OK: University of Oklahoma Press.

Blackburn, S. (1990) 'Filling in Space', *Analysis* 50: 62–5.

Blakeslee, S. (1996) 'The Brain in the Gut'. *New York Times* (*Science Times*), Tuesday, 23 Jan., b5 and b10.

Block, N. J. (1978) 'Troubles with Functionalism'. In C. W. Savage, ed. *Perception and Cognition: Issues in the Foundations of Psychology* (Minnesota Studies in the Philosophy of Science 9). Minneapolis: University of Minnesota Press: 261–325. Reprinted in Block (1980a): 268–305; O'Connor and Robb (2003): 222–33. Excerpted in Chalmers (2002): 94–8.

Block, N. J., ed. (1980a) *Readings in Philosophy of Psychology* 1, Cambridge: Harvard University Press.

Block, N. J. (1980b) 'What is Functionalism?', in Block (1980a): 171–84. Reprinted in Heil (2003b): 183–99.

Block, N. (2003) 'Mental Paint'. In Hahn and Ramberg (2003): 125–51.

Block, N. J., O. Flanagan, and G. Güzeldere, eds. (1997) *The Nature of Consciousness: Philosophical Debates*. Cambridge, MA: MIT Press.

Boghossian, P. A. (1990) 'The Status of Content'. *The Philosophical Review* 99: 157–84.

Borst, C. V., ed. (1970) *The Mind–Brain Identity Theory*. London: Macmillan.

Braddon-Mitchell, D. and F. Jackson. (1996) *The Philosophy of Mind and Cognition*. Oxford: Blackwell.

Brănquinho, J., ed. (2001) *The Foundations of Cognitive Science*. Oxford: Oxford University Press.

Broad, C. D. (1925) *The Mind and Its Place in Nature*. London: Routledge and Kegan Paul.

Burge, T. (1979) 'Individualism and the Mental'. *Midwest Studies in Philosophy* 4: 73–121. Reprinted in Heil (2003b): 428–77; Chalmers (2002): 597–607.

Burge, T. (1986) 'Individualism and Psychology'. *Philosophical Review* 45: 3–45. Reprinted in Rosenthal (1991): 536–67.

Butler, R. J., ed. (1965) *Analytical Philosophy*, 2nd series. Oxford: Basil Blackwell.

Campbell, K. (1976) *Metaphysics: An Introduction*. Encino: Dickenson.

Campbell, K. (1981) 'The Metaphysics of Abstract Particulars'. *Midwest Studies in Philosophy* 6: 477–88.

Campbell, K. (1990) *Abstract Particulars*. Oxford: Blackwell.

Carnap, R. (1938) 'Logical Foundations of the Unity of Science'. In Neurath *et al.* (1955) I, 1: 42–62. Reprinted in Feigl and Sellars (1949): 408–23.

Carruthers, P. (1989) 'Brute Experience'. *Journal of Philosophy* 86: 258–69.

Carruthers, P. (2000) *Phenomenal Consciousness: A Naturalistic Theory*. Cambridge: Cambridge University Press.

Caston, V. (1997) 'Epiphenomenalisms Ancient and Modern'. *Philosophical Review* 106: 309–63.

Chalmers, D. J. (1996) *The Conscious Mind: In Search of a Fundamental Theory*. New York: Oxford University Press.

Chalmers, D. J., ed. (2001) *Contemporary Philosophy of Mind: An Annotated Bibliography*. <http://www.u.arizona.edu/~chalmers/biblio.html> Tucson, AZ: University of Arizona.

Chalmers, D. J., ed. (2002) *Philosophy of Mind: Classical and Contemporary Readings*. New York: Oxford University Press.

Chalmers, D. J., and J. R. Searle. (1997) 'Consciousness and the Philosophers: An Exchange'. *New York Review of Books*, 15 May: 60–1.

Chomsky, N. (1959) 'Review of "Verbal Behavior"', *Language* 35: 26–58.

Chomsky, N. (1966) *Cartesian Linguistics: A Chapter in the History of Rationalist Thought*. New York: Harper and Row.

Christensen, S. M. and D. R. Turner, eds. (1993) *Folk Psychology and the Philosophy of Mind*. Hillsdale, NJ: Lawrence Erlbaum Associates.

Churchland, P. M. (1986) *Neurophilosophy*. Cambridge, MA: MIT Press.

Churchland, P. M. (1988) *Matter and Consciousness: A Contemporary Introduction to the Philosophy of Mind*, Revised ed. Cambridge, MA: MIT Press.

Churchland, P. S. (1979) *Scientific Realism and the Plasticity of Mind*. Cambridge: Cambridge University Press.

Churchland, P. S. (1981) 'Eliminative Materialism and the Propositional Attitudes'. *Journal of Philosophy* 78: 67–90. Reprinted in Heil (2003b): 382–400; O'Connor and Robb (2003): 391–412; Chalmers (2002): 568–80.

Clark, A. (1997) *Being There: Putting Brain, Body, and World Together Again*. Cambridge, MA: MIT Press.

Clark, A. (2001) *Mindware: An Introduction to Cognitive Science*. New York: Oxford University Press.

Corcoran, K., ed. (2001) *Soul, Body, and Survival: Essays on the Metaphysics of Human Persons*. Ithaca: Cornell University Press.

Cottingham, J. (1992) *The Cambridge Companion to Descartes*. Cambridge: Cambridge University Press.

Crane, T. (2001) *Elements of Mind: An Introduction to the Philosophy of Mind*. Oxford: Oxford University Press.

Crick, F. (1994) *The Astonishing Hypothesis: The Scientific Search for the Soul*. New York: Scribner.

Cummins, R. (1983) *The Nature of Psychological Explanation*. Cambridge, MA: MIT Press.

Cummins, D. D. and R. Cummins, eds. (2000) *Minds, Brains, and Computers: The Foundations of Cognitive Science: An Anthology*. Oxford: Blackwell.

Danziger, K. (1980) 'The History of Introspection Reconsidered'. *Journal of the History of the Behavioral Sciences* 16: 241–62.

Davidson, D. (1970) 'Mental Events'. In Foster and Swanson (1970): 79–101. Reprinted in Davidson (1980): 207–25; Heil (2003b): 685–99; Chalmers (2002): 116–25.

Davidson, D. (1973) 'Radical Interpretation'. *Dialectica* 27: 313–28. Reprinted in Davidson (1984): 125–39; and in Heil (2003b): 286–97.

Davidson, D. (1975) 'Thought and Talk'. In S. Guttenplan, ed. *Mind and Language: Wolfson College Lectures 1974*. Oxford: Clarendon Press: 7–23. Reprinted in Davidson (1984): 155–70; Heil (2003b): 321–33; O'Connor and Robb (2003): 355–69.

Davidson, D. (1980) *Essays on Actions and Events*. Oxford: Clarendon Press.

Davidson, D. (1982) 'Rational Animals'. *Dialectica* 36: 317–27. Reprinted in LePore and McLaughlin (1985): 473–80.

Davidson, D. (1984) *Inquiries into Truth and Interpretation*. Oxford: Clarendon Press.

Dennett, D. C. (1978) 'Current Issues in the Philosophy of Mind'. *American Philosophical Quarterly* 15: 249–61.

Dennett, D. C. (1987) *The Intentional Stance*. Cambridge, MA: MIT Press.

Dennett, D. C. (1991a) *Consciousness Explained*. Boston, MA: Little, Brown & Co.

Dennett, D. C. (1991b) 'Real Patterns'. *Journal of Philosophy* 89: 27–51.

Dennett, D. C. (1996) *Kinds of Minds: Toward an Understanding of Consciousness*. New York: Basic Books.

Dennett, D. C. and D. R. Hofstadter eds. (1981) *The Mind's I*. New York: Basic Books.

Descartes, R. (1641/1986) *Meditations on First Philosophy*. J. Cottingham, trans. Cambridge: Cambridge University Press. Excerpted in Heil (2003b): 36–50; Chalmers (2002): 10–21.

Dretske, F. I. (1988) *Explaining Behavior: Reasons in a World of Causes*. Cambridge, MA: MIT Press.

Dretske, F. I. (1995) *Naturalizing the Mind*. Cambridge, MA: MIT Press.

Eddington, A. S. (1928) *The Nature of the Physical World*. London: Macmillan.

Edelman, G. L. (1993) *Bright Air, Brilliant Fire: On the Matter of the Mind*. New York: Basic Books.

Eliasmith, C., ed. (2003) *Dictionary of Philosophy of Mind* <http://www.artsci.wustl.edu/~philos/MindDict/main.html> St. Louis: Washington University.

Feigl, H. (1958) 'The "Mental" and the "Physical"'. In Feigl *et al.* (1958): 370–497. Reissued in 1967 as a monograph, *The 'Mental' and the 'Physical'*. Minneapolis, MN: University of Minnesota Press. Excerpted in Chalmers (2002): 68–72.

Feigl, H. and W. Sellars, eds. (1949) *Readings in Philosophical Analysis*. New York: Appleton-Century-Crofts.

Feigl, H., M. Scriven, and G. Maxwell eds. (1958) *Concepts, Theories, and the Mind–Body Problem* (Minnesota Studies in the Philosophy of Science 2). Minneapolis, MN: University of Minnesota Press.

Fetzer, J. H. (1991) *Philosophy and Cognitive Science*. New York: Paragon House.

Feyerabend, P. K. (1963) 'Materialism and the Mind–Body Problem'. *Review of Metaphysics* 17: 49–66. Reprinted in Christensen and Turner (1993): 3–16.

Flanagan, O. J. (1984) *The Science of the Mind*. Cambridge, MA: MIT Press.

Fodor, J. A. (1968) *Psychological Explanation: An Introduction to the Philosophy of Psychology*. New York: Random House.

Fodor, J. A. (1975) *The Language of Thought*. New York: T. Y. Crowell.

Fodor, J. A. (1981) 'The Mind–Body Problem. *Scientific American* 244: 114–23. Reprinted in Heil (2003b): 168–82.

Fodor, J. A. (1988) *Psychosemantics*. Cambridge, MA: MIT Press.

Fodor, J. A. (1991) 'You Can Fool Some of the People All of the Time, Everything Else Being Equal: Hedged Laws and Psychological Explanation'. *Mind* 100: 19–34.

Fodor, J. A. (1994) *The Elm and the Expert: Mentalese and its Semantics*. Cambridge, MA: MIT Press.

Fodor, J. A. (1997) 'Special Sciences: Still Autonomous after All These Years'. *Philosophical Perspectives* 11: 149–63; reprinted in Fodor (1998): 9–24.

Foster, J. (1982) *The Case for Idealism*. London: Routledge and Kegan Paul.

Foster, J. (1991) *The Immaterial Self*. London: Routledge.

Foster, L. and J. Swanson, eds. (1970) *Experience and Theory*. Amherst, MA: University of Massachusetts Press.

Freeman, A., ed. (2006) *Consciousness and Its Place in Nature: Does Physicalism Entail Panpsychism*? Exeter, UK: Imprint Academic.

Garber, D. (2001) *Descartes Embodied: Reading Cartesian Philosophy through Cartesian Science*. Cambridge: Cambridge University Press.

Garfield, J. L., ed. (1990) *Foundations of Cognitive Science: The Essential Readings*. New York: Paragon House.

Geirsson, H. and M. Losonsky, eds. (1996) *Readings in Mind and Language*. Oxford: Blackwell.

Gennaro, R., ed. (2004) *Higher-Order Theories of Consciousness*. Philadelphia, PA: John Benjamin.

Gillett, C. and B. Loewer, eds. (2001) *Physicalism and Its Discontents*. Cambridge: Cambridge University Press.

Gleitman, L. R., M. Liberman, and D. N. Osherson, eds. (1995) *An Invitation to Cognitive Science*, 2nd ed., vol. 1 *Language*. Cambridge, MA: MIT Press.

Gopnik, A., and J. W. Astington. (1988) 'Children's Understanding of Representational Change and its Relation to the Understanding of False Belief and the Appearance–Reality Distinction'. *Child Development* 59: 26–37.

Graham, G. (1993) *Philosophy of Mind: An Introduction*. Oxford: Blackwell.

Greenblatt, S. (2011) *The Swerve: How the World Became Modern*. New York: W. W. Norton & Co.

Greenwood, J. D., ed. (1991) *The Future of Folk Psychology: Intentionality and Cognitive Science*. Cambridge: Cambridge University Press.

Gregory, R. L., ed. (1987) *The Oxford Companion to the Mind*. Oxford: Oxford University Press.

Guttenplan, S. D., ed. (1994) *A Companion to the Philosophy of Mind*. Oxford: Blackwell.

Hahn, M. and B. Ramberg, eds. (2003) *Essays on the Philosophy of Tyler Burge*. Cambridge, MA: MIT Press.

Harman, G. (1973) *Thought*. Princeton, NJ: Princeton University Press.

Harman, G. (1990) 'The Intrinsic Quality of Experience'. *Philosophical Perspectives* 4: 31–52. Reprinted in Heil (2003b): 641–56; O'Connor and Robb (2003): 491–509.

Harnish, R. M. (2001) *Minds, Brains, Computers: An Historical Introduction to the Foundations of Cognitive Science*. Oxford: Blackwell.

Harré, R. (2002) *Cognitive Science: A Philosophical Introduction*. London: Sage.

Haugeland, J., ed. (1981a) *Mind Design*. Cambridge, MA: MIT Press.

Haugeland, J. (1981b) 'Semantic Engines: An Introduction to Mind Design'. In Haugeland (1981a): 1–34.

Haugeland, J. (1985) *Artificial Intelligence: The Very Idea*. Cambridge, MA: MIT Press.

Heil, J. (1991) 'Being Indiscrete'. In Greenwood (1991): 120–34.

Heil, J. (1992) *The Nature of True Minds*. Cambridge: Cambridge University Press.

Heil, J. (1998) 'Supervenience Deconstructed'. *European Journal of Philosophy* 6: 146–55.

Heil, J. (2003a) *From an Ontological Point of View*. Oxford: Clarendon Press.

Heil, J., ed. (2003b) *Philosophy of Mind: A Guide and Anthology*. Oxford: Oxford University Press.

Heil, J. (2004) *Philosophy of Mind: A Contemporary Introduction*, 2nd ed. London: Routledge.

Heil, J. (2005) 'Dispositions'. *Synthese* 144: 343–56.

Heil, J. (2012) *The Universe as We Find It*. Oxford: Clarendon Press.

Heil, J. and A. R. Mele, eds. (1993) *Mental Causation*. Oxford: Clarendon Press.

Hempel, C. G. (1949) 'The Logical Analysis of Psychology'. In Feigl and Sellars (1949): 373–84. Reprinted in Heil (2003b): 85–95.

Hill, C. S. (1991) *Sensations: A Defense of Type Materialism*. Cambridge: Cambridge University Press.

Hobbes, T. (1651/1994) *Leviathan*. E. Curley, ed. Indianapolis: Hackett.

Hohwy, J. and J. Kallestrup, eds. (2008) *Being Reduced: New Essays on Reduction, Explanation, and Causation*. Oxford: Oxford University Press.

Hook, S., ed. (1960) *Dimensions of Mind*. New York: Collier Books.

Horgan, T. (1993) 'From Supervenience to Superdupervenience: Meeting the Demands of a Material World'. *Mind* 102: 555–86. Excerpted in Chalmers (2002): 150–62.

Horgan, T. and J. Woodward. (1985) 'Folk Psychology is Here to Stay'. *Philosophical Review* 94: 197–226. Reprinted in Christensen and Turner (1993): 144–66.

Hume, D. (1739/1978) *A Treatise of Human Nature*. L. A. Selby-Bigge and P. H. Nidditch, eds. Oxford: Clarendon Press.

Hume, D. (1748/1975) *Enquiries Concerning Human Understanding*. L. A. Selby-Bigge, ed. Oxford: Clarendon Press.

Huxley, T. H. (1901) *Methods and Results: Essays*. New York: D. Appleton.

Jackson, F. (1982) 'Epiphenomenal Qualia'. *The Philosophical Quarterly* 32: 127–36. Reprinted in Heil (2003b): 762–71; Chalmers (2002): 273–80.

Jackson, F. (1996) 'Mental Causation'. *Mind* 105: 377–41.

Jackson, F. and P. Pettit. (1990). 'In Defense of Folk Psychology'. *Philosophical Studies* 59: 31–54.

Jacquette, D. (1994) *Philosophy of Mind*. Englewood Cliffs, NJ: Prentice-Hall.

Kane, R. ed. (2011) *The Oxford Handbook of Free Will*, 2nd ed. Oxford: Oxford University Press.

Kant, I. (1787/1964) *The Critique of Pure Reason*. N. K. Smith, trans. London: Macmillan.

Kenny, A. J. (1970) *Descartes: Philosophical Letters*. Oxford: Clarendon Press.

Kenny, A. J. (1989) *The Metaphysics of Mind*. Oxford: Oxford University Press.

Kim, J. (1978) 'Supervenience and Nomological Incommensurables'. *American Philosophical Quarterly* 15: 149–56.

Kim, J. (1979) 'Causality, Identity, and Supervenience'. *Midwest Studies in Philosophy* 4: 31–49.

Kim, J. (1990) 'Supervenience as a Philosophical Concept'. *Metaphilosophy* 12: 1–27. Reprinted in Kim (1993): 131–60.

Kim, J. (1993a) *Supervenience and Mind: Selected Philosophical Essays*. Cambridge: Cambridge University Press.

Kim, J. (1993b) 'The Non-Reductivist's Troubles with Mental Causation'. In Heil and Mele (1993): 189–210. Reprinted in Kim (1993a): 336–57.

Kim, J. (1998) *Mind in a Physical World: An Essay on the Mind-Body Problem and Mental Causation*. Cambridge, MA: MIT Press.

Kim, J. (2001) 'Lonely Souls: Causality and Substance Dualism'. In Corcoran (2001): 30–43.

Kim, J. (2003) 'Blocking Causal Drainage, and Other Maintenance Chores with Mental Causation'. *Philosophy and Phenomenological Research* 67: 151–76.

Kim, J. (2005) *Physicalism, or Something Near Enough*. Princeton, NJ: Princeton University Press.

Kim, J. (2010) *Philosophy of Mind* 3rd ed. Boulder, CO: Westview Press.

Kirk, G. S., J. E. Raven, and M. Schofield. (1983) *The Presocratic Philosophers*, 2nd ed. Cambridge: Cambridge University Press.

Kirk, R. (1974) 'Zombies vs. Materialists'. *Proceedings of the Aristotelian Society*, Supplementary vol. 48: 135–52.

Kirk, R. (1996) *Raw Feeling*. Oxford: Clarendon Press.

Kolak, D., ed. (1997) *From Plato to Wittgenstein: The Historical Foundations of Mind*. Belmont, CA: Wadsworth.

Kriegel, U. (2006) 'The Same-Order Monitoring Theory of Consciousness'. In Kriegel and Williford (2006): 143–70.

Kriegel, U. and K. Williford, eds. (2006) *Self-Representational Approaches to Consciousness*. Cambridge, MA: MIT Press.

La Mettrie, J. O. de (1747 and 1748/1984) *Man a Machine* and *Man a Plant*. R. Watson and M. Rybalka, trans. Indianapolis: Hackett.

Leibniz, G. W. (1787/1973) *Monodology*. In M. Morris and G. H. R. Parkinson, trans., and G. H. R. Parkinson, ed. *Leibniz: Philosophical Writings*. London: J. M. Dent and Sons: 179–94.

Lepore, E. (ed.) (1986) *Truth and Interpretation: Perspectives on the Philosophy of Donald Davidson*. Oxford: Basil Blackwell.

Lepore, E., and B. Loewer. (1987) 'Mind Matters'. *Journal of Philosophy* 84: 630–42.

Lepore, E. and B. P. McLaughlin, eds. (1985) *Actions and Events: Perspectives on the Philosophy of Donald Davidson*. Oxford: Basil Blackwell.

Levin, J. (1986) 'Could Love be like a Heatwave?' *Philosophical Studies* 49: 245–61. Reprinted in Heil (2003b): 539–52.

Levine, J. (1983) 'Materialism and Qualia: The Explanatory Gap'. *Pacific Philosophical Quarterly* 64: 354–61. Reprinted in Heil (2003b): 772–80; O'Connor and Robb (2003): 427–37; Chalmers (2002): 354–61.

Lewis, C. I. (1929) *Mind and the World Order*. New York: Charles Scribner's Sons.

Lewis, D. K. (1966) 'An Argument for the Identity Theory'. *Journal of Philosophy* 63: 17–25. Reprinted in Lewis (1983): 99–107; in Heil (2003b): 150–7.

Lewis, D. K. (1972) 'Psychophysical and Theoretical Identifications'. *Australasian Journal of Philosophy* 50: 249–58. Reprinted in Block (1980a): 207–15; Chalmers (2002): 88–94.

Lewis, D. K. (1980) 'Mad Pain and Martian Pain'. In Block (1980a): 216–22. Reprinted in Lewis (1983): 122–9; and in Rosenthal (1991): 229–35.

Lewis, D. K. (1983) *Philosophical Papers*, vol. 1. New York: Oxford University Press.

Lewis, D. K. (1994) 'Reduction of Mind'. In S. Guttenplan, ed. *A Companion to the Philosophy of Mind*. Oxford: Basil Blackwell: 412–31. Reprinted in O'Connor and Robb (2003): 197–209.

Libet, B. (1985) 'Unconscious Cerebral Initiative and the Role of Conscious Will in Voluntary Action'. *Behavioral and Brain Sciences* 8: 529 66.

Locke, J. (1690/1978) *An Essay Concerning Human Understanding*. P. H. Nidditch, ed. Oxford: Clarendon Press. Excerpted in Heil (2003b): 59–63.

Lockwood, M. (1989) *Mind, Brain, and Quantum*. Oxford: Basil Blackwell.

Lockwood, M. (1993) 'The Grain Problem'. In Robinson (1993): 271–91. Reprinted in O'Connor and Robb (2003): 542–59.

Loux, M. (1998) *Metaphysics: A Contemporary Introduction*. London: Routledge.

Loewer, B. (2002a) 'Comments on Jaegwon Kim's Mind in a Physical World'. *Philosophy and Phenomenological Research* 65: 655–62.

Loewer, B. (2002b) 'Review of Jaegwon Kim's Mind in a Physical World'. *Journal of Philosophy* 98: 315–24.

Loewer, B. (2007) 'Mental Causation or Something Near Enough'. In McLaughlin and Cohen (2007): 243–64.

Lowe, E. J. (1994) 'Primitive Substances'. *Philosophy and Phenomenological Research* 54: 531–52.

Lowe, E. J. (1995) *Locke on Human Understanding*. London: Routledge.

Lowe, E. J. (1996) *Subjects of Experience*. Cambridge: Cambridge University Press.

Lowe, E. J. (1998) *The Possibility of Metaphysics: Substance, Identity, and Time*. Oxford: Clarendon Press.

Lowe, E. J. (2000a) *An Introduction to the Philosophy of Mind*. Cambridge: Cambridge University Press.

Lowe, E. J. (2000b) 'Locke, Martin, and Substance'. *The Philosophical Quarterly* 50: 499–514.

Lowe, E. J. (2002) *A Survey of Metaphysics*. Oxford: Clarendon Press.

Lycan, W. G. (1981) 'Form, Function, and Feel'. *Journal of Philosophy* 78: 24–50.

Lycan, W. G. (1987) *Consciousness*. Cambridge, MA: MIT Press.

Lycan, W. G. (1996) *Consciousness and Experience*. Cambridge, MA: MIT Press.

Lycan, W. G. (1998) 'In Defense of the Representational Theory of Qualia (Replies to Neander, Rey, and Tye)'. *Philosophical Perspectives* 12: 479–87.

Lycan, W. G., ed. (1999) *Mind and Cognition: An Anthology*, 2nd ed. Oxford: Blackwell.

Lyons, W. E. (2001) *Matters of the Mind*. London: Routledge.

Macdonald, C. (1989) *Mind–Body Identity Theories*. London: Routledge.

Macdonald, C. and G. Macdonald, eds. (2010) *Emergence in Mind*. Oxford: Oxford University Press.

McDowell, J. (1994) 'The Content of Perceptual Experience'. *The Philosophical Quarterly* 44: 190–205.

McGinn, C. (1982) *The Character of Mind*. Oxford: Oxford University Press.

McGinn, C. (1991) *The Problem of Consciousness: Essays Toward a Resolution*. Oxford: Blackwell.

McKirahan, R. (1994) *Philosophy Before Socrates: An Introduction with Texts and Commentary*. Indianapolis: Hackett.

McLaughlin, B. P. (1989) 'Type Epiphenomenalism, Type Dualism, and the Causal Priority of the Physical'. *Philosophical Perspectives* 3: 109–35.

McLaughlin, B. P. and J. Cohen, eds. (2007) *Contemporary Debates in Philosophy of Mind*. Malden, MA: Wiley-Blackwell.

Malcolm, N. (1959) *Dreaming*. London: Routledge and Kegan Paul.

Malebranche, N. (1688/1997) *Dialogues on Metaphysics and Religion*. N. Jolley and D. Scott, trans. Cambridge: Cambridge University Press.

Martin, C. B. (1980) 'Substance Substantiated'. *Australasian Journal of Philosophy* 58: 3–10.

Martin, C. B. (1987) 'Proto-Language'. *Australasian Journal of Philosophy* 65: 277–89.

Martin, C. B. (1992)'Power for Realists'. in Bacon *et al.* (1992): 175–86.

Martin, C. B. (1993) 'The Need for Ontology: Some Choices'. *Philosophy* 68: 505–22.

Martin, C. B. (1994) 'Dispositions and Conditionals'. *The Philosophical Quarterly* 44: 1–8.

Martin, C. B. (1997) 'On the Need for Properties: The Road to Pythagoreanism and Back'. *Synthese* 112: 193–231.

Martin, C. B. (2008) *The Mind in Nature*. Oxford: Clarendon Press.

Martin, C. B. and J. Heil. (1998) 'Rules and Powers'. *Philosophical Perspectives* 12: 283–312.

Martin, C. B. and J. Heil. (1999) 'The Ontological Turn'. *Midwest Studies in Philosophy* 23: 34–60.

Martin, C. B. and K. Pfeifer. (1986) 'Intentionality and the Non-Psychological'. *Philosophy and Phenomenological Research* 46: 531–54.

Maurin, A.–S. (2003) *If Tropes*. Dordrecht, Netherlands: Kluwer Academic Publishers.

Mele, A. (2011) 'Free Will and Science'. In Kane (2011) 499–514.

Mellor, D. H. (1974) 'In Defense of Dispositions'. *Philosophical Review* 83: 157–81. Reprinted in Mellor (1991): 104–22.

Mellor, D. H. (1991) *Matters of Metaphysics*. Cambridge: Cambridge University Press.

Millikan, R. G. (1984) *Language, Thought, and Other Biological Categories: New Foundations for Realism*. Cambridge, MA: MIT Press.

Millikan, R. G. (1989) 'Biosemantics'. *Journal of Philosophy* 86: 281–97. Reprinted in Chalmers (2002): 500–9.

Millikan, R. G. (2004) *Varieties of Meaning: The Jean Nicod Lectures*. Cambridge, MA: MIT Press.

Millikan, R. G. (2005) *Language: A Biological Model*. New York: Oxford University Press.

Molnar, G. (2003) *Powers: A Study in Metaphysics*. Oxford: Oxford University Press.

Morton, P., ed. (1997) *Historical Introduction to the Philosophy of Mind: Readings with Commentary*. Peterborough, UK: Broadview Press.

Moses, L. J. and J. H. Flavell. (1990) 'Inferring False Beliefs from Actions and Reactions'. *Child Development* 61: 929–45.

Nagel, T. (1974) 'What is it Like to be a Bat?' *Philosophical Review* 83: 435–50. Reprinted in Nagel (1979): 165–80; Block (1980a): 159–68; Heil (2003b): 528–38; Chalmers (2002): 219–26.

Nagel, T. (1979) *Mortal Questions*. Cambridge: Cambridge University Press.

Nani, M., ed. (2001) *A Field Guide to the Philosophy of Mind*. <http://host.uniroma3.it/progetti/kant/field/> Rome: University of Rome 3.

Neurath, O., R. Carnap, and C. Morris eds. (1955) *International Encyclopedia of Unified Science* vol. 1(1). Chicago: University of Chicago Press.

Nussbaum, M. C., and A. O. Rorty, eds. (1992) *Essays on Aristotle's* De Anima. Oxford: Clarendon Press.

O'Connor, J., ed. (1969) *Modern Materialism: Readings on Mind–Body Identity*. New York: Harcourt, Brace, and World.

O'Connor, T. and J. Jacobs (2003) 'Emergent Individuals'. *Philosophical Quarterly* 53: 540–55.

O'Connor, T. and D. Robb eds. (2003) *Philosophy of Mind: Contemporary Readings*. London: Routledge.

O'Connor, T. and H. Y. Wong. (2005) 'The Metaphysics of Emergence'. *Noûs* 39: 658–78.

O'Leary-Hawthorne, J. (1994) 'On the Threat of Elimination'. *Philosophical Studies* 74: 325–46.

Pereboom, D. (2002) 'Robust Nonreductive Materialism'. *Journal of Philosophy* 99: 499–531.

Pereboom, D. and H. Kornblith. (1991) 'The Metaphysics of Irreducibility'. *Philosophical Studies* 63: 125–45. Reprinted in Heil (2003b): 709–25.

Perner, J. (1991) *Understanding the Representational Mind*. Cambridge, MA: MIT Press.

Piccinini, G. (2007) 'Computational Modeling vs. Computational Explanation: Is Everything a Turing Machine, and Does It Matter to the Philosophy of Mind?' *Australasian Journal of Philosophy* 85: 93–115.

Piccinini, G. (2010) 'The Mind as Neural Software? Understanding Functionalism, Computationalism, and Computational Functionalism'. *Philosophy and Phenomenological Research* 81: 269–311.

Place, U. T. (1956) 'Is Consciousness a Brain Process?' *The British Journal of Psychology* 47: 44–50. Reprinted in Chalmers (2002): 55–60.

Place, U. T. (2001) 'Identity Theories'. In Nani (2001): <http://host.uniroma3.it/progetti/kant/field/mbit.htm>

Plato. *Parmenides*, in B. Jowett, trans. *The Dialogues of Plato*, 4th ed., vol. 2. Oxford: Clarendon Press, 1953.

Plato. *Phaedo*, in B. Jowett, trans. *The Dialogues of Plato*, 4th ed., vol. 1. Oxford: Clarendon Press, 1953. Excerpted in Heil (2003b): 21–30.

Plato. *Republic*, in B. Jowett, trans. *The Dialogues of Plato*, 4th ed., vol. 2. Oxford: Clarendon Press, 1953.

Poland, J. (1994) *Physicalism: The Philosophical Foundations*. Oxford: Clarendon Press.

Posner, M. I., ed. (1989) *Foundations of Cognitive Science*. Cambridge, MA: MIT Press.

Post, J. F. (1987) *The Faces of Existence: An Essay in Nonreductive Metaphysics*. Ithaca: Cornell University Press.

Presley, C. F., ed. (1967) *The Identity Theory of Mind*. Brisbane: University of Queensland Press.

Prior, E. W., R. Pargetter, and F. Jackson. (1982) 'Three Theses about Dispositions'. *American Philosophical Quarterly* 19: 251–7.

Putnam, H. (1960) 'Minds and Machines'. In Hook (1960): 138–64. Reprinted in Putnam (1975): 362–85.

Putnam, H. (1965) 'Brains and Behaviour'. In Butler (1965): 1–19. Excerpted in Heil (2003b): 96–104; Chalmers (2002): 45–54.

Putnam, H. (1967) 'Psychological Predicates'. In W. H. Capitan and D. D. Merrill, eds. *Art, Mind, and Religion*. Pittsburgh, PA: University of Pittsburgh Press: 37–48. Reprinted as 'The Nature of Mental States' in Putnam (1975b): 429–40. Reprinted in Heil (2003b): 158–67; O'Connor and Robb (2003): 210–21; Chalmers (2002): 73–9.

Putnam, H. (1975a) 'The Meaning of "Meaning"'. in Keith Gunderson (ed.), *Language, Mind, and Knowledge* (Minnesota Studies in the Philosophy of Science 7). Minneapolis: University of Minnesota Press: 131–93. Reprinted in Putnam (1975b): 215–71. Excerpted in Chalmers (2002): 581–96

Putnam, H. (1975b) *Mind, Language, and Reality: Philosophical Papers*, vol. 2. Cambridge: Cambridge University Press.

Putnam, H. (1981) *Reason, Truth, and History*. Cambridge: Cambridge University Press.

Quine, W. V. O. (1948) 'On What there Is'. *Review of Metaphysics* 5: 21–38. Reprinted in Quine (1961): 1–19.

Quine, W. V. O. (1960) *Word and Object*. Cambridge, MA: MIT Press.

Quine, W. V. O. (1961) *From a Logical Point of View*, 2d ed. Cambridge, MA: Harvard University Press. Reprinted in 1963 by Harper and Row.

Ramsey, F. P. (1929) 'Theories'. In Ramsey (1990): 112–36.

Ramsey, F. P. (1990) *Philosophical Papers*. Edited by D. H. Mellor. Cambridge: Cambridge University Press.

Ramsey, W., S. P. Stich, and J. Garon. (1991) 'Connectionism, Eliminativism, and the Future of Folk Psychology'. In Greenwood (1991): 93–119. Reprinted in Christensen and Turner (1993): 315–39.

Rey, G. (1997) *Philosophy of Mind: A Contentiously Classical Approach*. Oxford: Blackwell.

Robinson, D. N., ed. (1999) *The Mind*. New York: Oxford University Press.

Robinson, H., ed. (1993) *Objections to Physicalism*. Oxford: Clarendon Press.

Rorty, R. (1965) 'Mind–Body Identity, Privacy, and Categories'. *Review of Metaphysics* 19: 24–54.

Rorty, R. (1970) 'In Defense of Eliminative Materialism'. *Review of Metaphysics* 24: 112–21.

Rosenthal, D. (1986) 'Two Concepts of Consciousness'. *Philosophical Studies* 49: 329–59.

Rosenthal, D., ed. (1991) *The Nature of Mind*. New York: Oxford University Press.

Rosenthal, D. (2005) *Consciousness and Mind*. Oxford: Oxford University Press.

Rowlands, M. (2001) 'Consciousness and Higher-Order Thoughts'. *Mind and Language* 16: 290–310.

Russell, B. (1927) *Analysis of Matter*. London: Kegan Paul.

Ryder, T. D. (1996) 'Evaluating Theories of Consciousness Using the Autonomic Nervous System for Comparison'. MA thesis, University of Calgary.

Ryle, G. (1949) *The Concept of Mind*. London: Hutchinson.

Schechter, E. (forthcoming) 'The Unity of Consciousness: Subjects and Objectivity'. *Philosophical Studies*.

Schneider, S. (2011) *The Language of Thought: A New Philosophical Direction*. Cambridge, MA: MIT Press.

Schrödinger, E. (1958) *Mind and Matter*. Cambridge: Cambridge University Press.

Seager, W. (2004) 'A Cold Look at HOT Theory'. In Gennaro (2004): 255–75.

Searle, J. R. (1980) 'Minds, Brains, and Programs'. *Behavioral and Brain Sciences* 3: 417–24. Reprinted in Haugeland (1981a): 282–306; Dennett and Hofstadter (1981): 353–82; Heil (2003b): 235–52; O'Connor and Robb (2003): 332–52.

Searle, J. R. (1992) *The Rediscovery of the Mind*. Cambridge, MA: MIT Press.

Searle, J. R. (1997) 'Consciousness and the Philosophers'. *New York Review of Books*, 6 March: 43–50.

Shoemaker, S. (1975) 'Functionalism and Qualia'. *Philosophical Studies* 27: 291–315. Reprinted in Block (1980a): 251–67; in Shoemaker (1984a): 184–205; and in Rosenthal (1991): 395–407.

Shoemaker, S. (1980) 'Causality and Properties'. In van Inwagen (1980): 109–35. Reprinted in Shoemaker (1984a): 206–33.

Shoemaker, S. (1981) 'Some Varieties of Functionalism'. *Philosophical Topics*, 12: 83–118. Reprinted in Shoemaker (1984a): 261–86.

Shoemaker, S. (1984a) *Identity, Cause, and Mind: Philosophical Essays*. Cambridge: Cambridge University Press.

Shoemaker, S. (1984b) 'Absent Qualia are Impossible – A Reply to Block'. In Shoemaker (1984a): 309–26.

Shoemaker, S. (2007) *Physical Realization*: Oxford: Oxford University Press.

Siewart, C. (1998) *The Significance of Consciousness*. Princeton, NJ: Princeton University Press.

Simons, P. (1994) 'Particulars in Particular Clothing: Three Trope Theories of Substance'. *Philosophy and Phenomenological Research* 54: 553–75.

Skinner, B. F. (1953) *Science and Human Behavior*. New York: Macmillan.

Skinner, B. F. (1957) *Verbal Behavior*. New York: Appleton-Century-Crofts.

Skinner, B. F. (1963) 'Behaviorism at Fifty'. *Science* 140: 951–58. Reprinted with commentaries and Skinner's responses in *Behavioral and Brain Sciences* 7 (1984): 615–57.

Smart, J. J. C. (1959) 'Sensations and Brain Processes'. *Philosophical Review* 68: 141–56. Reprinted in Heil (2003b): 116–27; O'Connor and Robb (2003): 121–37; Chalmers (2002): 60–8.

Smart, J. J. C. (2000) 'The Identity Theory of Mind'. In Zalta (2002): http://plato.stanford.edu/entries/mind-identity/.

Sobel, D. (1995) *Longitude: The True Story of a Lone Genius who Solved the Greatest Scientific Problem of his Time*. New York: Walker.

Spinoza, B. de (1677/1982) *The Ethics*. S. Shirley, trans. Indianapolis: Hackett.

Staddon, J. (1993) *Behaviourism: Mind, Mechanism, and Society*. London: Duckworth.

Sterelny, K. (1990) *The Representational Theory of Mind: An Introduction*. Oxford: Blackwell.

Stich, S. P. (1983) *From Folk Psychology to Cognitive Science: The Case Against Belief.* Cambridge, MA: MIT Press.

Stich, S. P. and T. A. Warfield, eds. (2003) *The Blackwell Guide to Philosophy of Mind*. Oxford: Blackwell Publishing.

Strawson, G. (2006) 'Realistic Monism: Why Physicalism Entails Panpsychism'. In Freeman (2006): 3–31.

Strawson, G. (2008) *Real Materialism and Other Essays*. Oxford: Clarendon Press.

Strawson, G. (2009) *Selves: An Essay in Revisionary Metaphysics*. New York: Clarendon Press.

Swoyer, C. (1982) 'The Nature of Natural Laws'. *Australasian Journal of Philosophy* 60: 203–23.

Teller, P. (1986) 'Relational Holism and Quantum Mechanics'. *British Journal for the Philosophy of Science* 37: 71–81.

Teller, P. (1995) *An Interpretive Introduction to Quantum Field Theory*. Princeton, NJ: Princeton University Press.

Thagard, P. (1996) *Mind: Introduction to Cognitive Science*. Cambridge, MA: MIT Press.

Thomas, N. J. T. (1989) 'Experience and Theory as Determinants of Attitudes toward Mental Representation: The Case of Knight Dunlap and the Vanishing Images of J. B. Watson'. *American Journal of Psychology* 102: 395–412.

Thomas, N. J. T. (1999) 'Are Theories of Imagery Theories of Imagination? An *Active Perception* Approach to Conscious Mental Content'. *Cognitive Science* 23: 207–45.

Tolman, E. C. (1948) 'Cognitive Maps in Rats and Men'. *Psychological Review* 55: 189–208.

Turing, A. M. (1950) 'Computing Machinery and Intelligence'. *Mind* 59: 434–60. Reprinted in Dennett and Hofstadter (1981): 53–68; in Anderson (1964): 4–30; in Heil (2003b): 212–34.

Tye, M. (1991) *The Imagery Debate*. Cambridge, MA: MIT Press.

Tye, M. (1995) *Ten Problems of Consciousness: A Representational Theory of the Phenomenal Mind*. Cambridge, MA: MIT Press.

van Gulick, R. (2011) 'Consciousness'. In E. N. Zalta, ed. *Stanford Encyclopedia of Philosophy*. <http://plato.stanford.edu/archives/sum2011/entries/consciousness/>.

van Inwagen, P., ed. (1980) *Time and Cause*. Dordrecht: Reidel Publishing Co.

van Inwagen, P. (1993) *Metaphysics*. Boulder, CO: Westview Press.

Vesey, G. N. A. (1964) *Body and Mind: Readings in Philosophy*. London: George Allen and Unwin.

Watson, J. B. (1913) 'Psychology as the Behaviorist Views It'. *Psychological Review* 20: 158–177.

Wegner, D. (2004) 'Précis of "The Illusion of Conscious Will"'. *Behavioral and Brain Sciences* 27: 649–59.

Weinberg, S. (1997) 'Before the Big Bang'. *New York Review of Books*, 12 June: 16–20.

Wilson, M. D. (1978) *Descartes*. London: Routledge.

Wilson, M. D. (1999) *Ideas and Mechanism: Essays on Early Modern Philosophy*. Princeton, NJ: Princeton University Press.

Wilson, R. A. and F. Keil, eds. (1999) *MIT Encyclopedia of Cognitive Sciences* <http://cognet.mit.edu/MITECS/login.html>. Cambridge, MA: MIT Press.

Wimmer, H., and J. Perner. (1983) 'Beliefs about Beliefs: Representation and Constraining Function of Wrong Beliefs in Young Children's Understanding of Deception'. *Cognition* 13: 103–28.

Wittgenstein, L. (1922/1961) *Tractatus Logico-Philosophicus*. D. F. Pears and B. F. McGuinness, trans. London: Routledge and Kegan Paul.

Wittgenstein, L. (1953/1968) *Philosophical Investigations*. G. E. M. Anscombe, trans. Oxford: Basil Blackwell.

Wittgenstein, L. (1969) *On Certainty*. G. E. M. Anscombe and G. H. von Wright, eds.; D. Paul and G. E. M. Anscombe, trans. Oxford: Basil Blackwell.

Zalta, E. N., ed. (2002) *The Stanford Encyclopedia of Philosophy*. <http://plato.stanford.edu/>. Stanford, CA: Metaphysics Research Lab, Center for the Study of Language and Information.

Index